by Mahesh Krishnan and Philip Beadle

Wiley Publishing, Inc.

Silverlight™ 4 For Dummies®

Published by
Wiley Publishing, Inc.
111 River Street
Hoboken, NJ 07030-5774

www.wiley.com

Copyright © 2010 by Wiley Publishing, Inc., Indianapolis, Indiana

Published by Wiley Publishing, Inc., Indianapolis, Indiana

Published simultaneously in Canada

No part of this publication may be reproduced, stored in a retrieval system or transmitted in any form or by any means, electronic, mechanical, photocopying, recording, scanning or otherwise, except as permitted under Sections 107 or 108 of the 1976 United States Copyright Act, without either the prior written permission of the Publisher, or authorization through payment of the appropriate per-copy fee to the Copyright Clearance Center, 222 Rosewood Drive, Danvers, MA 01923, (978) 750-8400, fax (978) 646-8600. Requests to the Publisher for permission should be addressed to the Permissions Department, John Wiley & Sons, Inc., 111 River Street, Hoboken, NJ 07030, (201) 748-6011, fax (201) 748-6008, or online at http://www.wiley.com/go/permissions.

Trademarks: Wiley, the Wiley Publishing logo, For Dummies, the Dummies Man logo, A Reference for the Rest of Us!, The Dummies Way, Dummies Daily, The Fun and Easy Way, Dummies.com, Making Everything Easier, and related trade dress are trademarks or registered trademarks of John Wiley & Sons, Inc. and/or its affiliates in the United States and other countries, and may not be used without written permission. Silverlight is a trademark of Microsoft Corporation in the United States and/or other countries. All other trademarks are the property of their respective owners. Wiley Publishing, Inc., is not associated with any product or vendor mentioned in this book.

LIMIT OF LIABILITY/DISCLAIMER OF WARRANTY: THE PUBLISHER AND THE AUTHOR MAKE NO REPRESENTATIONS OR WARRANTIES WITH RESPECT TO THE ACCURACY OR COMPLETENESS OF THE CONTENTS OF THIS WORK AND SPECIFICALLY DISCLAIM ALL WARRANTIES, INCLUDING WITHOUT LIMITATION WARRANTIES OF FITNESS FOR A PARTICULAR PURPOSE. NO WARRANTY MAY BE CREATED OR EXTENDED BY SALES OR PROMOTIONAL MATERIALS. THE ADVICE AND STRATEGIES CONTAINED HEREIN MAY NOT BE SUITABLE FOR EVERY SITUATION. THIS WORK IS SOLD WITH THE UNDERSTANDING THAT THE PUBLISHER IS NOT ENGAGED IN RENDERING LEGAL, ACCOUNTING, OR OTHER PROFESSIONAL SERVICES. IF PROFESSIONAL ASSISTANCE IS REQUIRED, THE SERVICES OF A COMPETENT PROFESSIONAL PERSON SHOULD BE SOUGHT. NEITHER THE PUBLISHER NOR THE AUTHOR SHALL BE LIABLE FOR DAMAGES ARISING HEREFROM. THE FACT THAT AN ORGANIZATION OR WEBSITE IS REFERRED TO IN THIS WORK AS A CITATION AND/OR A POTENTIAL SOURCE OF FURTHER INFORMATION DOES NOT MEAN THAT THE AUTHOR OR THE PUBLISHER ENDORSES THE INFORMATION THE ORGANIZATION OR WEBSITE MAY PROVIDE OR RECOMMENDATIONS IT MAY MAKE. FURTHER, READERS SHOULD BE AWARE THAT INTERNET WEBSITES LISTED IN THIS WORK MAY HAVE CHANGED OR DISAPPEARED BETWEEN WHEN THIS WORK WAS WRITTEN AND WHEN IT IS READ.

For general information on our other products and services, please contact our Customer Care Department within the U.S. at 877-762-2974, outside the U.S. at 317-572-3993, or fax 317-572-4002.

For technical support, please visit www.wiley.com/techsupport.

Wiley also publishes its books in a variety of electronic formats. Some content that appears in print may not be available in electronic books.

Library of Congress Control Number: 2010924585

ISBN: 978-0-470-52465-7

Manufactured in the United States of America

10 9 8 7 6 5 4 3 2 1

About the Authors

Mahesh Krishnan has been a geek all his life and proud of it. He works as a Principal Consultant at Readify and is passionate about Software Architecture and new technologies. He has been working in the IT industry since 1992 and has worked on a range of projects, from shrink-wrapped products to large-enterprise applications across the globe. He is currently based in Melbourne, Australia, and runs the local .NET Developer user group. He also helped start the Silverlight Designer and Developers Network, a group that focuses on spreading the Silverlight message to both the developer and designer communities. He blogs at blogesh.wordpress.com, is very active in the developer community, and has presented a number of times at user groups, hands-on days, code camps, and Tech.Ed. He is married to Lakshmi and they have a wonderful three-year-old daughter, Riya.

Philip Beadle is a founding member of the DotNetNuke Core Team, a DotNetNuke Trustee, a Microsoft Certified Application Developer, and a Microsoft Certified Trainer. Philip now works for the DotNetNuke Corporation, an open source content management system built in ASP.NET, and was awarded the Microsoft Most Valuable Professional (MVP) award in ASP/ASP.NET in 2004. Philip also helped start the Silverlight Designer and Developers Network with Mahesh Krishnan and Jordan Knight. He speaks at many conferences, including Tech Ed, ReMIX, and DotNetNuke OpenForce, and speaks at local user group gatherings as well. Philip and Lorraine have a beautiful one-year-old daughter, Allegra Rose. You can visit Philip's Web site at http://www.philipbeadle.net.

Dedication

To my loving parents, without whom I wouldn't be who I am today, my daughter Riya, who constantly kept closing my notebook while writing the book so that I could play with her, and to my wife, Lakshmi, for putting up with me while I spent all my spare time on the book.

Mahesh Krishnan

To my wife, Lorraine, who supports me in all my endeavors, and to my darling daughter, Allegra Rose, who always brings a smile to my face and joy to my day.

Philip Beadle

Acknowledgements

Writing a book is hard. Writing a book for Dummies is even harder — trying to articulate something in a way for someone with very little or no knowledge of the topic to understand is not easy. Making the book easy to read and ensuring that it is technically correct is, as I said, hard. Thankfully, I had some help along the way.

First and foremost, I would like to thank Susan Christophersen, the Project Editor, for hand holding me through the entire process. Susan, thanks for the guidance and all the work you've put into this book. The book is a huge improvement from the first cut that I sent you and most of the credit for that should go to you.

I would also like to thank Jordan Knight and Russ Mullen for diligently reading through the content and looking for technical errors, as well as providing valuable feedback.

A big thanks also to Katie Feltman and Wiley Publishing for providing me an opportunity to write this book.

Mahesh Krishnan

Publisher's Acknowledgments

We're proud of this book; please send us your comments at http://dummies.custhelp.com. For other comments, please contact our Customer Care Department within the U.S. at 877-762-2974, outside the U.S. at 317-572-3993, or fax 317-572-4002.

Some of the people who helped bring this book to market include the following:

Acquisitions and Editorial

Project Editor and Copy Editor: Susan Christophersen

Acquisitions Editor: Katie Feltman

Technical Editors: Jordan Knight, Russ Mullen

Editorial Manager: Jodi Jensen

Media Development Project Manager: Laura Moss-Hollister

Media Development Assistant Project Manager: Jenny Swisher

Media Development Associate Producers: Josh Frank, Marilyn Hummel, Douglas Kuhn, Shawn Patrick

Editorial Assistant: Amanda Graham

Sr. Editorial Assistant: Cherie Case

Cartoons: Rich Tennant (www.the5thwave.com)

Composition Services

Project Coordinator: Katherine Crocker

Layout and Graphics: Joyce Haughey, Christin Swinford, Erin Zeltner

Proofreaders: Laura Albert, Laura Bowman, John Greenough

Indexer: BIM Indexing & Proofreading Services

Publishing and Editorial for Technology Dummies

    Richard Swadley, Vice President and Executive Group Publisher

    Andy Cummings, Vice President and Publisher

    Mary Bednarek, Executive Acquisitions Director

    Mary C. Corder, Editorial Director

Publishing for Consumer Dummies

    Diane Graves Steele, Vice President and Publisher

Composition Services

    Debbie Stailey, Director of Composition Services

Contents at a Glance

Introduction 1

Part I: Illuminating Silverlight 7
Chapter 1: Adding Silverlight to Your Web Development Toolkit 9
Chapter 2: Getting Started in Silverlight 23
Chapter 3: Enhancing the User Interface 49

Part II: Managing Your Silverlight Controls 81
Chapter 4: Working with Controls for UI Interactions 83
Chapter 5: Laying Out Controls 107
Chapter 6: Styling and Skinning Controls 127
Chapter 7: Creating Your Own Controls 149
Chapter 8: Creating Animations in Silverlight 171
Chapter 9: Updating Data the Easy Way with Data Binding 191

Part III: Connecting with Data 211
Chapter 10: Accessing Data in Silverlight 213
Chapter 11: Using WCF Data Services to Store and Manage Data 249
Chapter 12: Using WCF RIA Services in Silverlight 285
Chapter 13: Accessing Data with WCF RIA Services 297

Part IV: The Part of Tens 319
Chapter 14: Ten Cool Controls for Collecting and Displaying Data 321
Chapter 15: Ten Ways to Get More Out of Silverlight 329
Chapter 16: Ten Handy Tips for Writing Silverlight Applications 343

Index 351

Table of Contents

Introduction 1

What's in This Book 1
Foolish Assumptions 2
How This Book Is Organized 2
    Part I: Illuminating Silverlight 2
    Part II: Managing Your Silverlight Controls 2
    Part III: Connecting with Data 3
    Part IV: The Part of Tens 3
Conventions Used in This Book 4
Icons Used in This Book 4

Part I: Illuminating Silverlight 7

Chapter 1: Adding Silverlight to Your Web Development Toolkit 9

Obtaining and Running Silverlight 9
Checking Out Some Silverlight-Enhanced Sites 10
Grasping the Potential of Silverlight 12
Hosting a Silverlight Application in a Web Page 14
All the Stuff You Need to Create Silverlight Applications 15
    Visual Studio 16
    Silverlight Tools for Visual Studio 16
    Expression Blend 16
    Silverlight Toolkit 19
    WCF RIA Services 19
    Deep Zoom Composer 19
Creating Rich User Experiences in Silverlight 20
Silverlight Plays Well with Others 21
Silverlight Has More to Offer Than Just a Pretty Face 21

Chapter 2: Getting Started in Silverlight 23

Getting Started in Silverlight with Expression Blend 23
    Exploring the Expression Blend interface 26
    Menu bar 27
    Artboard 28
    Tools panel 28
    Workspace panels 28
    Adding a user interface element to the page 33
Introducing the Basics of the Extensible Application
    Markup Language 35
    Digging deeper into XAML 37
    Understanding elements and properties by category 39

Firing Up Visual Studio to Create a Silverlight Application 41
    Exploring Visual Studio... 42
    Creating the Hello, World application.. 44
    Exploring the Solution Explorer.. 44
    Specifying the startup file for the application................................ 46
    Understanding other files involved in the solution....................... 47
    Hosting the Silverlight application 47
Using Expression Blend and Visual Studio in Tandem 48

Chapter 3: Enhancing the User Interface 49

Getting to Know the Properties Panel 49
    Setting a property for an object.. 50
    Getting to know the Properties panel better.................................. 51
Drawing Shapes on the Artboard 53
    Drawing with ready-made shapes 54
    Drawing freehand... 54
    Understanding the XAML for shapes 56
Shaping, Sizing, and Positioning Your Object... 57
    Getting your object into shape using your mouse 57
    Reshaping and sizing an object using the Properties panel........... 58
    Rounding the corners of a Rectangle object 59
Rotating, Projecting in 3-D, and Doing Other Funky
    Things with Shapes.. 60
    Rotating a rectangle or other shape... 61
    Skewing an object 61
    Applying 3-D Perspective transformations..................................... 63
Painting Colors with Brushes in the Properties Panel.............................. 64
    Filling an object with color.. 65
    Using the Eyedropper tool... 66
    Mixing colors... 66
    Applying gradients for color transitions.. 67
    Using the Gradient tool instead of setting gradients
        through the Properties panel 69
    Manipulating gradients further with the Brush Transform tool.... 70
    Adding special effects 71
Playing Around with Some Special Effects 72
Adding Video and Audio to Your Pages 74
    Playing video and audio files.. 74
    Creating a video brush.. 76
    Displaying video from your Webcam 77
    Selecting the default webcam and microphone
        for your application 79

Part II: Managing Your Silverlight Controls 81

Chapter 4: Working with Controls for UI Interactions 83

Exploring the Text-Related Tools 83
    Displaying text with TextBlock 84
    Using the TextBox and PasswordBox to get
       input from the user 86
    Accessing TextBox values in XAML markup 88
Using Buttons in Your Application 91
    Setting the content of a button 92
    Adding an image as content for a Button 93
Jumping to another Web page using HyperlinkButton 96
Using RadioButtons to Present Options 96
Using the ListBox and ComboBox to Present a Large
   Number of Options 98
    Creating a list box 98
    Creating a combo box 101
Entering Rich Text into a RichTextBox Control 101
    Understanding the XAML behind RichTextbox 103
    Formatting text at runtime 103

Chapter 5: Laying Out Controls 107

Understanding Layout Containers 107
    The root container 109
    Manipulating properties that control layout 109
    Aligning controls to one side 110
    Setting the Height and Width of a UserControl at design time 112
    Clearing margins of an element from the Artboard 112
Laying Out Controls in Rows and Columns 113
    Setting up rows and columns 113
    Adding controls to the rows and columns 114
    Understanding the XAML 115
    Changing row heights and column widths on the Artboard 117
Stacking Controls Horizontally and Vertically 117
    Adding controls to a StackPanel 117
    Converting a Grid to a StackPanel 118
    Understanding the XAML for a StackPanel 120
Wrapping Controls 120
Arranging Controls by Absolute Positioning Using
   the Canvas Control 121
Using the ScrollViewer to Scroll Through the Contents 122
Using the Viewbox to Fit the Contents Snugly 122
Grouping Controls into a Tabbed Page 123
Docking Controls 125

Chapter 6: Styling and Skinning Controls 127

Applying Styles to Controls 127
    Creating default styles for a control 128
    Creating named styles for controls 130
    Understanding the Style property 130
    Understanding the XAML behind Style resources 131
    Understanding styles as resources in the Resources panel 132
    Applying styles to existing elements 132
    Creating controls with existing styles 134
    Creating new styles based on existing styles 134
Skinning a Control 134
    Editing the template visually 138
    Specifying state 140
    Binding values in the template 143
    Applying skins to existing controls 144
Using Themes to Change the Look of All Controls 144

Chapter 7: Creating Your Own Controls 149

Grouping Controls to Create a UserControl 149
    An example of creating an Address UserControl 150
    Reusing the User control 153
    Creating properties for your UserControl 154
Creating a Smiley Custom Control 156
    Using the custom control 166
    Adding events to your control 167
Controlling the Behavior of Controls without Writing Code 168

Chapter 8: Creating Animations in Silverlight 171

Creating a Simple Bouncing Ball Animation 171
    Create the ball and set the timeline in motion 172
    Switching to the Animation workspace 174
    Animating the ball 175
    Understanding the XAML behind the animation 177
Running the Animations You Create 180
    Controlling animations from code 180
    Easing the animation 182
    Understanding the different kinds of Easing functions 185
    Easing using KeySplines 186
Animating States of Controls 188

Chapter 9: Updating Data the Easy Way with Data Binding 191

Binding Controls to Each Other 192
Binding to a Data Object 195
    Creating a user control for data binding 195
    Data bind the controls in the UserControl
        to a property name 196
    Create a data class that can be databound 198

Table of Contents

Binding the data object to the control 198
Automatically updating changes to the data 199
Converting data while binding 201
Binding to Sample Data 205
Creating sample data 205
Binding a DataGrid to the sample data 207
Creating a Master-Detail view 209
Fooling around with the sample data 209

Part III: Connecting with Data 211

Chapter 10: Accessing Data in Silverlight 213

Downloading Files to Your Silverlight Application 214
Downloading files using the WebClient class 216
Using WebClient to include a progress bar
    with large downloads 219
Using the HTTPWebRequest class 222
Talking to Web Services 226
Accessing Web services that allow cross-domain exchanges 227
Programming against a Web service that has a WSDL 232
Creating your own WSDL Web service 234
Understanding Cross-Domain Security 236
Creating a cross-domain policy file 237
Accessing a Web service without a cross-domain policy file 237
Using the workaround: An example 238
Authenticating Users 244

Chapter 11: Using WCF Data Services to Store and Manage Data ... 249

Getting Started with WCF Data Services 250
What, Exactly, Is WCF Data Services? 251
Creating a WCF Data Service 254
Creating the database 254
Adding the ADO.NET Entity Framework 256
Adding the WCF Data Service 259
Using the WCF Data Service in a Silverlight Application 261
Generating the proxy classes in the Silverlight application 261
Reading data from the database 263
Updating data in the database 269
Adding new items to the database 274
Deleting entities from the database 275
Handling Data Concurrency 277
Using Query and Change Interceptors to
Control Data Querying and Updates 280
Controlling server-side queries with query interceptor 280
Enforcing rules using change interceptors 282
Controlling Access to Entity Sets 283

Chapter 12: Using WCF RIA Services in Silverlight ... 285

Getting Started with WCF RIA Services ... 285
Authenticating Your Users ... 286
    Authenticating users with the Business Application template ... 287
    Understanding the client side of the
        Business Application template ... 289
    Investigating the server side of the
        Business Application template ... 289
    Understanding how the template files work together ... 290
Creating a Custom Authentication System ... 292
    Implementing custom user validation logic ... 293
    Returning a custom user object to the Silverlight application ... 294

Chapter 13: Accessing Data with WCF RIA Services ... 297

Creating the Domain Data Service ... 298
    Understanding the generated files ... 300
    Creating the user interface ... 300
    Retrieving the data ... 301
    Updating your data ... 303
Writing Your Own Service Methods — LINQ to Entity Framework ... 304
    A common mistake (Psst — This won't work!) ... 305
    This, on the other hand, DOES work ... 305
Writing Your Own Service Methods — LINQ to SQL ... 306
Validating Data on the Client and Server Sides ... 309
    Adding validation attributes ... 311
    Using a DataForm for great validation ... 312
Securing Your WCF RIA Service ... 315

Part IV: The Part of Tens ... 319

Chapter 14: Ten Cool Controls for Collecting and Displaying Data ... 321

ListBox ... 321
DataGrid ... 322
DataForm ... 323
Expander ... 324
Chart ... 325
DatePicker ... 326
ProgressBar ... 326
TreeView ... 327
Rating ... 327
AutoCompleteBox ... 328

Chapter 15: Ten Ways to Get More Out of Silverlight 329

Using SketchFlow to Prototype Your Application................................330
Using Deep Zoom Composer..331
Creating Designs Using Expression Design...332
Importing Designs from Other Applications...334
Creating Your Own Behaviors 335
Running Silverlight Out of the Browser...337
Calling Silverlight Code via JavaScript..338
    Create a scriptable method 339
    Create and register the object 339
    Call the ScriptableMember function....................................339
Accessing HTML from Silverlight 340
    Using the WebBrowser control..341
    Using the DOM to access HTML...342
Storing Data Locally in the Client 342

Chapter 16: Ten Handy Tips for Writing Silverlight Applications...343

Resources about Silverlight Beyond This Book 343
Ten Handy Expression Blend Shortcuts 343
Ten Handy Visual Studio Shortcuts 344
Debugging Silverlight Applications 345
Looking Out for Performance Pitfalls...345
Building for Accessibility..346
Internationalization and Localization 347
Build Composite Applications Using Prism 347
Use the Model-View-ViewModel (MVVM) Pattern
  to Manage Large Applications..348
Handy Tools 349

Index 351

Introduction

Welcome to *Silverlight 4 For Dummies*. This book not only gives you an introduction to the bright new world of programming in Silverlight but is also loaded with hands-on steps and examples of using Expression Blend and Visual Studio with Silverlight to create rich Internet applications.

Silverlight is a cross-browser, cross-platform plug-in that runs rich interactive applications whose emphasis is on providing a rich user experience that incorporates audio, video, animation, and graphics.

What's in This Book

Silverlight 4 For Dummies aims to give you all the information you need to create full-fledged Silverlight applications that you can host on your Web site. In this book, rather than overload you with pages and pages of technical explanations, we get you started right away on creating a Silverlight application and working with the controls that make Silverlight such an exciting addition to the world of Web site design. Of course, we do put the tasks we show you in context so that you can understand how the various components work — but we've tried to keep the explanations interesting, too.

Although the book introduces the basic components of Silverlight, chapter by chapter, you don't have to read the chapters sequentially. If you already have a basic understanding of Silverlight, for example, and want to know more about creating animations for your Web site, just flip straight to Chapter 8 and dive in.

The examples in this book use XAML markup and C# code. If you're thinking, "Huh? What's XAML?" (which, by the way, is pronounced *zamel*), don't worry: We tell you all about it in due course. All you need to know to get started is that XAML is the markup language that you use to design a user interface. To specify the UI's *behavior,* you use a language such as C#. We show you examples of XAML many times throughout this book, and when you need to understand something about the C# code, we show you that, too.

C# and VB.NET are currently the two most popular languages that people working with Microsoft technologies use, and rather than confuse you by using both languages, we stick with just C#. If you are already familiar with VB.NET, you should be able to convert the sample code in this book line for line quite easily. Also, you'll find much of the sample code that appears in this book on the companion Web site at www.dummies.com/go/silverlight4fd. Download the code from there and cut and paste freely to make life easier.

Foolish Assumptions

Even if you have no background in programming, you can learn a lot about using Silverlight from this book. However, if you already have some understanding of a programming language, you'll have an easier time grasping the concepts introduced in this book.

We also assume that you know a little bit about HyperText Markup Language (HTML) and how to install and run applications. The tools required to create Silverlight applications run on Windows, so we assume that you are running Windows XP, Vista, or Windows 7.

Finally, we assume that you can obtain the tools you need to create Silverlight applications. Expression Blend and Visual Studio are not free, but you should be able to download evaluation versions of these programs to play around with if you are not prepared to invest in them just yet.

How This Book Is Organized

The book is divided into four parts, described next.

Part I: Illuminating Silverlight

In Part I, we introduce you to Silverlight and guide you to creating your first Silverlight application. We tell you in more detail what Silverlight is all about and what programs you need to install on your computer to get cracking in Silverlight.

Also in this part, you find out how to set properties on user interface elements, called *controls,* and you play around with drawing various shapes.

Part II: Managing Your Silverlight Controls

This part delves far more deeply into the world of controls than Part I does. In Chapter 4, you find out about some of the most commonly used controls such as text boxes and buttons, and in Chapter 5, we show you how to effectively arrange them on-screen.

With Silverlight, you can change a control's appearance without changing how it works. You find out how to do this in Chapter 6, which describes *styling* and *skinning*. *Styling* means to create a style by specifying property values for a certain control and reusing those values throughout your application for a consistent appearance. With *skinning*, you completely change the look of the control.

In Chapter 7, you find out how to create your own controls — whether by aggregating a set of controls to form a new control or creating a control from scratch.

Chapter 8 introduces you to the exciting world of animation, and we show you how to animate controls on-screen.

The final chapter in this part, Chapter 9, familiarizes you with the important concept of data binding, which connects user interface elements to data. Traditionally, programmers have been busy constantly setting properties, such as the Text property, when the data for an element displays changes. With data binding, however, you tell the control what kind of data it is bound to and let Silverlight take care of the rest. Not only does Chapter 9 give you an insight into this wonderful way of programming, it also shows you how you can create data sources and sample data to test your application.

Part III: Connecting with Data

No application is complete without getting data from somewhere and displaying it to the users.

Chapter 10 shows you how to connect to data sources through the Web and extract the data you need to have returned to your application, while Chapter 11 takes you a step further to show you how you can expose data from your databases using a technology called *WCF Data Services*. Chapters 12 and 13 introduce you to a data service called *WCF RIA Services*, which helps you create a large line of business applications. In these chapters, you see how to retrieve data from a database, validate user input, secure your site by authenticating site users, and much more.

Part IV: The Part of Tens

The Part of Tens, which is a staple of all *For Dummies* books, offers a fun way of discovering intriguing or useful items (ten in each chapter) that aren't covered in the other parts of the book.

In these chapters, we tell you about programs such as SketchFlow, which is a great tool to use for creating a prototype of your application, and Deep Zoom Composer, which helps you create an application with arresting images that visitors to your Web site can zoom into. This part is also packed with tips and other resources to explore.

Conventions Used in This Book

This book is saturated with how-to steps to follow for every topic we cover. These steps sometimes contain figures and sometimes source code. The figures may not match exactly what you see on your own screen. This is okay; the figures are meant as a guide in most cases and do not have to match your screen pixel by pixel.

You also find little figures in the margin like the one shown here. These figures help you easily identify a button referred to in the text.

Source code or XAML typically appears like this:

```
<Grid x:Name="LayoutRoot" Background="White"
    . . .>
</Grid>
```

Notice the ellipsis indicated with three dots. The ellipsis indicates that we've left out some of the code for brevity so that you can focus on just the important bits in the code that are relevant to what we're describing.

We use a special typeface to distinguish code terms in text, like so: The `Text` property. Also, when we present you with a series of menu commands to follow in sequence, it looks like this: Choose File⇨New Project. This means that you should choose File from the menu and, in the dialog box that appears, choose New Project.

Icons Used in This Book

When we want to draw your attention to an easy way to get something done, we include this icon in the margin.

Text with this icon next to it mentions points that you should keep in the back of your mind.

The Warning icon alerts you to a potential problem. Be on the lookout for these icons because they point out gotchas and Bad Things.

This icon serves up technical stuff that you don't have to pay attention to unless you're inclined to do so. If you are technically minded or are an experienced programmer, you will likely appreciate these technical bits. But if you are new to programming and want to skip over this technical stuff, feel free to do so.

Part I
Illuminating Silverlight

The 5th Wave   By Rich Tennant

"Look into my Web site, Ms. Carruthers. Look deep into its rotating spiral, spinning, spinning, pulling you deeper into its vortex, deeper...deeper..."

In this part . . .

This part gives you an introduction to Silverlight 4 and guides you to creating your first Silverlight application. We tell you what Silverlight is all about and what tools you need to install on your computer to get cracking in Silverlight.

The first chapter introduces Silverlight and provides an overview of what you can do with it. Chapter 2 takes off from there and helps you create simple applications using Visual Studio and Expression Blend. These two tools are the predominant tools covered in this book.

The final chapter of this part shows you how to set properties on user interface elements, or *controls,* and how to draw various shapes.

Chapter 1

Adding Silverlight to Your Web Development Toolkit

In This Chapter
- Understanding Rich Internet Applications (RIA)
- Seeing how Silverlight enables RIA development
- Understanding what you need to develop Silverlight applications
- Seeing what Silverlight can do beyond just creating a stylish user interface

*W*atch out, Adobe — Silverlight 4 is here to give you a run for your money. Web site designers and developers alike can find much to be excited about in Microsoft's answer to Adobe Flash. As we tell you in more detail in the Introduction to this book, Silverlight 4 is one of a new family of Web site applications that provide graphics, animation, audio, and video — all the features necessary for the kind of rich user experience people have come to expect on the Web. These applications are called Rich Internet Applications (RIA). Adobe Flash was one of the first in the RIA arena; more recently, Microsoft made its entry into this space with the launch of Silverlight.

In this chapter, we give you an overview of what Silverlight is, what it can do, and the tools you need to develop Silverlight applications.

Obtaining and Running Silverlight

As does Adobe Flash, Silverlight runs as a plug-in within the browser and needs to be installed the first time any Silverlight application is run. A plug-in is a piece of software that is not part of the Web browser but can be added to it to run additional applications. When a user visits a Web site that needs the Silverlight plug-in, the Web browser will prompt the user to install it.

After the plug-in is installed, visiting any site that hosts a Silverlight application causes Silverlight to start up in the browser seamlessly. The plug-in itself is around 4MB, and in addition to the Silverlight runtime (which is responsible for running the Silverlight application), the application itself needs to be downloaded from the site that hosts the application. Modern popular browsers such as Internet Explorer, Firefox, Safari, and Chrome support Silverlight while running on Microsoft's Windows operating systems 2003, XP, Vista, and 7) or on Apple's Mac OS X. Recently, Silverlight has also been rewritten to run on browsers in Linux-based operating systems. With Silverlight 4, the application can also run as a stand-alone application — that is, it can be run outside the browser.

Obtaining and installing Silverlight on your computer is quite simple. All you have to do is visit a Silverlight-enabled site and it will prompt you to install Silverlight. Figure 1-1 shows a site that uses Silverlight. As soon as you visit the site using a Web browser, the browser prompts you to install Silverlight.

Figure 1-1:
Site prompting Silverlight installation.

All you have to do is click the button to install and you are done. A Silverlight installation is around 4.7MB and needs to be installed only once. If you visit the same site again or another site that uses Silverlight, you are not prompted to reinstall it.

Checking Out Some Silverlight-Enhanced Sites

So, what do Silverlight applications look like? You can find a good example at the Hard Rock Café Memorabilia site (http://memorabilia.hardrock.com/), shown in Figure 1-2. This site contains photographs of some of the memorabilia that Hard Rock Café owns.

When the page comes up, the screen displays numerous small images of the memorabilia, but each time you click an image, you zoom in to it. As you zoom in to the image, it first appears blurred and progressively becomes sharper. This is because the whole photograph (which can be several megabytes in size) does not load in one go; instead, it loads progressively as you need it. You can also see several animations on the site. Creating an application like this using plain HTML would be very difficult and would lack the rich interactivity that is provided by Silverlight.

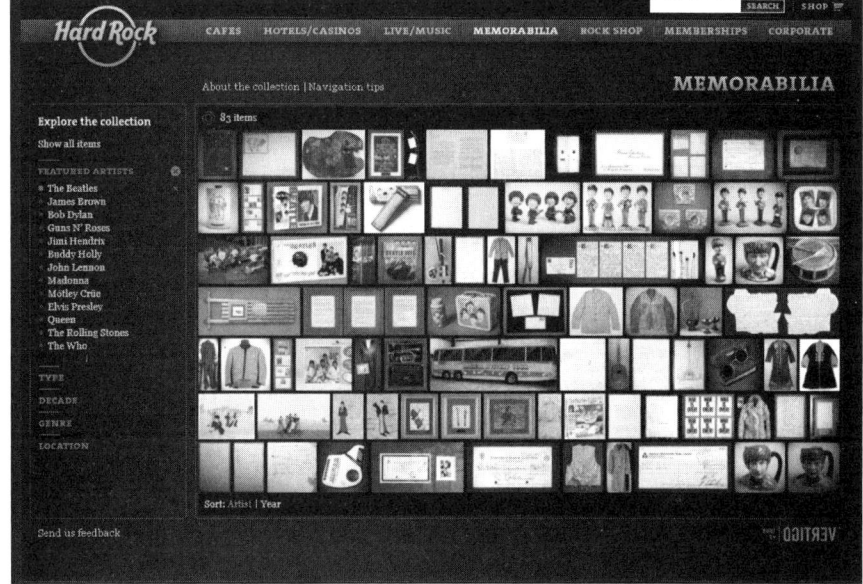

Figure 1-2: Silverlight running the Hard Rock Café Memorabilia site.

Another site that showcases Silverlight's user interface is the Woodgrove Financials sample application, shown in Figure 1-3. This application uses fly-out menus, dynamic graphs, and slick animation.

See the list of images to the left of the screen? On the site, as you move your mouse cursor over them, a menu slides out, giving additional information about what you can do. Clicking the Mortgage option, for example, brings up an interactive graph that shows you how much money you can save on your mortgage. Clicking Trade History brings up an interactive display of graphs and tables, where you can filter your stocks, find information on them, and review the stock prices over a period of time.

The sample application has several features, which you can explore by visiting http://cookingwithxaml.com/meals/financials/default.html. The application is highly interactive. As noted previously, creating a rich user interface for an application such as this would be extremely difficult using plain ol' HTML.

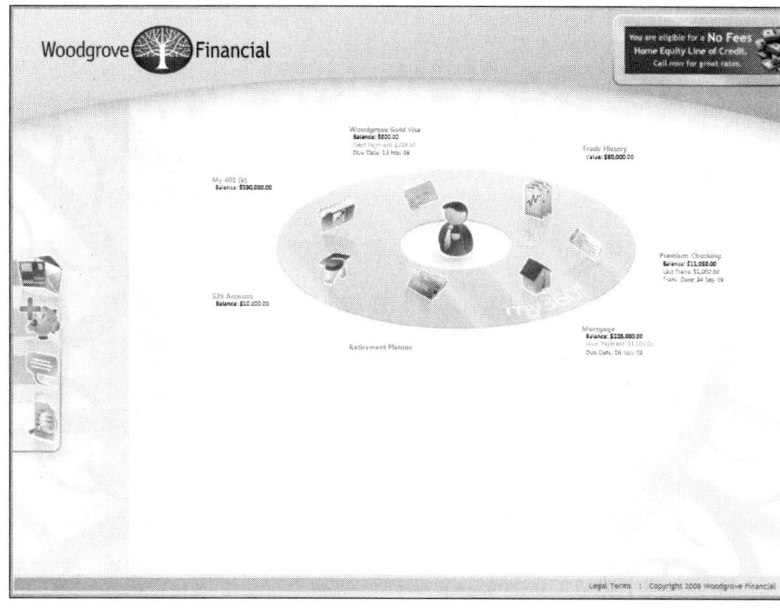

Figure 1-3: An example of a dynamic site with a rich user interface.

Grasping the Potential of Silverlight

One of the main advantages of Silverlight is that if you are a developer and have already been creating applications using Microsoft technologies, you do not have to learn something new to create Silverlight applications. You can program Silverlight applications using .NET languages such as C# and VB.NET. In fact, the Silverlight runtime is a scaled-down version of .NET, which is Microsoft's primary environment under which most applications run. The .NET framework contains all the libraries needed to run these applications and provides the Application Programming Interface (API) that programmers can call to use the various features.

The Silverlight team worked hard to trim down the .NET framework so that it contains all the good bits of the framework while at the same time ensuring that it doesn't get too big to be sent across the Internet when you download it for the first time. The user interface framework, which is a key part of the RIA user experience, is based on Windows Presentation Foundation (WPF) and Extensible Application Markup Language (XAML). We tell you more about XAML in Chapter 2 and show you many examples of it throughout this book. Silverlight contains a powerful graphics and animation engine, and the UI framework provides the following features:

- Support for drawing vector graphic images and doing 3-D perspective transformations
- Support for creating storyboards and animations
- A full suite of controls, such as text boxes and buttons, and support for creating your own controls
- Layout management support, which allows you to lay out controls in a variety of ways
- Styling of controls, which allows the properties of your controls to be standardized and reused
- Skinning, which allows you to change the complete appearance of controls
- Support for *data binding,* which seamlessly binds data and control properties
- Multi-touch support, which allows you to use hand gestures and touch interactions on hardware that supports it
- Support for hooking on to webcams and microphones to share video and audio with others
- Support for media streaming, allowing audio and video to be streamed according to the optimal bit rate based on the network speed
- The ability to create Silverlight applications to be run on mobile phones that are part of the Windows Phone 7 series.

This set of features helps developers easily provide a rich interactive user experience.

Although the base class library in Silverlight is a cut-down version of the .NET framework, it still uses the same namespaces as the full version and supports a wide variety of features such as multithreading, generics, and even Language Integrated Query (LINQ). In addition, the framework adds support for WCF RIA Services, which helps build Silverlight applications in a multitier environment while allowing applications to work in offline scenarios at the same time. Other feature highlights of Silverlight include support for connecting to Web services, peer-to-peer communication, and access to local storage.

In spite of all these features, Silverlight itself runs in a sandboxed environment. This means that for security reasons, the Silverlight application cannot access system resources or invoke API calls on the machine it is running on. This feature prevents malicious applications from taking over your computer without your knowledge.

> ### A brief history of the name "Silverlight"
>
> Silverlight was initially called WPF/e (for "WPF everywhere"), which would have been a terrible name for it. It needed a catchy and simple name, and eventually the name Silverlight was chosen. Version 1 was released in September 2007, and it mainly accomplished the delivery of rich media and programming that couldn't be done using languages like C# and VB.NET.
>
> Around the same time that version 1 was released, Microsoft also released a preview version of Silverlight. This 1.1 version of the program allowed developers to write Silverlight applications using .NET languages such as C# and VB.NET. It also made use of the Framework API.
>
> When version 1.1 was finally released in Oct 2007, it was rebranded as version 2.0. Silverlight 3 was announced in early 2009 and finally released in September 2009, soon followed by Silverlight 4 in the spring of 2010. In March 2010, Microsoft also announced that Silverlight will also be used to deploy applications for Windows Phone 7 series. Having four major releases in such a short time shows Microsoft's commitment to Silverlight and the RIA scene in general.

Hosting a Silverlight Application in a Web Page

Because Silverlight applications are run from a Web browser, they have to be hosted n a Web page. Silverlight applications have the extension .xap (pronounced "zap"), but the Silverlight file is actually nothing more than a .zip file. If you rename the file to have a .zip extension and open the file, you can still see all the compiled libraries, markup images, and other resources that the file contains.

To understand how a Silverlight application is hosted in HTML, you can navigate to a Web site that contains a Silverlight application and view the HTML source code by right-clicking and choosing View Source from the menu. The HTML source code will look something like the following:

```
<object data="data:application/x-silverlight-2,"
  type="application/x-silverlight-2" width="100%"
        height="100%">
    <param name="source" value="ClientBin/
        SilverlightApplication.xap"/>
    <param name="onerror" value="onSilverlightError" />
    <param name="background" value="white" />
    <param name="minRuntimeVersion" value="4.0.50303.0"
        />
    <param name="autoUpgrade" value="true" />
    <a href="http://go.microsoft.com/
        fwlink/?LinkID=149156&v=4.0.50303.0"
        style="text-decoration: none;">
```

Chapter 1: Adding Silverlight to Your Web Development Toolkit

```
            <img src="http://go.microsoft.com/
                fwlink/?LinkId=161376"
            alt="Get Microsoft Silverlight" style="border-style:
                none"/>
        </a>
</object>
```

The HTML tag is an `object` tag that specifies the data attribute and the type. These elements signify that a Silverlight object is being created. The `param name="source"` tag contains the relative location of the `.xap` file that will be run when the application starts.

Some of the other parameters contain values that specify where to get the latest versions of Silverlight.

If all this looks too complicated for you, don't despair. The `object` tags are created automatically when you use Visual Studio and Expression Blend.

All the Stuff You Need to Create Silverlight Applications

Microsoft provides all the programs needed to create Silverlight applications. Expression Blend and Visual Studio are the most commonly used applications to create Silverlight applications, and we cover these two products in depth in this book.

To start developing applications in Silverlight 4, you need to install the following programs and associated tools:

- Visual Studio 2010
- Silverlight 4 Tools for Visual Studio 2010
- Expression Blend for .NET 4
- Silverlight Toolkit
- WCF RIA Services
- Deep Zoom composer

Other than Visual Studio and Expression Blend, all the tools listed here are free for you to download and install. If you do not have Visual Studio 2010 installed on your machine, you can also use the free Visual Web Developer 2010 Express. There is, however, no free edition of Expression Blend.

Links to download the free tools can be obtained from www.silverlight.net.

Visual Studio

To write, compile, and debug programs, you need an Integrated Development Environment (IDE). Visual Studio is the IDE of choice for building applications that run in Microsoft's .NET environment. Visual Studio supports languages such as VB.NET and C#, and you can use it to create Silverlight applications, too.

Silverlight Tools for Visual Studio

Silverlight Tools for Visual Studio is responsible for adding all the necessary elements to get Visual Studio to build Silverlight applications. It adds the following: Silverlight project templates; the Silverlight Toolbox, which contains all the Silverlight controls such as buttons and text boxes; and the Silverlight Software Development Kit (the SDK). It also offers other useful features such as debugger support.

Expression Blend

You use Expression Blend to create user interfaces using visual tools for both WPF and Silverlight. It provides a much better environment for creating user interfaces than Visual Studio does. For instance, you can create a user interface just by dragging and dropping controls onto the design surface, whereas you would have to manually code most of this using Visual Studio.

Expression Blend is actually part of a suite of applications collectively known as Expression Studio. Although you can install just the applications you need, designers generally tend to install the entire suite of the Expression Studio applications because these tools help in visually designing the user interface. They complement each other quite well. The other applications in this suite are as follows:

- **Expression Web:** This application allows you to not only author Web pages in HTML but also design, build, and manage entire Web sites. It helps in creating Web sites that use Cascading Style Sheets (CSS), and it integrates with Microsoft's ASP.NET and PHP programming environments. Expression Web, shown in Figure 1-4, complies with Web standards endorsed by the World Wide Web Consortium (W3C). It also contains something called Super Preview, which enables you to see how pages look in different browsers at design time. Traditionally, designers have struggled to make their applications look the same across multiple browsers, and Super Preview allows them to look at these pages side by side or even overlap each other to observe and fix differences.

- **Expression Design:** This application allows designers to create graphics and artwork for use in Web and desktop applications. You can even export these designs into XAML so that they can be used in Silverlight applications. Figure 1-5 shows Expression Design in action.

- **Expression Encoder:** This application helps in preparing media files (such as videos and audios) so that they can be used with Silverlight. A video file being edited in Expression Encoder is shown in Figure 1-6.

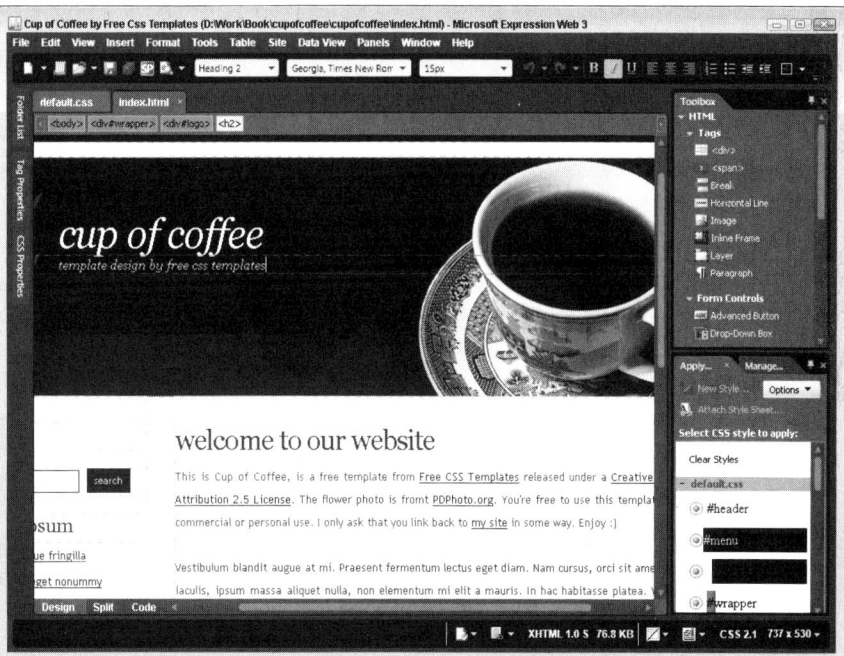

Figure 1-4: Expression Web in use.

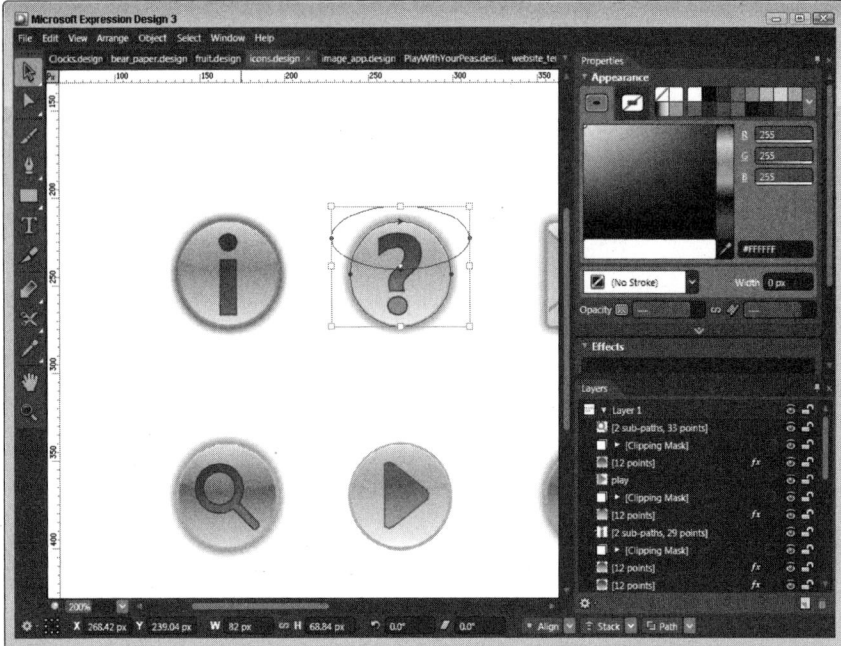

Figure 1-5: Graphics created using Expression Design.

Figure 1-6: A video file being edited in Expression Encoder.

Silverlight Toolkit

The Silverlight Toolkit is a collection of controls and utilities for Silverlight that supplements what is already present in the core Silverlight libraries. The Silverlight Toolkit includes additional controls (such as charts) that are very useful but aren't used daily by applications. If Microsoft had included these controls in the main Silverlight runtime application, it would have become unwieldy and too big to download in a reasonable amount of time. By separating this set of controls from the main application, Microsoft left it up to developers to decide which parts to include in their application. In addition, it allows Microsoft to make frequent updates to the toolkit outside the release cycle of Silverlight.

WCF RIA Services

When you start creating large applications that have multiple screens and that connect to a database to read and write data, you need to design your application well. As part of this design, you need to divide your application into multiple layers, or *tiers*. An application is typically divided into the following tiers:

- **Presentation:** Focuses on the user interface
- **Application:** Focuses on application logic, such as validating user input or performing calculations
- **Data:** Focuses on how to read and write the data used by the application

WCF RIA Services is a framework for creating multitier applications in Silverlight, incorporating data operations such as authentication, authorization, data validation, and other essential services across the different tiers. It integrates with ASP.NET and provides ways to share code among the different tiers. WCF RIA Services is explained in more detail in Chapters 12 and 13.

Deep Zoom Composer

Deep Zoom Composer helps in creating the zooming and panning effect of images that you see in the Hard Rock Café Memorabilia site mentioned earlier in this chapter. Figure 1-7 shows Deep Zoom Composer being used to create a similar application. We tell you more about using Deep Zoom Composer in Chapter 15.

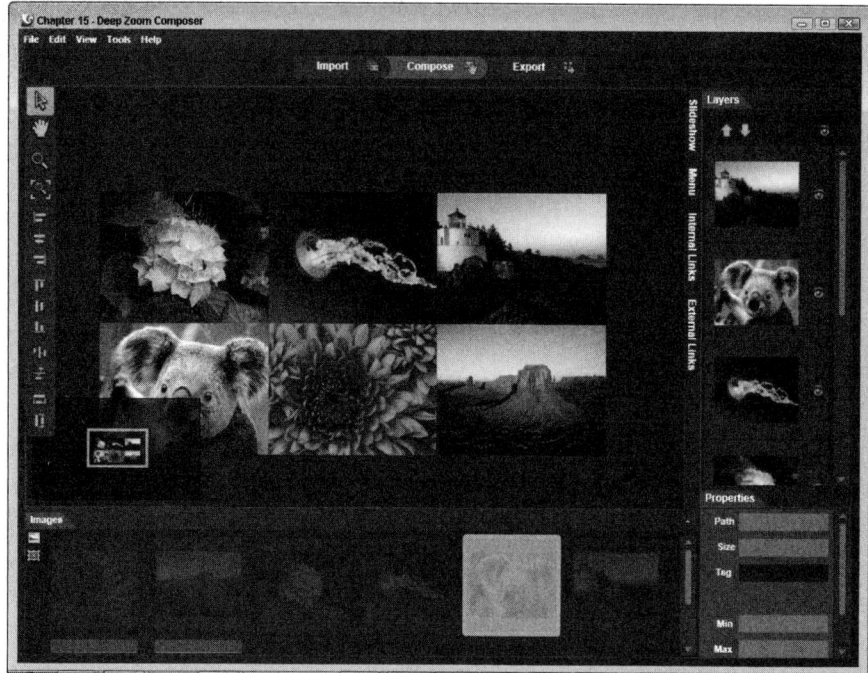

Figure 1-7: Deep Zoom composer in action.

Creating Rich User Experiences in Silverlight

Rich Internet applications such as Silverlight aim to provide a dynamic experience for Web site users. This dynamism comes in the form of graphics, animation, audio, and video, and Silverlight supports all these features. In fact, Silverlight 1.0 was all about playing audio and video files in a browser, and nothing more.

So what kind of audio and video files work in Silverlight? In addition to MP3 files for audio, Silverlight supports a range of audio and video formats, including High Definition (HD)-quality video. Even the formats that it does not currently support can be easily converted into a supported format using Expression Encoder.

Graphics is another key area for providing rich user interfaces. Silverlight provides shape objects such as an ellipse, a line, a polyline, a rectangle, and a polygon that designers can modify to suit their needs. In addition, you can draw complex shapes using an object in XAML called `Path`. You can apply transformations on these vector graphic images to create 3-D effects and animations.

In addition to all these features, Silverlight, out of the box, contains around 60 controls. *Control* is another name for tools such as text boxes, buttons, and other elements that appear on Web sites. Part II of this book covers all the fundamentals you need to get started on working with the most commonly used controls. We even show you how to create your own!

Accessibility for people with special challenges has become a very important aspect of modern Web sites, and Silverlight supports this user accessibility by providing features that allow applications to be read using screen readers and by helping developers create functionality and features, within applications, that do not depend on the mouse alone but can be accessed using keyboard shortcuts. So, for example, if you have a menu in an application that usually pops up when you right-click the mouse, the user can also access it using a keyboard shortcut.

Silverlight also supports internationalization and localization, which allow applications to be written to support other languages and cultures. Not all countries speak or even use English, of course, and even the countries that do use English have varying date formats and currencies.

Silverlight Plays Well with Others

Silverlight does not actually replace HTML, ASP.NET, or JavaScript. In fact, it can complement these technologies to provide a pleasing, rich user experience for existing Web sites. The Document Object Model (DOM), which is a standard model for accessing all the user interface objects in an HTML page, can be manipulated from Silverlight, and some Silverlight functionality can be triggered from JavaScript. All these technologies actually work well together. You can find out how to integrate these technologies together in Chapter 15.

Silverlight Has More to Offer Than Just a Pretty Face

The user interface is the primary focus of Silverlight. It is also the most visible part as far as the users are concerned. But there is more to Silverlight than just creating pretty user interfaces.

In Part III of this book, we tell you how you can use Silverlight to access data that is available on the Web. This data can be in the form of Web services, which are small units of functionality that can be accessed by other applications. Such a unit of functionality can be anything from providing weather information for a certain region to complex business functionality such as managing product inventory or an employee database.

Silverlight does not have any API calls to talk to the database directly. It can use Web services or use another technology called WCF Data Services. Using WCF Data Services, Silverlight can perform all the necessary database operations such as creating, reading, updating, and deleting (known collectively as CRUD) data using calls to a Web service.

WCF Data Services is accessed by applications as RESTful services. REST stands for Representational Transfer State, and RESTful services present data from the database to applications as resources that can be accessed using unique Universal Resource Indicators (URIs), which are HTTP addresses. In addition, commands in the HTTP protocols (such as GET, POST, PUT, and DELETE) are used to specify the type of action that needs to be performed on the data. For example, to get information about a book with an ISBN whose last six digits are 524657, the REST address could look something like http://servername/Book/524657. Rather than return an HTML page for this address, the REST service would return an XML document containing all the information about the book.

Chapter 2
Getting Started in Silverlight

In This Chapter
▶ Creating your first Silverlight application
▶ Seeing what you can do with Expression Blend
▶ Creating a user interface with Extensible Markup Language (XAML)
▶ Running the application in Visual Studio
▶ Understanding the various files involved in creating a Silverlight application

So, you're fired up about creating your first Silverlight application. Great, but first make sure that you have the applications described in Chapter 1 installed. At the very minimum, you need Expression Blend, Visual Studio 2010, and the Silverlight Tools for Visual Studio.

You can create Silverlight applications using either Visual Studio or Expression Blend. If you are a developer, at this point you would most likely get things under way using Visual Studio 2010, but in this chapter, we start with Expression Blend. As we tell you in Chapter 1, Expression Blend provides a much better environment for creating user interfaces than Visual Studio does. Also, if you are new to development, you're more likely to find Expression Blend easier to use for that purpose.

In this chapter, you find out how to create simple Silverlight applications using both Expression Blend and Visual Studio. In the course of creating these applications, you can also become more familiar with using both applications.

Keeping up with tradition, we start by creating a "Hello, World" application.

Getting Started in Silverlight with Expression Blend

When you start Expression Blend for the first time, you see a screen (shown in Figure 2-1) with three tabs, as follows:

✔ **Projects:** This tab lets you open any recently opened projects from a list, create a new project, or open existing projects.

✔ **Help:** This tab lets you open the User Guide, look at online tutorials, and visit the Microsoft Expression community Web site, which contains tutorials, articles, and community forums.

✔ **Samples:** This tab provides you with a set of sample projects that you can explore. These projects were created by the Expression Blend development team.

The Startup dialog box provides an option to make this initial window appear every time Expression Blend starts up.

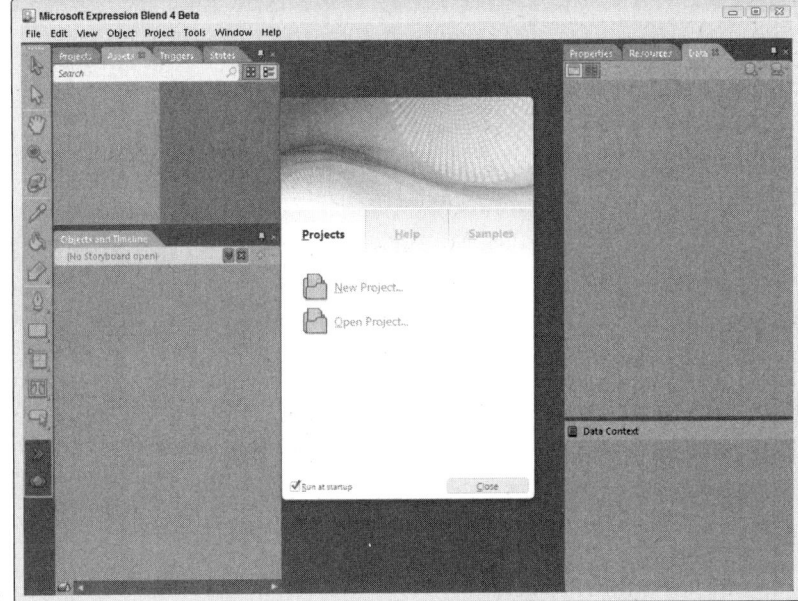

Figure 2-1: The Startup screen in Expression Blend.

To create a Hello, World application, start by clicking the Projects tab and then selecting the New Project option. The New Project dialog box appears; while you're there, make sure that the Silverlight 4 Application + Website option is selected in the list box. Then click OK.

Selecting the Silverlight 4 Application + Website option in the New Project dialog box ensures that a Web site with a startup page that hosts the Silverlight application is created along with the Silverlight application.

The New Project dialog box, shown in Figure 2-2, also has a chevron that you click to reveal a Project Types list. You can click items on the list to display only the types of projects you are interested in.

Chapter 2: Getting Started in Silverlight 25

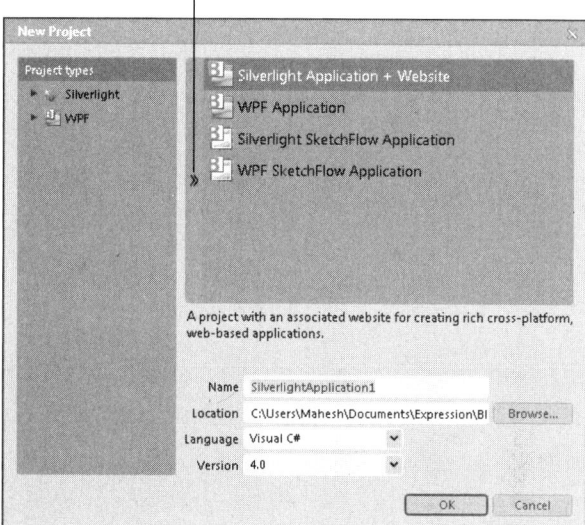

Click to Show/Hide project types

Figure 2-2: The New Project dialog box.

Expression Blend creates a Silverlight *solution* for you with two projects: one to hold the Silverlight-related files and another for a Web site project that will host your Silverlight application.

In both Expression Blend and Visual Studio, the "problem" of grouping together the files needed to create a Silverlight application is "solved" by creating a solution file (.sln). The solution file breaks down these collections even further into project (.prj) files that are specific to the type of application in use. For example, the Silverlight part of the application becomes a Silverlight project, and the Web part of the application becomes a Web project.

To run the project, just press the F5 button on the keyboard or choose Project➪Run Project.

When you run the project, Internet Explorer (or whatever your default browser is) opens up after a slight delay caused by Expression Blend compiling code and starting up the necessary applications. The application comes up in the Web browser as an empty screen. Despite the fact that it's just an empty page at the moment, you have successfully created and run your first Silverlight application. Congratulations!

How can you tell that it is running Silverlight? You can verify this by right-clicking the empty page and choosing Silverlight from the menu that appears. This brings up the Microsoft Silverlight Configuration dialog box, which shows what version of Silverlight you are using, among other things.

Part I: Illuminating Silverlight

But what about "Hello, World"? Patience, friend. You need to first get acquainted with some basic aspects of Expression Blend in order to start placing controls in the application. (A *control* is what you need to contain the "Hello, World" text.)

Exploring the Expression Blend interface

Expression Blend has been created primarily with designers in mind. That is one of the reasons it looks markedly different from other applications that developers use, such as Visual Studio. If you are already familiar with Visual Studio, the first thing you notice about Expression Blend, which is shown in Figure 2-3, is its dark color scheme. However, although everything looks different from Visual Studio, there are some similarities between the two applications.

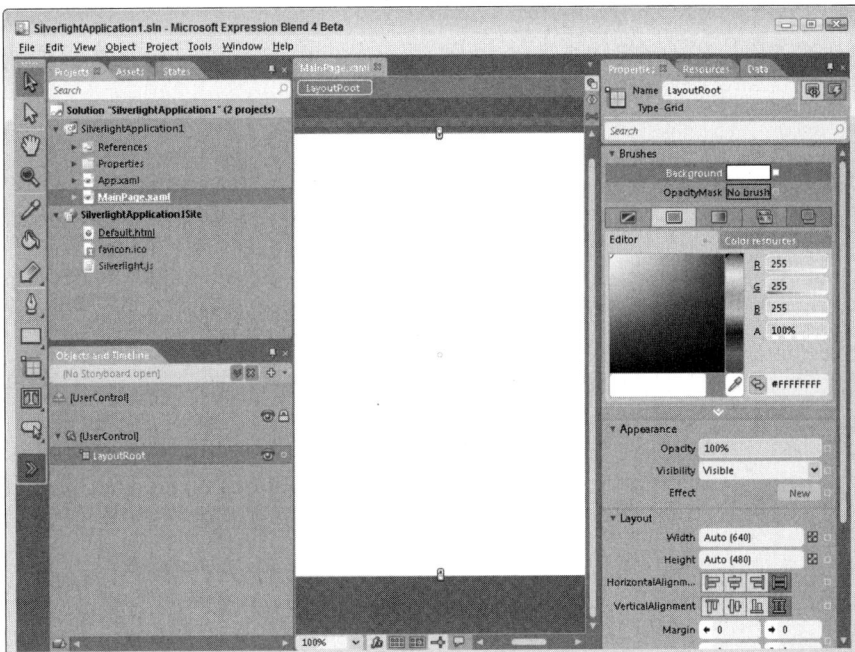

Figure 2-3: Expression Blend workspace.

The main window in the application, which contains the user interface, is called the *workspace*. The workspace contains four main parts:

- **Menu bar:** This is the element that sits at the top of the screen and is similar to the menu bar of other Windows applications.
- **Artboard:** The main portion of the screen is taken up by the design surface. This design surface, called the Artboard, is where you create the user interface for your Silverlight application.
- **Tools panel:** The left corner of the screen holds a toolbar called the Tools panel; it contains a bunch of tools for designing the user interface. This is also referred to as *Toolbox*.
- **Workspace panels:** The workspace contains a number of panels that allow you to do additional things such as create animations, open files, find tools easily, and so on. They appear as tabs and can be moved around, closed, and opened again at any time. You close panels by clicking the cross that appears at the top of the panel; you open them from the Window menu on the menu bar (which is described next).

Menu bar

The menu bar for Expression Blend contains the following top-level menus:

- **File:** Contains options to create new projects and files as well as to open existing ones.
- **Edit:** Contains options to cut, copy, and paste as well as to find items.
- **View:** Contains options to zoom, switch among the different views on the Artboard (explained in the next section), and other view-related options.
- **Object:** Contains options to manage the user interface objects that you have added to the Artboard. These options include aligning multiple objects, making the height and width of multiple objects the same, and others.
- **Project:** Contains options to manage the project, such as to add new projects to the existing project and to build and run the current project.
- **Tools:** Contains more advanced options such as the Font manager, which is used to manage fonts within the application.
- **Window:** This menu contains options to open and close workspace panels as well as switch to different workspace settings (which specify what panels are open and at what position).
- **Help:** Contains options to get help on different aspects of Expression Blend.

Artboard

The Artboard, shown in Figure 2-4, is the design surface for creating Silverlight applications; it contains the following components:

- **Documents tab:** The top of the Artboard shows the name of the file that is open. In your case, it should read MainPage.xaml because this file is automatically created by Expression Blend and opened when you create the project. You can open multiple files at the same time; these appear as tabs. You can switch among the different files by clicking these tabs. You close the files by clicking the *X* that appears next to the filename.
- **Artboard controls:** At the bottom of the Artboard are options that control the behavior of the Artboard. Some examples of what these options control include zooming, showing a grid, and setting options to snap controls to a grid when you add or move these objects around on the Artboard. Enabling the options to show the grid and snap to a grid helps in laying out controls on the screen.
- **View buttons:** At the top-right corner of the screen are three buttons for changing the view on the Artboard to Design, XAML, or Split. See the next bullet for more on these views.
- **Design, XAML and Split views:** In the Design view, you can add or manipulate controls on the Artboard visually. The XAML view shows the XAML for the markup that gets generated. The Split view is useful when you want to see both the XAML and the Design view at the same time.

Tools panel

The Tools panel contains a set of tools that you can use to add new controls to the Artboard as well as to modify existing ones. The Tools panel is shown in Figure 2-5. We discuss these controls throughout the book.

Workspace panels

There are eight workspace panels in Expression Blend, and each panel has its own functionality. But the panels all behave the same way when they are moved, closed, and opened.

If you feel so inclined, you can move a panel around by clicking the title of the tab and dragging it to another position. You can have the panel float wherever you want, or you can dock it to a side.

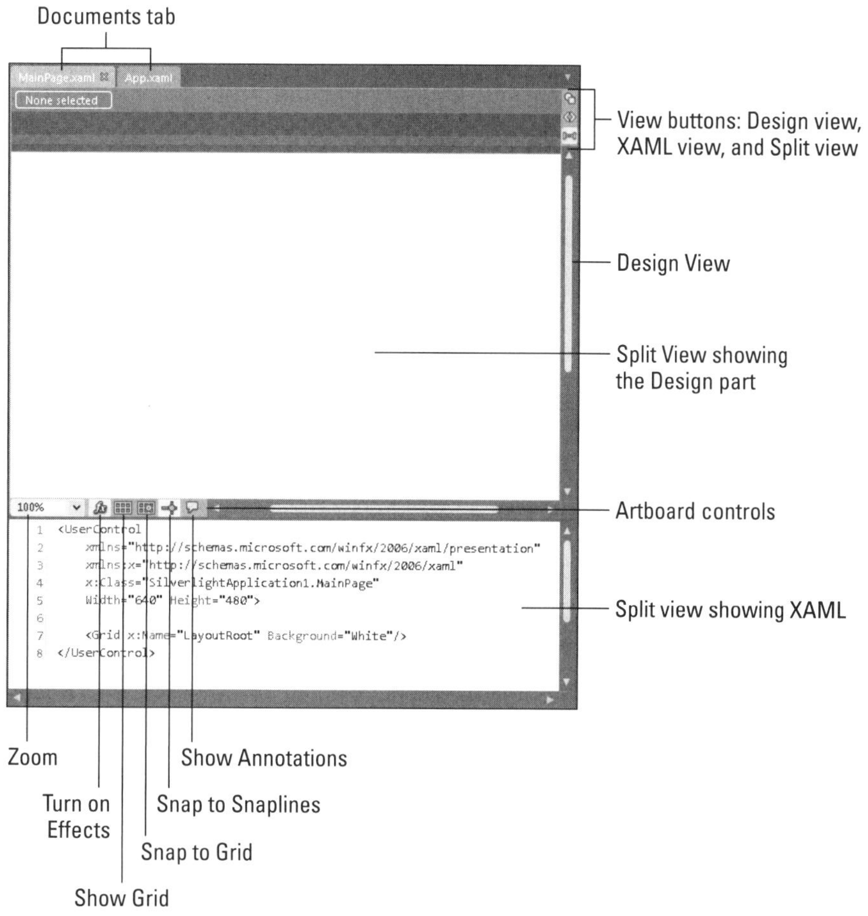

Chapter 2: Getting Started in Silverlight   29

Figure 2-4: The Artboard.

(Callouts: Documents tab; View buttons: Design view, XAML view, and Split view; Design View; Split View showing the Design part; Artboard controls; Split view showing XAML; Zoom; Turn on Effects; Show Grid; Snap to Grid; Snap to Snaplines; Show Annotations.)

As you drag the workspace panel around, a dark, transparent rectangle appears on the screen. This rectangle indicates that the panel will be docked in that location.

 Every panel also has a pin, shown here in the margin, at the top of the window. Clicking this pin auto-hides the window when it's not in use. The title of the panel then appears at the side of the location it was originally located in, and hovering the mouse cursor over the name makes the panel appear again. You normally set a panel to auto-hide mode when you need more space on the screen to work.

You save any changes you've made to the workspace by choosing Window➪ Save as New Workspace. After you've created multiple workspaces, you toggle between them by pressing F6. Expression Blend comes configured with two workspaces: Design and Animation.

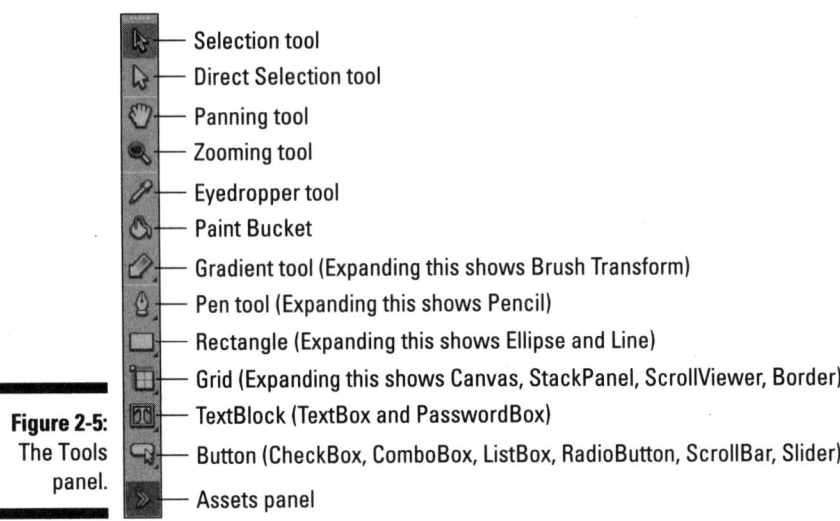

Figure 2-5: The Tools panel.

To reset the workspace panels to their default position, just press Ctrl+Shift+R.

Enough about how you move workspace panels around — far more interesting is what you can accomplish with them. The panels are as follows:

- **Projects panel:** This panel, shown in Figure 2-6, is similar to the Solution Explorer in Visual Studio and contains the projects and files used in the application. You can open files by double-clicking a filename. The file that is currently open on the Artboard appears selected in the Projects panel.

- **Assets panel:** This panel (see Figure 2-7) contains all the assets that you can use in your Silverlight application. *Assets* include controls, media files, behaviors, effects, and so on that we describe in later chapters. The panel also contains a Search box to help you find assets easily. Two buttons are used to display the items either in a grid mode, in which the items are arranged in rows and columns, or in a list mode, where they are displayed in a list.

- **Objects and Timeline panel:** This panel, shown in Figure 2-8, contains all the controls added to the Artboard, as well as the timeline for the animations that the objects are part of. We look at this panel in more detail in Chapter 8.

- **States panel:** This panel can be used to manage the visual states of controls. For instance, the Button control can have states such as Pressed and Disabled. Figure 2-9 shows the visual states for a button. We cover this topic in more detail in Chapter 7.

Chapter 2: Getting Started in Silverlight 31

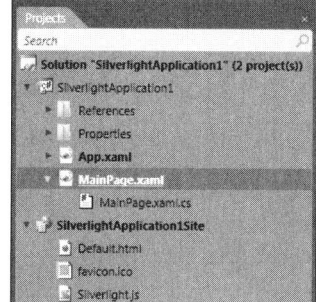

Figure 2-6: The Projects panel.

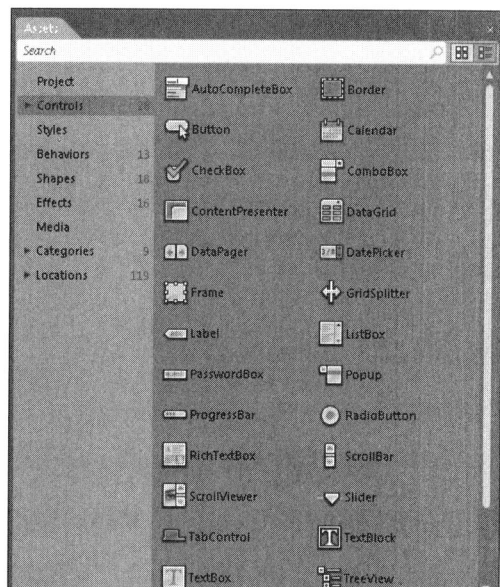

Figure 2-7: Assets panel.

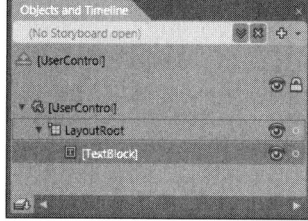

Figure 2-8: Objects and Timeline panel.

✓ **Properties panel:** You use the Properties panel (see Figure 2-10) to set properties, such as color, width, and height, for items that have been added to the page. You find out more about working with the Properties panel in Chapter 3.

Part I: Illuminating Silverlight

- **Resources panel:** Resources are items such as colors and styles that are shared between controls within the application. The Resources panel lists all these resources. Figure 2-11 shows a Resources panel that has a couple of brush resources. Brushes are used to set colors for controls, as we describe in Chapter 3.

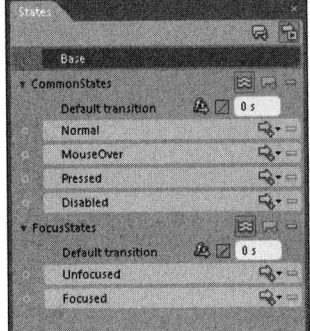

Figure 2-9: States panel for a Button control.

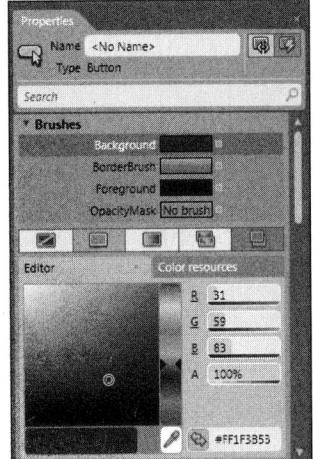

Figure 2-10: Properties panel

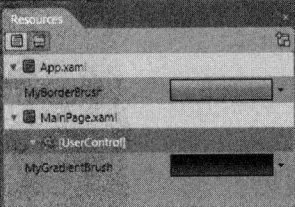

Figure 2-11: Resources panel.

✔ **Data panel:** The Data panel is used for creating sample data that you can use to help you design your application. You find out how to create sample data in Chapter 9. Figure 2-12 shows the Data panel with some sample data.

 ✔ **Results panel:** The Results panel displays information that you use to determine errors in your application. It contains two tabs: an Error tab that shows errors in your application, and a Build tab that shows the steps Expression Blend follows to build the application. Figure 2-13 shows the Results panel after you build the Hello, World application.

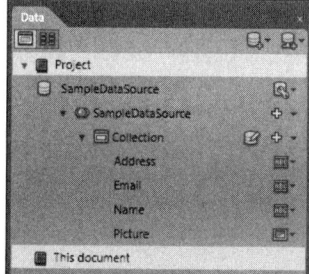

Figure 2-12: Data panel.

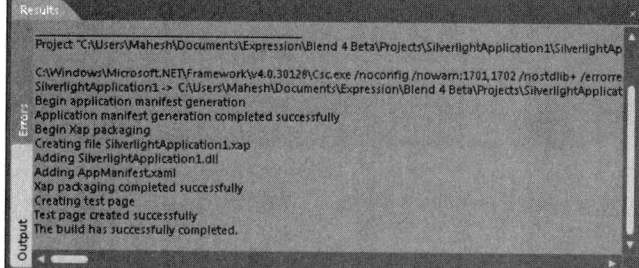

Figure 2-13: Results panel.

Adding a user interface element to the page

The previous sections give you a detailed look at the Expression Blend workspace. Here, we get you started on adding some UI elements and creating a "Hello, World" screen. You use the Tools panel at the side of the screen to add UI elements to your design.

 Among other items in the Tools panel is the TextBlock tool, shown here in the margin. Tools that you can add to a Silverlight application are also called *controls* (not a particularly intuitive name, but there you have it). So, the TextBlock tool is also referred to as the TextBlock control.

> ## What is XML?
>
> XML, which stands for Extensible Markup Language, is used primarily to exchange data over the Internet. It consists of markup and content. Markup begins with a left-pointing angle bracket (<) and ends with a right-pointing angle bracket (>). Anything that appears between two markups constitutes content. Here's an example of markup:
>
> ```
>     <Name ID="1234">
>        <LastName>Krishnan
>        </LastName>
>        <FirstName>Mahesh
>        </FirstName>
>     <Name>
> ```
>
> In this example `Name`, `LastName`, and `FirstName` constitute markup, while `Krishnan` and `Mahesh` constitute the content. Markups such as `Name` and `LastName` are also referred to as *elements*, and `ID`, which is part of the `Name` element, is called an *attribute*. Because the elements `LastName` and `FirstName` appear under another element (`Name`), they are called child elements. XML usually follows standard markup names so that different applications understand what elements to expect. You can find out more about XML by reading *XML For Dummies* by Ed Tittel, Norbet Mikula, and Ramesh Chandek (Wiley Publishing, Inc.).

You use the TextBlock control to display text, and this is the very control that you're about to create a Hello, World message with. To add the text "Hello, World" to the Artboard, follow these steps:

1. **Click the TextBlock control to select it as the default control.**

   After you select a control, it remains selected as the default control until you click another control in the Tools panel. You can then use it as many times as you want to perform actions within the Artboard.

2. **Click and drag your mouse on the Artboard.**

   A TextBlock control is added to the page and contains the text `TextBlock`. As the control is added, the dimensions (height and width) of the control are displayed along with some visual cue as to where the control is being added in relation to other existing controls. You can also add a TextBlock to the Artboard by double-clicking the TextBlock control in the Tools panel.

3. **After you have added the control, you change the contents of the TextBlock by typing** Hello, World.

4. **Press F5 to run the application.**

   The text `Hello, World` appears in the Web browser window.

Introducing the Basics of the Extensible Application Markup Language

As mentioned in Chapter 1, Silverlight uses the Extensible Application Markup Language, or XAML, which is pronounced "zamel." XAML is built on XML and looks very similar to HyperText Markup Language (HTML).

XAML allows you to create the look of the application without writing any code in C# or VB.NET. This new language was first introduced with Windows Presentation Foundation (WPF) and allows you to express how you want the user interface to look and behave.

When you add controls to the Artboard, or modify them using the tools provided, Silverlight stores them as XAML markup.

You can look at the XAML for the Hello, World application you just created by clicking the XAML button at the top-right corner of the Artboard. The view of the Artboard changes to reveal the XAML markup behind the application.

You can also look at both the Design view and the XAML at the same time by clicking the Split button (shown here in the margin), which can be found with the View buttons on the Artboard. This view is very useful when you want to learn how to write XAML without using a design tool.

Following is the XAML for the Hello, World application that you just created:

```
<UserControl
        xmlns="http://schemas.microsoft.com/winfx/2006/
        xaml/presentation"
        xmlns:x="http://schemas.microsoft.com/
        winfx/2006/xaml"
        x:Class="SilverlightApplication1.MainPage"
        Width="640" Height="480">

    <Grid x:Name="LayoutRoot" Background="White">
    <TextBlock Height="41" HorizontalAlignment="Left"
        Margin="33,40,0,0" VerticalAlignment="Top"
        Width="275" Text="Hello, World"
        TextWrapping="Wrap"/>
    </Grid>
</UserControl>
```

Here's a look at what's going on in this XAML:

- `UserControl`: This is the root element of XAML. Elements in XAML are hierarchical, meaning that elements are contained in other elements in a hierarchical fashion, but there is only one top-level element. This is known as the *root* element. In this example, `UserControl` contains references to namespaces that are used in the file. You don't need to know more about namespaces than the fact that namespaces are used to qualify element and attribute names with predefined resource names, which in this case are `http://schemas.microsoft.com/winfx/2006/xaml/presentation` and `http://schemas.microsoft.com/winfx/2006/xaml`. As is true of any other XML, XAML contains a bunch of elements and attributes associated with each element.

- `x:Class`: This is an attribute of `UserControl` that specifies the .NET class associated with the user control. This class contains code such as event handlers that are triggered by controls in the XAML file. An *event handler* is code that gets called when an event occurs, such as a button being pressed or text being changed.

- `Grid`: The `UserControl` in our Hello, World markup holds one `Grid` element, and the `Grid` element holds another element, `TextBlock`, which contains the "Hello, World" text. The `Grid` element is automatically added by Expression Blend to lay out controls in a grid-like fashion, which you learn about in more detail in Chapter 5.

    `Grid` contains attributes that dictate how the controls look and behave:

    `x:Name`: Specifies a name for the control so that it can be used in the code-behind file.

    `Background`: Specifies the background color of the grid, which is white in this case.

- `TextBlock`: As does `Grid`, this element contains attributes that tell controls how to look and behave. In the example, `TextBlock` contains the `Height`, `Width`, `Margin`, `HorizontalAlignment`, `VerticalAlignment`, `TextWrapping`, and `Text` attributes. These properties define the way the `TextBlock` element looks, and each of these attributes can be set directly from the Properties panel in either Expression Blend or Visual Studio. (Chapter 3 tells you much more about the Expression Blend Properties panel.)

Anything you do with XAML can also be done in code using languages such as C# and VB.NET. A declarative syntax is a lot easier to follow, however, and helps to separate the visual parts that a designer creates (XAML) from the actual workings of the application that the developer programs (C# or VB.NET).

Digging deeper into XAML

In this section, we change the XAML slightly from the Hello, World example to give you a feel for how elements and attributes fit together in XAML. Open the `MainPage.xaml` file if it is not already open and replace the XAML with the following markup:

```
<UserControl
        xmlns="http://schemas.microsoft.com/winfx/2006/
        xaml/presentation"
        xmlns:x="http://schemas.microsoft.com/
        winfx/2006/xaml"
        x:Class="SilverlightApplication1.MainPage"
        Width="640" Height="480">
        <TextBlock>Hello, World</TextBlock>
</UserControl>
```

If you press F5 and run the application, you should see that it behaves exactly as before and displays the `Hello, World` text. However, something is different: The `Grid` element is gone. Although the `Grid` element is useful for positioning multiple controls nicely in a grid-like fashion, you don't need it here because, at least so far, this page of the application contains only one control. So, you can completely eliminate the `Grid` element.

The new XAML here also eliminates all the attributes associated with the `TextBlock` control and puts the text `Hello, World` between beginning and ending `TextBlock` tags. Elements in XAML are the same as elements in XML. They contain a left-pointing angle bracket (<) followed by the name of the element and a space after it. After the space comes a forward slash(/) followed by a right-pointing angle bracket (>). Here's an example of a `TextBlock` tag:

```
<TextBlock />
```

Having an empty element usually doesn't make sense. Elements typically contain a value as well as other elements or attributes, such as in the following example:

```
<TextBlock FontSize="45" Foreground="Red">Hello, World</
        TextBlock>
```

When other elements or values are involved, the XAML element has a beginning tag (such as `<TextBlock>`) and an ending tag (such as `</TextBlock>`). Attributes are defined within the beginning tag. In the preceding example, the `TextBlock` tag contains two attributes: `FontSize` and `Foreground`. These attribute names are self-explanatory, specifying the size of the font used in the text and the foreground color of the text. The value specified for the control directly maps to the Text property for the TextBlock. The equivalent markup would look like the following:

```
<TextBlock FontSize="45" Foreground="Red" Text="Hello,
          World"> </TextBlock>
```

Or better still:

```
<TextBlock FontSize="45" Foreground="Red" Text="Hello,
          World" />
```

Removing the end tag in the preceding example reduces the clutter and makes the markup more readable.

Attributes are simply properties for an element, and you can set these properties using the Properties panel in both Expression Blend and Visual Studio. Apart from using attributes to set properties, you can also set them using child elements (the sidebar "What is XML?" explains what a child element is), as shown in the following example:

```
<TextBlock>
     <TextBlock.Foreground>Red</TextBlock.Foreground>
     <TextBlock.FontSize>45</TextBlock.FontSize>
     Hello, World
</TextBlock>
```

You wouldn't normally worry about whether Expression Blend uses properties or child elements to set properties, but when you are typing the XAML yourself, you will find that using child elements is particularly useful when setting complex properties such as gradient brushes (which make the color gradually change from one to another) and transformations (such as rotating a control), or when adding special effects. You can find out more about brushes, transformations, and special effects in Chapter 3, but the following example shows the syntax for a TextBlock element with a drop-shadow effect included:

```
<TextBlock Text="Hello, World" FontSize="40"
           Foreground="Red">
     <TextBlock.Effect>
         <DropShadowEffect/>
     </TextBlock.Effect>
</TextBlock>
```

Although you can get by without actually learning XAML at the early stages of Silverlight programming, understanding the syntax is a good idea so that you can directly jump into XAML markup and change it.

Understanding elements and properties by category

XAML contains a wide range of elements (far too many to detail in this book), but Table 2-1 gives you a sense of the basic types of elements and what you use them for.

Table 2-1	Types of Elements in XAML
Type of Element	**What It Does**
Layout containers	These controls are containers that contain other controls. In addition, these containers determine the way in which these controls are laid out for display.
Shapes	As the name suggests, these controls are responsible for drawing shapes such as Rectangles and Ellipses. We also include the Path element in this group because it can be used to draw complex shapes.
Media	Contains media elements such as videos, audios, and images.
Common controls	These elements are typically used to display things on the screen and/or take some input from users. Examples of common controls are Button, TextBox, TextBlock, ListBox, and so on.
Additional Controls	These are controls that have been created by you or others that you wish to use in your application. The Silverlight Toolkit contains a wide range of additional controls like Charts that you can use in your application.
Resources	These are elements such as colors and animations that control the look and feel of other elements.

Although every element contains its own properties, some properties are used by a wide range of controls. These common property types are described in Table 2-2.

Table 2-2 Types of Properties Shared by Various Controls

Property Type	What It Does
Color properties	These properties are used to set a certain color property on the element. Examples are `Foreground` and `OpacityMask` (which controls the transparency of the element).
Text properties	These properties set the various attributes associated with the text that is shown in the element. Examples of these properties include font size, font family properties, indents, and so on.
Layout properties	These properties are responsible for configuring how the element actually looks with respect to layout. They include properties such as `Height` and `Width`, as well as properties for horizontal and vertical alignments. If the control is in a grid, it may also contain properties such as the row and column in which the control appears.
Transformation properties	In some cases, a transformation is applied to elements to scale them up or down, skew them in an angle, rotate them, and so forth. The properties can be collectively grouped under Transformation properties.
Others	There are some properties that are quite common, such as `ToolTip`, `Cursor`, and `DataContext`. These types of properties are available for almost all controls but are too generic to be classified.

In some cases, additional properties become available on one element that is based on other elements. As an example, if you use a TextBlock within a Grid control (which you find out about in Chapter 5), you also need to specify the row and element of the grid in which the TextBlock should reside. But these properties show up only if the TextBlock is present within the Grid. The Grid *attaches* these properties to the elements that it contains, and these properties are called *attached properties.* An example of an attached property is the `Grid.Row` property in the following XAML:

```
<Grid>
    <Grid.RowDefinitions>
        <RowDefinition/>
        <RowDefinition/>
    </Grid.RowDefinitions>

    <TextBlock Text="Hello, World" FontSize="40"
        Foreground="Red" Grid.Row="1">
        <TextBlock.Effect>
            <DropShadowEffect/>
        </TextBlock.Effect>
    </TextBlock>
</Grid>
```

In this example, the `TextBlock` element does not contain a property for `Row` and `Column`, but to specify its position within the Grid, it sets the attached `Grid.Row` and `Grid.Column` properties.

Firing Up Visual Studio to Create a Silverlight Application

If you are a developer, you may already be at least somewhat familiar with Visual Studio and therefore feel more at home with it than with Expression Blend. Both programs use XAML to define the user interface, but they go about it differently. In this section, you find out the basics of creating a sample Silverlight application using Visual Studio.

First, you need to start Visual Studio 2010. Then follow these steps to create a Silverlight application:

1. **Choose File⇨New Project or click New Project from the Start Page that is displayed when Visual Studio opens up.**

    The New Project dialog box appears, as shown in Figure 2-14.

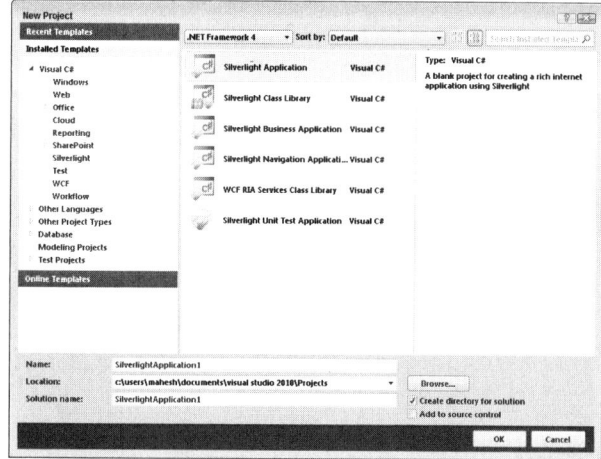

Figure 2-14: Creating a Silverlight project using the New Project dialog in Visual Studio.

2. **Select Silverlight Application from the list of project templates.**

    The New Silverlight Application dialog box appears, as shown in Figure 2-15.

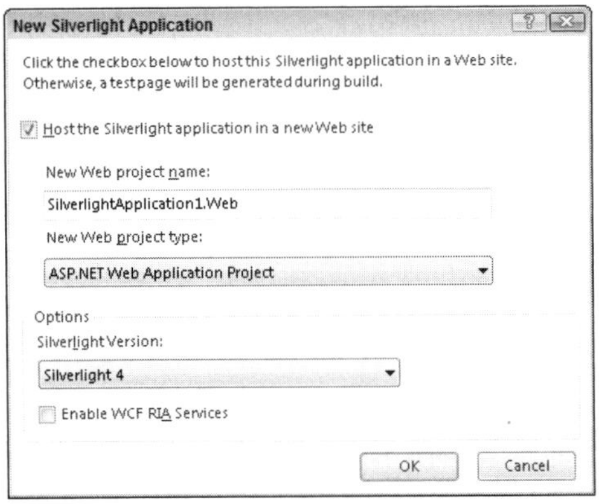

Figure 2-15: New Silverlight Application dialog box.

3. **In the New Silverlight Application dialog box, click OK without changing any options.**

    Visual Studio automatically creates the Silverlight project, the Web application project that hosts the Silverlight application, and the files for each of these projects.

4. **Press F5 to run the application.**

    Of course, the screen is empty at this point because you haven't added anything to the application yet. A little later in this section, we show you how to do that.

Exploring Visual Studio

Before you add the "Hello, World" text to the application, take a look at the Visual Studio Integrated Development Environment (IDE), which is shown in Figure 2-16. Here are its main features:

- The IDE contains a Toolbox panel on the left side that contains the Silverlight controls that you can add to the application. The controls in the list are split into Common Silverlight Controls and All Silverlight Controls.

- The top of the IDE contains menus and a toolbar, which enable you to do far more tasks than we have room to list here, but some examples include creating and opening files and projects, compiling and debugging applications, searching for text, and so on.

- The predominant area in the IDE is occupied by the Editor panel, where Silverlight project files can be opened for editing. The top of the panel contains a tabbed list of files that are open.

Chapter 2: Getting Started in Silverlight 43

✔ As in Expression Blend, the IDE contains a number of panels. Some are visible only during debugging, and others are used for seeing build or search results. The two most important ones are as follows:

The Solution Explorer: This shows all the projects and the files used for creating the Silverlight application. Double-clicking a file from the Solution Explorer opens the file in the Editor window.

The Properties window: This is similar to the Properties panel in Expression Blend and allows you to modify the properties for Silverlight control.

You can drag the various toolbars and panels in both Visual Studio and Expression Blend around and dock them to different parts of the screen. Although you may change the positions of these panels, their functionality remains the same.

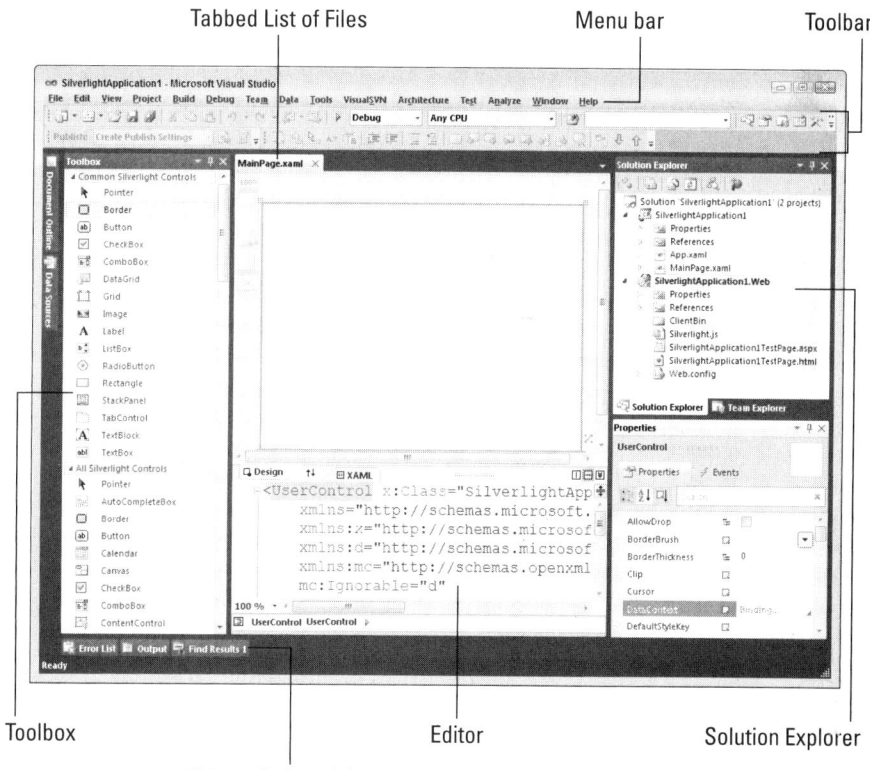

Figure 2-16: Visual Studio IDE showing all the panels.

Creating the Hello, World application

To create a Hello, World application from the project created earlier in this section, make sure that the `MainPage.xaml file` is open in Visual Studio. (Visual Studio automatically creates this file for you.) Then follow these steps:

1. **Double-click the TextBlock control in the Toolbox to add the control.**

   Alternatively, select the control from the Toolbox and then draw it on the design surface with the exact length and width that you want the control to have. Either way, the control appears on the design surface and displays the default text as `TextBlock`.

2. **Change the default Text property of the control to** `Hello World` **from the Properties window.**

3. **Press F5 to run the application in your browser.**

Exploring the Solution Explorer

As explained earlier in the chapter but worth mentioning again here, in both Expression Blend and Visual Studio, the problem of grouping together the files needed to create a Silverlight application is "solved" by creating a Solution file (`.sln`). The solution file breaks down these collections even further into projects (`.prj` files) that are specific to the type of application — for example, the Silverlight part of the application becomes a Silverlight project and the Web part of the application becomes a Web project.

The Solution Explorer, shown in Figure 2-17, is responsible for displaying and managing the solution file and displays all the projects and files associated with it. Notice that the solution you create in this section actually has two projects: SilverlightApplication1 and SilverlightApplication1.Web.

The SilverlightApplication1 project holds the Silverlight project and contains two main source code files: `App.xaml` and `MainPage.xaml`. The `MainPage.xaml` file contains the XAML responsible for displaying the Silverlight page. If you click the + (plus sign) in front of the `MainPage.xaml` file in the Solution Explorer, another file appears, called `MainPage.xaml.cs`.

XAML declares the way the user interface looks, but you also need code written in C# or VB.NET that complements the XAML markup and is responsible for running some code when a user interacts with the user interface, such as by pressing a button or even moving the mouse. The `MainPage.xaml` file contains this code and is referred to as the *code-behind* file.

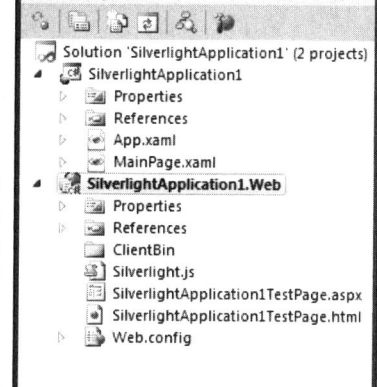

Figure 2-17: The Solution Explorer showing the files in the project.

You haven't added any event handlers (that is, code that gets called when an event occurs), so the file doesn't contain much code:

```
using System;
using System.Collections.Generic;
using System.Linq;
using System.Net;
using System.Windows;
using System.Windows.Controls;
using System.Windows.Documents;
using System.Windows.Input;
using System.Windows.Media;
using System.Windows.Media.Animation;
using System.Windows.Shapes;

namespace SilverlightApplication1
{
    public partial class MainPage : UserControl
    {
        public MainPage()
        {
            InitializeComponent();
        }
    }
}
```

The code for `InitializeComponent` will get auto-generated. This code contains the code to load the `MainPage.xaml` file and do other things that you don't need to worry about.

Specifying the startup file for the application

The other file in the Silverlight project, App.xaml, contains application resources. Open the file by double-clicking its name from the Solution Explorer, and you see the following XAML:

```
<Application xmlns="http://schemas.microsoft.com/
      winfx/2006/xaml/presentation"
       xmlns:x="http://schemas.microsoft.com/
      winfx/2006/xaml"
       x:Class="SilverlightApplication1.App"
       >
    <Application.Resources>

    </Application.Resources>
</Application>
```

The Application.Resources element tag contains all the resources that are shared among different Silverlight pages within the same application. As explained earlier, these resources can contain elements such as brushes or animations. In this case, it is empty because you have not yet added any resources.

The code-behind file for App.xaml - App.xaml.cs is used by Silverlight to start the application and to control the application behavior. In this file, you can enter code that is run on application startup, shutdown, or when your application encounters an error. To see what the code-behind file for App.xaml looks like, open the App.xaml.cs file by double-clicking it from Solution Explorer. It will look essentially like this (some lines have been left out for the sake of clarity here; these are indicated by the ellipses [. . .]):

```
namespace SilverlightApplication1
{
    public partial class App : Application
    {

        public App()
        {
            this.Startup += this.Application_Startup;
            this.Exit += this.Application_Exit;
            this.UnhandledException += this.Application_
      UnhandledException;

            InitializeComponent();
        }

        private void Application_Startup(object sender,
           StartupEventArgs e)
        {
```

```
            this.RootVisual = new MainPage();
        }

        private void Application_Exit(object sender,
          EventArgs e)
        {

        }
        private void Application_
          UnhandledException(object sender, ApplicationUn
          handledExceptionEventArgs e)
        {
            . . .
        }
        . . .
    }
}
```

Notice that the `App.xaml.cs` contains, among other things, the event handlers for handling three events: one for startup, one for exit, and one for handling exceptions. The event handler for `Startup` creates the `MainPage` object in this case. If multiple Silverlight user controls or pages are contained in the application, the `Startup` event can be used to initialize the class that you want the application to start with.

Understanding other files involved in the solution

The Solution Explorer also contains two folder icons with the headings Properties and References, as follows:

- **Properties:** This folder contains the files `AppManifest.xml` and `AssemblyInfo.cs`, which are used to set certain properties for the application. You do not have to worry about these files for now.
- **References:** This folder allows you to add assemblies to the project. Assemblies can contain controls and resources for your application, among other things, and are available as libraries. These libraries have the extension `.dll` and are created either by you or someone else to contain prebuilt code and functionality.

Hosting the Silverlight application

You will see another project in your Solution Explorer window: `Silverlight Application1.web`. Silverlight applications usually require a Web site to allow them to be hosted on the Internet. By default, Visual Studio and Expression Blend create a basic Web site to host your application for you. It is this Web site that runs and delivers your Silverlight application to the user for you. This project has numerous files that contain placeholders for the Silverlight application.

You do not really need the Web application for creating a Silverlight application, but having it helps in running and debugging the application.

Using Expression Blend and Visual Studio in Tandem

If you've followed along in this chapter and created the Hello, World application in both Expression Blend and Visual Studio, you may be wondering why we recommend that you know how to use both programs.

Expression Blend is primarily a designer's tool, but developers can use it, too. You will find that there are some things, such as creating animations, you can do with Expression Blend that you just can't do with Visual Studio. Similarly, there are things that you just can't do with Expression Blend. For instance, you can write code in a language such as C# using Expression Blend, but you cannot do more complex tasks such as setting breakpoints, debugging the application, and so on — for those tasks, you need Visual Studio.

These two programs actually complement each other quite well. In fact, you can open the same solution file (`.sln`) in both applications, and when you right-click a filename in the Solution Explorer in Visual Studio or in the Projects panel in Expression Blend, a menu to open the file in the other application shows up.

Chapter 3
Enhancing the User Interface

In This Chapter
- Understanding the Properties panel
- Drawing with shapes
- Changing dimensions of objects
- Painting with colors
- Applying transformations to objects
- Using audio and video in your pages

Silverlight applications are all about providing good user experiences on the Web, and building a good user interface plays a big part in creating that experience. A truly dynamic application, one that users find appealing, includes rich graphics, animations, audio, and video.

We look at how you use controls such as Buttons in Chapter 4 and animations in Chapter 8, but first, in this chapter, we show you how to jazz up your application by setting properties for objects such as shapes. We also show you how to transform an object by changing its dimension and position, filling it with various types of color, and doing complex things such as skewing, flipping, and projecting it into a 3-D axis. Finally, we show you how to add video and audio to your Silverlight application.

Getting to Know the Properties Panel

You set properties on user interface elements using the Properties panel in Expression Blend.

In Chapter 2, we show you how to create a simple Silverlight application called "Hello, World." If you haven't created an application yet, you can refer to that one to help you follow along in this chapter. To start familiarizing yourself with the Properties panel, make sure that you have an application open (by choosing File⇨Recent Projects and opening an existing project). Then select any element on the Artboard. If you open the Hello, World

Part I: Illuminating Silverlight

project that we show you in Chapter 2, you should see the TextBlock control containing the text Hello, World. Click the control to select it. The Properties panel then displays all the properties for that control.

If the Properties panel is not visible, press either the Tab key or F4.

Setting a property for an object

To set a property, follow these steps:

1. **Check to see whether the Selection tool, shown in the margin, is selected. Click the tool if it is not already selected.**
2. **Click the control on the Artboard for which you wish to set properties.**

    The control gets selected on the Artboard and shows selection handles to indicate that it is selected. The Objects and Timeline panel also highlights the control you've just selected.

3. **In the Properties panel, scroll up and down to find the property you want to change.**
4. **To find the property quickly, click the Search field in the Properties panel (shown in Figure 3-1) and start typing in the name of the property, such as Height or Width.**

    As you start typing, the Properties panel displays only those properties that contain the text you've typed. For instance, if you start typing the word *Width,* only the properties Width, MinWidth, and MaxWidth appear.

5. **If you are setting or changing a property that contains a string such, as** Text **or** Tooltip, **just click the field and start typing.**

    If the string property affects the way the control looks, the Artboard immediately updates that control.

6. **If you are setting or changing a property that contains a number, such as** Opacity, Width, **or** Height, **you again click the field and start typing the values.**

    Actually, an easier way to change the values is by using your mouse. As you move your mouse over the field, the cursor changes shape to a four-sided arrow, shown here in the margin. Click and drag the mouse left or down to reduce the value, and drag the mouse right or up to increase the value.

    If the property affects the way the control looks, the Artboard again updates it.

Getting to know the Properties panel better

There are a number of things in the Properties panel that you need to be aware of. They are indicated in Figure 3-1 and described in the following list.

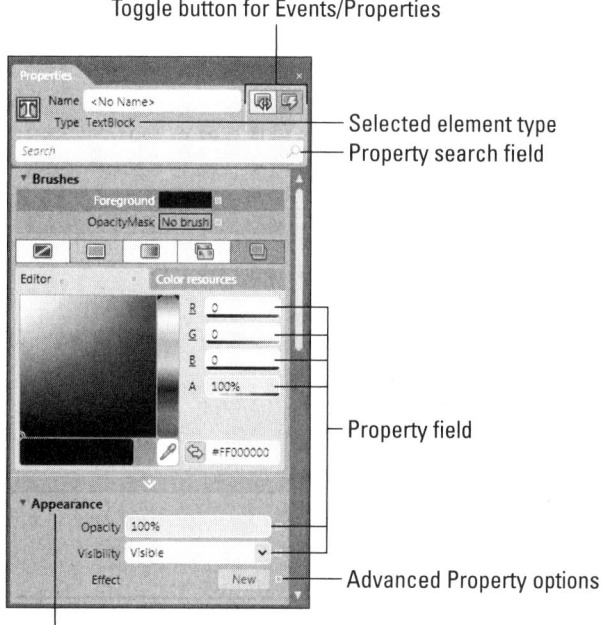

Figure 3-1: Properties panel.

✓ **The Search field:** The Properties panel also has a Search box that allows you to filter the property names as you type, as explained in the previous section.

To understand what we mean by filtering property names, type **Font** in the Search box. As you can see, the Properties panel displays only the properties that contain the text "Font" in them. You can cancel the search by clicking the X button at the right of the Search text box. Because the Properties panel can contain a great many properties, the search feature can help you find a property by name with ease.

- **Property groups:** The properties are also grouped together nicely to help you find what you are looking for quickly. Figure 3-2 shows some of the groups for the TextBlock control. You can expand and collapse these property groups by pressing the tiny triangle that appears in front of each group's name. For instance, if you expand the group called Appearance for the TextBlock control, you see the properties Opacity, Visibility, and Effect. Common group names are listed in Table 3-1.

Table 3-1	Common Groups of Properties
Group	*Description*
Brushes	This group contains properties that control the color of the control such as Foreground and Background.
Appearance	This group contains properties such as Visibility, Opacity, and BorderThickness.
Layout	This group contains properties such as Width and Height that control the position of the control.
Common	Properties such as Tooltip, Text, and Cursor appear under this group.
Text	Properties such as Font and FontSize for the Text component of the control are in this group.
Transform	Properties that apply transformations such as scaling and rotations are in this group.
Miscellaneous	Properties such as Style and Template are in this group. We look at these in more detail in Chapter 6.

- **Properties and Events buttons:** The Properties panel contains not only properties for the control but also its events. (An *event,* as we explain in Chapter 2, occurs when you interact with the element itself by moving a mouse over it or clicking it.) You can make the Properties panel display the list of events by clicking the Events button. Switch back to displaying properties by clicking the Properties button. These buttons appear here in the margin as well as in Figure 3-1.

- **Advanced Property options:** Most of the properties in the Properties panel contain a little square to the right of them that you can click to bring up Advanced Property options. The most commonly used Advanced Property option is Reset, which sets the property value to the default values of the control, thereby usually removing that property setting. For example, resetting a Margin property would remove the Margin attribute from the XAML for that control.

Drawing Shapes on the Artboard

Silverlight enables you to draw on the screen using vector graphics. This means that you specify the shapes, lines, and points using X-Y coordinates. Vector graphics display nicely on the screen irrespective of the screen resolution or whether the display is zoomed in or out, in contrast to the behavior of bitmapped graphics, whose shapes appear pixilated when displayed at a high resolution or when the display is zoomed in. Figure 3-2 shows the comparison between a vector graphic and a bitmapped graphic, when scaled. The figure contains three sets of images. From left to right, the first set displays an unscaled text and circle. The second set contains the vector graphic scaled up, and the third set contains the scaled-up bitmapped version. Notice that the bitmapped circle and text look pixilated when scaled up, whereas the vector graphic version appears clear.

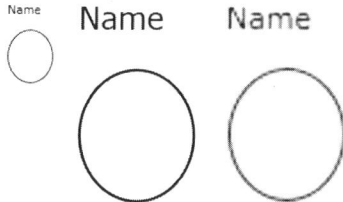

Figure 3-2: Comparison of vector and bit-mapped graphics.

Expression Blend allows you to add the following shapes as vector graphics:

- Rectangle
- Ellipse
- Line

You can also use the Pen and Pencil tools to draw freehand shapes on the Artboard. You select these tools from the Tools panel and add them to the Artboard the same way you add the TextBlock in the Hello, World example (as explained in Chapter 2).

Not all tools in the Tools panel are visible all the time. To display the additional shape tools, Ellipse and Line, click and hold the Rectangle tool (see Figure 3-3). Alternatively, right-click the Rectangle tool.

Part I: Illuminating Silverlight

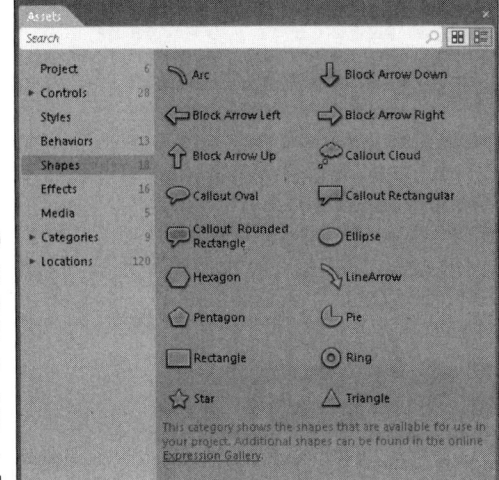

Figure 3-3: The Tools panel showing the Rectangle, Ellipse, and Line tools.

Drawing with ready-made shapes

To draw a shape, follow these steps:

1. **Create a new Silverlight project by choosing File**⇨**New Project, or open an existing project by choosing File**⇨**Recent Projects and picking a project from the menu.**
2. **Click the Rectangle, Ellipse, or Line tool to select it.**
3. **Click the Artboard and drag the cursor to get the size you need.**

   As you drag the cursor, the width and height of the shape appear next to the shape you are drawing. When you stop dragging, the shape appears on the Artboard.

Drawing freehand

The two Shape tools that work differently from the drawing tools in the previous section are the Pen and Pencil tools. You use these tools when you want to draw freehand sketches. These freehand sketches are drawn as vector paths, which are a series of points that are joined together.

The Pen tool

To draw a path with the Pen tool, click it in the Tools panel to select it. Then click the Artboard in different places to plot your shape. Try a star, for example. As you plot the star, notice that as you click the Artboard, the line from the previous point extends itself to the new point you just clicked. A star drawn with the Pen tool is shown in Figure 3-4.

Chapter 3: Enhancing the User Interface

The Pen tool allows you to also draw curves rather than just straight lines between the points you've drawn. To draw a curve, follow these steps:

1. **Click the Pen tool from the Tools panel to select it.**
2. **Click the Artboard and drag the mouse in the direction you want the curve to appear in.**

   A line appears on the screen with two selection handles — one square handle and one round handle. The round handle represents the direction in which the curve will appear.

3. **Click the Artboard again in the place where you want the curve to end.**

   A curve appears connecting the two points.

4. **Click the first point again.**

   This closes the curve shape that you just drew. Optionally, you can click another tool in the Tools panel to stop drawing.

The Pencil tool

The Pencil tool allows you to drag and draw any shape on the screen. Try drawing a star with the Pencil tool on the Artboard. The different shapes drawn with the available tools in Expression Blend are shown in Figure 3-4.

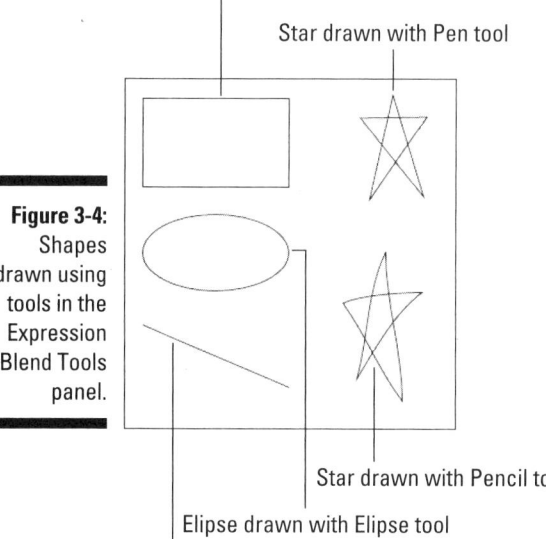

Figure 3-4: Shapes drawn using tools in the Expression Blend Tools panel.

Rectangle drawn with Rectangle tool
Star drawn with Pen tool
Star drawn with Pencil tool
Elipse drawn with Elipse tool
Line drawn with Line tool

Understanding the XAML for shapes

To see the XAML for the shapes you draw on the Artboard, click the XAML button on the Artboard. Be aware, though, that only two types of shapes show up by their name in the XAML: Rectangle and Ellipse.

When you create a rectangle using the Rectangle control, the XAML for it looks like the following:

```
<Rectangle Fill="White" Stroke="Black" Height="148"
        HorizontalAlignment="Left" Margin="58,51,0,0"
        VerticalAlignment="Top" Width="177"/>
```

The `Height` and `Width` properties along with `Margin` property determine where the Rectangle is placed and what dimension it takes, and the `Stroke` property determines the color with which it is drawn. All other properties in the preceding XAML are optional, but Expression Blend fills them in anyway, depending on the values these properties took when previous shapes were drawn.

Other shapes — those drawn with the Line, Pen, and Pencil tools — translate as `Path` elements in XAML.

A `Path` element is nothing more than a series of connected lines and curves and can be used to represent any freehand drawing. A simple Path that joins two points is represented in XAML as follows:

```
<Path Stretch="Fill" Stroke="Black" Height="60.5"
        Margin="284,72.5,248,0" VerticalAlignment="Top"
        UseLayoutRounding="False" Data="M284,72.5
        L391,132"/>
```

A more complex `Path` that draws a star may look something like this XAML snippet:

```
<Path Stretch="Fill" Stroke="Black "
        Margin="137.5,207.5,242.5,115.5"
        UseLayoutRounding="False" Data="M175,251
        L203,208 L215,248 L255,247 L222,280 L227,331
        L194,300 L160,326 L161,284 L138,253" />
```

The main information on how to connect the points in a `Path` is supplied in the `Data` parameter. The value for the parameter looks cryptic, but because Expression Blend automatically fills this out for you, don't worry too much about it.

Shaping, Sizing, and Positioning Your Object

After you've drawn a shape on the Artboard, you can play around with its shape and size to your heart's content. You do this by selecting the shape and manipulating it using your mouse or changing its properties in the Properties panel. Keep reading for the details.

Getting your object into shape using your mouse

You can reshape any object you've placed on your Artboard. To reshape a Rectangle object, for example, follow these steps:

1. **Click the Selection Tool in the Tools panel.**
2. **Click the Rectangle on the Artboard to select it.**

   The Artboard draws a bounding box with selection handles around the Rectangle, as shown in Figure 3-5.

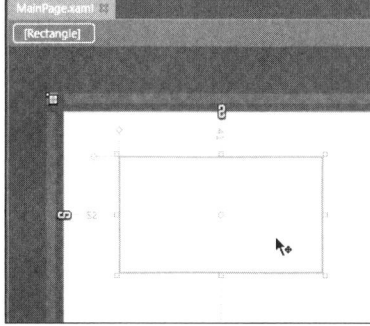

Figure 3-5: Rectangle showing bounding box and selection handles.

The selection handles appear on the four sides and four corners of the Rectangle. When you move the mouse over these handles and on top of the Rectangle, the cursor changes to a different shape depending on where it is. The different cursor shapes indicate the type of operation you can perform when you click and drag.

For example, you can resize the Rectangle when the cursor turns into a double-headed arrow. Click the double-headed arrow and drag the Rectangle to the required dimensions.

Part I: Illuminating Silverlight

When you want to move the Rectangle to a new position, simply click inside the Rectangle and drag it. The shape of the cursor again indicates the action that is available to you at that point.

Table 3-2 shows the different cursor shapes and what you can do with them.

Table 3-2	Using the Mouse for Shaping and Sizing an Object
Cursor Shape	Function
↕	Increase/decrease height
↔	Increase/decrease width
↘	Increase/decrease dimensions in the northwest or southeast direction
↗	Increase/decrease dimensions in the southwest or northeast direction
▶✥	Move the object to a new location

Reshaping and sizing an object using the Properties panel

The width, height, and position of a shape can also be set from the Properties panel. If you look under the Layout group in the Properties panel, you see the properties for Width and Height. The position attributes appear under Margin, as shown in Figure 3-6.

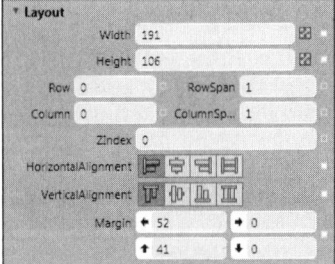

Figure 3-6: The Layout section of the Properties panel.

Chapter 3: Enhancing the User Interface 59

To see how the Height, Width, and Margin properties are tied together with an object on the Artboard, do the following:

1. **Use the Selection tool from the Tools panel and click an object, such as Rectangle, on the Artboard to select it.**

   The Rectangle is selected and shows the selection handles.

2. **Resize the Rectangle on the Artboard by dragging one of the selection handles.**

   The Rectangle's size changes. The Height and Width properties in the Properties panel also change.

3. **Move the Rectangle on the Artboard by dragging it.**

   The Rectangle moves position and while it is doing so, the Margin properties in the Properties panel also change.

You can constrain the movement of the shape to one direction by holding the Shift key while dragging. For instance, when you move the Rectangle, holding the Shift key restricts the movement either to the X-axis or Y-axis alone. Just try it to see for yourself.

Rounding the corners of a Rectangle object

To round the corners of a Rectangle, follow these steps:

1. **Use the Selection tool from the Tools panel and click a Rectangle object on the Artboard to select it.**

   The rectangle is selected and shows the selection handles. Notice the dotted lines that appear at the top-left corner of the Rectangle. These are the corner radius handles.

2. **Place the cursor on one of the corner radius handles at the end of the dotted line near the top-left corner of the Rectangle until the cursor turns into a plus sign, as shown in Figure 3-7.**

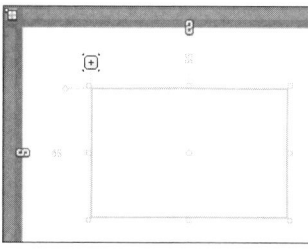

Figure 3-7: Rectangle with cursor on top of the corner radius handle.

Part I: Illuminating Silverlight

3. **Drag the mouse to set the length of the rounded rectangle.**

   Note that when you drag the mouse to set the rounded corner, the radius of both X and Y are always symmetrical. The rectangle with rounded corners is shown in Figure 3-8. If you want to change them individually, hold the Shift key while dragging.

You can also set the radius of the rounded corner by setting the RadiusX and RadiusY properties that appear under Appearance on the Properties panel.

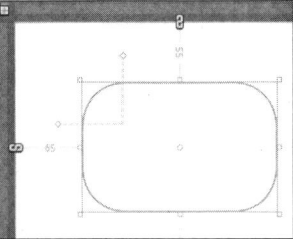

Figure 3-8: Rectangle with rounded corners.

Rotating, Projecting in 3-D, and Doing Other Funky Things with Shapes

Silverlight allows you to write applications that contain a lot of animation. This animation can be in the form of fly-out menus and games, for example. Animations are discussed in Chapter 8.

To bounce a ball up and down on the screen, you may need to be able to rotate the ball, change its position, or even stretch, contract, or skew it a little bit to produce a bouncing effect. These actions on the object are called *transformations*. You can perform a number of transformations to the object on the Artboard. These include the following:

- **Rotating:** You can rotate the object to change its angle.
- **Skewing:** This involves distorting the object to a certain angle.
- **Scaling:** You can scale an object up or down from its original shape.
- **Projection:** This involves giving an object the appearance of being three dimensional.

The following sections show you how to perform each of these actions, using a Rectangle object as an example.

Chapter 3: Enhancing the User Interface *61*

 Scaling and resizing are *not* the same thing. With *scaling,* everything in the object scales up or down. For example, the border thickness increases or decreases when you scale the object, but it doesn't change when you resize. It can be quite confusing sometimes if you do not know the difference.

Rotating a rectangle or other shape

To rotate a Rectangle (or other shape), you need to have the shape displayed on the Artboard. Then follow these steps:

1. **Click the Selection tool in the Tools panel and then click the Rectangle control.**

   The shape is selected and the selection handles appear.

 2. **Move the cursor to one of the edges until it changes into a two-sided arrow at an angle (shown here in the margin).**

   When the cursor changes shape, you can drag and rotate the Rectangle to any desired angle, as shown in Figure 3-9.

3. **Move the cursor to the axis of rotation, which is the small circle at the center of the object.**

   When the cursor changes shape to a four-headed arrow, drag the axis of rotation to another point.

4. **Repeat the rotation that you performed in Step 2.**

   The Rectangle rotates again, but on a new axis of rotation.

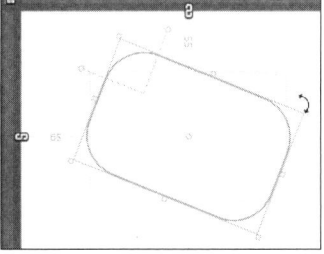

Figure 3-9: Rotating a Rectangle object.

Skewing an object

Skewing an object, as we mention at the start of this section, involves distorting the angles of the object. For example, you can create a parellelogram by skewing a square, or you can create shadow effects with skewed text (which we show you later in this chapter).

Part I: Illuminating Silverlight

To skew a shape to a new angle, follow these steps:

1. **Click the Selection tool in the Tools panel and then click the Rectangle control.**

   The shape is selected and the selection handles appear.

2. **Place the cursor near one of the side selection handles.**

   The shape of the cursor changes to the shape shown here in the margin, which indicates that the object can be skewed.

3. **Drag the cursor to skew the Rectangle to whatever angle you like.**

   The Rectangle appears skewed, as shown in Figure 3-10.

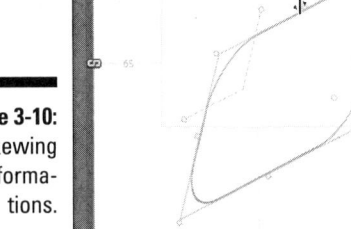

Figure 3-10: Skewing transformations.

You can skew an object on both the X-axis and the Y-axis. These transformations can also be directly applied from the Transform group in the Properties panel. For example, to perform a simple Translate transform, which moves an object from one position to another, follow these steps:

1. **Click the Selection tool in the Tools panel and then click the Rectangle control.**

   The shape is selected and the selection handles appear.

2. **Open the Properties panel and go to the Transform group, as shown in Figure 3-11.**

   The group contains tabs for Translate, Rotate, Scale, Skew, Center Point, and Flip.

3. **From the Translate tab, change the values of X and Y.**

   The position of the Rectangle on the Artboard changes.

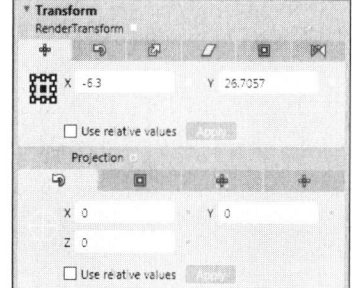

Figure 3-11: Transform properties.

Applying 3-D Perspective transformations

Silverlight supports 3-D projection. This means that you can take objects that are ordinarily limited to being manipulated in 2-D space and "project" them into 3-D space. These objects don't become 3-D objects, but they can be treated as if they live in 3-D space. For example, you can take the image of a photo that is in 2-D and rotate it in 3-D to provide illusions such as flipping a photo album.

To give a two-dimensional object the appearance of being a three-dimensional one, follow these steps:

1. **Create a new Silverlight Project by choosing File⇨New Project.**
2. **In the New Project dialog box, choose Silverlight 4 Application + Website.**

   A new Silverlight project is created and a blank Artboard is shown.
3. **From the Assets panel, type** Image **in the Search field. Then click the Image tool from the list to select it and draw it on the Artboard.**
4. **From the Properties panel, set the Source property by picking an image file.**

   The image is displayed in the Image control on the Artboard.
5. **Go to the Rotation tab under the Transform group in the Properties panel; this is the first tab (that is, the leftmost) that appears under Projection (see Figure 3-12).**

   When you move your mouse cursor over the circle in the tab, the circle changes to a blue color. This circle is called the Projection ball, and you can drag the mouse around to rotate the Projection ball to rotate the image on a 3-D plane.

Notice that the image on the Artboard performs a 3-D transformation as the mouse is moved. Figure 3-13 shows the transformation.

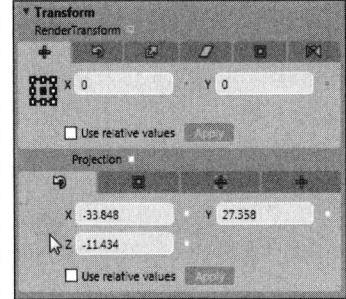

Figure 3-12: Rotating the Projection ball from the Rotation tab under the Transform group in the Properties panel.

Figure 3-13: Perspective transformation that has been applied to an image.

When you are doing 3-D perspective transformations, make sure you do them after setting all other properties on the object. Applying transformations first makes it hard to manipulate other properties from Expression Blend.

Painting Colors with Brushes in the Properties panel

Transformations, rotations, and so on look cool, but without any color, your objects still look pretty bland. You can add color to them by setting the properties that appear in the Brushes section of the Properties panel. You can also mix colors. To get a feel for playing with color, this section takes you through filling a shape with color and mixing different colors to create new shades from the Properties panel.

Filling an object with color

To fill an object (in this example, a rectangle) with color, follow these steps:

1. **Create a new Silverlight Project by choosing File➪New Project and selecting Silverlight 4 Application + Website, or open an existing project by choosing File➪Recent Projects and picking a project from the list.**

   A Silverlight project is opened and the Artboard is shown.

2. **From the Tools panel, select the Rectangle tool and draw a rectangle on the Artboard.**

3. **Go to the Brushes group in the Properties panel.**

   The Fill property should be highlighted by default, as shown in Figure 3-14. If it is not, click it. The section shows five brush tabs, which we describe in Table 3-3. Click the Solid color brush tab.

4. **In the color palette that appears in the Editor tab, select the color of your choice.**

   The fill color of the rectangle shows the color you just picked.

Figure 3-14: The Brushes group in the Properties panel.

Table 3-3	Color Brush Tabs
Tab Image	*Description*
	No brush.
	Solid color brush. Displays a single solid color.

(continued)

Table 3-3 *(continued)*

Tab Image	Description
	Gradient brush. Displays multiple colors that gradually change from one to another.
	Tile brush. Uses an image as a background and repeats the image as a tile.
	Brush resources. Uses a brush defined as a resource.

Using the Eyedropper tool

If you have a color anywhere in the screen that you would like to use, follow these steps:

1. **Click the Selection tool in the Tools panel and then click an object.**

   The shape is selected and the selection handles appear.

2. **Click the Fill property in the Properties panel.**

3. **From the Properties panel, click the Color Eyedropper button that appears at the bottom of the color palette in the Brushes group.**

   The cursor changes its shape to resemble an eyedropper, shown here in the margin.

4. **Move the cursor to a color on the screen and click it to select it.**

   The shape's color changes to the color you clicked, and the Fill Color property in the Properties panel displays the newly picked color.

Mixing colors

You can also alter colors, if desired, by changing the values under R, G, B, and A. R stands for Red, G for Green, B for Blue, and A for Alpha. These properties collectively make up a *brush*.

When you paint with colors in the real world, you make up new colors by mixing different colors together. Similarly, in Expression Blend, you mix up R, G, and B to make up new colors and new shades. The values for these colors can range between 0 and 255. For instance, if you set the value of 255 to R and set the value of 0 to both G and B, you get a pure red color. Similarly, when you set the value of 255 to G and set the value of 0 to R and B, you get a pure green color. You can start making the shade of green lighter by adding a bit more value to R and B, and even reducing the value of G.

When you set the value as 0 for all three color components, R, G and B, you get a pure black color, and when you set them all to 255, you get white.

The Alpha property specifies a transparency component to the brush you're painting with. The Alpha value is expressed as a percentage. Setting an Alpha value of 100 percent means that the object has no transparency (that is, it's opaque). Setting a value of 0 means that it is completely transparent.

The fill color is not the only property that has a brush associated with it. Depending on the type of control, you may have other properties as well. For instance, the Stroke property is used to set the color of the brush that draws the Rectangle object's border. The Foreground and Background properties also appear for many controls.

Applying gradients for color transitions

In addition to applying a solid color throughout an object, you can set the fill color using a gradient brush. A gradient brush gradually transforms one color into another color, and the smooth transition looks nicer than an abrupt change of color. Silverlight also allows you to specify multiple gradient stops or multiple color transitions to add more color effects. You specify a gradient stop at a location on the object where you want the brush to change from one color to another.

To set a gradient brush, follow these steps:

 1. **In the Properties panel, click the tab with the gradient image, shown here in the margin.**

    A gradient brush is immediately applied to the shape you're working with on the Artboard. At the same time, some new items appear on the Properties panel that are specific to the gradient brush. These new items include the following:

    - *Gradient slider:* This is used to show and set the gradient color changes.

    - *Buttons to select the type of gradient:* There are two types of gradient buttons: Linear gradient and Radial gradient. When the Linear Gradient button is selected, the color changes gradually from one side of the control to the other side. When the Radial Gradient button is selected, the gradient appears in a circular fashion, starting from a midpoint and gradually changing outward.

Part I: Illuminating Silverlight

- *Options to select the next gradient stop:* These appear as little arrows that you can click to set the previous and next gradient stops.
- *Selected gradient stop offset:* You use this field to change the position of the gradient stops.

Figure 3-15 shows the extended properties for gradients.

2. **To select the gradient colors, first click one of the two gradient stops in the gradient slider, shown here in the margin, and then pick a color from the Editor.**

You can add more gradient stops by clicking anywhere within the slider.

After you have selected the gradients, you can reverse the colors by clicking the Reverse Gradient Stops button, shown here in the margin.

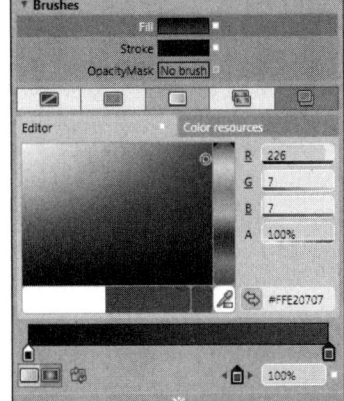

Figure 3-15: Setting gradient properties.

When the Linear gradient is selected, the gradient appears in a linear fashion. You can change this to the Radial gradient with the gradient appearing in a circular fashion by clicking the Radial Gradient button. The two gradients are shown in Figure 3-16.

Figure 3-16: Linear (left) and Radial (right) gradients.

TIP The Eyedropper can also be used to pick gradient shades. To do that, first click the Gradient eyedropper (refer to Figure 3-15) and then click and drag any portion of the screen that you would like to use for your color gradient. You can even open an image that has a nice gradient pattern (such as an image of a cloud or the sky, for instance) on your screen and, using the Eyedropper, select the gradient from a portion of the image.

Using the Gradient tool instead of setting gradients through the Properties panel

The Gradient tool, shown here in the margin, is in the Tools panel and can be used to specify gradient directions. It also helps you perform actions, such as adding gradient stops, more easily.

To use the Gradient tool, select the tool from the Tools panel first and then click the object on the Artboard that you want to apply the gradient to. An arrow appears on the selected object, as shown in Figure 3-17.

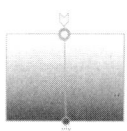

Figure 3-17: Gradient tool on a rectangle.

You have several ways to manipulate gradient properties, as follows:

- Click and move the arrow around. The position of the gradient changes accordingly.
- Click the circle that appears on the middle of the arrow and drag it to reposition the gradient stop.
- Hold the Alt key down and click along the length of the arrow to create more gradient stops.
- Click the arrow head or arrow bottom and resize the arrow. Resizing the arrow allows you to specify the length of the gradient color within the object selected.
- Move the cursor close to the arrow head or bottom until the shape of the cursor changes to show two arrow heads. At that point, you can drag and rotate the arrow to another direction.

✔ When the Radial gradient is set for the object, an oval appears with selection handles. You can also change the radius of the oval by dragging these handles.

When you double-click a gradient stop handle in the arrow, a small color selection editor pops up near the arrow to allow you to pick a new gradient color quickly and easily.

Manipulating gradients further with the Brush Transform tool

The Brush Transform tool, which is available from the Tools panel and is shown in Figure 3-18, lets you perform transformations on the gradient similarly to the way rotation, skew, and scale transformations can be done on regular objects.(See the section "Rotating, Projecting in 3-D, and Doing Other Funky Things with Shapes," earlier in this chapter, for more about transformations.)

Figure 3-18: Brush Transform tool in the Tools panel.

To select any hidden tool, you have to click and hold the tool under which the hidden tool is grouped. The Brush Transform tool is grouped with the Gradient tool. So, to reveal the Brush Transform tool, you have to click and hold the Gradient tool. Alternatively, right-click the Gradient tool.

To apply brush transformations, first click the tool from the Tools panel and then select the rectangle object on the Artboard. After the rectangle is selected, you can perform the following transformations on the gradient:

✔ **Size:** Resize the transformation bounding rectangle using the resize handles.

✔ **Rotation:** Rotate the transformation bounding rectangle by clicking the edges when the rotate cursor appears and rotating it with a drag motion of the mouse.

Chapter 3: Enhancing the User Interface

 ✔ **Move:** Just click in the middle of the bounding rectangle and drag it to a new position.

 ✔ **Skew:** Click the side selection handles when the Skew cursor appears, and then change the skew angle of the gradient's bounding rectangle, as shown in Figure 3-19.

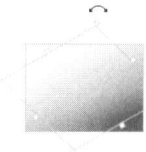

Figure 3-19: Brush transformations applied to a Rectangle.

Adding special effects

You can add effects such as a drop shadow to the objects on the Artboard by setting the `Effect` property on the object. Silverlight ships with two effects out of the box, but you can create your own. (Chapter 15 tells you how to create your own effects and where you can find other effects for free.) The effects shipped with Silverlight are as follows:

 ✔ **DropShadowEffect:** Adds a shadow to the control
 ✔ **BlurEffect:** Produces a blur effect on the control

Adding an effect is easy. Both the BlurEffect and DropShadowEffect appear in the Assets panel. Drag the tool from the Assets panel, and on the Artboard, drop it onto the control to which you want to add the effect. Alternatively, you can set it on the Properties panel by following these steps:

1. **Click the Selection tool to select the object.**

   The object is highlighted.

2. **Click the New button on the Effect property in the Properties panel, which appears in the Miscellaneous group.**

   The Select Object dialog box appears.

3. **Click the desired effect and then click OK.**

   The effect is applied to the object. Figure 3-20 shows what happens to a rectangle when the DropShadowEffect is selected.

72 Part I: Illuminating Silverlight

Figure 3-20: Drop shadow effect applied to a rectangle.

Playing Around with Some Special Effects

This section takes the tools described in previous sections of this chapter and puts them to use creating some text and adding shadow effects to it. Check out what happens when you follow these steps:

1. **Create a new Silverlight application by choosing File⇨New Project and selecting the Silverlight 4 Application + Website option.**

   A new Silverlight project is created and a blank Artboard is shown.

2. **Double-click the TextBlock tool from the Tools panel.**

   A TextBlock control is added to the Artboard.

3. **Replace the default text, "TextBlock," by typing** Silverlight Rocks **in its place.**

   You can also change the `Text` property to `Silverlight Rocks` from the Properties panel.

4. **Click the Selection tool, and if the TextBlock is not automatically selected, click the TextBlock to select it.**

5. **Go to the Text group on the Properties panel and increase the font size to 24, as shown in Figure 3-21.**

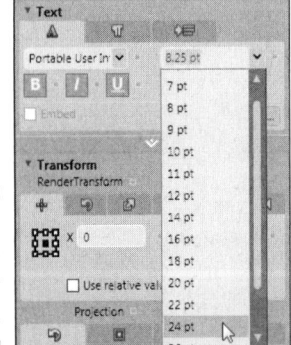

Figure 3-21: Setting the font size for the text.

Chapter 3: Enhancing the User Interface

6. Next, click the bold button, which is the button labeled B.

7. In the Brushes section of the Properties panel, click Foreground and then click the Gradient Brush button. Click a Red color on the Editor.

    The "Silverlight Rocks" text shows a gradient that moves from black to red.

8. While holding the Alt key, drag the TextBlock down to create a copy of it.

    A copy of the TextBlock is created and appears below the original TextBlock.

9. Holding down the selection handle at the top of the newly created copy, drag it down to flip it upside down, as shown in Figure 3-22.

    This creates a "mirror" effect with the text.

Figure 3-22: Flipping the text to create a mirror effect.

10. Move the two TextBlocks close to each other by dragging one of them up (or down).

11. Press Ctrl+A to select both TextBlocks and drag them to the center of the Artboard.

    This gives you more room to transform the controls in the following steps. Click anywhere on the Artboard to remove the multiple selections you made with Ctrl+A.

12. Using the Selection tool, select the inverted TextBlock and, after it's selected, move your cursor over the bottom middle selection handle.

    The cursor changes shape to a Skew cursor.

13. Drag the cursor to skew the selected TextBlock to an angle as shown in Figure 3-23 so that the second control looks like a shadow.

14. Click the Foreground property under Brushes in the Properties panel and click the Solid Color brush tab (shown in the margin).

    This sets the color of the second TextBlock to a black color.

15. From the Assets panel, select the BlurEffect and drag it to the second TextBlock on the Artboard.

    The second TextBlock appears blurred on the Artboard.

Part I: Illuminating Silverlight

Figure 3-23: Skewing the text to make it look like a shadow.

16. **Press F5 to run the application.**

    The application runs in a browser. The screen should look like Figure 3-24, showing a "Silverlight Rocks" text with a nice shadow effect. Pretty cool, huh?

Figure 3-24: Text with a shadow effect.

Adding Video and Audio to Your Pages

When Silverlight 1.0 was released, it was used mainly to play media files — that is, video and audio files. Although lots of features have been added to Silverlight, video and audio still form a big part of Silverlight. This section shows you how to add them to your Silverlight applications.

Playing video and audio files

To add media such as video and audio to your page, follow these steps:

1. **In Expression Blend, open the XAML page you would like to add media to.**
2. **Right-click the Silverlight project in the Projects panel and choose Add Existing Item from the menu.**

    The Add Existing Item Dialog box appears.

3. **Select the name of the media file, such as a WMV file, that you want to add to your page and click OK.**

   The media file gets added to the project and appears in the Projects panel.

4. **Drag and drop the file from the Projects panel into the XAML file on the Artboard.**

   A MediaElement control gets added to the Artboard and the `Source` property of the control gets set to the file you just added.

5. **Press F5 or choose Project➪Run Project from the menu.**

   The media file opens and automatically plays in the Silverlight page.

The media file plays automatically when the page opens because of a property in the MediaElement control called `AutoPlay`, which is set to `true` by default. You can set this property to `false` and control when and how the media file is played by calling the `Play` method from the MediaElement control in your VB.NET or C# code. Similarly to the controls of an actual media player, the MediaElement control also has methods such as `Pause` and `Stop`.

In addition to `Source` and `AutoPlay`, there are also other properties in MediaElement that you may find useful:

- ✔ `IsMuted`: This property specifies whether the audio is turned off.

- ✔ `Stretch`: This property specifies how the video is stretched within the bounds (height and width) of the MediaElement. It takes the values `None`, `Uniform`, `UniformToFill`, and `Fill`. A value of `Fill` makes the video take up the entire width and height of the control, and this is the default setting. But if the aspect ratio of the video does not match that of the MediaElement control, the images may end up looking too tall or too wide. The value `Uniform` takes up as much width and height of the control that it can while ensuring that the video is displayed with the right aspect ratio. `UniformToFill` displays the video centered within the control using the right aspect ratio, but it clips either the height or width of the video to ensure that it fits within the bounds of the MediaElement control. `None` displays the video in its native resolution and clips the video if it doesn't fit into the control's bounds.

- ✔ `Position`: This property can be used to move the media to a specific time. Not all media allows you to set the position, and you can determine whether it is supported by checking the value of the `CanSeek` property. If the value of this property is `true`, you can set the `Position` of the media.

- ✔ `Volume`: This property is used to set the volume of the audio and takes values between `0` and `1`. The default value of `Volume` is set to `0.5`.

Creating a video brush

To add a very special background to your control, such as a video or an image, you need to create a brush that contains the resource and set it as the Background brush. In fact, you can add the video or image brush to any property that accepts a brush, such as Fill, Stroke, Foreground, and BorderBrush. This section shows you how to add a video as a brush using Expression Blend.

1. **Add a video as a MediaElement to the XAML page by following the first four steps from the previous section, "Playing video and audio files."**

2. **From the menu, choose Tools➪Make Brush Resource➪Make VideoBrush Resource.**

    The Create VideoBrush Resource dialog box appears. You can optionally set the Name (Key) field to a meaningful name; then click OK.

3. **Set the Visibility property under Appearance in the Properties panel to Collapsed.**

    This hides the MediaElement control that you just added. You hide this element because you want to use the video as a brush and not as a MediaElement.

4. **Using the Selection tool from the Tools panel, select the control you want to set the Brush property for.**

5. **In the Properties panel, click the Brush property you want to set.**

    For example, if you are using a Rectangle control, click the `Fill` property under Brushes.

6. **Click the Brush Resources tab, shown here in the margin.**

    The Brush Resources tab appears and displays a list of Resource brushes, including the video brush you just created.

7. **Click the Resource Brush you wish to use from the list.**

8. **Press F5 or choose Project➪Run Project from the menu.**

    The application runs in the Web browser and the control shows the video as its brush.

Creating an image as a Resource Brush is similar to creating a video as a Resource Brush. Rather than select the MediaElement control and choose Tools➪Make Brush Resource➪Make VideoBrush Resource to create the Brush, you add an Image control, select it, and then choose Tools➪Make Brush Resource➪Make ImageBrush Resource.

You can also use an image as a brush in a control by clicking the Tile Brush tab for the Brush you want to set in the Properties panel and setting the `ImageSource` property.

Displaying video from your Webcam

With Silverlight 4, you can also connect your computer's webcam and microphone to your application. In this section, we show you how to display the video from your webcam in a Silverlight application. Just follow these steps:

1. **Create a new Silverlight application by choosing File⇨New Project; then, in the New Project dialog box, select Silverlight 4 Application + Website option and then click OK.**

2. **From the Tools panel, add a Rectangle to** `MainPage.xaml` **on the Artboard.**

3. **In the Properties panel, set the name of the Rectangle by entering** rctWebcam.

   By setting the name of the Rectangle, you can set its properties from code. Setting the properties from code is essential to linking the camera's image to the Rectangle's background.

4. **In the Properties panel, click the Events tab and double-click the MouseLeftButtonUp field.**

   A method called `rctWebcam_MouseLeftButtonDown` gets added to the `MainPage`, class and the `MainPage.xaml.cs` file opens on the Artboard. (You can find out more about events and event handlers in Chapter 4.)

5. **In the** `MainPage` **class, add a data member called** cameraSource **of type** CaptureSource, **as follows:**

   ```
   CaptureSource  cameraSource;
   ```

   You can use the `CaptureSource` class to start and stop the camera capture of the image coming from the webcam.

6. **Change the constructor of** `MainPage` **to the following code:**

   ```
   public MainPage()
   {
       // Required to initialize variables
       InitializeComponent();

       cameraSource = new CaptureSource();
       cameraSource.VideoCaptureDevice =
           CaptureDeviceConfiguration.
           GetDefaultVideoCaptureDevice();
       var brush = new VideoBrush();
       brush.SetSource(cameraSource);
       rctWebcam.Fill = brush;
   }
   ```

Part I: Illuminating Silverlight

The code that you've added initializes the `cameraSource` object from the default video capture device (which is the webcam) and sets the Rectangle's Fill brush to the video brush of the camera source. This displays the webcam's image in the rectangle.

7. **Change the `rctWebcam_MouseLeftButtonDown` method to the following code:**

```
private void rctWebcam_MouseLeftButtonDown(object
       sender, System.Windows.Input.
       MouseButtonEventArgs e)
{
    if (CaptureDeviceConfiguration.AllowedDeviceAccess
       || CaptureDeviceConfiguration.
       RequestDeviceAccess())
    {
        cameraSource.Start();
    }
}
```

This code starts the webcam after checking to see whether the device can be accessed and getting the user's permission.

8. **Press F5 or choose Project⇨Run Project.**

    The application runs in a browser.

9. **Click the Rectangle.**

    A message box, shown in Figure 3-25, appears, asking whether you want to allow camera and microphone access. Click the Yes button and notice the video from the webcam appearing on the rectangle.

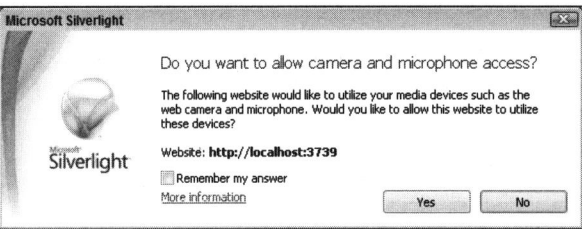

Figure 3-25: Silverlight requesting the use of a camera or microphone.

Hooking your microphone to your application works in the same way as that of a webcam. Instead of using the method `CaptureDeviceConfiguration.GetDefaultVideoCaptureDevice()`, you use CaptureDeviceConfiguration. GetDefaultAudioCaptureDevice() to set the source from which you capture the audio.

Selecting the default webcam and microphone for your application

In the previous section, we tell you how to get the default webcam installed on your machine to use within your Silverlight application. But you also need to know how to set these defaults in the application. To do so, just follow these steps:

1. **Right-click the Silverlight application when it is running in the Web browser and choose Silverlight from the pop-up menu that appears.**

    The Silverlight Configuration dialog box appears.

2. **Click the Webcam / Mic tab.**

    The Webcam / Mic dialog box appears, showing a list of available video sources (webcams) and audio sources (microphones), as shown in Figure 3-26.

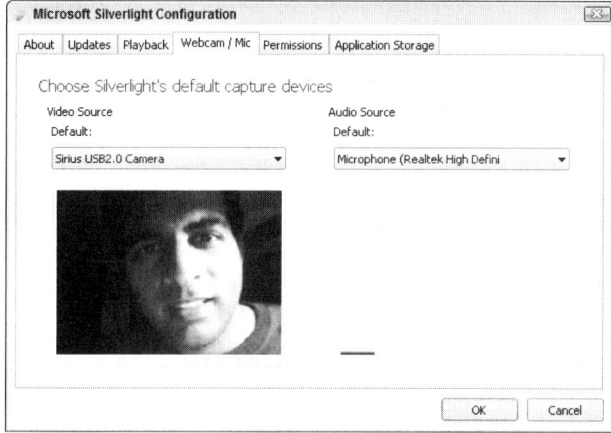

Figure 3-26: Selecting the default webcam and microphone to use in the Silverlight Configuration dialog box.

3. **Select the default webcam and default microphone from the two lists in the dialog box and click OK.**

Part II
Managing Your Silverlight Controls

The 5th Wave   By Rich Tennant

"You know, I've asked you a dozen times not to animate the torches on our Web page!"

In this part . . .

This part delves deeply into the world of controls. In Chapter 4, you find out about some of the most commonly used controls, such as text boxes and buttons, and Chapter 5 shows you how to arrange them effectively on-screen.

Silverlight allows you to change the appearance of a control without changing the way it works, and we give you the goods on this topic in Chapter 6. You can see how to create a style by specifying property values for a certain control and reuse that style throughout in your application, thereby providing a consistent look for your controls throughout.

In Chapter 7, you find out how to create your own controls, whether they are a collection of controls that you want to reuse in your application or something you create from scratch. Chapter 8 introduces you to the exciting world of animation, and you get a taste of animating controls on-screen.

Finally, Chapter 9 introduces you to the concept of data binding. When you write programs the "traditional" way, you are constantly setting properties when the data it displays changes. With data binding, however, you can tell the control what kind of data it is bound to, and Silverlight takes care of the rest. This chapter gives you a solid launch into this wonderful way of programming, and you see how to create data sources and sample data to test your application.

Chapter 4

Working with Controls for UI Interactions

In This Chapter

▶ Displaying text using TextBlock

▶ Reading text input with TextBox

▶ Triggering actions with Buttons

▶ Making selections using RadioButtons, ListBoxes, and ComboBoxes

▶ Entering rich text with RichTextBox

*M*ost applications need to have some kind of interaction with the user to be useful. For example, if you are creating a business application, you need to provide a whole bunch of screens to collect information from a user. These screens may contain a number of fields that require user interaction — for example, you can accept textual input from the user, or the user can pick an item from a list or trigger an action by clicking a button.

In this chapter, you see how you can use TextBox to collect text input from the user and how you can use a RadioButton and ListBox to get the user to pick an item from a list, a button to perform an action, and so on.

Exploring the Text-Related Tools

There are four different text-related controls in Expression Blend, as follows:

- ✔ TextBlock
- ✔ TextBox
- ✔ RichTextBox
- ✔ PasswordBox

You use the TextBlock predominantly for displaying a label for an input field or just to display some information to the user. The TextBox, RichTextBox, and PasswordBox controls, on the other hand, allow the user to type in some text that is used as input to perform an operation. An example of an operation using a TextBox is getting the users to fill in their names. If you are writing an application that requires users to sign in using a username and password, you use the TextBox to collect the username, and you use the PasswordBox to collect the password. When the user types the password into the PasswordBox field, it is not available for anyone to see; Silverlight hides it by replacing the characters the user types with unreadable characters.

The RichTextBox control allows you to format the text you type into it by specifying which parts have to be in bold and which ones have to be in italics. It also allows you to choose different fonts and specify other text attributes.

Displaying text with TextBlock

As its name suggests, the TextBlock displays a block of text. In its simplest form, the TextBlock looks like this in XAML:

```
<TextBlock>Hello World</TextBlock>
```

You can change the appearance of the text by changing its font and color, setting it in bold or italics, underlining, and so on — all by setting the properties for it. It is, of course, much easier to set these properties using Expression Blend than to manually type the XAML because you can manipulate these properties visually using the Properties panel. (Chapter 3 tells you all about using the Properties panel.) The XAML for a TextBlock with some of these properties set resembles the following:

```
<TextBlock FontFamily="Times New Roman" FontSize="36"
        FontStyle="Italic" FontWeight="Bold"> Hello
        World</TextBlock>
```

This is all fine, but when you want to write a paragraph of text that has individual words in italics or bold, or you want to vary the fonts for multiple words, stringing together a series of TextBlocks in XAML is a bit complex. Thankfully, however, you can use Expression Blend to take care of a lot of this for you by following these steps:

1. **Add a TextBlock to the Artboard (see Chapters 2 and 3 for how to add a control to the Artboard) and type a few lines of text, as shown in Figure 4-1.**
2. **Double-click a word to select it.**

   For this example, we selected *Joke*.

Chapter 4: Working with Controls for UI Interactions

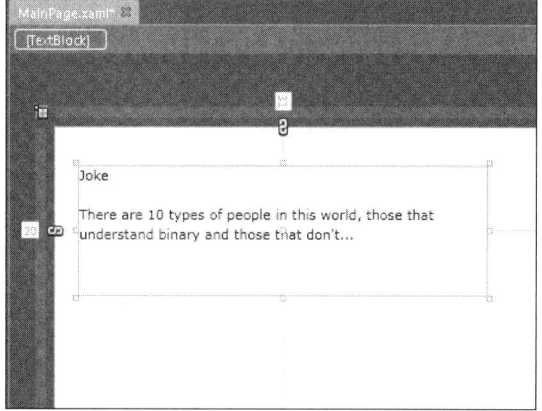

Figure 4-1: TextBlock with multiple lines.

   3. **In the Properties panel, select the properties you want to apply to the word you selected.**

      For example, set the font type as Times New Roman and the font size to 36; also, click the B button to make the text bold, as shown in Figure 4-2.

Figure 4-2: Setting properties for selected text.

   4. **To select multiple words together, click and drag to highlight the desired words; next, set their properties from the Properties panel.**

      In our example, we selected *those that don't . . .* and clicked the I button in the Properties panel to set these words in italics. We also selected the number *10* and made it bold.

   5. **Press F5 or choose Project**⇨**Run Project to run the application.**

      The application runs in the browser showing the TextBlock and looks like Figure 4-3.

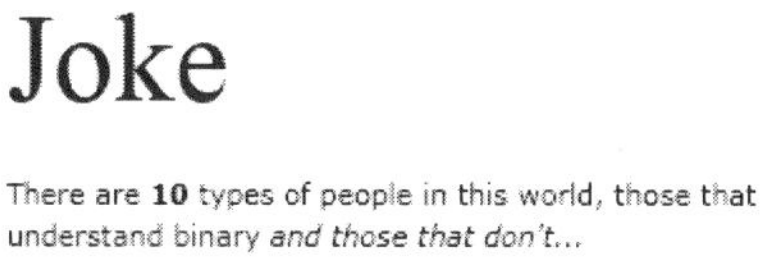

Figure 4-3: TextBlock showing inline formatting.

Joke

There are **10** types of people in this world, those that understand binary *and those that don't...*

 You can also use Ctrl+B to set the selected text to Bold, Ctrl+I to italicize it, and Ctrl+U to underline, and use the same combinations to toggle the text back to normal.

Using the TextBox and PasswordBox to get input from the user

The TextBox control in Silverlight is similar to text boxes used in other applications such as Windows programs and Web pages. The TextBox control also provides functionality for you to do things like the following:

- ✓ Click and drag to select text.
- ✓ Double-click to select a word.
- ✓ Press Ctrl+C to copy the selected text and Ctrl+V to paste it.

The TextBox, RichTextBox, and PasswordBox tools in Expression Blend are grouped along with the TextBlock tool in the Tools panel, as shown in Figure 4-4.

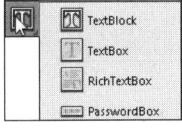

Figure 4-4: The tools available for text-related purposes.

To see how to use these tools, follow these steps:

1. **Create a new Silverlight project, add a TextBlock to the Artboard, and replace the default text in it with some text of your own.**

   In our example for these steps, we use the text `Enter Hogwarts location:`.

2. **Click and hold the TextBlock tool to reveal the other text-related tools in the Toolbox; then select the TextBox tool.**

3. **Draw a text box below the TextBlock you've already added.**

4. **Go to the Properties panel and assign a name, such as** `txtLocation`, **to the TextBox.**

5. **Add yet another TextBlock underneath the txtLocation (or whatever you named it) TextBlock and type new text into it.**

   In our example, that text is `Enter the password to enter:`.

Chapter 4: Working with Controls for UI Interactions

6. **Select the PasswordBox tool from the Toolbox, add it below the TextBlock that you just added, and set the name, such as** `txtPassword`, **for the new control in the Properties panel.**

   Your Artboard should now look like Figure 4-5.

7. **Press the F5 key or choose Project**➪**Run Project to run the application in the browser.**

   You can type the text for Hogwarts location and also enter the password. When you enter the password, the actual text you type is hidden. This is pretty much the main difference between the TextBox and the PasswordBox.

   To read the value typed into a TextBox from C# or VB.NET, you need to access the `Text` property. For a PasswordBox, instead of `Text`, you need to access the `Password` property. You find out how to do this in the next section.

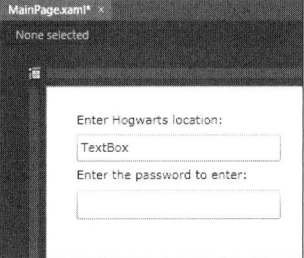

Figure 4-5: The Artboard showing the TextBlock, TextBox, and Password fields.

Consider naming the controls you place on the Artboard using a prefix that tells you what kind of control it is. For example, use the prefix *txt* to denote that the control is a text box. For a button, use the prefix *btn*. This convention of naming controls with a prefix is called Hungarian notation and was once very popular when people used languages such as C and C++ for the Windows environment. It is no longer used in C# and VB.NET, but it can help you to find the controls used in the page easily while using IntelliSense. IntelliSense is a feature in both Expression Blend and Visual Studio that tries to figure out what you are typing based on the first few characters. For instance, you may not remember whether you named a button SearchButton or FindButton, but if you use Hungarian notation for all your controls, as soon as you type **btn** in your C# code, IntelliSense will prompt you with all the controls that start with *btn,* including btnSearch.

Accessing TextBox values in XAML markup

The previous sections discuss creating a simple application that accepts text input using Expression Blend. In this section, we look at how to read the text values you typed into the TextBox and Password fields and also to set the `Text` property of a TextBlock programmatically from C#. To illustrate how to do so, we use the example from the previous section and add another TextBlock after the txtPassword control to the Artboard and name it lblOutput. We use this TextBlock to show how its `Text` property is set from code. Your XAML should look something like this:

```xml
<UserControl
  xmlns="http://schemas.microsoft.com/winfx/2006/xaml/
        presentation"
  xmlns:x="http://schemas.microsoft.com/winfx/2006/xaml"
  x:Class="Chapter4.MainPage"
  Width="640" Height="480">
  <Grid x:Name="LayoutRoot" Background="White">
    <TextBlock Height="24" Margin="38,8,0,0"
          HorizontalAlignment="Left"
          VerticalAlignment="Top" Width="274" Text="Enter
          Hogwarts location:" TextWrapping="Wrap"/>
    <TextBox x:Name="txtLocation" Height="24"
          Margin="38,26,312,0" VerticalAlignment="Top"
          Text="TextBox" TextWrapping="Wrap"/>
    <TextBlock Height="24" Margin="38,60,0,0"
          HorizontalAlignment="Left"
          VerticalAlignment="Top" Width="274" Text="Enter
          the password to enter:" TextWrapping="Wrap"/>
    <PasswordBox x:Name="txtPassword" Height="24"
          Margin="38,78,312,0" VerticalAlignment="Top"
          Password=""/>
    <TextBlock x:Name="lblOutput" Height="24"
          Margin="38,106,312,0" VerticalAlignment="Top"
          Text="TextBlock" TextWrapping="Wrap"/>
  </Grid>
</UserControl>
```

The TextBox and PasswordBox controls both have a set of events attached to them that get triggered automatically when you perform an action, such as typing or even just moving your mouse over the control. You can look at all the events that are available by clicking the Events button in the Properties panel. The available events for the TextBox are shown in Figure 4-6.

The name of a given event typically gives you an idea of the event's purpose. For example, the `MouseEnter` event is called when a mouse enters the control; likewise, the `KeyDown` event is called when a user presses a key while in the control.

Chapter 4: Working with Controls for UI Interactions

To validate the location and password whenever it is changed, add an event handler for `TextChanged`, which will be triggered every time the value of the `Text` in the `TextBox` field changes. (No points for guessing that the equivalent trigger for a `PasswordBox` is `PasswordChanged`!)

To add an event handler when the text in a control changes, just double-click the field for `TextChanged` in the Properties panel. Expression Blend creates an empty function called `txtLocation_TextChanged` and adds it to the `MainPage.xaml.cs` file. Expression Blend also opens and displays the file. The code generated looks like this:

```
private void txtLocation_TextChanged(object sender,
        System.Windows.Controls.TextChangedEventArgs e)
{
    // TODO: Add event handler implementation here.
}
```

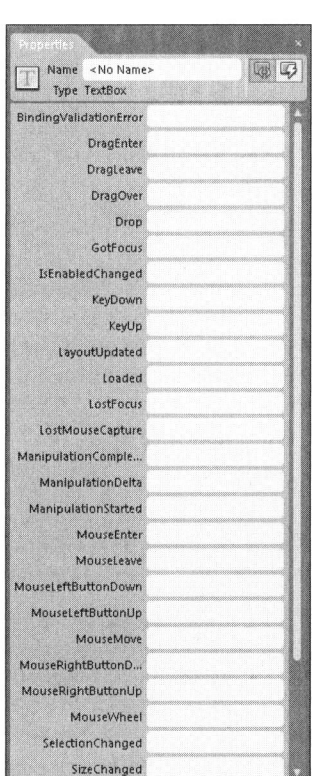

Figure 4-6: Events available for a TextBox.

Type `ValidateEntry();` to replace the placeholder that says `TODO: Add event handler implementation here`. Then add a function called `ValidateEntry`, as shown:

```
private void txtLocation_TextChanged(object sender,
            System.Windows.Controls.TextChangedEventArgs e)
{
    ValidateEntry();
}
private void ValidateEntry()
{
    if(txtLocation.Text == "Griffindor Common room" &&
         txtPassword.Password == "Caput Draconis")
    {
        lblOutput.Text = "Correct password. Please enter";
    }
    else
    {
        lblOutput.Text = "Tut, Tut! Wrong password";
    }
}
```

Similar to the `TextChanged` event handler for `txtLocation`, add a `PasswordChanged` event handler for `txtPassword`. Again replace the TODO comment with a call to `ValidateEntry()`, as shown in the following code:

```
private void txtPassword_PasswordChanged(object sender,
            System.Windows.RoutedEventArgs e)
{
    ValidateEntry();
}
```

Press F5 or choose Project⇨Run Project to run the application. When the application shows up in the browser, type **Griffindor Common room** in the text box and enter **Caput Draconis** in the password field; you should see the text `Correct password. Please enter` displayed on the screen, as shown in Figure 4-7.

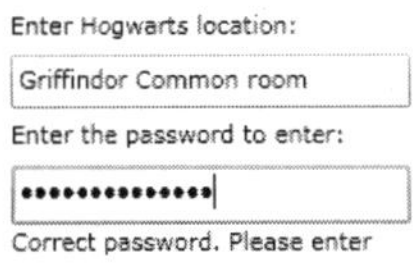

Figure 4-7: Screen showing output when the correct values are entered.

Using Buttons in Your Application

Another frequently used tool in the Toolbox is the Button. Typically, in any environment, clicking a button fires an action. The Button control is grouped along with the CheckBox, ComboBox, ListBox, RadioButton, ScrollBar, and Slider controls in the Tools panel, as shown in Figure 4-8.

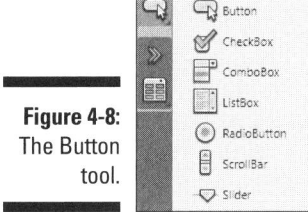

Figure 4-8: The Button tool.

To add a button in Expression Blend, follow these steps:

1. **Create a new Silverlight application by choosing File⇨New Project and then selecting the Silverlight 4 Application + Website option (or continue with the existing project that you've been working on in the previous sections).**

2. **Select the Button tool from the Tools panel and, using the mouse, draw it on the Artboard, placing it to the right of any TextBlocks and TextBoxes you've already added.**

3. **Click the Selection tool in the Tools panel.**

    This selects the button that you just added to the Artboard.

4. **Double-click the button and replace the default text *Button* by typing Enter. Press Esc after you've made the change.**

    The button text on the Artboard shows the word *Enter* that you typed into the Content property field.

You can also change the button's text from the Properties panel by setting the `Content` property.

To write an event handler for the button that performs an action when the button is pressed, follow these steps:

1. **Click the Selection tool from the Tools panel to select it.**
2. **Click the button for which you want to add the event handler.**
3. **From the Properties panel, click Events and double-click the Click Event field to generate the `Button_Click` event handler.**

The event handler function shows up in the Editor window. You can modify the event handler to run any code. If you've been continuing from the previous example, replace the event handler with a call to the `ValidateEntry` function, as shown in the following code:

```
private void Button_Click(object sender, System.
        Windows.RoutedEventArgs e)
{
    ValidateEntry();
}
```

4. **Remove the two event handlers for `txtLocation` and `txtPassword` that you added previously (if you followed along with the examples in earlier sections of this chapter).**

    You can do that easily by removing the following text from the XAML source code for the TextBox txtLocation and the Password field txtPassword: `TextChanged="txtLocation_TextChanged"` and `PasswordChanged="txtPassword_PasswordChanged"`. Alternatively, go to the Events tab for both controls and remove the text that appears for txtLocation's `TextChanged` event and txtPassword's `PasswordChanged` event from the Properties panel.

5. **Press F5 or choose Project⇒Run Project to run the application.**

    The application runs in a browser. Now instead of validating the input at every key press, the application will validate only when the button is pressed.

Setting the content of a button

In the previous section, we describe how to set the text to appear in the Button control. When you do that, you set a property called `Content`, not `Text`, in contrast to what you set for text in the TextBox and TextBlock controls. The reason the property is called `Content` instead of `Text` for this control is that the Button can have more than just text; it can contain an image, a video, or even a bunch of other controls.

The Button is one of a large set other controls such as CheckBox, ScrollViewer, and others that allow you to add any type of content to them. This group of controls is based on another control called `ContentControl`, which represents any control that can hold any type of content.

If you switch to the XAML view for the page by clicking the XAML button on the Artboard, the markup for the button will look something like this:

```
<Button Height="76" HorizontalAlignment="Right"
        Margin="0,26,185,0" VerticalAlignment="Top"
        Width="97" Content="Enter"/>
```

Rather than express the text of a button or any other control based on `ContentControl` in the `Content` property, you can set the value of the Button element as shown in the following snippet:

```
<Button Height="76" HorizontalAlignment="Right"
        Margin="0,26,185,0" VerticalAlignment="Top"
        Width="97">
    Enter
</Button>
```

The button is displayed the same way on the screen using both code snippets, but the second snippet is interesting because it lets you specify some text that appears as the button's content or even another XAML element such as a Button, as shown in the following example:

```
<Button Height="76" HorizontalAlignment="Right"
        Margin="0,26,185,0" VerticalAlignment="Top"
        Width="97">
    <Button Height="26" Width="79" Content="Inner
        button"/>
</Button>
```

You are not restricted to having just one control within the content of a `ContentControl` — you can have complex XAML with multiple controls, and if some of these controls happen to be based on `ContentControl`, they can have complex content, too.

Adding an image as content for a Button

The previous sections provide the concepts important to creating content and using ContentControl. Here, we show you how to add an image to a button as content. Just follow these steps:

1. **Create a new Silverlight application by choosing File⇨New Project and then selecting the Silverlight 4 Application + Website option (or continue with the example project from the previous sections).**

2. **If you are creating a new project, add a button to the Artboard by using the Button tool from the Tools panel.**

3. **Click the Asset Library icon in the Tools panel, which is represented by a chevron image.**

   A pop-up menu with all the available tools in Expression Blend appears, but the Image tool may still not be available. To find it quickly, just start typing into a text field. A Search field will appear as you type, and you can type **Image** in that Search field.

   Figure 4-9 shows the Asset Library window.

Part II: Managing Your Silverlight Controls

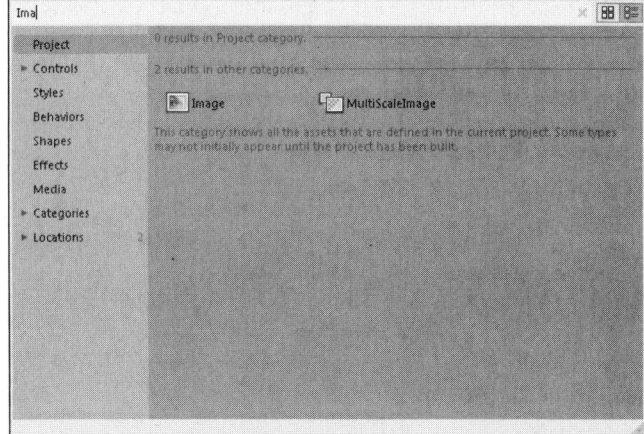

Figure 4-9: Asset Library.

You can also click the Assets tab in Expression Blend to go to the Assets panel and search for the Image control there, as shown in Figure 4-10.

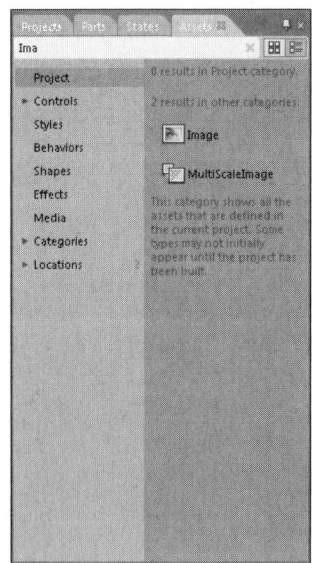

Figure 4-10: The Assets panel.

   4. **When you've located the Image tool from either the Assets Library or the Assets panel, click and drag it onto the Artboard.**

   The image gets added to the button as content.

Chapter 4: Working with Controls for UI Interactions

5. **Go to the Properties panel and locate the Source property that appears under the Common Properties group. Click the ellipses (. . .) button, shown here in the margin; this button appears next to the field.**

   The Add Existing Item dialog box is displayed.

6. **Select the image you would like to add to the button and click OK.**

   The selected image is now displayed in the control.

7. **Click the Selection tool in the Tools panel to select the Image control. Then drag the Image control over the button.**

   A tooltip should appear with the message `Press Alt to place inside [Button]`, as shown in Figure 4-11.

8. **Press the Alt key while dropping the image on top of the button to replace the text in the button with the image.**

9. **Press F5 or choose Project⇨Run Project to run the application.**

   The application opens in a browser and displays the image inside the button.

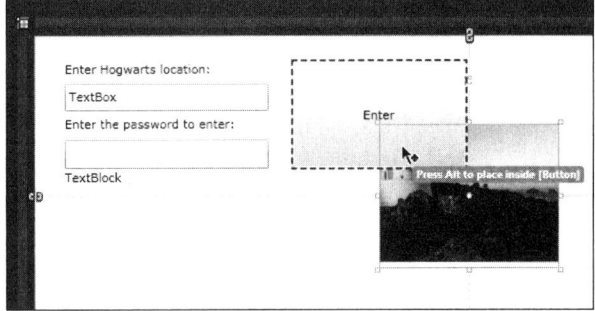

Figure 4-11: Dragging an image into a button.

The XAML for the button should look something like this:

```
<Button Height="94" HorizontalAlignment="Right"
        Margin="0,8,142,0" VerticalAlignment="Top"
        Width="135" Click="Button_Click">

    <Image Source="Lighthouse.jpg" Stretch="UniformToFill"
           Height="96" Width="133"/>

</Button>
```

Notice that the Image XML tag sits between the start and end Button tags. This effectively makes it the content for the button. With the image selected, you can go to the Properties panel and reset the `Height` and `Width` properties for it by going to the Advanced Property options (click the little square to the right of the property's field) and choosing Reset to make the image fill the whole area of the Button.

Jumping to Another Web Page Using HyperlinkButton

Standard Web pages typically contain a lot of hyperlinks. When you click these links, the browser takes you to a new page. You can get the same result in Silverlight using a special kind of button called HyperlinkButton.

To see how a HyperlinkButton works, follow these steps:

1. **Create a new Silverlight application by choosing File➪New Project. In the New Project dialog box, select Silverlight 4 Application + Website option and press OK.**
2. **In the Assets panel, type Hyper in the Search field.**

    Only controls that have the string *Hyper* in their name are displayed in the panel. HyperlinkButton should be one of those controls.
3. **Drag the HyperlinkButton from the Assets panel and drop it in a suitable location on MainPage.xaml on the Artboard.**
4. **Change the Content property of the HyperlinkButton found under Common properties in the Properties panel to indicate the link you want to add.**

    For example, you might enter `Go to Dummies.com`.
5. **Set the NavigateUri property under Common properties in the Properties panel to `http://www.dummies.com`.**
6. **Press F5 or choose Project➪Run Project to run the application.**

    When the application opens, click the `Go to Dummies.com` link found on the page. Silverlight takes you straight to the `Dummies.com` Web site.

Using RadioButtons to Present Options

Sometimes it doesn't make sense to have the user type information into a text box if only a few options are available. For example, if you are looking for a "Yes" or "No" answer to a question, it doesn't make sense to have the user type that into a text box. Or say that you want the user to fill in Male or Female in a Sex field without having to type in that information. In such cases, you (and your users) would be better off having options available to select from a set of radio buttons.

Radio buttons provide the user with a list of values to pick from that are mutually exclusive, meaning that if you select one item from a set, the other items are automatically deselected.

Chapter 4: Working with Controls for UI Interactions

To see how radio buttons work in a Silverlight application, follow these steps:

1. **Create a new Silverlight application by choosing File⇨New Project. In the New Project dialog box, select Silverlight 4 Application + Website option and press OK.**

2. **Select the TextBlock tool from the Tools panel and drag the mouse on the Artboard to the position you want to add the text.**

3. **Double-click the TextBlock and replace the default text with the word *Sex*.**

4. **Select the RadioButton tool (shown here in the margin) from the Tools panel and drag the mouse on the Artboard to where you want to add the radio button.**

5. **Double-click the RadioButton and change the Content value to *Male*.**

6. **Repeat Steps 4 and 5, but set the Content value of the second radio button to *Female*.**

7. **Using the Selection tool, Ctrl+click the two radio buttons.**

   Both the radio buttons get selected, and the selection handles appear on both.

8. **In the Properties panel, set the `GroupName` property that appears under Common Properties to *Sex*.**

   This ensures that when multiple radio button groups such as Sex and Age Group appear on the same screen, selecting an item in one group doesn't deselect an item from the other group.

9. **Press F5 or choose Project⇨Run Project to run the application.**

   The application shows up with the two radio buttons, as shown in Figure 4-12. The radio buttons within the same group are mutually exclusive. So when you click one radio button to select it, the other radio button gets deselected.

As is the Button item, `RadioButton` is derived from `ContentControl`, and its content is not limited to just text — it can contain images or even a group of other controls. The property that determines whether the radio button appears selected or not is called `IsChecked`, and you can set this property from the Properties panel under the Common Properties group.

Figure 4-12: Radio buttons in action.

In addition to the RadioButton, Silverlight also contains a CheckBox, which works similarly to the RadioButton but can be used to make multiple selections. For example, if you presented users with a choice to enter their favorite music, they may choose Rock, Classical, and Alternative, among a number of choices. In contrast to choices allowed by the radio button, choices presented with the CheckBox aren't mutually exclusive. To add a CheckBox to your application, follow exactly the same steps as defined for the radio button, but instead of using the RadioButton control from the Tools panel, use the CheckBox control.

Using the ListBox and ComboBox to present a large number of options

A radio button is ideal when you have a small number of options — say, between two and five. When you have a large number of options, you should consider using a list box. The ListBox control in Silverlight provides a list of values in a scrollable box that you can employ for displaying a large number of options such as a list of countries or states. The ListBox also allows the user to make multiple selections by holding the Ctrl key when clicking an item in the list.

Silverlight also has a ComboBox, which acts like a drop-down list that displays only one item at a time but lets the user click a down arrow to reveal more items in the list.

Creating a list box

To create a list box, follow these steps:

1. **Create a new Silverlight application by choosing File➪New Project. In the New Project dialog box, select Silverlight 4 Application + Website option and click OK.**
2. **Select the TextBlock tool from the Tools panel and drag the mouse on the Artboard to where you want to add the text.**
3. **Double-click the TextBlock and replace the default text with**
   `Favorite Sport:.`
4. **Select the ListBox tool from the Tools panel and draw a list box on the Artboard, as shown in Figure 4-13.**

Chapter 4: Working with Controls for UI Interactions   99

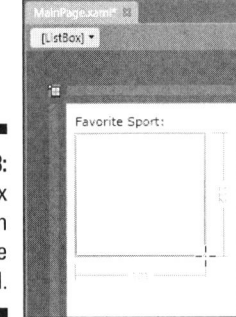

Figure 4-13: A list box drawn on the Artboard.

5. **From the Properties panel, click the ellipses button next to the Items property under the Common Properties group.**

   An Object Collection Editor: Items dialog box appears, as shown in Figure 4-14. This dialog box lets you add items that will be displayed in the list box.

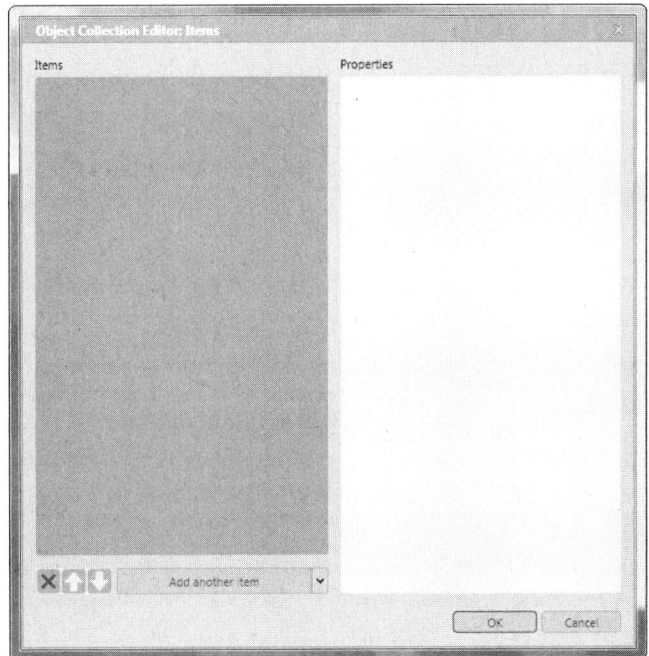

Figure 4-14: The Object Collection Editor: Items dialog box.

6. **In the dialog box, click the arrow next to the Add Another Item drop-down list and select ListBoxItem.**

   A ListBoxItem gets added to the Items list box, and properties appear in the Properties box located on the right side of the dialog box.

7. **In the Properties box, set the Content properties to say** `Football`.
8. **Repeat Steps 6 and 7 six times, but set the Content properties to the following values:** `Baseball, Basketball, Hockey, Soccer, Cricket, Tennis`.
9. **Press OK to close the dialog box.**

   The list box on the Artboard shows the list items you've just added.

10. **Press F5 or choose Project**⇨**Run Project to run the application.**

    The application opens in a browser window, as shown in Figure 4-15, and shows the list box with the different items you added. The list box allows you to make a selection and scroll up and down the list.

Figure 4-15: Selecting items from a ListBox.

To set or determine the index of the selected list box item, you use the `SelectedIndex` property. If the value of this property is set to –1, it means that no items are selected.

To allow the user to set multiple selections, you can use the SelectionMode property, which is set to `Single` by default.

The XAML for a list box looks like the following:

```
<ListBox Height="112" HorizontalAlignment="Left"
         Margin="8,31,0,0" VerticalAlignment="Top"
         Width="121">
....<ListBoxItem Content="Football"/>
....<ListBoxItem Content="Baseball"/>
....<ListBoxItem Content="Basketball"/>
....<ListBoxItem Content="Hockey"/>
....<ListBoxItem Content="Soccer"/>
....<ListBoxItem Content="Cricket"/>
....<ListBoxItem Content="Tennis"/>
</ListBox>
```

Notice that the ListBox contains several `ListBoxItem` properties as child elements. The `ListBoxItem` property also has a property called `IsSelected`, which when set to true determines whether the item is selected. A `ListBoxItem` is based on `ContentElement` and can contain any UI element inside it.

Chapter 4: Working with Controls for UI Interactions 101

TIP: You can directly select a ListBoxItem control from the Artboard using the Selection tool and set its properties from the Properties panel.

TIP: You can also right-click the list box you've added and choose Add ListBoxItem from the Properties panel to add an item to the list box. This selects the ListBoxItem on the Artboard, allowing you to change its content and set other properties.

Creating a combo box

The steps to create a combo box are exactly the same as those for creating a ListBox (see the previous section). The only difference is that instead of selecting a ListBox control from the Tools panel in Step 4 in the previous section, you select the ComboBox tool.

A combo box that replaces the list box is shown in Figure 4-16.

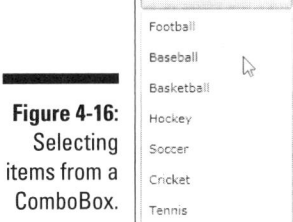

Figure 4-16: Selecting items from a ComboBox.

Entering Rich Text into a RichTextBox Control

We explore the Text-related tools in the first section of this chapter, where we also briefly introduce you to the RichTextBox control. In this section, we delve more deeply into using this handy control, which is new as of Silverlight 4.

The RichTextBox control not only allows you to display "rich" text that may contain multiple fonts, formatting, images, and other rich text elements, but also allows your users to change those elements.

To allow your users to format the text at runtime, you need to write code in addition to the XAML markup, and we tell you more about that in the upcoming "Formatting text at runtime" section. But first, to display rich text in the control, follow these steps:

1. **Create a new Silverlight application by choosing File➪New Project. In the New Project dialog box, select Silverlight 4 Application + Website option and click OK.**

2. **In the Assets panel, type** RichTextBox **in the Search field, and when the control appears in the panel, select it and drag the mouse on the Artboard to where you want it to appear.**

3. **Switch the Artboard to the XAML view by clicking the XAML button at the top-right corner of the Artboard.**

   The Artboard switches to the XAML view. Although you can format the contents of the RichTextBox via a series of steps from the Properties panel, it's easier to do this by directly changing the markup.

4. **Change the markup for the RichTextBox so that it looks similar to the following:**

   ```
   <RichTextBox x:Name="txtNotes" Height="161"
           Margin="39,64,0,0" VerticalAlignment="Top"
           HorizontalAlignment="Left" Width="246">
      <Paragraph>
        <Bold>Text In Bold</Bold>
        <LineBreak/>
        <Italic>Text in Italics</Italic>
        <LineBreak />
        <InlineUIContainer>
          <Image Source="Autumn Leaves.jpg"
            Stretch="UniformToFill" Height="100" >
          </Image>
        </InlineUIContainer>
      </Paragraph>
   </RichTextBox>
   ```

   Make sure that the Source attribute in the Image element points to the location of an actual image resource. The markup is used to display a line of text in bold, followed by a line of text in italics and an image. (We explain the markup in the next section.)

5. **Press F5 or choose Project➪Run Project to run the application.**

   The application runs, showing a text box that displays rich formatting including an inline image, as shown in Figure 4-17.

Figure 4-17: RichText Area showing formatted text and an inline image.

Understanding the XAML behind RichTextBox

The RichTextBox control can contain zero or more Paragraph elements, and each Paragraph element can contain zero or more of the following elements:

- Bold: This is used to make the text enclosed within this tag appear bold.
- Italic: This is used to make the text enclosed within this tag appear italicized.
- Underline: This is used to underline the text enclosed within this tag.
- LineBreak: This introduces a line break in the running text.
- InlineUIContainer: This can be used to add UI elements such as Images and Buttons.
- Hyperlink: This is used to display a hyperlink in the text.
- Run: This is used to represent a section of text.
- Span: This is used to group other elements, such as Bold and Italics, within the paragraph.

The XAML Paragraph element allows multiple paragraphs to be displayed within the control.

The RichTextBox also contains a property called Xaml, which returns the XAML string that represents the contents of the RichTextBox with all the special formatting information included.

Formatting text at runtime

The previous two sections show you how to format text using a RichTextBox control. If you want your users to be able to change the formatting of text at runtime, however, you have a fair amount of coding to do. To serve as an example, the following steps show you how to set the selected text to Bold, Italics, and Underline:

1. **Follow the steps that appear at the start of "Entering Rich Text into a RichTextBox Control" to add a RichTextBox to** `MainPage.xaml` **on the Artboard.**

2. **Add three buttons to the Artboard: one to represent bold; one to represent italics; and one to represent underline, as shown in Figure 4-18. (Or see Step 4.)**

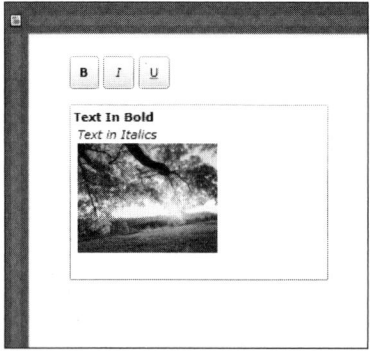

Figure 4-18: Artboard showing buttons added for Bold, Italics, and Underline.

3. **In the Properties panel, set the Name property for the three buttons to** btnBold, btnUnderline, **and** btnUnderline, **respectively.** (Or see Step 4.)

4. **As an alternative to Steps 2 and 3, switch to XAML view on the Artboard and just add the following markup after the RichTextBox element:**

```
<Button x:Name="btnBold" Content="B"
        HorizontalAlignment="Left" Height="30"
        Margin="39,20,0,0" VerticalAlignment="Top"
        Width="29" FontWeight="Bold" />
<Button x:Name="btnItalics" Content="I"
        HorizontalAlignment="Left" Height="30"
        Margin="72,20,0,0" VerticalAlignment="Top"
        Width="29" FontStyle="Italic" />
<Button x:Name="btnUnderline"
        HorizontalAlignment="Left" Height="30"
        Margin="105,20,0,0" VerticalAlignment="Top"
        Width="29" >
  <TextBlock TextDecorations="Underline">U</TextBlock>
</Button>
```

5. **From the Tools panel, click the Selection tool and click the first button (btnBold) to select it.**

6. **In the Properties panel, switch to the Events tab by clicking the Events button; then double-click the Click field.**

   The `MainPage.xaml.cs` file opens and the `btnBold_Click` method is displayed. Change the method so that the button-click event handler looks like the following code:

   ```
   private void btnBold_Click(object sender, System.
           Windows.RoutedEventArgs e)
   {
       txtNotes.Selection.ApplyPropertyValue (TextElement.
           FontWeightProperty, FontWeights.Bold);
   }
   ```

   This code will make the current text selection in the RichTextBox appear bold when the btnBold button is clicked.

7. **Repeat Steps 5 and 6 but select btnItalics instead of btnBold.**

   A method called `btnItalics_Click` gets created. Replace the method with the following code:

   ```
   private void btnItalics_Click(object sender, System.
           Windows.RoutedEventArgs e)
   {
       txtNotes.Selection.ApplyPropertyValue (TextElement.
           FontStyleProperty, FontStyles.Italic);
   }
   ```

   This code ensures that when the user clicks the btnItalics button, the selected text shows up italicized.

8. **To underline the selected text in the RichTextBox control, repeat Steps 5 and 6 again but select btnUnderline instead of btnBold.**

   A method called `btnUnderline_Click` gets created in the MainPage.xaml.cs file. Replace the method with the following code:

   ```
   private void btnUnderline_Click(object sender, System.
           Windows.RoutedEventArgs e)
   {
       txtNotes.Selection.ApplyPropertyValue (Inline.
           TextDecorationsProperty, TextDecorations.
           Underline);
   }
   ```

9. **Press F5 or choose Project⇨Run Project to run the application.**

   The application runs in the browser. When you select a piece of text in the RichTextBox control and press the **B** button, the selected text changes to Bold. Similarly, pressing the *I* button changes the selected text to italics, and pressing U underlines the selected text.

You can add more functionality to the application by adding more buttons and even changing the event handler code. For example, rather than always changing the currently selected text to bold, you can toggle the selected text between bold and normal by changing the `btnBold_Click` function to the following code:

```
private void btnBold_Click(object sender, System.Windows.
        RoutedEventArgs e)
{
    if((FontWeight)txtNotes.Selection.
            GetPropertyValue(TextElement.FontWeightProperty)
            == FontWeights.Bold)
    {
        txtNotes.Selection.ApplyPropertyValue (TextElement.
            FontWeightProperty, FontWeights.Normal);
    }
    else
    {
        txtNotes.Selection.ApplyPropertyValue (TextElement.
            FontWeightProperty, FontWeights.Bold);
    }
}
```

Chapter 5

Laying Out Controls

In This Chapter
▶ Working with container controls
▶ Displaying things in a tabular way
▶ Stacking up controls the easy way
▶ Laying out controls with absolute positioning using the Canvas control
▶ Using the ScrollViewer to view more of the control
▶ Using the Viewbox to squeeze controls into a given space
▶ Grouping controls together in tabs
▶ Docking controls

Designing a good user interface includes paying close attention to how the contents of your screen are organized and laid out. You can lay out the user interface elements using *absolute positioning,* which means to specify the exact position an element should occupy. This approach is not always practical, however, because your users may have different screen resolutions and may even run the application on a variety of devices. Uh-oh, did we say a *variety* of devices? Yes, it's true: Remember that Silverlight actually runs on a browser, and the plug-in can be ported to different devices, including mobile phones.

Laying out your controls on your screen with a range of devices in mind therefore presents a challenge. Thankfully, Silverlight contains a range of layout containers — controls that help you manage the way your on-screen controls are laid out. In this chapter, we look at a few of the commonly used containers and how they can be used to control the layout of the screen.

Understanding Layout Containers

A *container* in Silverlight is simply a control that can contain other user interface elements (or controls). The controls that the container holds are referred to as *children,* whereas the container itself is called the *parent.* The parent typically has a layout behavior defined that determines how the children are sized, positioned, and drawn within the parent.

Part II: Managing Your Silverlight Controls

Silverlight offers a set of layout containers that are available for you to use, and Table 5-1 lists the ones you're most likely to need.

Table 5-1	Commonly Used Layout Containers
Container	**Purpose**
Grid	Provides columns and rows in which children can be placed
Canvas	Provides an area in which children can be explicitly positioned using relative coordinates and absolute dimensions
ScrollViewer	Provides a container that can contain scrollbars and the ability to scroll up and down to view more of its contents
Viewbox	Provides a container that fits the entire control within its bounds and has the ability to resize its content when it is resized
StackPanel	Provides a container for children in which they are stacked either horizontally or vertically
WrapPanel	Places children sequentially, and if there is no space to fill them all in one line, wraps subsequent children in the next line; continues until all the controls are laid out
DockPanel	Allows the children to be "docked" or attached to one side of the parent

All these containers are derived from a class called `Panel`. These layout panels work out the dimensions and position of the children.

In addition to the seven containers described in Table 5-1, another commonly used container is the Border. The Border is a very simple container that simply draws a border around its content. Some containers, such as the ScrollViewer, the Viewbox, and the Border, can contain only one child. But this is not a big restriction. You can use another container as a child to these containers and use that to hold more child controls.

The more children in the container, the more difficult it is for the parent to work out how to organize them. Similarly, a simple layout container such as the Canvas spends less time laying out the containers than a more complex one, such as a Grid, does. That is why it is important to pick the container that is right for the screen you're building.

Every control in Silverlight has some basic properties that help in positioning and sizing the control. For instance, `MinHeight` and `MinWidth` specify the minimum dimensions of the control, whereas `MaxHeight` and `MaxWidth` specify the maximum dimensions it can take. The layout containers take these properties into consideration while setting the actual height and width of controls when they are laid out.

The root container

If you look at the XAML of a blank Silverlight page, you see something like this:

```
<UserControl
    xmlns="http://schemas.microsoft.com/winfx/2006/
       xaml/presentation"
    xmlns:x="http://schemas.microsoft.com/winfx/2006/xaml"
    x:Class="SilverlightApplication13.MainPage"
    Width="640" Height="480">

    <Grid x:Name="LayoutRoot" Background="White"/>

</UserControl>
```

The UserControl element contains a property called Content, which, as the name suggests, holds the contents of the control. In this case, it holds the Grid element. The Grid element is actually a layout container and lets you have more than one child control. The Grid element also lays out controls in rows and columns that are easy to work with.

The layout container that is used as the content for the UserControl element is usually referred to as the *root container,* and you do not always have to use the Grid for it. The Grid control is just what Expression Blend adds by default; it can be a Canvas or a StackPanel instead, or any other layout container you want to use.

You can also have other layout containers as children. That is, you can have nested containers and design very complex layouts.

Manipulating properties that control layout

Controls have a number of properties that determine how an object is laid out within a layout container. These properties are as follows:

- ✔ Height: Used to specify the height of the control.
- ✔ Width: Used to specify the width of the control.
- ✔ Margin: Used to specify the left, top, right, and bottom margins of the control. Specifying a top margin of 10 ensures that the control is placed 10 pixels below the top-left corner of the parent.
- ✔ MinHeight: Used to specify that the height of the control cannot be any lower than the value specified in this property.

- **MinWidth:** Used to specify that the width of the control cannot be any lower than the value specified in this property.
 - **MaxHeight:** Used to specify that the height of the control cannot be any larger than the value specified in this property.
 - **MaxWidth:** Used to specify that the width of the control cannot be any larger than the value specified in this property.
 - **Z-Index:** Used to determine whether the control should appear on top of another control. A higher Z-Index for your control means that it will be placed on top of another control with a lower value.
 - **HorizontalAlignment:** Specifies where an element should be placed horizontally within its layout slot. It takes the values Left, Right, Center, or Stretch.
 - **VerticalAlignment:** Specifies where an element should be placed vertically within its layout slot. It takes the values Top, Bottom, Center, or Stretch.

The way these properties work depends on the type of layout container you use, whether a property is set, and certain precedence rules. For example, if you specify values for Height and Width, they take precedence over HorizontalAlignment and VerticalAlignment values set to Stretch.

Aligning controls to one side

Setting some properties but not others may have considerable impact on the layout of your screen. For example, if you just set the right and bottom margin, but not the left and top one, the control will always be aligned to the bottom-right margin of the parent, even when the parent is resized. To see how aligning controls works, follow these steps:

1. **Create a new Silverlight application by choosing File⇨New Project. In the New Project dialog box, select Silverlight 4 Application + Website option and click OK. Alternatively, open an existing project and then open the XAML file on the Artboard by double-clicking the file in the Projects panel.**

2. **If your Artboard is empty, add an item such as a Rectangle to it.**

   You can do that by selecting the Rectangle tool from the Tools panel and drawing a rectangle on the Artboard with your mouse.

3. **Click the Selection tool to select an object, such as the Rectangle.**

   The object gets selected and the screen (a Rectangle, in this case) looks like Figure 5-1.

   Notice that the lines at the sides of the Rectangle show a value. This is the margin for the Rectangle. Each side has a margin value, but if any

Chapter 5: Laying Out Controls

lines appear as dotted and do not show a value, this means that the margin for that side isn't specified. When you don't set a margin for a certain side, you tell the layout container to use any value it sees fit.

4. **Set the left and top margin of the Rectangle to 0 and the right and bottom margin to 50.**

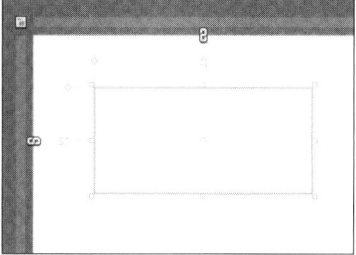

Figure 5-1: Rectangle showing margin values.

5. **Press F5 or choose Project⇨Run Project to run the application.**

   The application opens in a Web browser. Try resizing the browser window to see whether doing so affects the Rectangle in any way. (*Hint:* It doesn't.) The reason it doesn't is that the Width and Height properties of the UserControl are fixed. Although you are resizing the browser window, the size of the UserControl does not change as a result. Because the UserControl does not resize, the Rectangle you have created doesn't move, either.

6. **Close the application, and from the Objects and Timeline panel, click the UserControl object to select it.**

7. **In the Properties panel, click the Set to Auto button next to both the Height and Width property fields.**

   This sets both the values to Auto, which means that the values are automatically assigned based on the layout.

8. **Press F5 or choose Project⇨Run Project to run the application.**

   The application runs in the browser, and as you change the size of the browser window, the position of the Rectangle changes as well.

Clicking a control in the Objects and Timeline panel is another way of selecting controls, particularly ones that are hard to select from the Artboard. They can be hard to select when they're not visible or one control completely obscures another one on the Artboard. Using the Objects and Timeline panel is also the easiest way to set the default container — that is, the container to which controls are added from the Tools panel and Assets panel.

Setting the Height and Width of a UserControl at design time

After you set the Height and Width properties of the UserControl to Auto, the size of the control reduces, and adding new controls or even working with existing controls on the Artboard may become difficult. To fix this problem, follow these steps:

1. **Select the UserControl by clicking it on the Objects and Timeline panel.**

   The UserControl is selected and shows design-time resizing handles, one of which is shown here in the margin as an example.

2. **Move the cursor over these handles.**

   The shape of the cursor indicates the direction in which you can resize.

3. **Click the handle and resize to the size required.**

   The design time size of the UserControl changes, but this size is not applied when the application is actually run.

Clearing margins of an element from the Artboard

Expression Blend allows you to change the margin of controls by setting the values from the Properties panel. But there is also an easier way of manipulating them directly on the Artboard. Just follow these steps to change the margins of a control:

1. **Click the Selection tool on the Artboard and then click the control whose margins you want to manipulate.**

   The control is selected on the Artboard and shows the selection handles. In addition to the lines that show the margin values, margin adorners (shown here in the margin next to this paragraph) are also displayed. *Margin adorners* are used to display whether a margin is set or not.

2. **Click one of the margin adorners.**

   The shape of the margin adorner changes from a closed knot to an open one. The closed margin adorner indicates that the margin is set. An open one indicates that the margin is not set. You can toggle between the two values just by clicking the margin adorner.

Laying Out Controls in Rows and Columns

To lay out controls in a tabular fashion using rows and columns, you need to use the Grid. By default, when you create a project, Silverlight includes the Grid as the root container in the empty XAML pages it creates. (You can change the default control to a different one if you want, but not to create rows and columns, as we're doing here.) Before you add any controls to the page, you have to add rows and columns. This is because in an empty Grid, no rows and columns are specified, and Silverlight assumes that you have just one row and one column, which means that you just have one big cell. The following section tells you how to add rows and columns to a Grid.

Setting up rows and columns

To add rows and columns to the Grid control, follow these steps:

1. **Create a new Silverlight project in Expression Blend by choosing File⇨New Project; then, in the New Project dialog box that appears, select Silverlight 4 Project + Website option and click OK.**

   Alternatively, open an existing project and open its XAML file on the Artboard by double-clicking the file in the Projects panel.

   The Artboard is displayed, showing a light-blue strip at the top as well as at the right of the white rectangle. These blue strips are called *rulers*.

2. **Hover the cursor over the top ruler.**

   A vertical line appears on the design surface, as shown in Figure 5-2. (You can't tell here, but the line should be yellow.) This yellow line is called a *grid divider*. The shape of the cursor also changes to an arrow with a plus sign next to it.

3. **Move the cursor to a suitable position and click.**

   The yellow line turns blue and a column is added to the Grid.

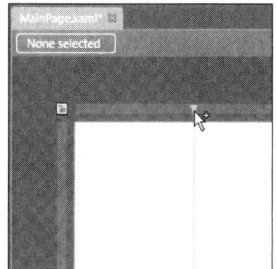

Figure 5-2: Adding a column to the Grid.

Part II: Managing Your Silverlight Controls

   4. **To add a row, click the blue strip along the side.**

      You can add multiple rows by clicking at various positions in the blue strip so that the Grid looks something like Figure 5-3.

Figure 5-3: Grid showing multiple rows and columns.

Adding controls to the rows and columns

After you've created a Grid with rows and columns (as described in the previous section), you should be ready to add controls to the Grid. Just follow these steps:

   1. **Select the control you want from the Tools panel, such as a TextBlock. Then click the cell in which you want the control to appear and drag the mouse to draw the control.**

      For the example in this section, we've selected the TextBlock tool and drawn a TextBlock in the first column and the first four rows.

   2. **Replace the default text in the TextBlocks by clicking each TextBlock with the Selection tool from the Tools panel and typing the text you want into each one.**

      For the example, we added the following text: First Name, Last Name, Sex, and Income Group.

   3. **Continue adding controls this way until you fill out the Grid the way you want it.**

      For example, we added two TextBox controls to the columns next to First Name and Last Name. We used the TextBox controls so that when

Chapter 5: Laying Out Controls   115

we run the application, it looks like a form with labels appearing in the first column and Text fields that accept input appearing in the second column.

You can also add rows and columns after you have added your controls to the Artboard. Expression Blend is smart enough to figure out which row and column each control should be placed in based on its location.

Figure 5-4 shows the Artboard with the controls we added.

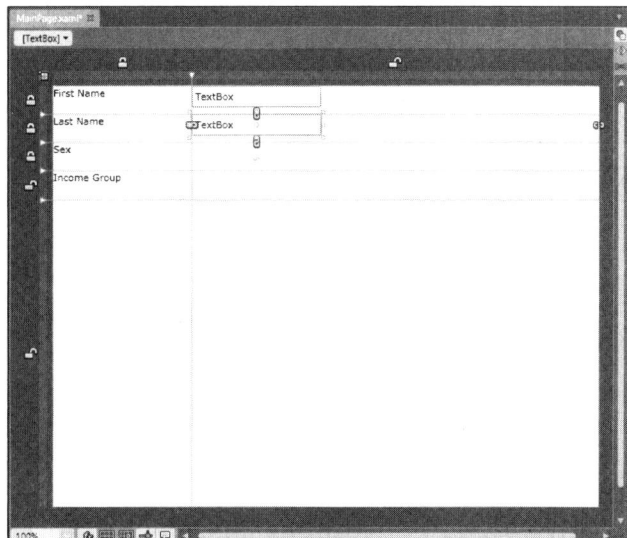

Figure 5-4: Grid with controls laid out.

Understanding the XAML

The XAML view for the page we created in the preceding section's example shows the following (with the part of the markup that's not relevant to this discussion replaced by an ellipsis [. . .]):

```
<UserControl . . .>
    <Grid x:Name="LayoutRoot" Background="White">
        <Grid.RowDefinitions>
            <RowDefinition Height="0.106*"/>
            <RowDefinition Height="0.108*"/>
            <RowDefinition Height="0.11*"/>
            <RowDefinition Height="0.116*"/>
            <RowDefinition Height="0.559*"/>
        </Grid.RowDefinitions>
        <Grid.ColumnDefinitions>
            <ColumnDefinition Width="0.265*"/>
            <ColumnDefinition Width="0.735*"/>
        </Grid.ColumnDefinitions>
```

```
            <TextBlock Margin="8" Text="First Name"
                TextWrapping="Wrap"/>
            <TextBlock Margin="8" Grid.Row="1" Text="Last
                Name" TextWrapping="Wrap"/>
            <TextBlock Margin="8" Grid.Row="2" Text="Sex"
                TextWrapping="Wrap"/>
            <TextBlock Margin="8" Grid.Row="3" Text="Income
                Group" TextWrapping="Wrap"/>
            <TextBox Margin="8,0,197,8" Grid.Column="1"
                Text="TextBox" TextWrapping="Wrap"/>
            <TextBox Margin="8,8,197,8" Grid.Column="1" Grid.
                Row="1" Text="TextBox" TextWrapping="Wrap"/>
    </Grid>
</UserControl>
```

When you click the blue strip along the side and top of the white rectangle to create rows and columns (as described in "Setting up rows and columns," earlier in this chapter), Expression Blend creates row and column definitions. In the XAML, each row gets a `RowDefinition` element added to `Grid.RowDefinitions`, and each column gets a `ColumnDefinition` element added to `Grid.ColumnDefinitions`. The row definitions specify the height of each row, and the column definitions specify the width.

By default, Expression Blend adds relative widths and heights to the column and rows — relative, that is, to the width of the parent control. So, for example, when the value of the width appears as `0.265*`, this indicates that the width of the column is 0.265 times the width of the grid. The use of asterisks (or stars) to set relative sizes is also known as *star size*. Using a star size helps in making the row heights and column widths bigger when the page is viewed on a bigger screen or smaller when viewed on a smaller screen.

You can also specify absolute width in pixels by specifying a value without the asterisk.

If you want to set the value of `Width` (or `Height`) to "Auto," Silverlight will automatically calculate the width (or height) of the column (or row).

The Grid adds two attached properties to all its children: `Row` and `Column`. (See Chapter 2 for more about attached properties.) These properties are used to determine which cell of the grid a control is placed in.

The `Row` and `Column` values are zero based. This means that if the `Row` value is set to 0, the control is placed in the first row, and if set to 1, the control is placed in the second row.

Changing row heights and column widths on the Artboard

After you've added rows and columns to your XAML page, you can easily adjust a cell's height and width by dragging the column and row lines, but to toggle the height and width values between star sizes, pixel sizes, and automatic sizes (as mentioned in the previous section), all you need to do is click the padlock image that appears to the side and on top of the light-blue strips.

 A closed padlock indicates that it uses pixel widths (pixel sized). An open padlock indicates relative widths (star sized), and an auto icon, which is shown here in the margin, indicates automatic widths (auto sized). You can toggle between values by clicking each image as it appears.

Stacking Controls Horizontally and Vertically

The StackPanel in Silverlight allows you to stack your controls either vertically or horizontally. When you stack controls vertically, the controls appear one below the other, and when you stack controls horizontally, they appear one after the other.

Using the StackPanel with a vertical layout is like having a Grid control with just one column and multiple rows, and with each control having a row to itself. Similarly, a StackPanel with a horizontal layout is like having a Grid control with one row and multiple columns.

Adding controls to a StackPanel

To stack controls vertically, follow these steps:

1. **Open the XAML page for which you would like to add the StackPanel from Expression Blend.**

   The page opens and is shown on the Artboard.

2. **In the Tools panel, right-click the Grid tool (or the currently selected Layout tool). The StackPanel is grouped with the Grid, Canvas, ScrollViewer, and Border controls in the Tools panel, as shown in Figure 5-5. Click the StackPanel to select it. Then double-click the Stack Panel tool.**

The StackPanel is added to the Artboard. Rather than double-click the StackPanel tool, you can click to select the tool and drag the mouse on the Artboard to draw the StackPanel at the exact position you want to place it.

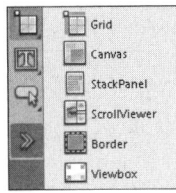

Figure 5-5: The Tools panel showing the StackPanel control.

   3. **In the Tools panel, double-click a control, such as the TextBlock or TextBox.**

      The control you clicked is added to the StackPanel.

   4. **Repeat Step 3 to add more controls.**

      Notice that the controls are placed one below the other. If you want to change this and stack them horizontally instead, select the StackPanel using the Selection tool, and in the Properties panel, change the `Orientation` property under the Layout group to Horizontal.

Converting a Grid to a StackPanel

Expression Blend allows you to change from one layout container to another easily. This feature is very useful if you've already added your controls to a certain layout container, such as the Grid, and realize that you are better off using another container, such as the StackPanel. In this example, you convert a Grid layout to a StackPanel by following these steps:

   1. **Open an existing Silverlight project in Expression Blend, and from the Projects panel, double-click the XAML file for which you want to change the layout container.**

      In this example, we use a page that has a Grid control with various TextBlocks and TextBoxes. In addition, we have a set of radio buttons for Sex — Male, Female, and Unknown. The three radio buttons are placed within a nested Grid, that is, a grid within a grid, as shown in Figure 5-6.

      Notice how Expression Blend supports nested grids by showing the rulers around the Grid that you are currently working with.

   2. **Click the Selection tool from the Tools panel, and then in the Objects and Timeline panel, click the layout container that you want to change.**

Chapter 5: Laying Out Controls **119**

In the example shown here, the Grid containing the three radio buttons is selected.

3. **Right-click the Grid on the Objects and Timeline panel and choose Change Layout Type⇨Stack Panel to change the Grid into a StackPanel, as shown in Figure 5-7.**

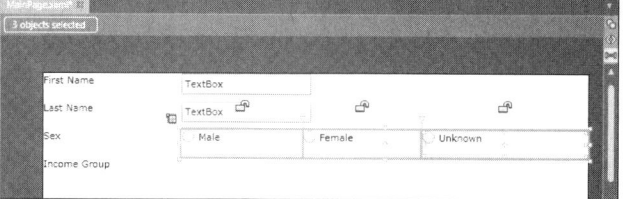

Figure 5-6: Artboard showing a nested Grid.

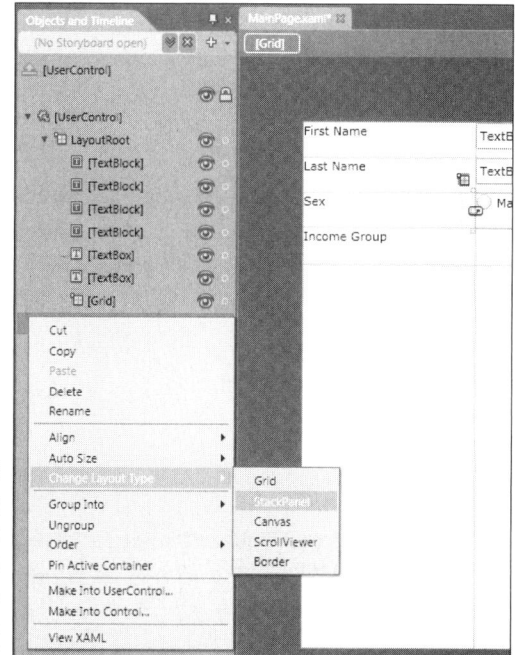

Figure 5-7: Changing the Grid into a StackPanel.

4. **Change the Orientation of the StackPanel to Horizontal or Vertical depending on whether you want the controls to appear one after the other on the same line, or one below the other.**

When you are dealing with nested containers such as a Grid nested within a grid, you can find the currently selected container by looking at the Objects and Timeline panel, which is the control with a blue border surrounding it.

Understanding the XAML for a StackPanel

If you open the XAML view from the Artboard by clicking the XAML button at the top, the XAML for a StackPanel should look something like this (based on the example in the previous section):

```
<StackPanel Grid.Column="1" Grid.Row="3"
            Orientation="Horizontal">
    <RadioButton Content="Male"/>
    <RadioButton Content="Female"/>
    <RadioButton Content="Unknown"/>
</StackPanel>
```

Notice the simplicity in the XAML, as compared to the XAML for Grid (shown in a previous section). Unlike the Grid, which has lots of elements to configure the rows and columns, the StackPanel contains only the controls you add to it. The StackPanel is one of the simplest layout containers in Silverlight, and all you need to do is add the controls one after the other in it, which are arranged either vertically or horizontally based on the Orientation property you choose.

Wrapping Controls

There is another layout container in Silverlight that is just as easy to use as the StackPanel control described in the previous section. This layout container, WrapPanel, is available as part of the Silverlight Toolkit. The Toolkit doesn't come with the original Silverlight installation, but you can obtain it from http://silverlight.net. (See Chapter 1 for more about the Silverlight Toolkit.)

As with the other layout container controls, the WrapPanel serves as a parent control. It displays its children one after the other, and when it cannot fit any more controls into the same line, it wraps them into the next line. It repeats the same layout method for each line until all the child controls are laid out.

To add a WrapPanel, follow these steps:

1. **Open the XAML file to which you want to add the WrapPanel.**

2. **From the Assets panel, locate the WrapPanel control by typing WrapPanel in the Search field. When the control appears in the search results, add it to the Artboard by dragging it onto the location on the Artboard where you want the WrapPanel to appear.**

    The WrapPanel gets added to the Artboard. The WrapPanel tool also shows up in the Tools panel.

3. Add a few controls to the WrapPanel by double-clicking those controls from the Tools panel or the Assets panel.

4. Select the WrapPanel by using the Selection tool from the Tools panel and clicking the WrapPanel.

    The WrapPanel gets selected.

5. Press the Set to Auto button next to Width and Height properties under the Layout group in the Properties panel.

6. Press the Advanced property options button for the Margin property under the Layout group in the Properties panel.

    The WrapPanel resizes to occupy just enough space to fill in the controls it contains. If you resize the WrapPanel by dragging the resizing handles, the controls in the panel wrap to the next line if there isn't enough space to fill all the controls in one line.

Arranging Controls by Absolute Positioning Using the Canvas Control

Another very simple layout container in Silverlight is the Canvas. You can use the Canvas layout container whenever you need absolute positioning of child controls. You can also use it when you want your controls to overlap or when you don't want the dimensions and positions to change when you resize the Canvas.

To see how a Canvas control works, follow these steps:

1. Open the XAML file for which you want to add the Canvas in Expression Blend.

2. Choose the Canvas tool from the Tools panel, shown here in the margin, and add it to the Artboard by clicking and dragging it to the desired position and size.

3. Now add controls to the Canvas by selecting them from either the Tools panel or the Assets panel and clicking and dragging them to the desired position and size within the Canvas.

    The controls get added to the Canvas and have absolute positioning. The XAML for a Canvas that contains two buttons will look something like this:

```
<Canvas HorizontalAlignment="Left" Margin="0,8,0,41"
        Width="340" Grid.Column="1" Grid.Row="5">
    <Button Width="75" Content="OK" Canvas.Left="8"
        Canvas.Top="8"/>
    <Button Width="75" Content="Cancel" Canvas.Left="97"
        Canvas.Top="8"/>
</Canvas>
```

The Canvas adds the attached properties, Left and Top, which you can set either from the Properties panel or just by moving the controls around on the Artboard. Of course, you can also edit the XAML manually to update the values.

Using the ScrollViewer to Scroll Through the Contents

Sometimes, the screen real estate you have may not be enough to display what you want to show to your users. In these scenarios, you can use a ScrollViewer. The ScrollViewer just displays scrollbars that the user can use to scroll up or down to display more of the contents that the ScrollViewer holds. To use a ScrollViewer, open the XAML file that you want to add the ScrollViewer to in Expression Blend and follow these steps:

 1. **Choose the ScrollViewer tool (shown here in the margin) from the Tools panel and add it to the Artboard by clicking and dragging it to the desired position and size.**

 2. **From the Properties panel, set the value on both the properties** `HorizontalScrollBarVisibility` **and** `VerticalScrollBarVisibility` **to Auto.**

 3. **Right-click the project name in the Projects panel and choose Add Existing Item from the menu.**

    The Add Existing dialog box opens. Select a fairly large image file from your computer and click Open to add it to the project.

 4. **Drag the image file you just added from the Project file and drop it onto the ScrollViewer control on the Artboard.**

 5. **Press F5 or choose Project⇨Run Project to run the application.**

    The application runs in the browser and displays the image in a ScrollViewer with scrollbars. Moving the scrollbars will scroll the image up or down.

Using the Viewbox to Fit the Contents Snugly

If you want your control to take up as much or as little space as is available, you need to use the Viewbox control. The Viewbox control automatically readjusts the size of the content to fit into its bounds. To use a Viewbox in your page, just follow the steps mentioned in the previous section, but use the Viewbox control instead of the ScrollViewer control. You also do not have to set `HorizontalScrollBarVisibility` and `VerticalScrollBarVisibility` because they are specific to the ScrollViewer control. When you increase or decrease the size of the Viewbox control, the image will automatically resize.

Both the ScrollViewer and Viewbox containers can hold only one control, but you can add a container such as Grid or StackPanel as this control and add more controls to them.

Grouping Controls into a Tabbed Page

When you have a lot of controls on a page, the screen can get very cluttered and may even end up confusing the user. This problem is usually solved by using tabs in a page. For example, if you are getting users to fill out their details before a checkout, you may be collecting a lot of information such as personal details, shipping address, payment details, and so on. Each of these details may consist of a large number of fields. Using a tabbed page, you show the fields for collecting personal details in only one tab, and you show the fields to collect shipping details in another tab, and so on.

Each tab is visible only when you are entering details for that tab, and this makes the screen less cluttered.

To see how to create an application that uses tabbed pages, follow these steps:

1. **Create a new Silverlight application by choosing File⇨New Project. In the New Project dialog box, select the Silverlight 4 Application + Website option and click OK.**

2. **In the Assets panel, type** TabControl **in the Search field to find the TabControl. When it appears, drag and drop it onto the Artboard or double-click it to add it to the Artboard.**

    The TabControl appears on the page. By default, Expression Blend adds two tabs for you to work with. A tab page in Silverlight is implemented as a TabItem control, and the default header text for this control is `TabItem`. You can add another tab by right-clicking inside one of the tabs and, in the drop-down list that appears, choosing Add Tab Item. (You can also delete unwanted tab items by selecting them and pressing the Del key.)

    You need to change the header text on both tabs and also fill each tab with controls. But first, you need to make the TabControl occupy the entire page (as described in the next step).

3. **To make the TabControl fill up the entire page, open the Properties panel. Click the Advanced property options button**

next to Margin and choose Reset from the menu. Then set both the `HorizontalAlignment` and `VerticalAlignment` **properties under Layout to** `Stretch`.

4. **Click the Selection tool from the Tools panel and click the first TabItem on the screen. In the Properties panel, change the** `Header` **property value to a suitable value, such as** `Page 1`.

5. **Click the second TabItem and change the** `Header` **property to** `Page 2`.

6. **From the Objects and Timeline panel, click Grid, which appears under the first TabItem, as shown in Figure 5-8.**

   The Grid becomes the current container and allows you to add controls to it.

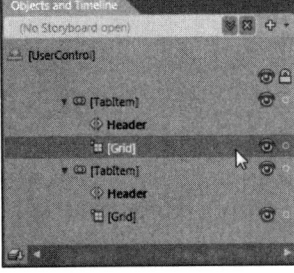

Figure 5-8: Selecting the Grid to be the current container under TabItem.

7. **From either the Tools panel or the Assets panel, add controls that need to go into the first tab to the Grid.**

   As an example, we've added a TextBlock and set the `Text` property to `This is page 1`, as shown in Figure 5-9.

8. **Select the Grid under the second TabItem from the Objects and Timeline panel, and add controls from the Tools panel or Assets panel that need to go into the second Tab.**

   As an example, we've added a TextBlock and set the `Text` property to `This is page 2`.

9. **Press F5 or choose Project**➪**Run Project to run the application.**

   The application runs in the browser and displays the two tabs. Clicking the first tab header displays the contents of the first tab; clicking the second tab header displays the contents of the second tab.

   An example of an application having one tab for Person Details and one for Image Details is shown in Figure 5-10.

Figure 5-9: Artboard showing controls being added to the first tab.

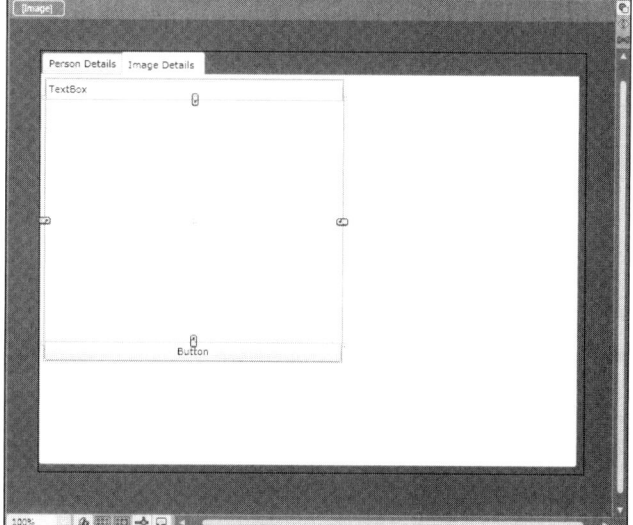

Figure 5-10: Application showing one tab for Person Details and one for Image Details.

Docking Controls

The DockPanel allows you to dock a control to one of the sides of the container: top, left, bottom, or right. You might want to use the DockPanel to set toolbars at the top or side of a page, or include something like a status bar at the bottom of the page.

To add a DockPanel to your page, open the Assets panel and type **DockPanel** in the Search field to find the DockPanel control. You can then drag and drop it into the Artboard to add it as a container.

After you've added a DockPanel to your page, you can add other controls to the page and set the `DockPanel.Dock` property to values such as `Top` or `Button`, depending on where these controls should go.

Picking the wrong layout container may sometimes complicate the way the controls are laid out. You may still be able to place controls where you want them, but the process may end up being far more complex and time consuming than you'd like.

Chapter 6

Styling and Skinning Controls

In This Chapter
- Changing the look of controls using styling
- Applying styles in Expression Blend
- Skinning the controls using templates
- Using themes to change the look of your application

An important aspect of providing a good experience for users of a Web site is presenting an appealing, professional-looking interface. A key to achieving this kind of presentation is consistency. By consistency, we mean using the same font and color schemes, setting the same margins, and so on throughout the application. To achieve consistency, you can painstakingly set the properties on every individual control, but that's not the best way to do it. What happens if you decide to change something like the font style? You're faced with the tedious, time-consuming chore of changing that property for every control you've used in your application.

This is where the styling and skinning features in Expression Blend come to your rescue. In this chapter, we show you how to create styles and templates (which is another name for skins) as well as how to apply them to your controls.

Applying Styles to Controls

You can change the way a control looks by setting its various properties. Some of the typical properties on a TextBlock that you may set include:

- `VerticalAlignment` and `HorizontalAlignment`
- `FontFamily`, `FontSize`, and `FontWeight`
- `Margin`
- `TextAlignment` and `LineHeight`

You can set these items quite easily by selecting multiple TextBlocks simultaneously using the Selection tool and then setting all their properties in the Properties panel. Although this approach would work, it would become unmanageable when you have multiple screens in your application or you need to add another TextBlock at a later stage.

A much better way is to create a *style* that includes all the properties you want your control to have, and then, again for the sake of consistency, apply that style to each of the TextBlock controls in the application. You can do this through the Properties panel or in the XAML itself. The following sections describe both methods.

Creating default styles for a control

To create a style, you can start off with a new Silverlight project or open an existing project that contains controls that you want to style. For the example in this section, we use an existing application that has three controls in the `MainPage.xaml` file: a TextBlock, a TextBox, and a Button, as shown in the following XAML:

```xaml
<UserControl
    xmlns= "http://schemas.microsoft.com/winfx/2006/xaml/
        presentation"
    xmlns:x= "http://schemas.microsoft.com/winfx/2006/
        xaml"
    x:Class="Chapter6.MainPage"
    Width="640" Height="480">
  <StackPanel x:Name="LayoutRoot" Background="White">
    <TextBlock Text="Enter Search Term:"
        TextWrapping="Wrap" />
    <TextBox TextWrapping="Wrap" />
    <Button Content="Search" />
  </StackPanel>
</UserControl>
```

To create a style for a control, follow these steps:

1. **Click the Selection tool from the Tools panel and click the control whose style you want to change.**

   In this example, we have selected a TextBlock.

2. **Right-click the control and from the main menu, choose Object⇨Edit Style⇨Create Empty.**

   A Create Style Resource dialog box pops up, as shown in Figure 6-1.

3. **Change the Name(Key) radio button to Apply to All. Also, select the Application radio button that appears under the Define In radio button group and press OK.**

Chapter 6: Styling and Skinning Controls

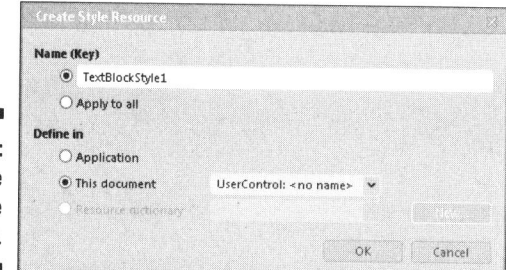

Figure 6-1: Create Style Resource dialog box.

The `App.xaml` file opens automatically and displays the as-yet-unstyled control, which is a TextBlock in this case.

4. **In the Properties panel, change the properties you want set for the style. To set a TextBlock's font to 14pt and color to a shade of blue, set the Foreground color property to a shade of blue and the Font size property to 14 pt, as shown in Figure 6-2.**

5. **On the Artboard, click the tab page that contains the control for which you are applying the style (MainPage.xaml, in this example).**

The page opens and shows the control with the style applied. Any new TextBlock you add to the page will also have the style automatically applied to it.

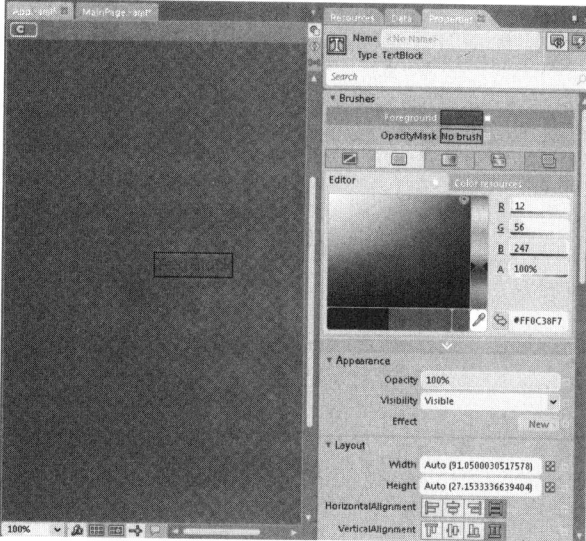

Figure 6-2: TextBlock being styled.

Creating named styles for controls

In the previous section, you saw how to create styles that are implicitly applied to all controls of a certain type. If you want to create a style that doesn't apply to all controls of a type, you need to create a named style.

To create a named style, you need to follow all the steps from the previous section, with a slight change: In Step 3, rather than change the Name (Key) field to Apply to All, you need to specify a name. In the case of the TextBlock, set the name to something meaningful, such as Caption.

A common mistake people make is to name the style they use based on how it looks. For instance, if you call your style BlueText and later decide to change the color from blue to red, the style would require a name change, too. So it is much more useful if you named a style based on what it does or what it represents (such as Caption) rather than how it looks (BlueText).

Understanding the Style property

Every control has a `Style` property that can be used to specify the named style for the control. To understand this in more detail, press the XAML button on the Artboard to view the XAML for the `MainPage.xaml` file after you've created a named style as described in the previous section. The XAML should look something like this (some markup has been left out for the sake of clarity here; these are indicated by the ellipses [...]):

```
<UserControl ...>
  <StackPanel x:Name="LayoutRoot" Background="White">
    <TextBlock Text="Enter Search Term:"
          TextWrapping="Wrap" Style="{StaticResource
          Caption}" />
    <TextBox TextWrapping="Wrap" />
    <Button Content="Search" />
  </StackPanel>
</UserControl>
```

If you look closely at the TextBlock element, you will notice that a property called `Style` has been added and has a value set within curly brackets. The value in the curly brackets specifies that the style is bound to a static resource called Caption. A *static resource* is a resource that gets replaced in the XAML when the application is being built.

Understanding the XAML behind Style resources

A style is nothing but a resource that can be specified either in the App.xaml file or in another file. To understand how styles are created as resources in Silverlight, open the XAML view for App.xaml to look at the markup that gets created for a style. The Application markup that specifies a style for a TextBlock would look like this (some markup has been left out for the sake of clarity here; these are indicated by the ellipses [. . .]):

```
<Application . . . >
  <Application.Resources>
    <!-- Resources scoped at the Application level should
          be defined here. -->
    <Style TargetType="TextBlock">
      <Setter Property="Foreground" Value="#FF1053DE"/>
      <Setter Property="FontSize" Value="18.667"/>
    </Style>
  </Application.Resources>

</Application>
```

Basically, to declare a style, you need to declare a Style element and specify the type of control that it can be applied on using the TargetType attribute. Setter child elements are declared under Style to specify the various properties for that control. Any property that you can set directly on a control can also be set in a Style declaration using the Setter element. The Setter element contains a name and value pair combination specified in the attributes Property and Value.

If you created a named style, the Style element will also have another attribute, x:Key, which can be used to specify the name for the Style as follows:

```
<Style x:Key="Caption" TargetType="TextBlock">
    <Setter Property="FontSize" Value="18.667"/>
    <Setter Property="Foreground" Value="#FF3D6AE0"/>
</Style>
```

The properties for each control differ, which is one of the reasons that you need to specify the Control type in a Style declaration.

Understanding styles as resources in the Resources panel

As we show in the previous section, a style in Silverlight is created as a resource. In addition to a style, you can add brushes, templates, and animation storyboards (which we describe in Chapter 7) as resources. The Resources panel lists all the resources that are available for use on the current page, as shown in Figure 6-3.

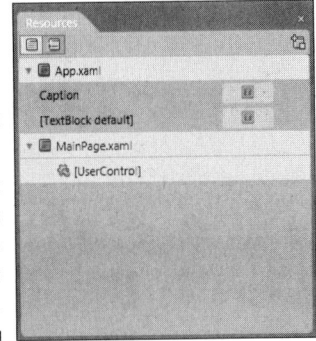

Figure 6-3: Looking at resources in the Resources panel.

 The Resources panel contains two buttons (shown here in the margin) at the top-right corner of the screen. The top button in the margin allows you to see all the resources; the bottom one shows only the resources used by the selected control on the Artboard.

 You would normally put all the resources you want to share in your `App.xaml` file. If you put any resources in your page (such as `MainPage.xaml`), then these resources can only be used in that page. If you want to share resources among different pages, you can also create separate resource dictionaries. A *resource dictionary* is another XAML file whose sole purpose is to store resources. You can also add resource dictionaries by clicking the New Resources Dictionary button (shown here in the margin), which is on the top-right corner of the panel.

Each item on the panel is clickable, and you can right-click any style and choose Edit to edit the style quickly. Each style entry in the list also shows the tool type as a little image next to its name.

Applying styles to existing elements

You can apply styles that you've already created to a control by dragging the resources from the Resource panel onto the control or by setting the Style property of the control from the Properties panel. They are explained in more detail in the following sections.

Applying a style from the Resources panel

From the Resources panel, drag the style you want to use and drop it onto the field on the Artboard that you want to apply the style to. A menu pops up, as shown in Figure 6-4. Choose the Style menu item that appears below Select Property on "[TextBlock]". This changes the style of the control to that found in the Resource panel.

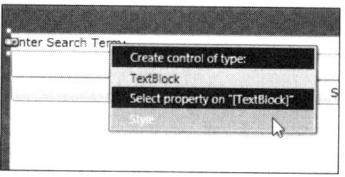

Figure 6-4: Pop-up menu that appears when a style is dropped onto a control from the Resources panel.

Applying a style from the Properties panel

In the Properties panel for the control that you want to add the style to, click the Advanced Property Options rectangle for the Style property; you find this under Miscellaneous. A menu is displayed, as shown in Figure 6-5. Choose Local Resource followed by the name of the style you want to apply. Figure 6-5 shows how you can apply the previously created Caption style to a TextBlock.

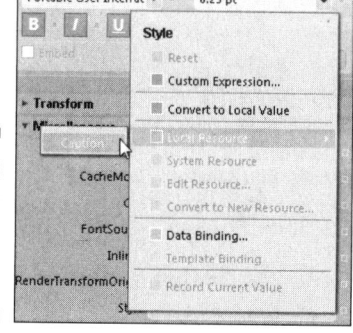

Figure 6-5: Binding the style to an existing control.

Creating controls with existing styles

You do not have to add a control such as a TextBlock to the Artboard first and then apply a style to it afterward. If a previously created style already exists on the Resource panel, you can just drag and drop the style from the Resources panel onto the Artboard. Doing so automatically creates the control you chose with the right style.

Creating new styles based on existing styles

You can create a new style based on an existing style quite easily. Just follow these steps:

1. **Open an existing XAML file that contains the control for which you want to create a new style.**

2. **Click the Selection tool from the Tools panel and click the control on the Artboard for which you want to create a style.**

3. **From the menu, choose Object⇨Edit Style⇨Edit a Copy.**

    The Create Style Resource dialog box appears.

4. **Enter a suitable name for the style in the Name field and select the Application radio button.**

5. **Press OK to create the new style.**

    A new style is created in App.xaml based on the existing style. Properties that were set for the control that you selected will automatically be set in the new style you just created.

You can edit an existing style by selecting a control using the Selection tool and choosing Object⇨Edit Style⇨Edit Current from the main menu.

Skinning a Control

A control in Silverlight is essentially made up of other controls. For example, a Button control is made up of several controls such as Rectangles, Borders,

Chapter 6: Styling and Skinning Controls   135

Grids, and so on that are placed in such a way that they look like a button. This arrangement of the controls is called a *template*. The process of changing the template is known as *skinning* (or even *templating*).

You can completely change the template to make it look anyway you want — you can make a button look spherical or the lines in a textbox look crooked. In fact you can change all the building blocks of the template that make up the control without changing how it works. So, when you change the template for a button control, Silverlight still generates button-click events or mouse-over events when you click the button or move your mouse over it.

A *style*, on the other hand, is essentially a collection of Properties settings. You can easily change particular aspects of an element's style, such as its font or color, but you can't change the actual building blocks of the element.

The template for a control is present in a XAML definition that defines the visual appearance and behavior of the control.

You can see how the template for a button looks by following these steps:

1. **Open a XAML file that contains a button in Expression Blend.**

2. **Click the Selection tool from the Tools panel and click the button control on the Artboard to select it.**

3. **Right-click the button, and when a menu appears, choose Edit Template➪Edit a Copy.**

    The Create Style Resource dialog box pops up.

4. **Change the text in the Name field to** `MyButton`, **and under Define In, select the Application radio button. Then click OK.**

    The App.xaml file opens, and you should see an empty screen with a button, as shown in Figure 6-6. Notice that the Objects and Timeline panel shows the other controls that have been used to make a button.

 Just as you can create an implicit style that can apply to all instances of a control, so can you create an implicit template as well. When the Create Style Resource dialog box appears while you're creating a new template, just select the Apply to All radio button rather than give the template a name.

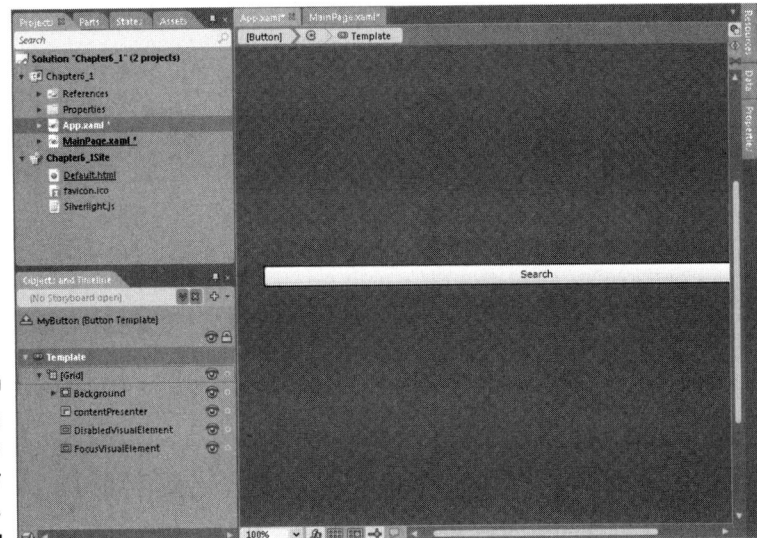

Figure 6-6:
Editing the template for a button.

Switch to the XAML view to see what the template looks like in XAML. The XAML that specifies the style for MyButton should look something like this (some markup has been left out and is represented by ellipses [...] for brevity):

```
<Style x:Key="MyButton" TargetType="Button">
  <Setter Property="Background" Value="#FF1F3B53"/>
  . . .
  <Setter Property="Template">
    <Setter.Value>
      <ControlTemplate TargetType="Button">
        <Grid>
          <VisualStateManager.VisualStateGroups>
            <VisualStateGroup x:Name="CommonStates">
              <VisualState x:Name="Normal"/>
              <VisualState x:Name="MouseOver">
                . . .
              </VisualState>
              <VisualState x:Name="Disabled">
                . . .
              </VisualState>
            </VisualStateGroup>
            <VisualStateGroup x:Name="FocusStates">
              . . .
            </VisualStateGroup>
          </VisualStateManager.VisualStateGroups>
          <Border x:Name="Background" ...>
            <Grid Margin="1" . . .>
```

```
            . . .
          </Grid>
        </Border>
        <ContentPresenter . . ./>
        . . .
      </Grid>
    </ControlTemplate>
  </Setter.Value>
 </Setter>
</Style>
```

The XAML shown here basically defines a style called MyButton, and the most important property that it sets is the `Template` property. The template defines how the button looks. The root container of the Button template is the `ControlTemplate`. (See Chapter 5 for more explanation of a root container.)

The control template for a button defines a Grid under which the other UI controls are placed. The button actually can exist in many states, which are described in Table 6-1.

Table 6-1	Button States
Button State	*Description*
Normal	Default state of the button
MouseOver	State when a mouse hovers over a button
Disabled	State of the button when it is disabled
Focused	State of the button when it has the keyboard focus
Unfocused	State when the button does not have the keyboard focus

These states are defined as Visual State groups in the template, and you can specify in the XAML how the button should look for each state.

If you look more closely at the XAML, you see that the visual states — Normal, MouseOver, and Disabled — are placed in a group called CommonStates; also, the Focused and Unfocused states are defined in a group called FocusStates.

The reason for these two groups is that the states in a certain group are mutually exclusive — that is, if you have a Normal state, you cannot have a MouseOver or Disabled state. Similarly, if your button is in the Disabled state, it cannot have the other two states in the same group. It can, however, have another state in the other Visual State Group, which in this case can be either Focused or Unfocused.

Editing the template visually

It is usually easier to start editing the control from an existing template, but we offer this example of starting from scratch to give you a better understanding of the elements involved. In this example, we skin a Button control to make it look oval.

 If you are continuing from the previous section, then to begin, click the Palette icon (shown here in the margin) at the top of the Artboard under the App.xaml tab and choose Edit Template➪Create Empty, as shown in Figure 6-7. Alternatively, select a button using the Selection tool and right-click to bring up the menu; next, choose Edit Template➪Create Empty.

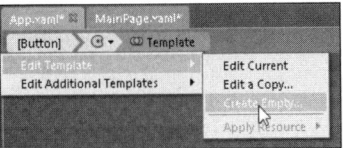

Figure 6-7: Creating an empty Button skin, or template.

In both cases, the Create Control Template Resource dialog box appears. Change the Name(Key) field by entering the new name OvalButton (for this example). Next, select the Application radio button and click OK.

An empty template gets created. To create the oval button, follow these steps:

1. **Double-click the Ellipse tool in the Tools panel.**

   This adds an oval shape to the template on the Artboard. (The section about drawing shapes on the Artboard in Chapter 3 tells you how to work with shapes such as the Ellipse.)

2. **In the Properties panel, set the Fill to Gradient Color and select the Radial Gradient. Also, click Reverse gradient stops so that the white color starts from the inside and gradually turns black as it moves outward, as shown in Figure 6-8. Now, click Advanced Property options for Margin and choose Reset.**

   The oval fills up the entire space of the control.

3. **From the Assets panel, find the ContentPresenter tool and double-click it to add it to the Control template.**

4. In the Properties panel for the ContentPresenter, reset the Margin and set both HorizontalAlignment and VerticalAlignment to Center. Your screen should now look like Figure 6-9.

 5. Set the `MinHeight` and `MinWidth` properties of the Grid to 50 each so that the buttons have a minimum height and width when used.

 6. Click the MainPage.xaml tab on the Artboard to switch back to the `MainPage.xaml` file.

    The Search button now has the newly created OvalButton control's shape and properties.

 7. Select the Button control using the Selection tool, and in the Properties panel, set the `Height` and `Width` properties to a suitable value, such as 40 and 100, respectively.

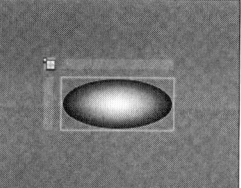

Figure 6-8: The newly created Button on the Artboard.

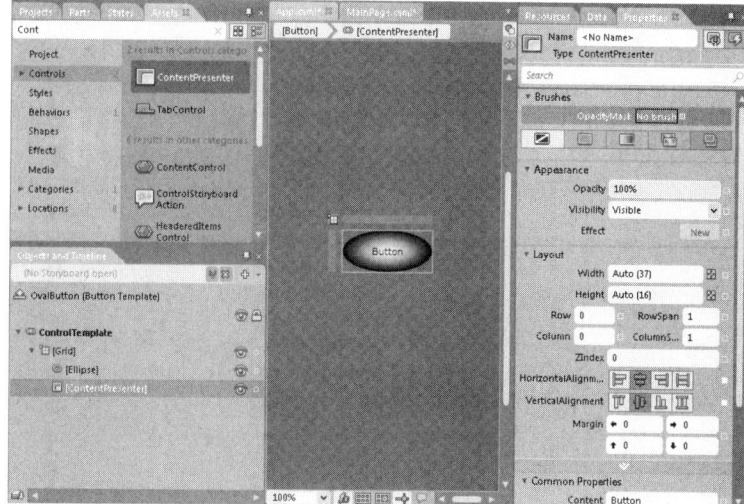

Figure 6-9: Expression Blend showing the newly created OvalButton.

8. **Switch to the Events view in the Properties panel and add a** `Click` **event by double-clicking the Click field.**

    The `MainPage.xaml.cs` file opens and shows the `Button_Click` function. Replace the comment

    ```
    // TODO: Add event handler implementation here.
    ```

    in the `Button_Click` function with the following code:

    ```
    private void Button_Click(object sender, System.
            Windows.RoutedEventArgs e)
    {
        MessageBox.Show("Search button pressed");
    }
    ```

9. **Press F5 or choose Project⇨Run Project to run the application.**

    The application shows up in the browser. Click the Search button to determine whether the `Click` event is being called. The MessageBox appears, proving that the event is in fact being called, but you don't get any visual cue that the button has actually been pressed.

    To get that visual cue, you have to start playing with the states of the button. Read on to see how to do that.

Specifying state

To work with the state of a control, continue from the previous section and open the Resources panel. Double-click `App.xaml`, shown in the panel, to expand it. When `OvalButton` shows up in the panel, double-click it to open it for editing; then open the States panel.

The States panel, shown in Figure 6-10, displays all the available Visual State groups and the Visual States under them. (See the beginning of the "Skinning a Control" section for more details about Visual State groups.) You can click any of the states in this panel and start changing how that state looks.

To change how the button looks when you move your mouse over it, select the `MouseOver` state from the panel first. A red border appears in the Artboard and you get a little message at the top of the Artboard that reads `MouseOver state Recording is on`. Next, select the Ellipse using the Selection tool and go to the Properties panel. Change the Stroke color to a solid black and Stroke Thickness to 5, and click the red button that appears to the left of the `MouseOver state Recording is on` text on the Artboard, as shown in Figure 6-11.

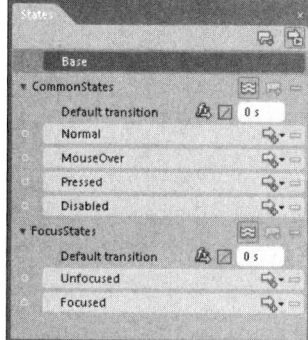

Figure 6-10: The States panel showing the states available for the control.

To change the way the button looks when it is clicked, select the Pressed state in the States panel and change both ends of the Fill Brush gradient to white. Press the red button again to stop the recording.

To test the changes you've made, go to `MainPage.xaml.cs` to get rid of the MessageBox code you added earlier (if you followed the example in the previous section).

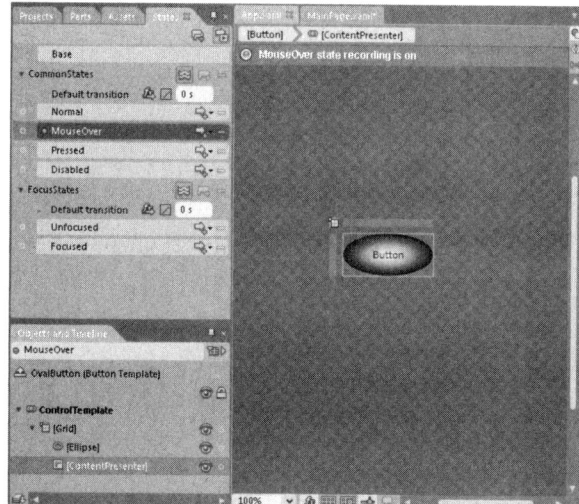

Figure 6-11: Recording the MouseOver state.

Press F5 or choose Project➪Run Project to run the application. You now get a visual cue when the mouse rolls over the button as well as when the button is pressed. The transition from Normal state to Pressed state does not, however, happen smoothly.

To fix that problem, close the application, go back to Expression Blend, and click the App.xaml tab.

 In the Pressed state in the State panel, press the arrow image (shown in the margin). This brings up a pop-up menu, as shown in Figure 6-12.

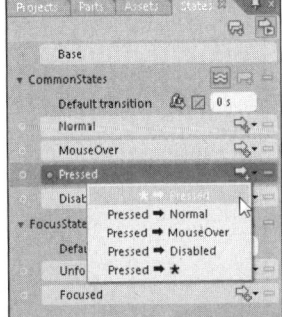

Figure 6-12: Menu items to specify transitions.

This menu allows you to specify the transition time from one state to another. An asterisk (*) indicates any state. Choose *➪Pressed. Doing so opens the setting that allows you to specify the transition time in seconds. Type **0.2** (for this example) to specify that you want the transition from any state to the Pressed state to happen in 0.2 seconds.

Press F5 or choose Project➪Run Project to run the application. If you press and hold the button, notice that the transition to the pressed state now happens slowly rather than abruptly.

You can enhance the Button template design by building the look for other states in the CommonStates group as well as for states in the FocusStates group. (You can find more information about the two groups in the "Skinning a Control" section, earlier in this chapter.) As you can see in the example, changing the state just alters the look of the control without altering the behavior.

 You can also add a special transition effect when you change from one state to another. Click the image that says fx, which appears after Default Transition in the States panel. A small window pops up that allows you to pick a transition effect. Choose a value such as Ripple and check out what happens when you run the application and move your mouse over the button.

Binding values in the template

There may be a couple of things you've hard-coded in the template, such as the gradient transform color in the Button, but that is okay because that is what you may actually want. In some cases, however, it would be nice to set certain values based on the Button's property values. For instance, you may want the border color of the Ellipse to be the same as the border color of the Button.

To set this property, start from where you left off in the previous section by opening the States panel. Click the Base state to select it.

Using the Selection tool on the Artboard, select the Ellipse, and in the Stroke brush, click the Advanced Property Options rectangle next to the field. When the menu pops up, choose Template Binding⇨BorderBrush, as shown in Figure 6-13. This binds the `Stroke` property of the Ellipse specified in the template to the `BorderBrush` property of the button. (For more about data binding, see Chapter 9.)

To test the binding you've just done, click the MainPage.xaml tab and select the Button using the Selection tool. Change the Border brush to a solid brush color, such as Red.

Now, run the application by pressing F5 or choosing Project⇨Run Project to see whether everything still works as before.

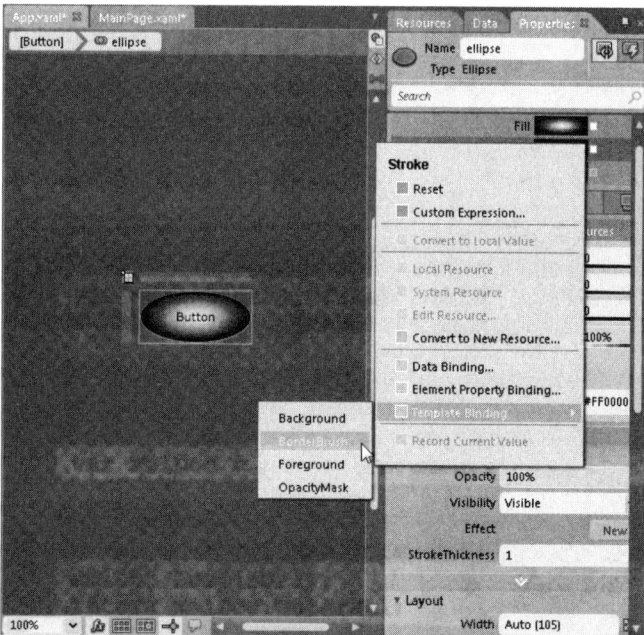

Figure 6-13: Binding the Stroke color of the Ellipse to that of the Button's BorderBrush.

Applying skins to existing controls

Applying a template/skin to an existing control is exactly the same as setting its style. From the Resource panel, just drag the resource (such as the OvalButton created previously in this chapter) onto an existing control, and it will automatically be added after you're asked whether you want to add another control or set the Template property.

The XAML for how the template is being applied should look like this:

```
<Button Content="Button" Template="{StaticResource
        OvalButton}"/>
```

It is a good idea to create a style and set the newly created template in the style as a property. To do that click Advanced Property Options for the Template field, found under Miscellaneous when the menu pops up; then choose Local Resource, under which all the template names (such as OvalButton) are listed. Choose the template you want to apply.

Dave Crawford (blogs.msdn.com/dave/) and Corrina Barber (blogs.msdn.com/corrinab/), who are Microsoft designers, provide blogs with some good examples of styles that you can use in your own application. We highly recommend that you check out those designs to get an idea of how to create your own styles and templates.

Using Themes to Change the Look of All Controls

Silverlight Toolkit contains numerous predefined themes that you can apply to your page. Using a theme alters the look of all your controls to match that theme. Figures 6-14 and 6-15 show the Bubble Creme Theme and the Expression Dark theme, respectively, from the Theme Browser sample that ships with the Silverlight Toolkit.

You can install the Silverlight Toolkit from www.silverlight.net. It is a free download and contains a lot of useful controls.

Notice how the same control looks so different between the two themes? Theming can be done without much work.

Chapter 6: Styling and Skinning Controls 145

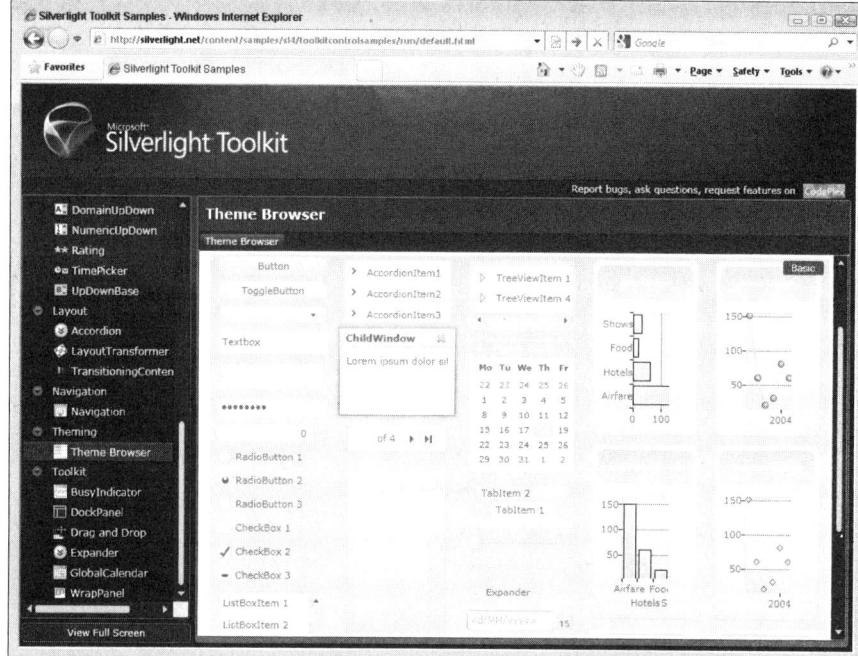

Figure 6-14: The Bubble Creme theme.

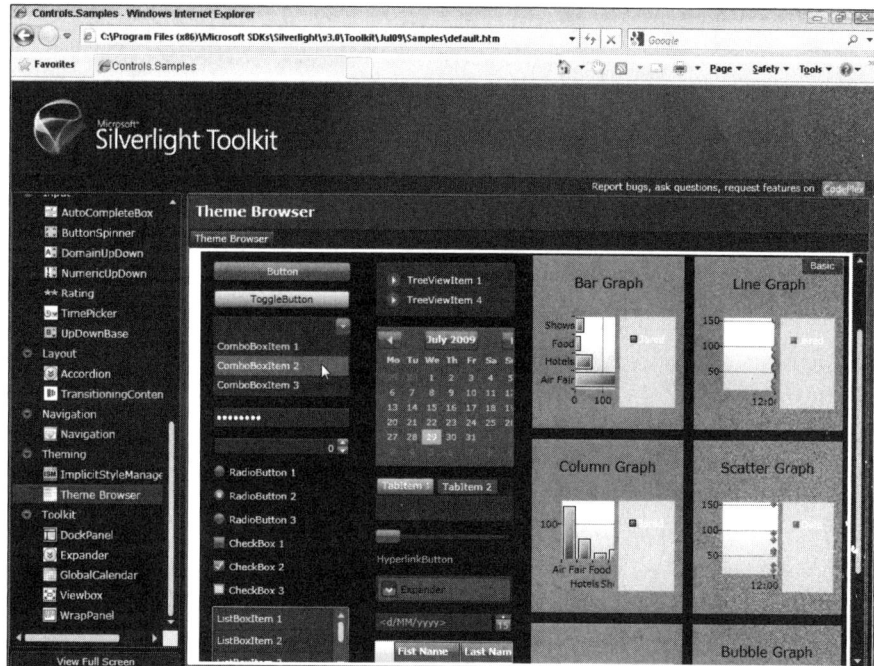

Figure 6-15: The Expression Dark theme.

To see how a theme works, follow these steps:

1. **Start a new Silverlight project in Expression Blend.**
2. **From the Assets panel, type the word** theme **to search for all the installed themes. Click the theme you want and drag it onto the Artboard.**

    For this example, we've chosen the Expression Dark theme.

3. **Add a control, such as a Button, by finding it in the Assets panel and dragging it on top of the theme you added to the Artboard. Then press F5 or choose Project**⇨**Run Project to run the application.**

    The application runs, showing a control that you added using the Expression Dark theme. All controls in this theme resemble the controls that are used in Expression Blend.

Go to the XAML view in Expression Blend to examine the XAML. It should look something like this:

```
<Grid x:Name="LayoutRoot" Background="White">
    <expressionDark:ExpressionDarkTheme>
        <Button … Content="Button"/>
    </expressionDark:ExpressionDarkTheme>
</Grid>
```

Basically, anything appearing in between the `expressionDark:Expression DarkTheme` element is styled according to the Expression Blend theme you chose.

However, you cannot add more than one control to the ExpressionDarkTheme element. So, you need to add a layout container to it if you want to add more controls. Examples of layout containers are the Grid and the StackPanel controls. (We tell you much more about layout containers in Chapter 5.)

To see how you add more controls to a theme, follow these steps:

1. **Create a new Silverlight application in Expression Blend.**
2. **From the Assets panel, search for a theme, such as ExpressionDarkTheme, and drag it onto the Artboard.**
3. **Increase the size of the Theme control to a suitable height and width by dragging the resizing handles.**

Chapter 6: Styling and Skinning Controls   147

4. **From the Tools panel, select a suitable layout container such as Grid, StackPanel, or Canvas. Click and drag in the Theme control to add the container.**

5. **Add a few controls such as Button, TextBox, Slider, and CalenderItem to the Artboard. Press F5 or choose Project**➪**Run Project to run the application.**

   The screen with the added controls shows up in the Expression Blend theme, as shown in Figure 6-16. Notice that all the added controls now have the theme you've used.

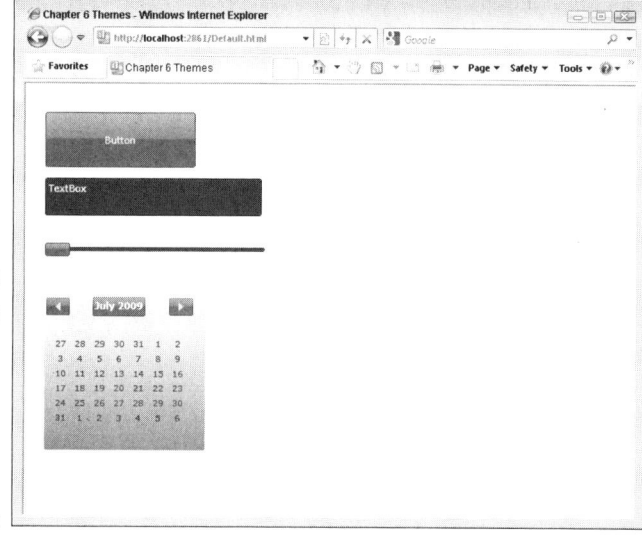

Figure 6-16: Screen running the chosen Expression Blend theme.

Chapter 7
Creating Your Own Controls

In This Chapter
- Creating a new control by grouping other controls
- Creating custom controls
- Creating and managing states for controls
- Creating your own events
- Adding behavior to controls

Silverlight comes with a wide array of controls. And if that weren't enough, you also have more controls available in the Silverlight Toolkit. But sometimes, you may have to create your own controls to accomplish something very specific, such as to display weather information that graphically displays the outlook for the day.

Or you may need to create a control that does something very simple, such as collect address information, but you may want to use the same data over and over again — for the delivery address, postal address, and so on.

Silverlight caters to both these needs. Controls that you create from scratch or by extending existing controls are called custom controls. Controls that group a bunch of other controls to form a new control are called user controls.

Grouping Controls to Create a UserControl

When you are writing any application, the application consists of some basic building blocks that you may want to use again and again. This building block may be some logic that exists as a piece of code (maybe in the form of a class or a method) or in the form of a user interface (which is the subject of discussion here).

For example, your application may contain a simple user interface that lets users of your Web site type in address information. You may be using this in multiple pages; for instance, you can use it to gather the user's home address, work address, shipping address, and so on. The address may itself consist of multiple fields, such as street address, city, and so on. Silverlight allows you to create a user interface element that contains other user interface elements to form a composite element called a UserControl. In addition to the user interface elements, UserControls allows you to add some logic such as validation in the code.

In this section, we show you how to create such a control, as well as how to use it.

An example of creating an Address UserControl

In this example, we show you how to create a type of control that many business Web sites use routinely — a control to collect address information.

To create an Address control, you need the following fields:

- Street Number
- Street Name
- City
- State
- ZIP or Postal Code
- Country

For the sake of simplicity, you can set all these fields as Text fields. Read on to see how.

1. **Create a new Silverlight project by choosing File⇨New Project from the menu, and when the New Project dialog box appears, select Silverlight 4 Application + Website and give it a suitable name such as AddressUserControlExample. Then click OK.**

    A new project is created and `MainPage.xaml` file is shown on the Artboard.

2. **Double-click the StackPanel in the ToolsPanel to add it to the MainPage. Drag the resizing handles to set the height and width of the StackPanel to a suitable dimension.**

    Using a StackPanel makes it easier to lay out controls. (See Chapter 5 for more details on the StackPanel.)

3. **Add six pairs of TextBlocks and TextBoxes to the Artboard to display the six address fields. Replace the default text in the TextBlocks by double-clicking and typing over them so that they read Street Number, Street Name, City, State, Postal Code, and Country, as shown in Figure 7-1.**

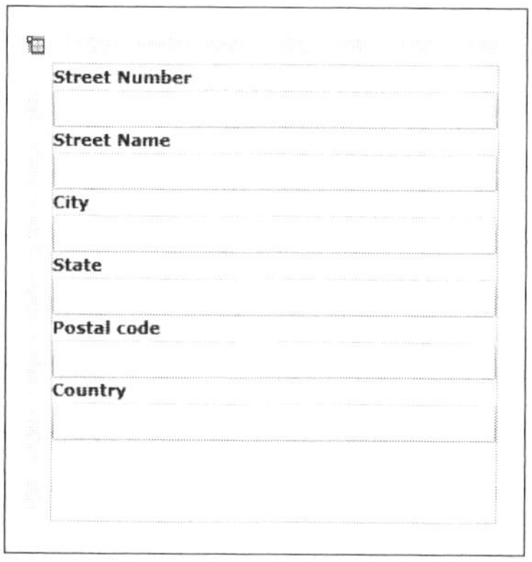

Figure 7-1: Example Address fields on the Artboard.

4. **Ctrl+click the TextBlocks one after the other until you have clicked all the TextBlocks on the Artboard.**

   This selects all the TextBlocks and allows you to change all the properties simultaneously.

5. **Go to the Properties panel and press the Bold button under the Text group to make the text in all the TextBlocks bold.**

   All the TextBlock controls change to bold on the Artboard. When you use the control in the next section, you will notice that these properties carry over.

6. **Ctrl+click the TextBox controls one after the other until you have clicked all the TextBlocks on the Artboard.**

7. **Click the Advanced Properties option next to the Text field in the Properties panel, and in the menu, choose Reset.**

   The default text in the TextBox controls gets reset and the XAML for the operations you just did should now look something like this (some markup has been replaced with ellipses[...] for brevity):

   ```
   <UserControl . . .>
     <Grid x:Name="LayoutRoot" Background="White">
       <StackPanel HorizontalAlignment="Left"
           Margin="8,22,0,167" Width="291">
         <TextBlock Text="Street Number"
           TextWrapping="Wrap" FontWeight="Bold"/>
         <TextBox TextWrapping="Wrap"/>
   ```

```
            <TextBlock Text="Street Name"
                TextWrapping="Wrap" FontWeight="Bold"/>
            <TextBox TextWrapping="Wrap"/>
            <TextBlock Text="City" TextWrapping="Wrap"
                FontWeight="Bold"/>
            <TextBox TextWrapping="Wrap"/>
            <TextBlock Text="State" TextWrapping="Wrap"
                FontWeight="Bold"/>
            <TextBox TextWrapping="Wrap"/>
            <TextBlock Text="Postal code"
                TextWrapping="Wrap" FontWeight="Bold"/>
            <TextBox TextWrapping="Wrap"/>
            <TextBlock Text="Country" TextWrapping="Wrap"
                FontWeight="Bold"/>
            <TextBox TextWrapping="Wrap"/>
        </StackPanel>
    </Grid>
</UserControl>
```

8. **Using the selection tool, select the Street Number TextBox control from the Artboard and set its name to txtStreetNumber in the Properties panel. Similarly, set the Street name, City, State, PostalCode, and Country text boxes to the names txtStreetName, txtCity, txtState, txtPostalCode, and txtCountry, respectively.**

    Giving a name to these fields will be helpful when you set values for them later.

9. **Select the StackPanel either by clicking it from the Objects and Timeline panel or by using the Selection tool and selecting the StackPanel from the Artboard.**

10. **Right-click and choose Make Into User Control.**

    A Make Into UserControl dialog box appears, as shown in Figure 7-2.

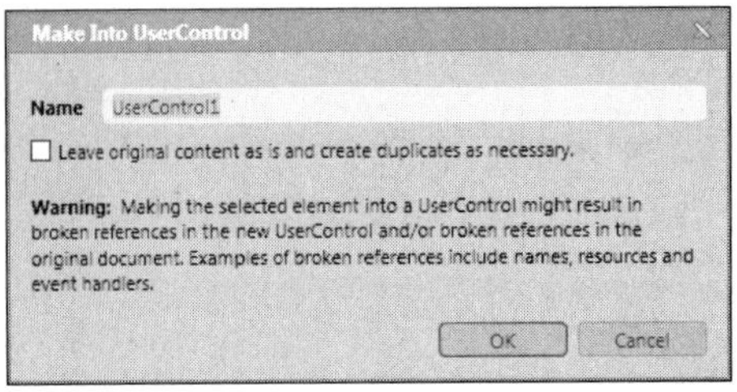

Figure 7-2: Make Into UserControl dialog box.

11. **Replace UserControl1 in the Name field by entering AddressUserControl; then click OK.**

    A new file called `AddressUserControl.xaml` gets added and all the contents of the StackPanel get moved to this new control.

Chapter 7: Creating Your Own Controls

12. **Click the MainPage.xaml tab on the Artboard.**

    The `MainPage.xaml` file opens and shows an exclamation mark on top of the Address fields. This is shown because the project needs to be built. You can build the project by pressing Ctrl+Shift+B, or you can simply press F5 to run the project.

13. **If you ran the project, close the browser, and in Expression Blend, click the XAML button on the Artboard to open the XAML view of the `MainPage.xaml` file.**

    In the XAML file, notice that all the address fields you added have been replaced with a single line that contains an element called `local:AddressUserControl`:

    ```
    <UserControl ...
            xmlns:local="clr-namespace:UserControls"
            x:Class="AddressUserControlExample.
        MainPage"
            Width="640" Height="480">

      <Grid x:Name="LayoutRoot" Background="White">
        <local:AddressUserControl
            HorizontalAlignment="Left" Margin="8,8,0,181"
            Width="291"/>
      </Grid>
    </UserControl>
    ```

    Notice that in the `UserControl` element, a line starting with the text `xmlns:local` has been added. This element helps Silverlight find out where the `AddressUserControl` you just added is located.

Reusing the User control

In the previous section, you created a new UserControl (AddressControl) for typing in Address information. By converting a portion of `MainPage.xaml` into a UserControl, Expression Blend automatically created the references and added the element to the page. But what if you wanted to add the same UserControl again on the same page? This section shows you how.

To add a UserControl, in this case the AddressControl, to `MainPage.xaml`, just follow these steps:

1. **Continue from the previous section and ensure that `MainPage.xaml` is open on the Artboard.**

2. **Open the Assets panel in Expression Blend and go to the Project category by clicking it.**

    The AddressUserControl appears under this category, as shown in Figure 7-3.

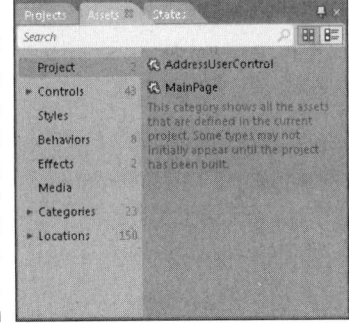

Figure 7-3: The Assets panel showing the newly added AddressUserControl.

Having the AddressUserControl here may not be surprising, but what you may find surprising is that MainPage also shows up here. It's in this category because MainPage, like AddressUserControl, is also a User control. You can open the XAML view for AddressUserControl and MainPage to verify this. As you've seen, all the pages you've created in XAML serve as reusable components and allow you to nest them in other user controls.

3. **Drag and drop AddressUserControl onto MainPage.xaml on the Artboard.**

   Another AddressUserControl gets added to MainPage.

4. **Press F5 to run the application.**

   The application runs in the browser window and shows the two AddressUserControls in the same page. These two address controls look and work the same but allow you to store and display two sets of addresses.

There are several advantages of putting something like an address into a UserControl, but one of our favorite reasons is that after it becomes a UserControl, it can be independently managed and maintained. For instance, if you change the layout container from the StackPanel to a GridPanel and rearrange the way the fields are displayed, they will be automatically updated in every page in which the AddressUserControl is used.

Creating properties for your UserControl

After you've created a UserControl, it would be good to set and read some values that you've typed into each field. One way of accomplishing that is to create properties for each and every field. This section shows you how to do that. (The other way of accomplishing this is through something called data binding, which we cover in Chapter 9.)

To add properties for each of the fields (namely StreetNumber, StreetName, City, State, PostalCode, and Country) from the AddressUserControl created in the previous sections, open the `AddressUserControl.xaml.cs` file on the

Artboard and add the following code snippet into the `AddressUserControl` class:

```
public string StreetNumber
{
    get
    {
        return txtStreetNumber.Text;
    }
    set
    {
        txtStreetNumber.Text = value;
    }
}
public string StreetName
{
    get
    {
        return txtStreetName.Text;
    }
    set
    {
        txtStreetName.Text = value;
    }
}
public string City
{
    get
    {
        return txtCity.Text;
    }
    set
    {
        txtCity.Text = value;
    }
}
public string State
{
    get
    {
        return txtState.Text;
    }
    set
    {
        txtState.Text = value;
    }
}
public string PostalCode
{
    get
    {
        return txtPostalCode.Text;
    }
```

```
        set
        {
            txtPostalCode.Text = value;
        }
    }
    public string Country
    {
        get
        {
            return txtCountry.Text;
        }
        set
        {
            txtCountry.Text = value;
        }
    }
```

Press Ctrl+Shift+B to build the application; then, open the `MainControl.xaml` file in Design view. Select the first AddressUserControl in it and open the Properties panel. Under the Miscellaneous section, you will now find all the properties that you just added. Change the values of these properties and press F5 to run the application and check whether the values show up in the AddressUserControl.

Creating a Smiley Custom Control

UserControls are, as you saw in the previous section, very good for creating reusable components such as the Address control. They can be repeatedly on the same page or even on different pages. However, after you create something like an AddressUserControl, application authors cannot change what the control looks like. You can expose some properties so that the application authors can customize the look and feel to a certain extent, but you cannot skin the control, as you did in Chapter 6.

To create a control that can be skinned and has a template, you have to create a custom control. (They are also referred to as a *templatable* or *templated* control for that reason.)

To show you how to create a custom control from scratch, we use an example of a Smiley control. The Smiley control displays a smiley face and has two "emotion" states: Happy and Sad. Setting the state of the control to `Happy` displays a happy face; conversely, `Sad` displays a sad face. Pretty simple, really.

However, creating a custom control from scratch can be somewhat difficult compared to creating the same control as a UserControl. Therefore, it is easier

Chapter 7: Creating Your Own Controls

to start your control as a UserControl and then convert it to a custom control. In our upcoming example, we show you in detail how to do the following:

1. Create a SmileyUserControl that looks like a Smiley face in Expression Blend.
2. Create states for the Smiley face to show sad and happy emotions, again using Expression Blend.
3. Create a SmileyCustomControl with Visual Studio, using the XAML from the first two steps to create your default template.
4. Add states and events to SmileyCustomControl.

Read on to find out the details for each task.

Creating a SmileyUserControl

To create the SmileyUserControl in Expression Blend, follow these steps:

1. **Create a new Silverlight project by choosing File⇨New Project from the menu, and when the New Project dialog box appears, select Silverlight 4 Application + Website and give it a suitable name, such as Smiley, and click OK**

    A new project is created and the `MainPage.xaml` file is shown on the Artboard.

2. **Choose File⇨New Item, and in the New Item dialog box that appears, select UserControl and set its name to** `SmileyUserControl`.

    Expression Blend creates a new file called `SmileyUserControl.xaml` and opens it on the Artboard.

3. **Using the Ellipse tool and the Pencil tool from the Tools panel, draw a smiley face in** `SmileyUserControl.xaml`, **as shown in Figure 7-4.**

Figure 7-4: Smiley face drawn on the Artboard.

4. **As an alternative to Step 3, open the XAML view on the Artboard and replace the XAML with the following markup:**

```xml
<UserControl
    xmlns= "http://schemas.microsoft.com/winfx/2006/
        xaml/presentation"
    xmlns:x= "http://schemas.microsoft.com/winfx/2006/
        xaml"
    xmlns:d= "http://schemas.microsoft.com/expression/
        blend/2008"
    xmlns:mc= "http://schemas.openxmlformats.org/
        markup-compatibility/2006"
    mc:Ignorable="d"
    x:Class="Smiley.SmileyUserControl"
    d:DesignWidth="250" d:DesignHeight="350">

<Grid x:Name="LayoutRoot">
  <Grid HorizontalAlignment="Left" Margin="0,0,0,0"
        Width="252">
    <Ellipse Fill="#FFF4BF0D" Stroke="Black"
        Margin="25,50,25,50"/>
    <Ellipse Fill="#FF1C0303" Stroke="Black"
        Margin="65,96,154,166" MaxWidth="60"
        MaxHeight="60" MinWidth="5" MinHeight="5"/>
    <Ellipse Fill="#FF1C0303" Stroke="Black"
        Margin="154,96,65,166" MaxWidth="60"
        MaxHeight="60" MinWidth="5" MinHeight="5"/>
    <Path x:Name="path" Stretch="Fill"
        Stroke="Black" Margin="80,160,80,80"
        UseLayoutRounding="False" Data="M82,169
        C96.198021,186.03763 102.84956,223.09027
        138,202 C152.23703,193.45778
        154.76633,184.11137 162,168"
        RenderTransformOrigin="0.5,0.5" MinWidth="5"
        MinHeight="5" MaxWidth="300" MaxHeight="60">
      <Path.RenderTransform>
        <TransformGroup>
          <ScaleTransform/>
          <SkewTransform/>
          <RotateTransform/>
          <TranslateTransform/>
        </TransformGroup>
      </Path.RenderTransform>
    </Path>
  </Grid>
</Grid>

</UserControl>
```

This XAML creates the smiley face using `Ellipse` and `Path` elements. (To see how you can use the Ellipse and Pencil tools to create the smiley face in Expression Blend, read through Chapter 3. The control shown here contains three Ellipse controls and a smile drawn with the Pencil tool.)

Chapter 7: Creating Your Own Controls 159

Rather than type all the markup or code shown in this book, you can visit www.dummies.com/go/mssilverlight4fd to look at an online version of the source code and markup text. You can then copy and paste them into your application.

Adding states to SmileyUserControl

As stated earlier, the next step is to add two states, Happy and Sad, to the UserControl to store the emotions. For each state, we change the expression on the face to reflect the type of emotion.

In Chapter 6, we demonstrate how to create a template for a Button control and tell you about the various states it can have, such as Normal, MouseOver, and others. By creating states, you can let other people customize your own control using templates, the way you can customize the Button template as explained in Chapter 6.

To add these two states, follow these steps:

1. **Go to the States panel and click the Add States Group Button.**

   A new group with a default name of VisualStateGroup is added to the list in the States panel and is highlighted, allowing you to change the name. It is usually a good idea to change the default name to something more meaningful, such as Emotion.

2. **Type Emotion and press Enter.**

   The name of the Visual State Group changes to Emotion.

3. **Click the Add State button to add a state.**

   A new state default named VisualState is added under the Emotion visual state group and is highlighted, allowing you to change the name. The top of the Artboard also displays the message VisualState recording is on. When the state recording is on, it allows you to record the visuals of the control for that state. When the control switches to that state, Silverlight plays back the recording for that state.

4. **Change the name of VisualState by typing Happy and then press Enter.**

5. **Press the red button in front of it to stop the recording.**

   Because the Happy state is your default state, you don't need to change it. Stop the recording without changing the way the control looks.

6. **Add another state by pressing the Add State button, but this time change the name of the state to Sad.**

7. **Using the Selection tool from the Tools panel, click the path on the Artboard that represents the mouth.**

   The mouth in the SmileyUserControl gets selected.

8. **In the Properties panel, go to the Transform group and click the Flip tab (shown here in the margin).**

9. **Click the Flip Y axis button (shown here in the margin) to flip the path that represents the mouth.**

   The mouth flips on the y-axis and the face resembles a sad face, as shown in Figure 7-5.

10. **Click the red recording button at the top of the Artboard to stop the recording.**

    You have now stopped the recording of the Sad emotion state. When the SmileyUserControl's state changes to Sad, the control's appearance changes to the visuals you've just finished recording.

11. **In the States panel, change the Default transition field to 0.3s.**

    By changing the transition time, you are telling Silverlight that when the emotion changes to the Sad state, the appearance of the control should change to the recording you've made gradually over a period of .3 seconds rather than abruptly. This is usually more pleasing visually. (You can find out more about transitions in Chapter 8.)

    You should now have added two emotion states to the SmileyUserControl.

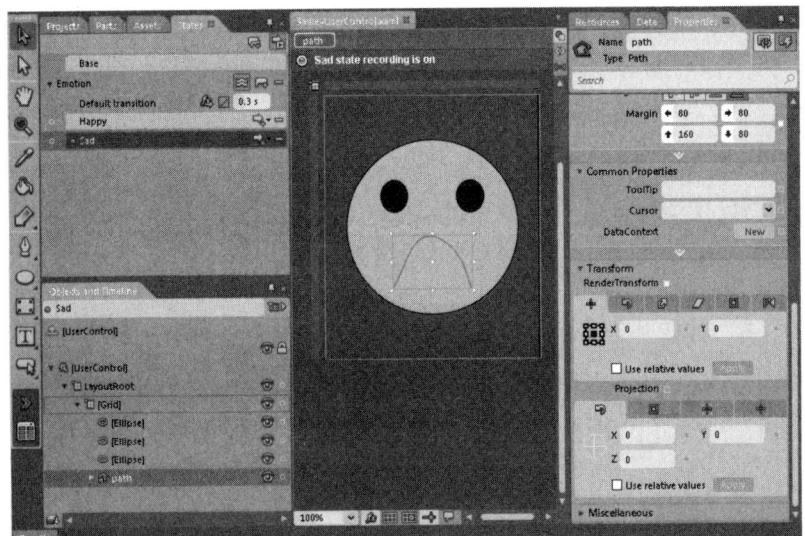

Figure 7-5: Flipping the mouth to make it a sad face.

Testing the UserControl and switching the states

After you create the SmileyUserControl, you need to test it. To test the UserControl, you need to first add methods in code to the SmileyUserControl to switch the states. You then need to add it to your page to test it.

You can accomplish all this by following these steps:

1. **Continuing from the previous section, open the** `SmileyControl.xaml.cs` **file in Expression Blend and add the two functions** `BeHappy` **and** `BeSad`**, as shown in the bold lines in the following code:**

    ```
    public partial class SmileyUserControl : UserControl
    {
        public SmileyControl()
        {
            // Required to initialize variables
            InitializeComponent();
        }

        public void BeHappy()
        {
            VisualStateManager.GoToState(this, "Happy",
                true);
        }

        public void BeSad()
        {
            VisualStateManager.GoToState(this, "Sad",
                true);
        }
    }
    ```

    The `VisualStateManager` is a class in Silverlight that helps you to change the visual state of your control.

2. **Press Ctrl+B to build the project to ensure that there are no errors in code.**
3. **After the build has finished, open** `MainPage.xaml` **in Design view.**
4. **From the Assets panel, find SmileyUserControl and drag it onto** `MainPage.xaml` **on the Artboard.**
5. **From the Tools panel, add two Buttons to the Artboard. Set the name of the SmileyUserControl to** `SmileyFace`**.**
6. **Double-click the first Button and type** Be Happy.

    This changes the Content property of the button to the text Be Happy.

7. **In the Properties panel, enter** `btnHappy` **to change the name of the button to** `btnHappy`. **Then switch to the Events tab and double-click the Click field.**

   This takes you to the `btnHappy_Click` method in the `MainPage.xaml.cs` file. Change the method as shown in the following line in bold:

   ```
   private void btnHappy_Click(object sender, System.
           Windows.RoutedEventArgs e)
   {
       SmileyFace.BeHappy();
   }
   ```

8. **Go back to the** `MainPage.xaml` **file and use the Selection tool to select the second button. Then, change the content of the button to Be Sad, set the name of the button in the Properties panel to btnSad, and double-click the Click field in the Events tab.**

   This takes you to the `btnSad_Click` method in the `MainPage.xaml.cs` file. Change the function as shown in the following bold line:

   ```
   private void btnSad_Click(object sender, System.
           Windows.RoutedEventArgs e)
   {
       SmileyFace.BeSad();
   }
   ```

9. **Press F5 to run the application, and click the buttons to see how the states change.**

Creating the custom control

The smiley face we show you how to make as a UserControl in the previous sections has a few drawbacks. For instance, you cannot skin it as you can a Button control — for that you need to derive your `SmileyCustomControl` class from either an existing control or a generic `Control` class in Silverlight.

Creating a custom control using Visual Studio 2010 is a lot easier than creating it using Expression Blend because Visual Studio automates a few steps for you. Follow these steps to create a SmileyCustomControl:

1. **Continuing from the previous sections, open the Projects panel, right-click Solution, and choose Edit in Visual Studio.**

   The solution opens in Visual Studio 2010.

2. **Right-click Solution in the Solution Explorer and choose Add**➪**New Project from the menu.**

   The Add New Project dialog box appears, as shown in Figure 7-6.

Chapter 7: Creating Your Own Controls **163**

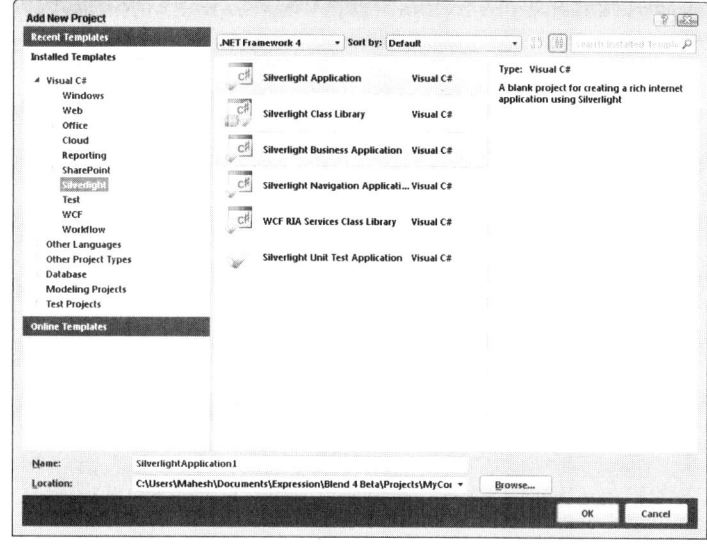

Figure 7-6:
The Add New Project dialog box in Visual Studio.

3. **Select Silverlight Class Library from the list of projects and change the name to** CustomControlLibrary; **then click OK. When the Add Silverlight Class Library dialog box appears, click OK.**

   This creates a new project in the solution. Although you can add the custom control to your existing Silverlight project, it is a good idea to create it in a separate project so that it can be shared with other Silverlight applications.

4. **In the Solution Explorer, select the** Class1.cs **file and press Del to delete the file. Click OK when the confirmation dialog box pops up.**

   This deletes the default file Class1.cs that gets automatically added when a new project is created.

5. **Right-click the CustomControlLibrary project name in the Solution Explorer and choose Add⇨New Item.**

   The Add New Item dialog box appears.

6. **Select Silverlight Templated Control from the list of items and change the name to** SmileyCustomControl.cs, **as shown in Figure 7-7.**

   This creates a class called SmileyCustomControl that derives from the Control class. Visual Studio also creates a directory called Themes and adds the file Generic.xaml. This file contains the default template for the SmileyCustomControl. You need to copy the XAML you used in Smiley UserControl to this template so that when you add the SmileyCustom Control to a page, Silverlight uses this template to draw the control.

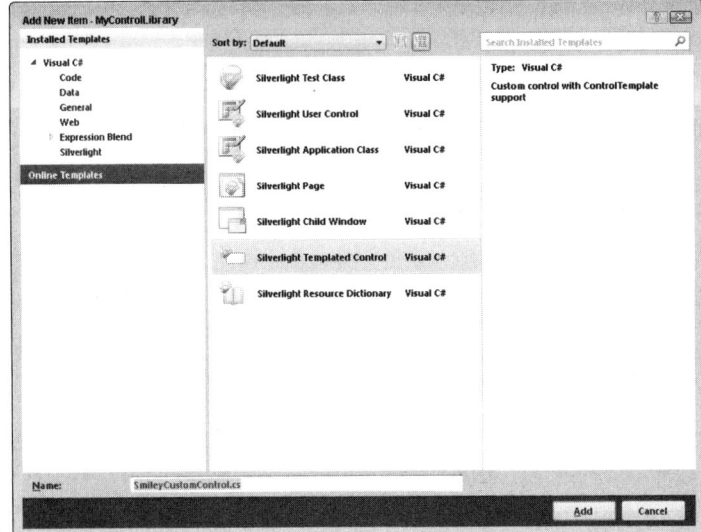

Figure 7-7:
The Add New Item dialog box in Visual Studio 2010.

7. **Click the little arrow that appears in front of the Smiley project in the Solution Explorer to expand and show all the files contained in the project. Then, double-click the** `SmileyUserControl.xaml` **file to open it. When the file is open, select all the lines between the** `UserControl` **tag. Press Ctrl+C to copy the markup.**

8. **Open the** `generic.xaml` **file again and paste the markup you copied by pressing Ctrl+V between the** `ControlTemplate` **XAML begin and end tags. The copied markup should now look like this, with the pasted markup shown in bold:**

```
<ResourceDictionary
  xmlns="http://schemas.microsoft.com/winfx/2006/xaml/
      presentation"
  xmlns:x="http://schemas.microsoft.com/winfx/2006/xaml"
  xmlns:local="clr-namespace:CustomControlLibrary">

  <Style TargetType="local:SmileyCustomControl">
    <Setter Property="Template">
      <Setter.Value>
        <ControlTemplate TargetType="local:SmileyCusto
          mControl">
          <Grid x:Name="LayoutRoot">
            <VisualStateManager.VisualStateGroups>
              <VisualStateGroup
  x:Name="Emotion">
                <VisualStateGroup.Transitions>
                  <VisualTransition
  GeneratedDuration="0:0:0.3"/>
                </VisualStateGroup.Transitions>
```

```xml
                    <VisualState x:Name="Happy"/>
                    <VisualState x:Name="Sad">
                        <Storyboard>

<DoubleAnimationUsingKeyFrames Storyboard.TargetProperty="(UIElement.RenderTransform).(TransformGroup.Children)[0].(ScaleTransform.ScaleY)" Storyboard.TargetName="path">

<EasingDoubleKeyFrame KeyTime="0" Value="-1"/>
                            </DoubleAnimationUsingKeyFrames>
                        </Storyboard>
                    </VisualState>
                </VisualStateGroup>
            </VisualStateManager.VisualStateGroups>
            <Grid HorizontalAlignment="Left" Margin="0,0,0,0" Width="252">
                <Ellipse Fill="#FFF4BF0D" Stroke="Black" Margin="25,50,25,50"/>
                <Ellipse Fill="#FF1C0303" Stroke="Black" Margin="65,96,154,166" MaxWidth="60" MaxHeight="60" MinWidth="5" MinHeight="5"/>
                <Ellipse Fill="#FF1C0303" Stroke="Black" Margin="154,96,65,166" MaxWidth="60" MaxHeight="60" MinWidth="5" MinHeight="5"/>
                <Path x:Name="path" Stretch="Fill" Stroke="Black" Margin="80,160,80,80" UseLayoutRounding="False" Data="M82,169 C96.198021,186.03763 102.84956,223.09027 138,202 C152.23703,193.45778 154.76633,184.11137 162,168" RenderTransformOrigin="0.5,0.5" MinWidth="5" MinHeight="5" MaxWidth="300" MaxHeight="60">
                    <Path.RenderTransform>
                        <TransformGroup>
                            <ScaleTransform/>
                            <SkewTransform/>
                            <RotateTransform/>
                            <TranslateTransform/>
                        </TransformGroup>
                    </Path.RenderTransform>
                </Path>
            </Grid>
        </Grid>
      </ControlTemplate>
    </Setter.Value>
  </Setter>
 </Style>
</ResourceDictionary>
```

9. **Open the** `SmileyUserControl.cs` **file and add the lines of code shown in bold, as follows:**

```
public class SmileyCustomControl : Control
{
    public SmileyCustomControl()
    {
        DefaultStyleKey = typeof(SmileyCustomControl);
    }

    public void BeHappy()
    {
        VisualStateManager.GoToState(this, "Happy",
            true);
    }

    public void BeSad()
    {
        VisualStateManager.GoToState(this, "Sad",
            true);
    }
}
```

10. **Press Ctrl+Shift+B to build the solution.**

You should have now successfully created a custom control.

Using the custom control

For this section's example, you need to return to Expression Blend. You may have to reload the project if you had Expression Blend open while working in Visual Studio. It will automatically prompt you when you switch to Expression Blend.

Now, follow these steps to add the custom control to `MainPage.xaml` and test it:

1. **Right-click References in the Smiley project in the Projects panel and choose Add Project References⇨CustomControlLibrary.**

   This adds the reference to CustomControlLibrary, which contains the newly added custom control.

2. **Open the** `MainPage.xaml` **file.**

3. **Delete the SmileyUserControl by selecting it with the Selection tool and pressing Del.**

   You are deleting this control so that you can add the SmileyCustomControl instead.

Chapter 7: Creating Your Own Controls

4. **From the Assets panel, as shown in Figure 7-8, drag and drop the SmileyCustomControl onto the** `MainPage.xaml` **file on the Artboard.**

5. **Using the Selection tool, select the SmileyCustomControl, and from the Properties panel, set the name to SmileyControl.**

6. **Press F5 to run the application.**

   The application runs the same as the example with the SmileyUserControl. But application authors who use your control can now skin the control.

You can actually create a CustomControl in Expression Blend because it allows you to code in C# or VB.NET. You can also create a class library from it. However, you do not have the option to add a templated control to it — you will have to manually add the Themes directory, create the `generic.xaml` file, and so on. Visual Studio automates these tasks for you.

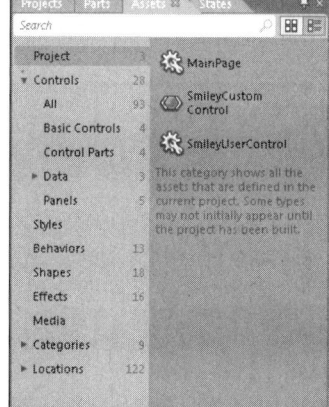

Figure 7-8: Smiley-Control in the Assets panel.

Adding events to your control

As you can with properties, you can also add your own custom event to the controls you create. For instance, to add a custom event called ClickFace that gets generated every time the user clicks the SmileyCustomControl, open the `SmileyCustomControl.cs` file in either Visual Studio or Expression Blend.

First add the following line of code to the class:

```
public event RoutedEventHandler ClickFace;
```

The `RoutedEventHandler` adds an event called `ClickFace` that will be visible in the Property panel under Events. But this never gets fired because you haven't associated anything with it yet. You can do that by adding an event handler for the `MouseLeftButtonUp` event, which gets fired when the left mouse button is released on top of your control. Add the line shown in bold in the following code to the `SmileyCustomControl` constructor.

```
public SmileyCustomControl()
{
    DefaultStyleKey = typeof(SmileyCustomControl);

    this.MouseLeftButtonUp += new
    MouseButtonEventHandler(LeftButtonUp);
}
```

This calls the function `LeftButtonUp` whenever the mouse button is released. Add that function to the class, too, using the following code snippet:

```
void LeftButtonUp(object sender, MouseButtonEventArgs e)
{
    if (ClickFace != null)
        ClickFace(this, new RoutedEventArgs());
}
```

Controlling the Behavior of Controls without Writing Code

Sometimes you may want to process events for your controls, but you may not be able to write the event handlers for them because doing so requires some C# coding. Maybe you're a designer and not comfortable with writing C#, or maybe, like most of the rest of us, you're in a hurry and want the easiest way to do things. (Okay, maybe you're just lazy, too!) Is there a way to fire events without writing event handlers for them? The answer is yes! Enter the world of behaviors.

Although this is stating the obvious, behaviors enable you to add certain types of, well, behaviors to your control. A *behavior* is nothing more than a piece of code that you can add to your application to set properties that further decide how this piece of code behaves.

For instance, you can have behavior that lets you navigate to a certain URL or play a sound — or even change the state of a control.

To change the state of a control, you need to use a behavior called GoToStateAction.

We show you how to put this behavior into action using the example in the previous section of this chapter. First, get rid of the two buttons on the Artboard, and add two new buttons with the same contents: Be Happy and

Chapter 7: Creating Your Own Controls *169*

Be Sad. (Alternatively, you can go to Events in the Properties panel for both buttons and remove the event association for clicking in them.)

Press F5 to run the application. Notice that when you click the two buttons, nothing happens. Why? There is no event handler associated with the new buttons. But we're about to remedy that situation.

First, close the application and go back to Expression Blend. Next, from the Assets panel, click Behaviors. A few behaviors show up on the Assets panel, as shown in Figure 7-9.

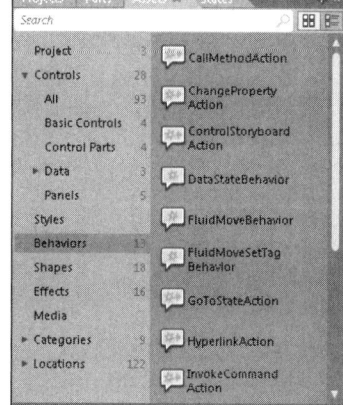

Figure 7-9: Assets panel showing behaviors.

Select GoToStateAction and drag and drop it onto the Be Happy button.

Now go to the Properties panel, shown in Figure 7-10, and click the Artboard element picker in the TargetName property (shown here in the margin).

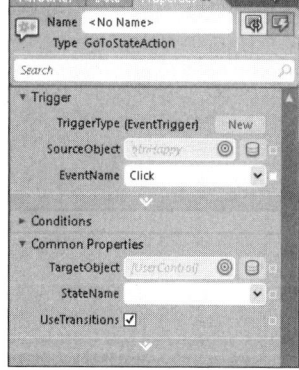

Figure 7-10: Properties panel for the GoToState-Action behavior.

The cursor shape changes. As you hover your mouse over different elements, Expression Blend displays the name of the element. Click the SmileyFace control, as shown in Figure 7-11.

The TargetName on the Properties panel changes to `SmileyFace`. Click the StateName drop-down list and select Happy.

Repeat the same steps for the Sad button, but instead of selecting the Happy state, select Sad from the drop-down list this time.

Run the application by pressing F5. The two buttons should now change the emotions on the Smiley Face. You have achieved this without writing any code!

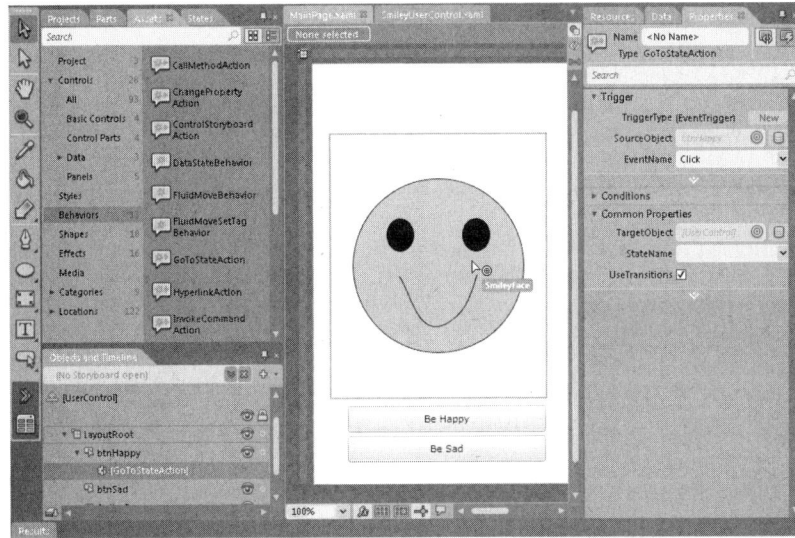

Figure 7-11: The Artboard element picker as you hover over the Smiley-Control.

Chapter 8
Creating Animations in Silverlight

In This Chapter

▹ Creating a simple animation

▹ Exploring the different kinds of animations

▹ Animating states for controls

*W*hen one of the authors was a child, he was given a flip book that had a slightly different picture on each page. Flipping the pages rapidly created the illusion that the character in the picture performed an action. This is the most primitive form of animation.

Likewise, an animation in a software application is nothing more than a sequence of images displayed in rapid succession, thereby creating the illusion that an object is moving or changing.

To create an animation in Silverlight, you change the value of certain properties over a duration of time. Those special properties relate to an object's size, position, or color, and in this chapter, we show you how you can create animations using Expression Blend.

Creating a Simple Bouncing Ball Animation

Using Expression Blend, animation can be performed very easily in Silverlight by recording the objects over a period of time and playing them back.

For example, to animate the height of an object, you "record" what the object's height is over a period of time; that is, you specify that at the one-second mark, the object's height should be 300, and at the five-second mark, it should be 500, and so on.

When you play back the animation, Silverlight automatically calculates what the height of the object should be between the two recorded property values.

In this section, we show you how to create a ball and bounce it across the screen.

Create the ball and set the timeline in motion

The first step in creating a bouncing ball animation is to create the ball itself. To get started, follow these steps:

1. **Create a new Silverlight application by choosing File**⇨**New Project. In the New Project dialog box, select Silverlight 4 Application + Website option and click OK.**

   A new Silverlight project is created and the `MainPage.xaml` file opens on the Artboard.

2. **Select the Ellipse tool from the Tools panel and draw an ellipse on the Artboard.**

3. **Click the Fill property on the Properties panel, select the Gradient brush, and set the color ranges to start at white and end with a shade of red. Then click the Radial Gradient button.**

4. **Select the Gradient tool from the Tools panel and reposition the center of the gradient to start from the upper-left corner, as shown in Figure 8-1.**

   This makes the ellipse you've added look like a 3-D ball. The XAML for the ellipse should look something like this:

   ```
   <Ellipse HorizontalAlignment="Left" Height="106"
           Margin="8,8,0,0" Stroke="Black"
           VerticalAlignment="Top" Width="108">
       <Ellipse.Fill>
           <RadialGradientBrush
           GradientOrigin="0.279,0.268">
               <GradientStop Color="#FFF9F7F7"/>
               <GradientStop Color="#FFF10B0B"
           Offset="1"/>
           </RadialGradientBrush>
       </Ellipse.Fill>
   </Ellipse>
   ```

Figure 8-1: Creating a ball to animate.

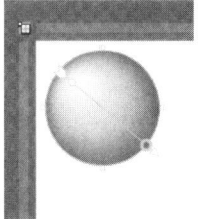

5. **In the Objects and Timeline panel, click the + (plus) button.**

   The Create Storyboard Resource dialog box appears. It displays a default name for the animation as Storyboard1.

6. **Type** BouncingBall **in the Name (Key) field in the dialog box and click OK.**

   Expression Blend turns on the Timeline Recording mode and the animation timeline shows up. At the same time, the message `BouncingBall timeline recording is on` appears at the top of the Artboard, as shown in Figure 8-2, along with a red border around the Artboard.

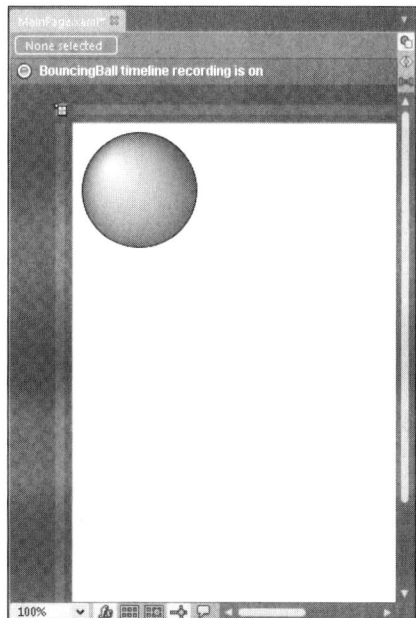

Figure 8-2: Expression Blend in Animation mode.

So far, so good. You have your ball on the Artboard and your animation timeline going. Before you continue, though, this is a good time to switch to another workspace. We tell you why and how in the next section.

Switching to the Animation workspace

When you are working with animations, you need to specify how an object looks or where it is positioned during different points in time, and you may need to display the timeline for a fairly long time. When you display the Objects and Timeline panel to the left of the Artboard, very little space is left on the screen to display a large timeline. To solve this problem, Expression Blend comes with a preconfigured Animation workspace. To switch to this workspace, choose Window⇨Workspaces⇨Animation.

The workspace now looks like Figure 8-3, making it more conducive to working with animations because it places the Objects and Timeline panel under the Artboard and gives you more space to work with the timeline.

You can also press F6 to quickly switch among different workspaces and to switch to the Animation workspace.

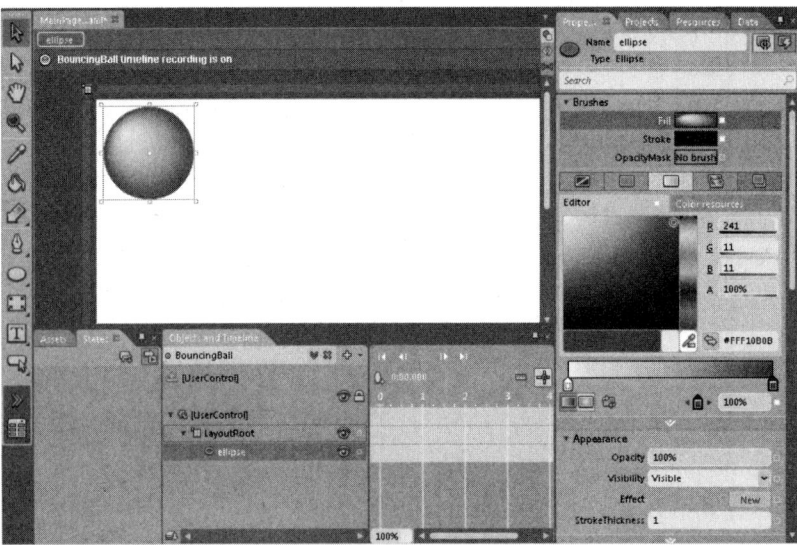

Figure 8-3: Expression Blend Animation workspace.

Animating the ball

The Objects and Timeline panel contains a timeline on which you can define keyframes. In Silverlight, a *keyframe* is the set of visual properties at a given point in time.

You specify what these properties should be at specified time intervals, and Silverlight automatically calculates and transitions the property values to create an animation.

To create an animation of a bouncing ball, follow these steps:

1. **Click the Selection tool from the Tools panel and click the ellipse you just created (if you did the steps in the earlier section, "Create the ball and set the timeline in motion") to select it.**

2. **In the Objects and Timeline panel, click the Record Keyframe button (shown here in the margin).**

   An oval appears in the timeline in the same row as the selected object. The oval indicates that a keyframe has been created at that point in the timeline.

3. **To specify what the properties should be after a period of time — say, four seconds — click 4 on the Objects and Timeline panel, as shown in Figure 8-4.**

   This places a yellow line at the 4-second mark, as shown in Figure 8-4, and you can now specify what the properties of the selected object should be at the 4-second mark. You can not only change the properties via the Properties panel but also manipulate the object directly on the Artboard.

4. **Drag the ball to the right side of the screen boundary on the Artboard, as shown in Figure 8-5.**

   Expression Blend automatically creates a keyframe for you at the 4-second mark and shows a dotted line to indicate the path in which the ellipse will move.

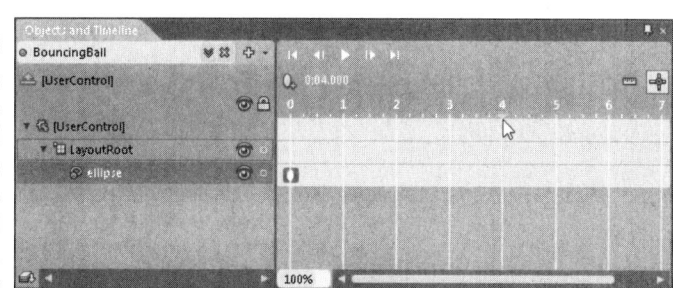

Figure 8-4: The Objects and Timeline panel at the 4-second mark.

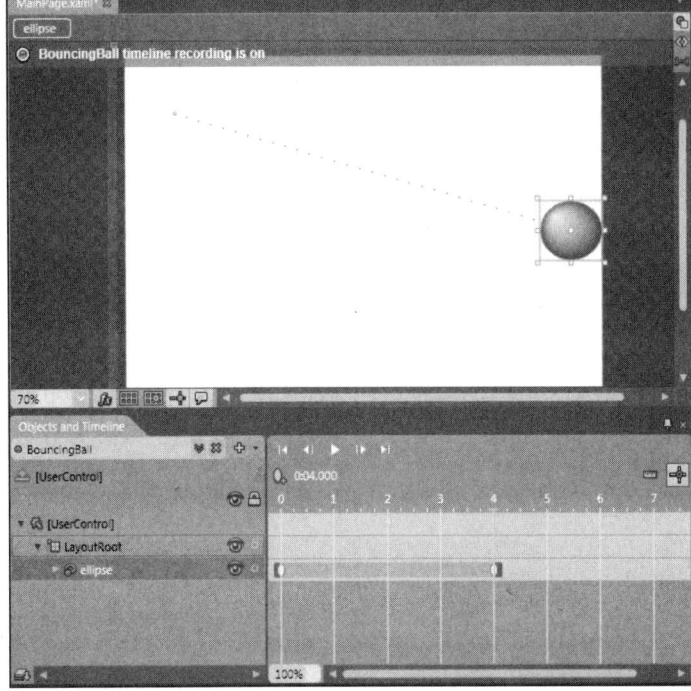

Figure 8-5:
The ball moved to the right side of the screen during animation.

5. **Now click the 6-second mark in the Objects and Timeline panel and move the ball to the left side to mimic a bounce motion.**

   Expression Blend creates another keyframe at the 6-second mark and visually shows the bouncing path of the ball. You can also manipulate the height and width of the button at these keyframes to simulate the ball's getting compressed at the point of impact, or you can do other funky things such as change the fill brush at different keyframes to animate the changing of colors.

6. **Click the Play button in the Objects and Timeline panel to see a preview of the animation.**

   The animation gets played and the ball appears to fall down, bounce, and go up again.

One thing to keep in mind as you watch the animation is that you created just two keyframes — one at the 4-second mark and the other at the 6-second mark; Silverlight takes care of the rest by automatically calculating the position (and possibly other property values) of the control for the time between these keyframes.

You can experiment further by adding keyframes and changing more properties to see how these properties are animated.

When you are finished recording keyframes, click the red ball (shown here in the margin) at the top of the Artboard to stop the recording.

 You can also click the Close Storyboard button in the Objects and Timeline panel (shown here in the margin) that appears next to the BouncingBall storyboard name to exit the Timeline-recording mode and get back to where you started.

Understanding the XAML behind the animation

Click the XAML view for the page to look at the XAML that Expression Blend has created for the animations. The part that contains the animation should look something like this:

```
<UserControl.Resources>
    <Storyboard x:Name="BouncingBall">
        <DoubleAnimationUsingKeyFrames
          BeginTime="00:00:00" …>
            <EasingDoubleKeyFrame KeyTime="00:00:00"
            Value="0"/>
            <EasingDoubleKeyFrame KeyTime="00:00:04"
            Value="532"/>
            <EasingDoubleKeyFrame KeyTime="00:00:06"
            Value="-33.333"/>
        </DoubleAnimationUsingKeyFrames>
        …
    </Storyboard>
</UserControl.Resources>
```

Did you notice the XAML element called `Storyboard`? The `Storyboard` element is nothing but a container for animations, and Silverlight supports two types of animations:

- Simple animation
- Animation using keyframes

Simple animation

In simple animation, you specify the property that needs to be animated, the start and end property values, and the duration for which the property needs to be animated. Three types of properties can be animated in Silverlight:

- `Double`: A `Double` denotes a floating-point number that has a very high precision. This means that any property that has a number, such as `Height` or `Width`, is stored as `Double`.

- **Point**: Properties that are represented as coordinates are typically stored as `Point`s.
- **Color**: This pertains to any property that contains a brush, such as Fill or Foreground.

To accommodate these three property types, there are three types of XAML elements: `DoubleAnimation`, `PointAnimation`, and `ColorAnimation`.

If you want to animate a property such as `Height` for a Rectangle control, the XAML for that would look like this:

```
<Storyboard x:Name="MyStoryboard">
    <DoubleAnimation
        Storyboard.TargetName="rect1"
        Storyboard.TargetProperty="Width"
        From="100" To="200"
        Duration="0:0:5">
    </DoubleAnimation>
</Storyboard>
```

The `DoubleAnimation` element typically needs five attributes for animation:

- **Storyboard.TargetName**: Specifies the name of the control that needs to take part in the animation.
- **Storyboard.TargetProperty**: Specifies the name of the property that needs to be animated. In this section's example, it happens to be `Width`.
- **From**: Specifies the starting value of the property that needs to be animated.
- **To**: Specifies the ending value of the property that needs to be animated.
- **Duration**: Specifies the time span in which the value has to change from the start value specified in the `From` attribute to the end value specified in the `To` attribute.

The classes `PointAnimation` and `ColorAnimation` also have similar properties, but they work on Point and Color properties, respectively.

Keyframe animation

Keyframe animation is what Expression Blend adds by default. It is a bit more complex but a lot more flexible. It lets you set a series of values as well as set the time interval for the property to have these values. It is like creating multiple simple animations, with the `From` property being the same as the `To` property of the previous animation.

In addition, you can specify the kind of interpolation to use. *Interpolation* allows you to specify how the values change over a period. There are three types of interpolations:

- **Linear:** The animation progresses at a constant rate from the start to the end.
- **Discrete:** The animation jumps from the start to the end at the specified time.
- **Splined:** Lets you control the animation progression in much finer detail. For instance, you can make the animation start slowly, accelerate, and then finish slowly again.

There are three types of animation keyframes (`DoubleAnimationUsing-KeyFrames`, `PointAnimationUsingKeyFrames`, and `ColorAnimation-UsingKeyFrames`), and combining the key animation types with the three interpolation types, you get the following keyframe types:

- `LinearDoubleKeyFrame`
- `DiscreteDoubleKeyFrame`
- `SplineDoubleKeyFrame`
- `LinearPointKeyFrame`
- `DiscretePointKeyFrame`
- `SplinePointKeyFrame`
- `LinearColorKeyFrame`
- `DiscreteColorKeyFrame`
- `SplineColorKeyFrame`

There is an additional `ObjectAnimationUsingKeyFrames`, which contains `DiscreteObjectKeyFrame`, but this is not supported in Expression Blend and would have to be coded manually. These keyframes are beyond the scope of this book.

The XAML for a keyframe animation looks like this:

```
<Storyboard x:Name="MyStoryboard">
    <DoubleAnimationUsingKeyFrames
        Duration="0:0:4.5"
        Storyboard.TargetName="rect1"
        Storyboard.TargetProperty="Width">
        <LinearDoubleKeyFrame Value="100"
            KeyTime="0:0:0"/>
        <LinearDoubleKeyFrame Value="200"
            KeyTime="0:0:2.2"/>
        <LinearDoubleKeyFrame Value="100"
            KeyTime="0:0:3"/>
    </DoubleAnimationUsingKeyFrames>
</Storyboard>
```

In this example, the value of the `Width` goes from 100 to 200 and then back to 100 at different time intervals, and the animation happens linearly. Notice that some of the properties on `DoubleAnimationUsingKeyFrames`, such as `Storyboard.TargetName` and `Storyboard.TargetProperty`, are the same as the ones for `DoubleAnimation`. In addition, the element contains a series of `LinearDoubleKeyFrame` elements with the value and the time at which the `Width` should be changed to that value in this example.

Running the Animations You Create

Building the animation is one thing, but running it is another. You can easily create animations interactively in Expression Blend, but to run them, you have to write some C# or VB.NET code. To run the animation that we show you how to create in the previous sections of this chapter, follow these steps:

1. **Select the Button tool from the Tools panel and add a button to the** `MainPage.xaml` **file (which should be open on the Artboard).**

2. **Click the Selection tool from the Tools panel, double-click the button, and type** Start Animation.

    This changes the default content of the button to the new text you typed.

3. **Click the Events tab in the Properties panel and double-click the Click event for the button.**

    The `MainPage.xaml.cs` file opens and displays the newly added event handler `Button_Click`.

4. **Change the** `Button_Click` **method so that it looks like the following code:**

    ```
    private void Button_Click(object sender,
        System.Windows.RoutedEventArgs e)
    {
        BouncingBall.Begin();
    }
    ```

    The `Begin` method of the `Storyboard` class starts the animation.

5. **Press F5 to run the application and click the Start Animation button.**

    The ball bounces on the screen according to the storyboard you just created.

Controlling animations from code

The `StoryBoard` class has a whole bunch of useful methods to control the animation when the application is running. As we show you in the earlier example, you can use the `Begin` method to start an animation. Similarly, you can use the `Stop` method to end an animation. There are also `Pause` and `Resume` functions to apply to the storyboard programmatically.

Just by looking at the methods of the class, you can see that working with animations is very similar to working with audio/video files.

This section contains a few other methods and events that you will also find useful.

AutoReverse property

You can reverse the animation quite easily using the `AutoReverse` property in the `StoryBoard` class. To see how it works, open the `MainPage.xaml.cs` file from the previous example, and in the method `Button_Click` method in the `MainPage.xaml.cs` file, set the `AutoReverse` property of the BouncingBall to true, as shown in bold in the following code snippet:

```
private void Button_Click(object sender, System.Windows.
        RoutedEventArgs e)
{
    BouncingBall.AutoReverse = true;
    BouncingBall.Begin();
}
```

This makes the animation go in reverse and return to its original position after it has finished traversing in the forward direction.

Completed event

The StoryBoard class contains an event called `Completed` that gets triggered when the Animation finishes. To run the animation continuously by restarting the Storyboard as soon as it completes, add the code in bold to the `MainPage.xaml.cs` file as follows:

```
public partial class MainPage : UserControl
{
    public MainPage()
    {
        // Required to initialize variables
        InitializeComponent();
        BouncingBall.Completed +=new
            System.EventHandler(BouncingBall_Completed);
    }

    private void Button_Click(object sender,
                    System.Windows.RoutedEventArgs e)
    {
        BouncingBall.AutoReverse = true;
        BouncingBall.Begin();
    }

    private void BouncingBall_Completed(object sender,
```

```
                           System.EventArgs e)
    {
        BouncingBall.Begin();
    }
}
```

RepeatBehavior property

You would never use the kind of code shown in the preceding section to loop your animation continuously, because there is a better way of achieving the same result.

The `Storyboard` class has a property called `RepeatBehavior` that you can use instead. This property also lets you control a few other things, such as the number of times the animation has to repeat.

Continuing from the previous example in this chapter, remove the code we told you to add for the event handling and add the line of code shown in bold to the `Button_Click` method:

```
private void Button_Click(object sender, System.Windows.
        RoutedEventArgs e)
{
    BouncingBall.RepeatBehavior =
            new RepeatBehavior(2);
    BouncingBall.AutoReverse = true;
    BouncingBall.Begin();
}
```

By setting the parameter value in the `RepeatBehavior` constructor to 2, you are saying that you want the animation to run twice, and by also having the `AutoReverse` property set to true, the animation will run twice and end where it actually started.

Press F5 to run the application and test this behavior.

You can also specify a `TimeSpan` as a parameter in the `RepeatBehavior` constructor to specify the duration in which the animation has to be repeated.

You can set properties such as `RepeatBehavior` and `AutoReverse` in XAML. We've just used it in code to show you how.

Easing the animation

You have likely realized that animation does not always happen in the linear fashion shown in our example in the previous sections. That is, a ball never bounces at the same speed, and things don't stop abruptly. If you want to create an animation that looks realistic, you need the easing feature. *Easing*

Chapter 8: Creating Animations in Silverlight 183

lets you control the speed of the animation so that it is different at different points in time.

To see how to apply easing to animations, continue from the previous example in this chapter and follow these steps:

1. **Using the Selection tool, select the ellipse that represents the bouncing ball.**
2. **Click the + button in the Objects and Timeline panel.**

   The Create Storyboard Resource dialog box appears.
3. **Set the name to BouncingBall2 and click OK.**

   A new storyboard called BouncingBall2 is created.

4. **In the Objects and Timeline panel, click the Record Keyframe button (shown here in the margin).**
5. **Click 5 in the timeline to record the properties at the 5-second mark.**
6. **Drag the ball down to the bottom of the screen, as shown in Figure 8-6.**

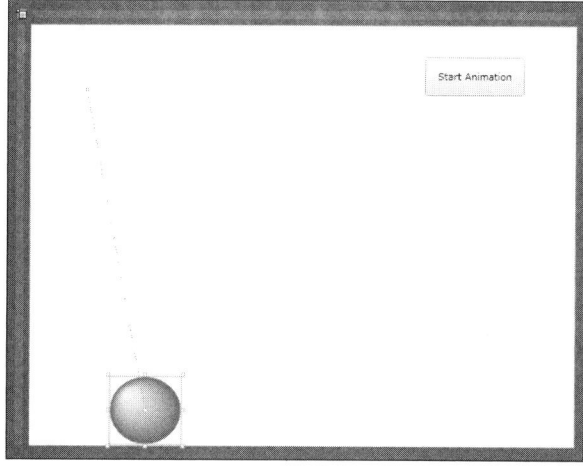

Figure 8-6: Dragging the ball down to create another animation.

7. **Click the Play button in the Objects and Timeline panel.**

   A preview of the animation is displayed on the Artboard, and the motion is even throughout.
8. **Click the second keyframe oval at the 5-second mark.**

   The properties panel shows an Easing group with the Easing function set to None, as shown in Figure 8-7. The graphic in front of the Easing function name shows the kind of easing that is performed in a graphical form with the speed of animation on the y-axis and the time in the x-axis. A straight line at a 45-degree angle denotes that the motion is linear throughout.

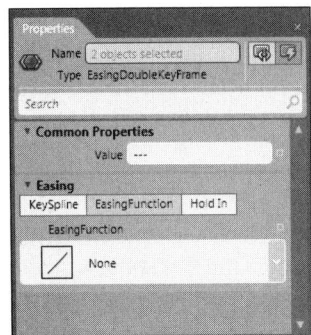

Figure 8-7: Easing function for the animation.

9. **Click the drop-down arrow of the Easing function.**

   The drop-down list opens and reveals a list of built-in Easing functions, as shown in Figure 8-8.

   Each of the Easing functions has the name to the side and has three motion types — In, Out, and InOut — specified at the top. Choosing one of these types specifies when the Easing function is applied: on the way in, on the way out, or both.

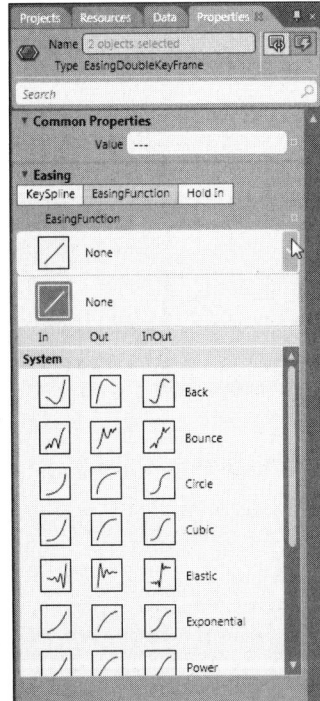

Figure 8-8: Built-in Easing functions.

10. **Click the Bounce Out function to select it; then click the Play button again.**

    A Bounce animation is displayed and the bounce speed looks more realistic. You can select other functions to see how the animation looks for these as well.

When you select one of the Easing functions, the Properties panel shows other properties that can be changed for that specific function. For instance, the Bounce function shows Bounces and Bounciness. By setting the Bounces to 6, as shown in Figure 8-9, you can see that the number of bounces has actually increased.

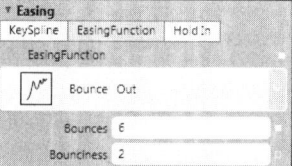

Figure 8-9: Properties for the Bounce Easing function.

Understanding the different kinds of Easing functions

In the previous section, we discuss the different kinds of Easing functions that are displayed in the EasingFunction drop-down list in Expression Blend. The following list shows the Easing functions in Silverlight and what they would do to the bouncing ball we have you create earlier:

- **Back:** Moves the ball back and then forward. You can specify how much the ball has to move back by using the `Amplitude` property.
- **Bounce:** This simulates a bouncing ball. You can control how many bounces the ball should have using the `Bounces` property. You can also set how bouncy it should be using the `Bounciness` property.
- **Circle:** This accelerates or decelerates the motion of the ball using a circular function.
- **Cubic:** This is similar to the Circle ease but uses a cubic function to calculate the easing.
- **Elastic:** This simulates a spring oscillation, where the ball oscillates in, out, or both according to the setting. You can control the number of oscillations using the `Oscillations` property; the `Springiness` property is similar to the `Bounciness` property used in the Bounce easing.

✔ **Exponential:** This uses an exponential function to control the easing of the ball.
 ✔ **Power:** Uses a power-of-time equation to accelerate or decelerate the ball's animation. You can specify the power you want to use by setting the Power property.
 ✔ **Quadratic:** This is similar to Power easing, but with the Power property set to 2.
 ✔ **Quartic:** This is similar to Power easing, but with the Power property set to 4.
 ✔ **Quintic:** This is similar to Power easing, but with the Power property set to 5.
 ✔ **Sine:** Uses a sine equation to control the easing of the ball.

Easing using KeySplines

Rather than use the built-in Easing functions, you can use something known as KeySplines to get more control over how the easing works.

Click the KeySpline button in the Easing section of the Properties panel. This brings up the KeySpline editor, shown in Figure 8-10. The KeySpline editor shows a Bezier curve through which you can specify the first and second control points.

A *Bezier curve* is a curve calculated using a complex mathematical equation that allows you to model smooth curves by specifying two points. The default values of the two points used to calculate the curve in Expression Blend are (0,0) and (1,1), and these show up as either a linear curve or a straight line. (The straight line is shown in Figure 8-11.)

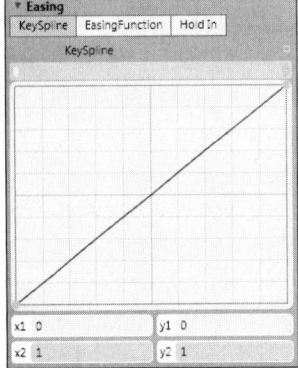

Figure 8-10: Setting KeySpline for easing.

Chapter 8: Creating Animations in Silverlight

The two yellow dots in the graph represent the two points that are used to calculate the curve. You can click and drag the curve to change the way the curve looks, and your changes, in turn, determine how the easing is performed.

You have endless options concerning how you can perform easing. For instance, if you want to create a slide show of photos, you may want the animation to have a fast start and fast exit but display the photo a bit longer toward the middle so that you can have a good look at it. To create a similar easing with the ball, you need to click the two yellow dots on the KeySpline Editor and drag them to the positions shown in Figure 8-11. Click the play button in the Objects and Timeline panel to see how the ball accelerates initially, slows down, and then accelerates again.

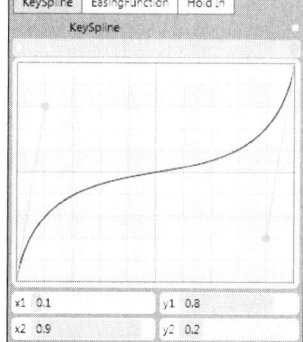

Figure 8-11: Fast start and fast finish.

Or if you want to create something like a page flip, you may want an animation that starts and ends slowly but speeds up in the middle. To simulate something similar for the ball, drag the yellow dots to the position shown in Figure 8-12. Click the play button again in the Objects and Timeline panel to see how the ball has a slow start, accelerates, and then decelerates toward the end.

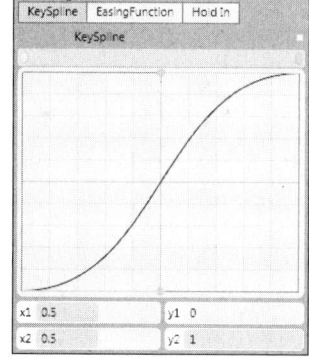

Figure 8-12: Slow start and slow finish.

Animating States of Controls

In Chapter 6, you create a Button template and specify how a button should look for various states. You also specify how to animate the change of states so that when you click a button, the button press happens in a smooth manner.

But you can do more! For starters, you can do more complex animations as well as apply easing to the animation when a state change occurs. To give you a feel for how all this works, we provide an example of animating the caption in a button by rotating it when the button is clicked. Follow these steps to animate the button:

1. **Create a new Silverlight application by choosing File⇨New Project. In the New Project dialog box, select Silverlight 4 Application + Website option and click OK.**

   This creates a new Silverlight project for the Button animation.

2. **Using the Selection tool from the Tools panel, add a button to the Artboard.**

3. **Select the button using the Selection tool and choose Object⇨Edit Template⇨Edit a Copy.**

   The Create Style Resource dialog box appears.

4. **In the Create Style Resource dialog box, select the Application radio button and click OK. If you are in the Animation workspace, press F6 to switch to the Design workspace.**

5. **Open the States panel and click the Add Transition arrow for the Pressed state, as shown in Figure 8-13.**

   A drop-down list appears.

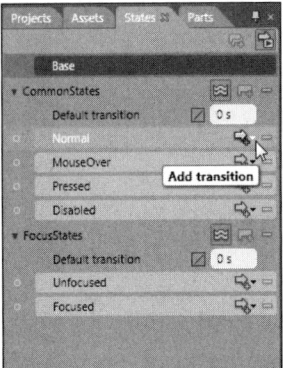

Figure 8-13: Adding a transition for the button.

6. **In the drop-down list, choose *→Pressed.**

 A transition gets added in the States panel under Pressed and shows the asterisk (*) followed by the arrow.

 7. **Click the line that shows *→, as shown in Figure 8-14.**

 Expression Blend switches to Timeline Recording mode and the Artboard shows the text *→Pressed transition recording is on.

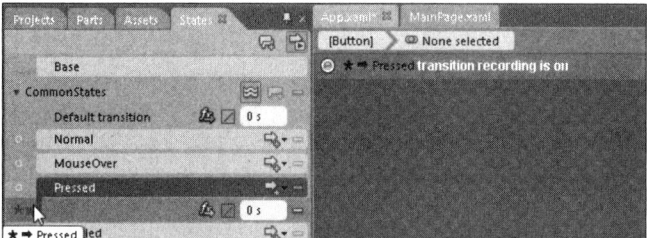

Figure 8-14: Adding animation to the *→Pressed state.

 8. **Select the contentPresenter in the Objects and Timeline panel and click the timeline at the 2-second mark. Rotate the contentPresenter using your mouse so that it makes one whole circle and returns to where it started, as shown in Figure 8-15.**

Figure 8-15: Animating the content-Presenter by rotating it.

 9. **Click the red bullet at the top of the Artboard to stop the recording.**

 10. **Press F5 to test the application.**

 When the application runs, click and hold the button you added. Notice how the text rotates and makes one full circle.

All the animation features are also available when you try to animate your control template to move the control from one state to another. This even includes features such as easing. You can click the Easing function button that appears next to the Default Transition field to display the Easing function drop-down list.

Chapter 9
Updating Data the Easy Way with Data Binding

In This Chapter
- Understanding the purpose of data binding
- Binding to controls
- Creating domain objects that can be bound to data
- Creating sample data for data binding

*U*ser interface elements are meant to display some kind of information to the user of a Web site. This information can be in the form of text or some other visual cue. For instance, to display a temperature value, you might display it as text or as a graphical representation of a thermometer or gauge. You might also include several other properties within the control that may provide additional information to the user. The color of the text could be Red to indicate that it is hot or Blue to indicate that it is too cold.

Whenever you write XAML to display these values, you have to set a property in your code-behind file using C# or VB.NET. For instance, if you want to use a TextBlock control to display the temperature, you may just set the `Text` property on it. This is fine. But what if the value of the temperature changes? The most common way of fixing this problem is to set the property of `Text` again with the updated value. And if you used the foreground color to show whether it is hot or cold, then you need to set that value as well.

If you have numerous controls, and several properties on these controls need to be changed every time the data it represents changes, the whole business can get very tedious.

Wouldn't it be nice if all you had to do was change the value, and the control would automatically update the user interface for you? That's what data binding is for.

In this chapter, we show you how you can bind user interface controls to data, even when the data originates from other controls. We also show you how to create sample data that you can bind to your application to see how your application will look when you run it.

Binding Controls to Each Other

An easy way for you to grasp how binding works is by jumping right in and binding one control to another. In this section, you create a simple project that contains a NumericUpDown control and a Slider control and binds the value of one control to another.

The NumericUpDown control is a special control for entering numbers easily. It consists of a TextBox and two buttons for increasing and decreasing the numeric value in the TextBox. The Slider control is another way of displaying and entering numeric value. It consists of a scroll thumb that can be dragged on a line to increase or decrease the numeric value. In this example, you bind the value of the NumericUpDown control to the Slider so that when you update one control, the value of the other one automatically gets updated.

To create and bind the two controls together, follow these steps:

1. **Create a new Silverlight project in Expression Blend and call it Chapter9 (very original, we know).**

2. **In the Assets panel, type** NumericUpDown **into the search field Control. When the control shows up in the Assets list, drag and drop it onto the Artboard at a convenient location.**

3. **In the Properties panel, set the FontSize property under the Text group to a high value, such as 24pt, so that it is easy to look at in this demo.**

4. **Again from the Assets panel, find the Slider control and add it to** `MainPage.xaml`**, as shown in Figure 9-1. Set the Maximum property value to 100.**

   The default `Maximum` value for the NumericUpDown control is 100. By matching the Slider control's `Maximum` to the same value as the NumericUpDown control, you ensure that when the two controls are databound together, the value of one cannot get higher than the other.

Chapter 9: Updating Data the Easy Way with Data Binding   193

5. **Click Advanced Property Options for the Value property and choose Element Property Binding.**

   The cursor changes to an element picker (shown in the margin) as you move it over the Artboard.

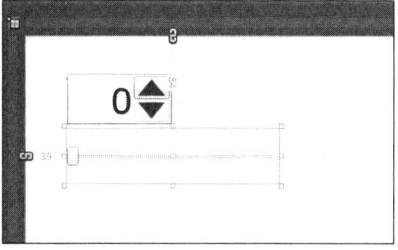

Figure 9-1: Adding a Slider control to the Artboard.

6. **Click the NumericUpDown control.**

   The Create Data Binding dialog box (see Figure 9-2) appears.

7. **In the dialog box, select Value from the drop-down list.**

   This binds the Value property of the selected control, which is the Slider to the Value property of the NumericUpDown control.

8. **Click Show Advanced Properties, which shows up as a small arrow, shown here in the margin.**

   Additional advanced property fields are shown on the screen.

9. **Set the Binding direction to TwoWay and click OK.**

   Setting the `Binding` to TwoWay ensures that changes in values to either control update the other.

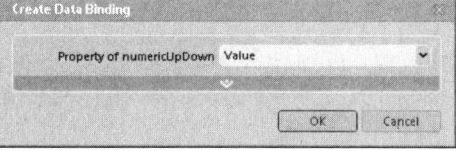

Figure 9-2: Creating a binding.

10. **Press F5 or choose Project➪Run Project to run the application.**

    Notice that when you change the value of the NumericUpDown control, the value in the Slider changes as well. Similarly, when the Slider is moved up or down, the value in the NumericUpDown control changes. This is the TwoWay binding at work.

Data binding is nothing more than establishing a connection between a user interface property, such as text in a TextBox or items in a ListBox, and any other object. This object can be a domain object, which is just a fancy name for an object that contains business-related data, such as customer or product information. Or the object can be another user interface element, such as the one created with the NumericUpDown control and Slider in the previous section.

To see the XAML generated in the previous section that shows data binding between two user interface elements, go to the XAML view for MainPage.xaml. The main statement that has the data binding markup looks like this:

```
<Slider Margin="72,176,246,234" Maximum="100"
        Value="{Binding Value,
        ElementName=numericUpDown, Mode=TwoWay }"/>
```

Notice that the Value attribute is enclosed by curly brackets with the wording Binding in the attribute. This part of the XAML specifies the source from which the data is bound, as well as some additional parameters that should be used in the binding.

The first parameter specifies the source object's property name that the Slider's Value property should bind to. In this case, it is set to Value. This means that the Value of the Slider is bound to the Value of the source object.

The source object is specified in the ElementName property. In this case, it is the numericUpDown object. If you are not binding to another UI element, this can be completely omitted. If this is omitted, the source is specified in the DataContext property of the Slider.

The next parameter is Mode, which can contain one of three values, as follows:

- OneWay: This value means that whenever the source object's Value changes, the Value of the Slider changes as well.
- TwoWay: With TwoWay, the changes are bidirectional, meaning that the values on the source and target are dependent on each other, and a change in one value affects the other.
- OneTime: This value means that the value of the Slider is updated only once, and any subsequent changes to the source's value do not affect the Slider's value.

You set the Mode to OneTime if you want to initialize the fields with certain values and these values do not change over a period of time. You use OneWay if these values change dynamically. For example, if you are showing live scores for an NBA game on your site, you use `OneWay`, whereas you use `OneTime` if you are showing the scores of games already completed. `TwoWay` is typically used when you are creating a form that you use to display as well as edit data. You bind the controls to data such as `Address`, and the screen gets updated when the value of `Address` changes. The `Address` object also gets updated if you change the values displayed on the screen.

Binding to a Data Object

In the previous sections, we tell you how to bind properties in a control to properties on other controls. In this section, we show you how you can bind properties such as `Text` in a TextBox to data from data such as Address fields. The task involves the following general steps:

1. Create a user control to display the address fields.
2. Bind the address fields in the control to specific property names.
3. Create a class that can be databound to the address control.
4. Data bind the class you created to the address control in code.

We describe these steps in more detail in the following sections.

Creating a user control for data binding

To create a control that binds to an Address, follow these steps:

1. **Create a new Silverlight project by choosing File⇨New Project from the menu, and when the New Project dialog box appears, select Silverlight 4 Application + Website and click OK.**

    A new project is created and the `MainPage.xaml` file appears on the Artboard.

2. **Double-click the StackPanel control in the Tools panel to add it to the `MainPage.xaml` file; then drag the resizing handles to set the height and width of the StackPanel to a suitable dimension.**

    Using a StackPanel makes it easier to lay out controls. (See Chapter 5 for more details on using the StackPanel.)

3. **Add six pairs of TextBlocks and Text Boxes to display address details. Change the text in the TextBlocks to Street Number, Street Name, City,**

State, Postal Code, and Country, and set their FontWeight to Bold from the Properties panel.

(Chapter 7 uses a similar example to create an Address user control, so if you're not sure how to do this step, refer to that chapter.)

The XAML should look like this (some markup has been left out for brevity and replaced by an ellipsis [...]):

```
<UserControl . . .>
  <Grid x:Name="LayoutRoot" Background="White">
    <StackPanel HorizontalAlignment="Left"
        Margin="8,22,0,167" Width="291">
      <TextBlock Text="Street Number"
        TextWrapping="Wrap" FontWeight="Bold"/>
      <TextBox TextWrapping="Wrap"/>
      <TextBlock Text="Street Name"
        TextWrapping="Wrap" FontWeight="Bold"/>
      <TextBox TextWrapping="Wrap"/>
      <TextBlock Text="City" TextWrapping="Wrap"
        FontWeight="Bold"/>
      <TextBox TextWrapping="Wrap"/>
      <TextBlock Text="State" TextWrapping="Wrap"
        FontWeight="Bold"/>
      <TextBox TextWrapping="Wrap"/>
      <TextBlock Text="Postal code"
        TextWrapping="Wrap" FontWeight="Bold"/>
      <TextBox TextWrapping="Wrap"/>
      <TextBlock Text="Country" TextWrapping="Wrap"
        FontWeight="Bold"/>
      <TextBox TextWrapping="Wrap"/>
    </StackPanel>
  </Grid>
</UserControl>
```

4. **Create a UserControl by right-clicking the StackPanel in the Objects and Timeline panel and choosing Make into UserControl. In the Make into UserControl dialog box, set the name to `AddressControl` and click OK.**

   A UserControl named AddressControl is created in the file `AddressControl.xaml` and is opened on the Artboard.

   This UserControl is now ready to be used.

Data bind the controls in the UserControl to a property name

Using the Selection tool from the Tools panel, select the Street Number TextBox control in the `AddressControl.xaml` file and click the Advanced Property Options for the Text property in the Properties panel.

Choose Custom Expression and type **{Binding StreetNumber}**, as shown in Figure 9-3; then press Enter.

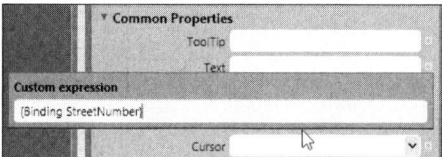

Figure 9-3: Custom expression for the Text property.

Repeat this step for every TextBox in the UserControl, setting the custom expression for the Text property to read `{Binding StreetName}`, `{Binding City}`, `{Binding State}`, `{Binding PostalCode}`, and `{Binding Country}` for the Street name, City, State, Postal Code, and Country text boxes.

When you're finished, the XAML for AddressControl should like the following (some markup has been left out for brevity and replaced by an ellipsis[. . .]):

```
<UserControl . . . >
  <Grid x:Name="LayoutRoot">
    <StackPanel>
      <TextBlock Text="Street Number" TextWrapping="Wrap"
          FontWeight="Bold"/>
      <TextBox TextWrapping="Wrap" Text="{Binding
          StreetNumber}"/>
      <TextBlock Text="Street Name" TextWrapping="Wrap"
          FontWeight="Bold"/>
      <TextBox TextWrapping="Wrap" Text="{Binding
          StreetName}"/>
      <TextBlock Text="City" TextWrapping="Wrap"
          FontWeight="Bold"/>
      <TextBox TextWrapping="Wrap" Text="{Binding City}"/>
      <TextBlock Text="State" TextWrapping="Wrap"
          FontWeight="Bold"/>
      <TextBox TextWrapping="Wrap" Text="{Binding
          State}"/>
      <TextBlock Text="Postal Code" TextWrapping="Wrap"
          FontWeight="Bold"/>
      <TextBox TextWrapping="Wrap" Text="{Binding
          PostalCode}"/>
      <TextBlock Text="Country" TextWrapping="Wrap"
          FontWeight="Bold"/>
      <TextBox TextWrapping="Wrap" Text="{Binding
          Country}"/>
    </StackPanel>
  </Grid>
</UserControl>
```

The AddressControl UserControl is now ready to be databound to any class that has the properties `StreetName`, `City`, `State`, `PostalCode`, and `Country`.

Create a data class that can be databound

Now that you've bound the text fields to certain property names, you need to create a class that contains these properties. To do so, follow these steps:

1. **Choose File⇨New Item, and in the New Item dialog box that appears, select Class and then set the Name field to `Address.cs` and click OK.**

   The file `Address.cs` opens on the Artboard and shows the `Address` class.

2. **When the `Address.cs` file opens, add the following code to the class:**

   ```
   public string StreetNumber { get; set; }
   public string StreetName { get; set; }
   public string City { get; set; }
   public string State { get; set; }
   public string PostalCode { get; set; }
   public string Country { get; set; }
   ```

   The `Address` class is now ready to be databound to the UserControl you created in the previous section.

3. **Press Ctrl+Shift+B to build the solution.**

Binding the data object to the control

To bind the `Address` data that is stored in the class you created with the AddressControl, follow these steps:

1. **Open the `MainPage.xaml` file, and using the Selection tool, select the AddressControl.**

2. **From the Properties panel, set the Name property to suitable text such as `ctlAddress`.**

3. **Open the `MainPage.xaml.cs` file by double-clicking the file from the Projects panel. Then change the `MainPage` class as shown in the following code that appears in bold:**

   ```
   public partial class MainPage : UserControl
   {
       Address _address = new Address
       {
           StreetNumber = "100",
   ```

```
        StreetName = "Silverlight Way",
        City = "Melbourne",
        State = "Victoria",
        PostalCode = "3000",
        Country = "Australia"
    };

    public MainPage()
    {
        // Required to initialize variables
        InitializeComponent();

        ctlAddress.DataContext = _address;
    }
}
```

This creates an instance of the Address class and data binds it to the UserControl. You use the `DataContext` property to specify the source data object. After you set the data context of the parent window, that property is set automatically for all its child controls.

4. **Press F5 or choose Project**⇨**Run Project to run the application.**

   The Address that you have set in code is automatically set in the `Address` UserControl.

Automatically updating changes to the data

In traditional programming, when you want to change the value for a field such as a TextBox to display on-screen, you set the TextBox's `Text` property to the new value. But as mentioned earlier in this chapter, you don't have to do this in Silverlight; instead, you update changes automatically using data binding.

To show you how this works, the following steps have you change the value of the `StreetName` property in the `Address` class (created in the previous section) when a button is clicked. You can then observe whether the AddressControl changes on the screen:

1. **Add a button to** `MainPage.xaml` **in the Design view and set its content property to** `Change Data`**. In the Properties panel, open Events and double-click the Click field.**

   The `MainPage.xaml.cs` file opens and displays the `Button_Click` event handler. (As noted elsewhere in this book, an *event handler* is code that gets called when an event occurs, such as a button being pressed or text being changed.)

2. **Change** `_address.StreetName` **to the value** `"Silverlight Avenue"`, **being sure to include the quotation marks, as shown in the following code:**

   ```
   private void Button_Click(object sender, System.
           Windows.RoutedEventArgs e)
   {
      _address.StreetName = "Silverlight Avenue";
   }
   ```

3. **Press F5 or choose Project**⇨**Run Project to run the application.**

   The application shows up in a browser window. Click the Change Data button. Although the Street Name value was changed in the event handler, note that the value on the screen is not updated. (Read on!)

The reason the field on the screen is not updated is that the TextBox control does not know that the field's value has changed. To take care of that issue, you need to implement an interface called `INotifyPropertyChanged` on the `Address` class. This interface has an event called `PropertyChanged` that needs to be fired every time you change the value of a databound field.

To add the necessary code, open the `Address.cs` file on the Artboard from the Projects panel and follow these steps:

1. **Add the following line to the top of the file:**

   ```
   using System.ComponentModel;
   ```

   You need to add this line because the `INotifyPropertyChanged` is in the System.ComponentModel namespace.

2. **In the class definition of the Address, add :
   INotifyPropertyChanged (be sure to include the spaces and the colon) as follows:**

   ```
   public class Address : INotifyPropertyChanged
   ```

3. **Add the following piece of code in the class:**

   ```
   public event PropertyChangedEventHandler
           PropertyChanged;
   ```

   Data binding uses the event defined to get notified whenever a data field changes.

4. **Write a method in the class to fire the event, as follows:**

   ```
   private void NotifyPropertyChanged(string p)
   {
       if (PropertyChanged != null)
       {
           PropertyChanged(this, new
           PropertyChangedEventArgs(p));
       }
   }
   ```

This method will fire the `PropertyChanged` event that you create in Step 3.

5. **Remove the existing `StreetName` property in the `Address` class and replace it with the following code snippet:**

    ```
    private string _StreetName;

    public string StreetName
    {
        get
        {
            return _StreetName;
        }
        set
        {
            _StreetName = value;
            NotifyPropertyChanged("StreetName");
        }
    }
    ```

    This ensures that when the `StreetName` property is set, the `PropertyChanged` event is fired.

6. **Press F5 or choose Project⇨Run Project to run the application. When the application starts up, click the Change Data button.**

    Notice that the Street Name now changes to Silverlight Avenue because of the data binding.

You need to replace all the other properties in the `Address` class so that all of them can be auto updated the way the StreetName property is.

Converting data while binding

Sometimes, the data that you wish to bind to your user interface element may not be compatible with the property that you want to bind to. For example, you may have a property that stores a date field as a string, but the control may require a `DateTime` field to be databound. Or you may have a string that stores the value Yes or No, but the CheckBox to which the data is bound may require a Boolean property. In these scenarios, you need to create a converter that converts the property value from its original data type to the data type that the databound control expects.

In the following example, you add a string property called `UseAsMailing Address` to the `Address.cs` file to store a value as "Yes" or "No". You then write a converter in C# that converts the string values `"Yes"` to `true` and `"No"` to `false`. Finally, you use the converter in the data-binding XAML. Follow these steps:

1. **Open the `Address.cs` file in Expression Blend or Visual Studio and add the following code snippet to the class:**

   ```
   private string _UseAsMailingAddress;

   public string UseAsMailingAddress
   {
       get
       {
           return _UseAsMailingAddress;
       }
       set
       {
           _UseAsMailingAddress = value;
           NotifyPropertyChanged("UseAsMailingAddress");
       }
   }
   ```

   This adds a new property called `UseAsMailingAddress` that can take the string values of `"Yes"` and `"No"`.

2. **Open `MainPage.xaml.cs` and modify the code where you set the values for `Address` by adding the line shown in bold:**

   ```
   Address _address = new Address
   {
       StreetNumber = "100",
       StreetName = "Silverlight Way",
       City = "Melbourne",
       State = "Victoria",
       PostalCode = "3000",
       Country = "Australia",
       UseAsMailingAddress = "Yes"
   };
   ```

   This sets the value for `UseAsMailingAddress` to `"Yes"` while creating the `Address` object.

3. **Open `AddressControl.xaml` in the Design view in Expression Blend and add a CheckBox control to the end by double-clicking the CheckBox control from the Tools panel. Set the `Content` property of the check box by double-clicking the control and typing** Use as mailing address.

   The CheckBox has a property called `IsChecked` that can be set to map to the `UseAsMailingAddress` property in the `Address` object. But the two types are incompatible because `IsChecked` takes a Boolean value, whereas `UseAsMailingAddress` is a `String` property type. To fix this incompatibility, you need to create a `Converter` class.

4. **From the menu, choose File⇨New Item. When the New Item dialog box shows up, select Class, and in the Name field, type StringToBooleanConverter.cs. Then click OK.**

   A new class called `StringToBooleanConverter` opens on the Artboard.

Chapter 9: Updating Data the Easy Way with Data Binding

5. **Replace the class definition that was generated with the following code:**

```
public class StringToBooleanConverter :
        IValueConverter
{

    #region IValueConverter Members

    public object Convert(object value,
            Type targetType, object parameter,
            System.Globalization.CultureInfo culture)
    {
        string data = value as string;

        if (data != null)
        {
            return (data == "Yes" || data == "True") ?
            true : false;
        }
        else
        {
            new ArgumentException("Conversion
        failed");
        }
        return false;
    }

    public object ConvertBack(object value,
            Type targetType, object parameter,
            System.Globalization.CultureInfo culture)
    {
        try
        {
            bool data = (bool)value;
            return (data) ? "Yes" : "No";
        }
        catch (Exception)
        {
            new ArgumentException("Conversion
        failed");
        }
        return false;
    }

    #endregion
}
```

This code converts the string value `"Yes"` or `"True"` to Boolean `true` and everything else to `false`. It also converts back Boolean `true` to `"Yes"` and `false` to `"No"`.

6. **To data bind** `UseAsMailingAddress` **to the CheckBox control using the StringToBooleanConverter in XAML, open** `AddressControl.xaml` **in Design view and select the CheckBox control. From the**

Properties panel, click Advanced Properties Options for the `IsChecked` **property. Choose Data Binding from the menu option.**

The Create Data Binding dialog box pops up.

7. **Select the Data Type tab. Then select the Use a Custom Path Expression check box and type** `UseAsMailingAddress` **in the text field next to it.**

8. **Click Show Advanced Properties (shown here in the margin) to reveal more of the Create Data Binding dialog box, as shown in Figure 9-4.**

9. **Click the Add New Value Converter button, which is denoted by an ellipsis (. . .) next to the Value Converter drop-down list.**

The Add Value Converter dialog box pops up. Select `StringToBooleanConverter` from the list and click OK.

10. **Click OK in the Create Data Binding dialog box and press F5 or choose Project**➪**Run Project to run the application.**

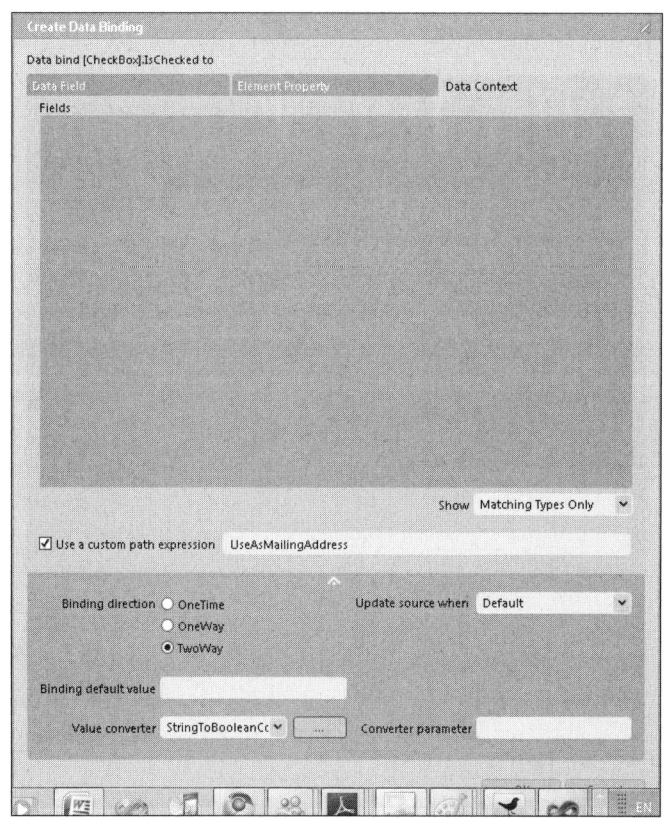

Figure 9-4:
The Create Data Binding dialog box.

Chapter 9: Updating Data the Easy Way with Data Binding *205*

The application starts up in a browser. Notice that the Use As Mailing Address check box is now selected with the StringToBooleanConverter converting the "Yes" property to a Boolean true and setting the IsChecked property in the control.

Binding to Sample Data

While designing the user interface of your application in Expression Blend, it is important to see how a screen will look while displaying actual data, and this is where creating sample data helps. For example, if your application displays a user's profile information such as name, e-mail, address, phone numbers, and photos, you need to figure out how to format all this in a page, including what font to use, what length to use for each field, and so on. Creating sample data gives you a realistic idea of how the screen will look at design time. You need to do this in a two-step process: First create the sample data and then bind user interface elements to the sample data.

Creating sample data

To see the process involved in creating some sample data that contains Name, Address, Email, and Picture, start a new Silverlight project in Expression Blend. Then follow these steps:

1. **Open the Data panel and click the Add Sample Data Source button, as shown in Figure 9-5.**

Figure 9-5: Adding a sample data source from the Data panel.

2. **Choose Define New Sample Data from the menu.**

    A Define New Sample Data dialog box appears.

3. **Ensure that the Enable Sample Data When Application Is Running check box is selected and click OK.**

    The SampleDataSource item is added to the Data panel, as shown in Figure 9-6.

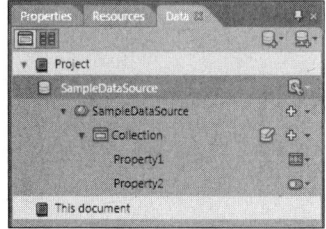

Figure 9-6: SampleDataSource added to the project.

4. **Double-click Property1 and change its name to *Name*.**

5. **Double-click Property2 and change its name to *Address*.**

6. **Click the Add Simple Property button, shown here in the margin, on the Collection line to add a new property. Change the name of the property to *Email*.**

7. **Click the Add Simple Property button again to add another property. This time change its name to *Picture*.**

   Note that all the properties in the collection arrange themselves in alphabetical order.

8. **Click the Change Property Type drop-down arrow that appears at the end of the Address property; then, change the Type to *String* in the drop-down list.**

   A few other fields appear on the screen, as shown in Figure 9-7. These fields include Format.

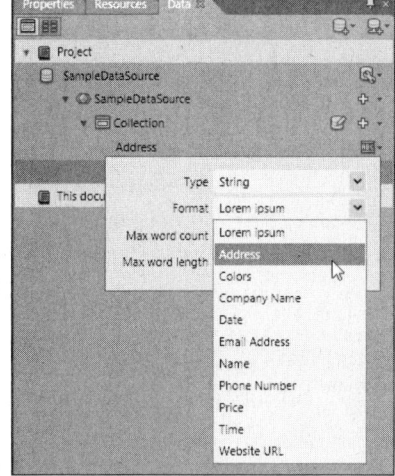

Figure 9-7: Changing the type of sample data.

Chapter 9: Updating Data the Easy Way with Data Binding

9. Click the Format drop-down list and choose the value *Address;* then, click anywhere outside the pop-up window to close it.

10. Click the Change Property Type button for Email, and in the pop-up window, click the Format drop down-list. Choose the value *Email Address* from the list and close the pop-up window.

11. Click the Change Property type button for Name, and set the Format to *Name*.

12. Finally, click the Change Property type button for Picture, and change the Type to *Image*.

    If you have a directory with images on your computer, you can change Location to point to that directory. If you do not fill this, Expression Blend loads its own set of sample images.

You have now created some sample data that you can data bind to controls to see how they will look when the application is run.

Binding a DataGrid to the sample data

After you create some sample data, as described in the previous section, you need to bind it to some controls in the page. Silverlight comes with a control called DataGrid that can be used to display data in rows and columns. In the example in the following steps, we show you how to bind the sample data you just created to a DataGrid:

1. Open `MainPage.xaml` **by clicking the MainPage.xaml tab.**

2. **In the Objects and Timeline panel, right-click the LayoutRoot item and, in the pop-up menu that appears, choose Change LayoutType**⇨**StackPanel.**

3. **From the Assets panel, type** DataGrid **in the Search box to find the control, and when it appears in the list, double-click it to add it to the** `MainPage.xaml` **file.**

    The DataGrid provides a tabular view of the data, with each column representing the object's properties and each row representing a single item from a collection.

4. **Drag the resizing handles on the DataGrid to set a suitable height and width to the control.**

5. **From the Data panel, select the Collection under SampleDataSource and drag it onto the DataGrid.**

    Expression Blend provides you with a notification that says `Bind [DataGrid].ItemsSource to Collection`, as shown in Figure 9-8.

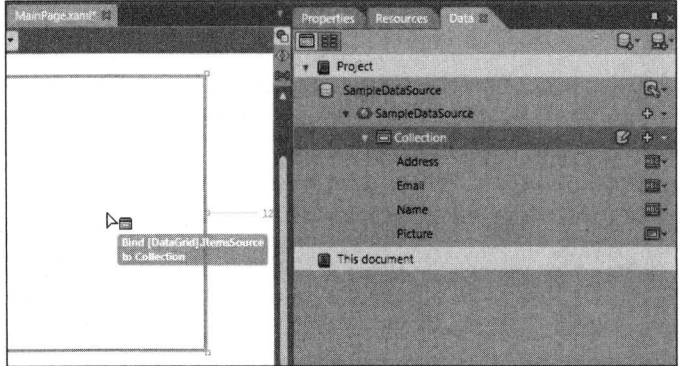

Figure 9-8: Dragging the sample data on to a DataGrid.

After you drop the Collection onto the DataGrid, the DataGrid automatically adds the right columns and displays the data, as shown in Figure 9-9.

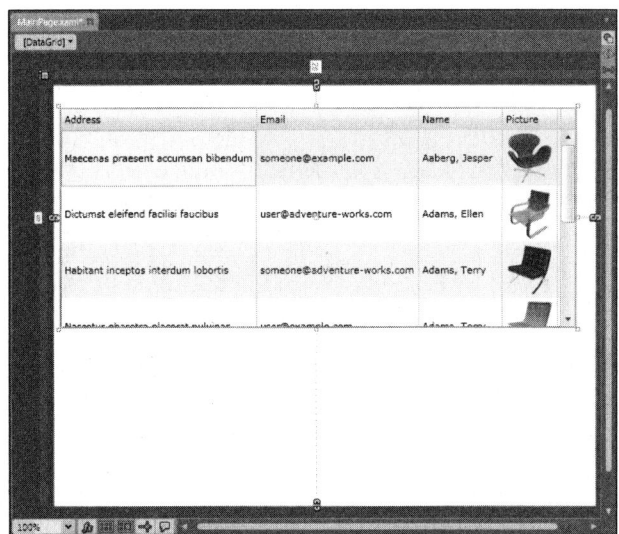

Figure 9-9: DataGrid displaying the sample data.

6. **Press F5 or choose Project**➪**Run Project to run the application.**

If you select the Enable Sample Data When Application Is Running check box when you're creating the data source, as we have you do in the previous section, "Creating sample data," the sample data will also be available for you when you run the application.

When you're ready to roll out your application, change the data binding to point to real data.

Creating a Master-Detail view

The DataGrid control displays all the items in rows, and when you have lots of columns, this is not the best way to edit individual items. You may have to create a Master-Detail view, in which you use the DataGrid to display the master record, and you click a row to see the details for that row.

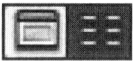

To create a Master-Detail view, open the Data Panel in Expression Blend. At the top of the panel are two buttons: one represents the ListMode and the other represents the Details mode.

Click the Details mode button. Then hold down the Ctrl key while clicking each of the properties you have added under Collection (as described in the "Creating sample data" section, earlier in this chapter) to select them all. Drag and drop them to the empty area under the DataGrid.

A Details view with all the controls is automatically created.

You can further change the layout of the Details view by repositioning the different controls or even removing the ones you don't want displayed.

Press F5 or choose Project⇨Run Project to run the application. Notice that as you select a different row in the DataGrid, the Details view automatically displays the data corresponding to the row you selected.

Fooling around with the sample data

The sample data that Expression Blend creates for you is quite useful for visualizing how the screens will look when real data is used, and you can customize the data further if what Expression Blend generates doesn't meet your needs.

To customize the data, open the Data panel and click the Edit Sample Values button in the Collections line. An Edit Sample Values dialog box appears, as shown in Figure 9-10.

You can change the sample data three ways within this dialog box:

- ✔ **Properties:** Click the Change Property Type button that appears at the top of each column to change the property type, Format, and other properties of the data.
- ✔ **Records:** Change the number of sample data items you want to generate by changing the Number of Records field at the bottom of the dialog box.
- ✔ **Data values:** Double-click any cell in the DataGrid to change the actual values of the sample data.

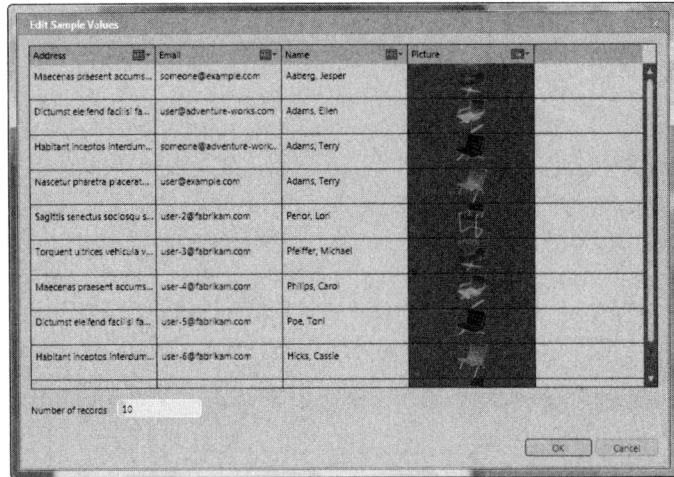

Figure 9-10: Edit Sample Values dialog box.

Part III
Connecting with Data

In this part...

No Web application is complete without retrieving data from somewhere and displaying it to users.

Chapter 10 shows you how to connect to data sources on the Web and extract data, while Chapter 11 takes you a step further to show you how you can expose data from your databases using a technology called WCF Data Services.

The final two chapters in this part discuss WCF RIA Services, which is a Web service with a variety of advantages of WCF Data Services. In these chapters, you find out how to retrieve data from a database, validate user input, and authenticate your users.

Chapter 10

Accessing Data in Silverlight

In This Chapter

▶ Connecting to the Web to get data

▶ Downloading files to your application

▶ Talking to Web services

▶ Understanding cross-domain security

Silverlight is a client-side technology that runs in the Web browser and is therefore disconnected from the server. This fundamental aspect of Silverlight plays a major part in how Silverlight applications "talk" to the server. Your Silverlight application runs inside your user's browser, so to get data from the server, you as the application developer need to communicate with it through some sort of service.

Your application data and certain types of resources are kept on the server for a number of reasons. For starters, your application probably needs only some of the data in a database. Downloading all of the data in the database not only takes a very long time but could also compromise your application if the wrong data is shown to the wrong user. If your application is media-intensive, you want to show only the media that the user wants, rather than downloading your whole media library to them. One site that is an example of this scenario is YouTube (www.youtube.com). You download only the videos you want to watch, not all of the millions of videos available. With media such as videos, you can also set up a streaming service to stream videos to the user before they have finished downloading.

When you are developing your Silverlight application, you will quite often build the service as well, so it will be located on your development machine. However, if you're part of a team, another team member may be developing that service, so you may be developing against an already-published service. This scenario is the same for when you develop applications for a public service such as Flickr.

The services you may use in your Silverlight Application could be a simple ASP.NET Web Service, commonly referred to as an .asmx service, a Windows Communication Foundation (WCF) service, or a service that is not part of your application, such as the Flickr photo service. If the service your Silverlight Application is talking to is not on the same domain as your Silverlight application, you have to set up a cross-domain policy, which we cover in "Understanding Cross-Domain Security" at the end of this chapter.

The other type of data you can connect to from your Silverlight application is file-based data, such as a text (.txt) file, a compressed (.zip) file, or even an image or movie file. This is the simplest way to get data into your application, so we start the chapter with a discussion of that.

In this chapter, we also cover the basics of getting server-side resources into your Silverlight application. Resources include files, fonts, streams, strings, and services. We show you how to download files to your application as well as include Web services in your application. We also give you a workaround for working with services that do not have a cross-domain policy (which is outlined in a cross-domain policy file) in place. This chapter also covers how to use the authentication system built into ASP.NET to make sure that you serve information only to logged-in users.

Downloading Files to Your Silverlight Application

Your Silverlight application runs in the user's browser and isn't connected to the Web server that holds the data it needs. So when you need server-side resources such as fonts, strings, images, and videos, you need to download them to your Silverlight application before you can use them. Another point to remember is that your Silverlight application does not begin to run until it has completely downloaded to the browser. Therefore, you want to try to keep the base application as small as possible and download the resources that your users need only when they need them. Deciding what to include initially and what to hold off on until later can be tricky, and you need to experiment with how you set up your application. You often have to make a trade-off of longer wait times to get started versus waiting for resources later in the application life. Generally, you should include resources in your application that are required for the first few actions and then later download anything else in a separate execution thread. That way, the later downloads don't block the main user interface thread and the user's experience is not affected.

You do get some things for free, meaning that you don't have to do the work. The most common scenario for the Image control and Media Element control is to get their source files directly from the server. As such, both controls support getting their sources directly from the server, so you don't need to write any download code for those elements. Instead, you just specify the source using a URL such as http://www.domain.com.au/MyVideoFile.wmv.

Silverlight comes with two very handy ways to download files to your application: the `WebClient` class and the `HttpWebRequest` class. They're built into the Silverlight runtime and easily accessible. The `WebClient` is quite simple to use. The `HttpWebRequest` has more options, but using it is a bit more work. The `WebClient` and the `HttpWebRequest` can both do a `GET` request, but only the `HttpWebRequest` can do a `POST` request. The `WebClient` class actually uses the `HttpWebRequest` class to do all of its work. Typically, you use the `WebClient` class unless you need to use the `POST` method to access your resource on the server.

What is a `POST` method, you ask? When an application calls a service or a user clicks on a Web page, two main types of requests are made: `GET` and `POST` requests. A `GET` request doesn't send any data to the Web server — it only uses information in the URL to process the request, such as www.domain.com/deafult.aspx?Id=3. The `GET` request would use the address and the `Id=3` part to return the correct data. You can have only 2,000 characters in the part of the URL that follows the question mark, which limits you in some cases.

A `POST` request, on the other hand, allows you to send much more data in a less visible way. You've done plenty of `POST` requests on the Internet already: Every time you fill out a form online and press the Submit button, you're making a `POST` request. Think about this scenario: Your Silverlight application is a system that allows people to apply for a passport online. Your users can fill out a series of forms and then, at the end your application, create a document to print and take to the post office to finish the process. This would be a good time to use `HttpWebRequest` and a `POST` operation to submit the information entered online. Your server-side operation would then create the file and let your Silverlight application download the file.

With the `WebClient` class, you can perform only an `HTTP GET` request. The `GET` request is excellent for downloading files and strings; however, if you need to post some data to the URL to get to your resources, you have to use `HttpWebRequest`. You often have to use `POST` when calling Web services, as we discuss in "Talking to Web Services," later in this chapter.

Downloading files using the WebClient class

The `WebClient` class is a class built into the Silverlight framework that provides a simple way to access remote resources with very little code. You typically use it to download files such as fonts, text files, images, and other media that your application needs to run. You need to do only four things to use the `WebClient`. To do those things, you need to use Visual Studio in an open Silverlight application and open the code-behind file. (Remember that a code-behind file is the file with a `.cs` or `.vb` extension that is associated with a `.xaml` file. For example, the `MainPage.xaml.cs` file is the code-behind file for `MainPage.xaml`.) Next, follow these steps:

1. **Create a new instance of the class using the following code:**

    ```
    var wc = new WebClient();
    ```

2. **Tell the instance of `WebClient` what to do when it has finished downloading the file, as follows:**

    ```
    wc.OpenReadCompleted += OpenReadCompleted;
    ```

3. **Write the event handler for the `OpenReadCompleted` to tell Silverlight what to do with the file after you have downloaded it, as follows:**

    ```
    void OpenReadCompleted(object sender,
            OpenReadCompletedEventArgs e)
    {
        //Do something with your downloaded file here
    }
    ```

4. **Tell Silverlight to open the file asynchronously. This is how you start the download:**

    ```
    OpenReadAsync(new Uri("myfile.txt", UriKind.
            Relative));
    ```

    The `UriKind.Relative` part of the `OpenReadAsync` method tells Silverlight that the file `myfile.txt` is located in the ClientBin folder on the server. You can see this folder in the Web application part of the solution as soon as you build your application for the first time. This folder is automatically generated by Visual Studio and is the folder that the compiled Silverlight application will be built into.

Here's an example of downloading a file that you have to get from the server because it's not a standard font in Silverlight. In the example, we use a Wingdings font:

1. **Create a new Silverlight application in Visual Studio by selecting File**⇨**New Project and selecting Silverlight Application from the dialog box shown. Call the new application** SilverlightData.

    A dialog box asking where to host the Silverlight Application appears.

2. **Click OK in the dialog box.**
3. **Press F6 or Ctrl+Shift+ B to build your solution.**

    This generates a ClientBin folder in the Web application project of your solution.

4. **Go to your Windows folder and locate the Fonts folder.**
5. **Copy the** webdings.ttf **file and paste it into the ClientBin folder in the Web application project of the solution.**

    You need to copy the font file into the ClientBin folder because you will specify that the address of the file is UriKind.Relative, which makes Silverlight look in the ClientBin folder.

Now that the file you want your user to be able to download is in the right folder, you need to create a new instance of the WebClient class. In doing so, you also have to tell it what to do when it has finished downloading the file and where to download the file from. To do so, follow these steps:

1. **Open the** MainPage.xaml **file by double-clicking the** MainPage.xaml **file in the Solution Explorer.**
2. **Now add a new TextBlock control, name it ContentText, and set its** Text **property to** Home page content **by adding the following code between the** Grid **tags in the XAML:**

    ```
    <TextBlock x:Name="ContentText" Text="Home page
        content" FontFamily="Wingdings"/>
    ```

3. **Open the code-behind file for the** MainPage.xaml **by double-clicking the** MainPage.xaml.cs **file in the Solution Explorer.**
4. **Declare a new instance of the** WebClient **class immediately after the code line** InitializeComponent **by using the following code:**

    ```
    var wc = new WebClient();
    ```

5. **Create an event handler for the** OpenReadCompleted **event, which tells your Silverlight application what to do after the file has been downloaded. In this example, we apply the downloaded font to the** TextBlock **element** ContentText **by setting its** FontSource **property. Use the following code:**

```
void wc_OpenReadCompleted(object sender,
        OpenReadCompletedEventArgs e)
{
        ContentText.FontSource = new FontSource(e.
        Result);
}
```

6. **Tell the instance of the** `WebClient` **which event handler to use when it finishes downloading the font file. Add the following code directly below the line for creating a new instance of** `WebClient`:

```
wc.OpenReadCompleted += wc_OpenReadCompleted;
```

7. **Call the** `OpenReadAsync` **method and set the URL to the** `wingding.ttf` **file using the following code placed immediately after the line from Step 6:**

```
wc.OpenReadAsync(new Uri("wingding.ttf", UriKind.
    Relative));
```

After you have followed the previous steps, your code should look like the following. Here you can see that we added the call to create a new `WebClient`, told the instance which event handler to use, and then called the `OpenReadAsync` method, all in the constructor for the `MainPage` of the application. We also added the event handler for when the file has finished downloading and applied the font file to the `FontSource` property of the `ContentText` TextBlock control.

```
public MainPage()
{
    InitializeComponent();
    var wc = new WebClient();
    wc.OpenReadCompleted += wc_OpenReadCompleted;
    wc.OpenReadAsync(new Uri("wingding.ttf", UriKind.
        Relative));
}
void wc_OpenReadCompleted(object sender,
        OpenReadCompletedEventArgs e)
{
        ContentText.FontSource = new FontSource(e.
        Result);
}
```

Now when you run the application, the text `Hello Silverlight` in the `ContentText` TextBlock control has the Wingdings font applied, as shown in Figure 10-1.

Chapter 10: Accessing Data in Silverlight 219

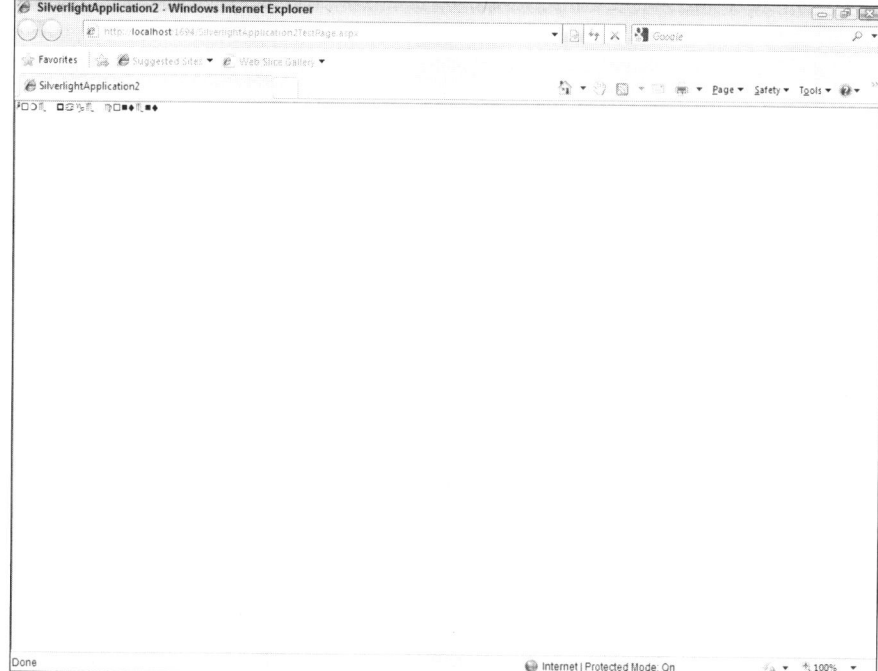

Figure 10-1: The Wingding font applied to text.

Using WebClient to include a progress bar with large downloads

When you download something small and simple such as a font file, the download occurs rapidly, so users don't have time to wonder what's going on. Sometimes, though, you have a massive file, such as a video file or a huge photograph, to download. In such a case, it's a good idea to provide some visual feedback on-screen to reassure your users that something is happening. To let your users know how much of the file has downloaded, you need to use the `WebClient` class. The `WebClient` class has a nice feature that lets you know each time a portion of the file has been downloaded.

Each time a portion of the file is downloaded, the `DownloadProgressChanged` event is fired and you can find out how many bytes have been downloaded and how many bytes of data the file contains in total. If you divide the number of bytes already received by the total number of bytes in the file, and then multiply the result by 100, you get the percentage downloaded. The `Download ProgressChanged` event makes it easy to display a progress bar that shows the download's progress.

When your application is running on the Internet, the download speeds are much lower than when it is running locally on your development machine, so for this example, you need a very large file of at least 500MB. Otherwise, the download goes so quickly that you won't get to see it properly.

In this example, you add a new ProgressBar control to the example from the previous section. This allows you to indicate to the user how much of your large file has been downloaded using a familiar control. Each time the `DownloadProgressChanged` event fires, you then calculate how much of the file has been downloaded and update the ProgressBar control to show that more of the file has been downloaded.

To add a new ProgressBar control, follow these steps:

1. **Open the SilverlightData solution you created in the previous section.**
2. **Find a very large file (at least 500MB) on your computer and copy it into the ClientBin folder just as you did for the font file in the previous example.**
3. **Open the `MainPage.xaml.cs` file by double-clicking it.**
4. **Find the `OpenReadAsynch` method that you used to download the font file and change the name of the file to the name of the file you are going to download. Your code should now look like this:**

    ```
    wc.OpenReadAsync(new Uri("mymassivevideofile.wmv",
            UriKind.Relative));
    ```

5. **Open the `MainPage.xaml` file by double-clicking it.**
6. **Add a new StackPanel control just inside the Grid control.**
7. **Find the existing TextBlock control called `ContentText` and drag it inside the new StackPanel control.**
8. **Add a new ProgressBar control immediately below the `ContentText` TextBlock control.**
9. **Set the `x:Name` property of the ProgressBar control to `DownLoadProgress` by typing `x:Name="DownLoadProgress"` so that you can refer to it in the code-behind file easily.**
10. **Set the `BackGround` property to `Blue` by typing `BackGround="Blue"`.**
11. **Set the `ForeGround` property to `White` by typing `ForeGround="White"`.**
12. **Set the `Maximum` property to `1` and the `Minimum` to `0`.**
13. **Set the `Height` to `50` by typing `Height="50"`. At this point, the XAML should look like this:**

```xml
<Grid x:Name="LayoutRoot">
   <StackPanel>
      <TextBlock x:Name="ContentText" Text="Home page
         content" FontFamily="Wingdings"/>
      <ProgressBar x:Name="DownLoadProgress"
         Minimum="0" Maximum="1" Background="Blue"
         Foreground="White" Height="50"/>
   </StackPanel>
</Grid>
```

14. **Add the** `DownLoadProgressChanged` **event immediately after the** `OpenReadCompleted` **event you added in the previous example.**

    You can get Visual Studio to write the event code for you by typing **wc.DownLoadProgressChanged** and then pressing the plus key, the equal sign key, and the Tab key twice. This is a Visual Studio shortcut key combination for generating the event handler for you.

15. **Inside the event handler, get the value of** `BytesReceived` **by using the following code:**

    ```
    var received = e.BytesReceived;
    ```

16. **Do the same for the** `TotalBytesToReceive` **by using the following code:**

    ```
    var toReceive = e.TotalBytesToReceive;
    ```

17. **Now divide** `Received` **by** `toReceive` **to get the value to apply to the DownLoadProgress ProgressBar by adding the following code:**

    ```
    DownLoadProgress.Value = received / toReceive;
    ```

Now every time a portion of your massive file is downloaded by the `WebClient`, the user sees a progress bar with updates on the progress of the download.

After you complete the preceding steps, your code looks like this:

```
public Home()
{
    InitializeComponent();
    var wc = new WebClient();
    wc.OpenReadCompleted += wc_OpenReadCompleted;
    wc.DownloadProgressChanged +=   wc_
        DownloadProgressChanged;
    wc.OpenReadAsync(new Uri("mymassivevideo.wmv",
        UriKind.Relative));
}

void wc_DownloadProgressChanged(object sender,
        DownloadProgressChangedEventArgs e)
{
    double received = e.BytesReceived;
    double toReceive = e.TotalBytesToReceive;
    DownLoadProgress.Value = received / toReceive;
}
```

Using the HTTPWebRequest class

In this section, we look at using the `HttpWebRequest` class to perform a `POST` request and send data to the server. To be able to `POST` some data to the server, you need to create a new `HttpWebRequest` object, write your data to the newly created request object, and then send the request to the server.

In this example, we create a new ASP.NET Web page called `PostForm.aspx`, which processes the data we `POST` from our Silverlight application. This is exactly the scenario we discuss earlier in this chapter about submitting a passport application online. The `PostForm.aspx` page reads FirstName and LastName out of the data we post to it. After the Form Variables are read, the processing formats the FirstName and LastName into a string that the Silverlight application displays on the screen.

We build the sample in three stages: First, we build the XAML needed to gather the first name and last name for the server. Second, we build the server page. The third and final step is to use the `HttpWebRequest` class to `POST` data to the new server page.

Follow these steps to build the XAML for the example:

1. **Open Visual Studio.**

2. **Choose File➪New Project and select Silverlight Application from the dialog box. Name the new application** SilverlightForDummiesHttpWebRequest.

3. **If the** `MainPage.xaml` **file is not already open, double-click it in the Solution Explorer to open it.**

4. **Add a StackPanel control between the** `Grid` **tags by adding the following XAML:**

    ```
    <StackPanel>
    </StackPanel>
    ```

5. **Add two TextBox controls between the** `StackPanel` **tags and call one** `FirstName` **and the other** `LastName` **by adding the following code:**

    ```
    <TextBox x:Name="FirstName"/>
    <TextBox x:Name="LastName" />
    ```

6. **Add a Button with a Click event after the two TextBox controls with the following code:**

    ```
    <Button Click="Button_Click" Content="Submit"/>
    ```

Chapter 10: Accessing Data in Silverlight   223

7. Add a TextBlock to show the formatted string you get back from the server page:

```
<TextBlock x:Name="ContentText" />
```

After you have the XAML set up, create the server page. This server page reads the Form variables posted to it and then writes a formatted string based on those variables. Follow these steps:

1. In the Solution Explorer, right-click the SilverlightForDummiesHttpWebRequest.Web project and select Add New Item from the menu that appears.

2. Click the WebForm option in the Add New Item dialog box and call it `PostForm.aspx`.

This adds a new `.aspx` file to the Web application.

3. If the new `PostForm.aspx` **file is not already open, double-click it in the Solution Explorer to open it.**

4. Add a Page Load event to the page by adding the following code:

```
<script runat="server">
void Page_Load(object sender, EventArgs e){
}
</script>
```

5. Read the Form variables and write the formatted string to the page with the following code. Write this code inside the `Page_Load` **event:**

```
if(Request.Form["FirstName"] != null )
{
Response.Write("FirstName : " + Request.
       Form["FirstName"] + " ");
}
if(Request.Form["LastName"] != null )
{
Response.Write("LastName : " + Request.
       Form["LastName"]);
}
```

You have now created a server page that will read the Form variables FirstName and LastName and then format them to your requirements. If you have done any ASP.NET programming or even any classic ASP programming, you will recognize the code here as standard forms programming. This technique gives you a good way to integrate Silverlight into existing ASP.NET applications.

The last step is to write the code that Silverlight uses to post the data to this form and get the results back. Follow these steps:

1. **Open the `MainPage.xaml` file.**
2. **Find the Button and the Click event code.**
3. **Right-click the word Button_Click and select Navigate to Event Handler from the menu that appears.**

   This takes you to the `MainPage.xaml.cs` file inside the event handler for the `Button_Click` event.

4. **Declare a byte array variable at the top of the class by adding the following code immediately under the public partial class `MainPage` : `UserControl`:**

   ```
   private byte[] byteArray;
   ```

5. **Go back to the `Button_Click` event handler and create the form data to post to the server page by adding the following code:**

   ```
   byteArray = Encoding.UTF8.GetBytes("FirstName=" +
           FirstName.Text + "&LastName=" + LastName.
           Text);
   ```

6. **Specify the server page address you want to POST your data to by adding the following code:**

   ```
   Uri address = new Uri(HtmlPage.Document.DocumentUri,
           "/PostForm.aspx");
   ```

7. **Create a new request object with the following code:**

   ```
   var request = (HttpWebRequest)HttpWebRequest.
           Create(address);
   ```

8. **Specify that you want to do a POST with the following code:**

   ```
   request.Method = "POST";
   ```

9. **Specify the content type (a very important step — without this step, the server doesn't know that you are posting Form variables to it) by adding the following code:**

   ```
   request.ContentType = "application/x-www-form-
           urlencoded";
   ```

10. **Add the following code to start the process of POSTing the data:**

    ```
    request.BeginGetRequestStream(GetRequestStream,
            request);
    ```

This step is the first part of a two-step process. Here, you get the `RequestStream` so that you can write your data to it before it is POSTed. Notice that you pass the request object that is making the call to `BeginGetRequestStream` as well. You will use the request object shortly.

11. **Create the new `GetRequestStream` method by adding the following code immediately underneath the `Button_Click` event code:**

    ```
    private void GetRequestStream(IAsyncResult ar)
    {
    }
    ```

12. **Get a reference to the request that is making the call to this method by adding the following code:**

    ```
    var request = (HttpWebRequest)ar.AsyncState;
    ```

    Remember that this is an asynchronous task, so you need to know which request object you are working on. That's why you pass it to the method in Step 10.

13. **Write the data from your TextBoxes into the request object with the following code:**

    ```
    using (Stream post = request.EndGetRequestStream(ar))
    {
    post.Write(byteArray, 0, byteArray.Length);
    post.Close);
    }
    ```

14. **Now that the request object has the data, start the process of getting a response from the server with the following code:**

    ```
    request.BeginGetResponse(GetResponseResult, request);
    ```

    Notice that you pass the request through again so that you can keep your method calls synchronized using the same request.

15. **Process the response from the server by creating a new method called `GetResponseResult` with the following code:**

    ```
    private void GetResponseResult(IAsyncResult ar)
    {
    }
    ```

16. **Get a reference to the response from the server by adding the following code to the `GetResponseResult` method:**

    ```
    var request = (HttpWebRequest)ar.AsyncState;
    var response = (HttpWebResponse)request.
            EndGetResponse(ar);
    ```

17. **Retrieve the value of the response from the response object with the following code:**

    ```
    var responseValue = new StreamReader(response.
            GetResponseStream()).ReadToEnd();
    ```

18. **Get the returned value and set it as the value of the TextBlock on the page so that you can see it:**

    ```
    ContentText.Dispatcher.BeginInvoke(() =>{ContentText.
            Text = responseValue;});
    ```

    Remember that you're doing asynchronous programming — you need to make sure that you use the correct processing thread to set the `Text` property. You can do that easily by using the TextBlock's `BeginInvoke` method on its `Dispatcher` property. If you don't do it this way, you will get cross-threading errors. Threading is a complicated issue, so for the purpose of this book, the following explanation is sufficient to explain why you use the `Dispatcher` property to update the `Text` property of the `ContentText` TextBlock control.

    The Silverlight application is running in what is known as the UI (user interface) Thread, or the Main Thread. Each time the application makes a call to a method such as `BeginGetResponse`, a new thread is created so that the time that request takes to execute does not stop the user interface from responding to the user. If the second thread then tries to update a property of a control on the Main Thread, a cross-threading error will occur. This is why controls have the `Dispatcher` property that can be used to update properties from different threads.

19. **Run the application by pressing F5 or clicking the green Play button.**

    You should see two text boxes and a button.

20. **Type your name into the text boxes and click the button.**

    Under the button, you should see what you typed appearing in the following format:

    First Name: Philip Last Name: Beadle

Using the `HttpWebRequest` class with `POST` is a very valuable technique for integrating Silverlight into existing sites and is an excellent way to interact with Web services. It is more complicated to use than the `WebClient` class, however, so use the `WebClient` class where you can.

Talking to Web Services

Web services are the connecting glue of the Internet. Many companies around the world expose their data and services via Web services for you to use in your applications. Some examples are Flickr, PhotoBucket, and

Windows Live, which allow applications such as Silverlight to interact with their systems via Web services. However, Silverlight does not allow this access unless the Web service has a cross-domain policy file in place. A *cross-domain policy file* is a small XML file that lets Silverlight know that it's okay to call the service even though the service is on a different domain than the one that the Silverlight application is running on. Silverlight requires services to have this policy because it's a strong security feature to protect users from malicious code that can damage files on their computer.

Just because a Web service doesn't have a cross-domain policy, however, doesn't automatically mean that you can't get your application to access that service. As with just about everything in the .NET world, an effective workaround exists. In this section, we first show you how to use Web services that Silverlight can automatically access. Later, in the section "Accessing a Web service without a cross domain policy file," you find out how to get Silverlight to allow access to the services that have no cross-domain policy in place.

Accessing Web services that allow cross-domain exchanges

Think of a Web service as a pre-existing piece of your application that runs all the time on the Internet. You don't need to create it because it's already been created and used by others. That Web service conforms to the standard way Web services are published, so that you can easily add that functionality into your application without having to worry about how it was implemented. All you care about are the results.

There are several different ways to build and access Web services that have all sorts of acronyms and sound pretty complicated but essentially all do the same thing. Web services expose data, such as photographs, and methods to act on that data for you, such as uploading. Think of a popular Web site such as Flickr (www.flickr.com). Flickr allows people to upload photos to their servers and then show the photos to their friends. Flickr also publishes a Web service that allows developers like you to access their systems to upload and manipulate photos with code. Flickr also has a cross-domain policy in place that allows a Silverlight application to access it directly. The Flickr Web service can be accessed through several different protocols. A *protocol* is the way in which you access the Web service.

If you have a look at the Services API page on Flickr, www.flickr.com/services/api/, you can see under the Format section that Flickr has several different protocols for talking to the Web service. The first one is called REST, which stands for Representational State Transfer. All that really means is that you can open a Web browser and type in the Web service URL with some parameters, such as a search term, and you will see the data as XML on your screen. REST is one of the easiest protocols to use, so we start off with it.

Before you begin building the following example, you need to get a Flickr developer's account so that you can get your own key and password, called a secret, that you use when you craft the requests to the Web service. To get your own Flickr developer account, follow these steps:

1. **Open a Web browser.**
2. **Navigate to** www.flickr.com/services.

   This is the Flickr Services page, with a list of all the methods the Web service makes available to you as a developer. The list of methods is often called an API, which stands for Application Programming Interface.

3. **To log in to Flickr, you must have a valid Yahoo! account. If you have one, click the Sign In link and supply your Yahoo! e-mail address and password in the pop-up dialog box that appears, and then click the Sign In button to log in.**

   If you don't yet have a Yahoo! account, go to www.yahoo.com, click the Sign Up link, and follow the instructions for creating an account. Then go back to Flickr and enter your new e-mail address and password.

4. **Click the button that says Get API Key and fill out the form that asks you about your application.**

   This generates a new key and secret that we use in the example to access the Web service.

After you have created a Flickr developer account, try the following:

1. **Open a new Web browser.**
2. **Type** http://api.flickr.com/services/rest/?method=flickr.photos.search&api_key=yourkeygoeshere&text=australia **in the address box.**
3. **Press Enter.**

   You now see the XML data that comes back from the Flickr Web service when you use the REST format. The return data is XML, which means you can use the new Language Integrated Query (LINQ) syntax in your code to make it really easy to turn that raw XML into a useful list of items.

If you haven't used LINQ before, don't worry: The example is very simple, and we are using LINQ to easily create a list of items that we can add to the list box. (LINQ is a very valuable tool to use when programming in .NET.)

After you have seen the raw data, you are ready to write some code against the API and show the photos in your Silverlight application. The example pulls down a list of photos based on a search tag and displays them in a list box that uses an Image control to show the photo.

To access the Flickr Web service, follow these steps:

1. **Open Visual Studio.**
2. **Choose File⇨New Project, select Silverlight Application from the dialog box, and call it SilverlightForDummiesFlickrREST.**
3. **Click OK in the next dialog box that appears.**

   You should now have a new Visual Studio Solution with two projects in it: the Silverlight application and a Web site.

4. **Open the** `MainPage.xaml.cs` **file by double-clicking it in the Solution Explorer.**
5. **Create a new instance of a** `WebClient` **class as we did in the section "Downloading files using the WebClient class" by adding the following code immediately after** `InitializeComponent`:

   ```
   var service = new WebClient();
   ```

6. **Tell the service instance what to do when it is completed by typing the following code on the next line:**

   ```
   service.DownloadStringCompleted
   ```

7. **On the same line, type a plus sign and then an equal sign, and then press Tab twice.**

   This automatically generates the event handler code for the `DownloadStringCompleted` event.

   You should see the code for the event handler and event assignment generated for you by Visual Studio.

8. **Call the Web service by adding the following code immediately after the line that assigns the DownloadStringCompleted event to the service:**

   ```
   service.DownloadStringAsync(new Uri("http://api.
       flickr.com/services/rest/?method=flickr.
       photos.search&api_key=use your own
       key&text=australia"));
   ```

9. **In the event handler for the** `DownloadStringCompleted` **event, remove the exception that is automatically added for you and replace it with the following code so that you can see what is returned:**

   ```
   MessageBox.Show(e.Result);
   ```

10. **Run the application by pressing F5 or by clicking the green Play button.**

    A pop-up box with the same XML data you saw in the browser window previously appears.

That's how easy it is to access a Web service using the REST protocol. That wasn't a very interesting example, however, so we're going to take it a step further and process the returned XML and display the photos in a ListBox control. We do this in two stages. First, we add a simple ListBox control and process the XML into a list of Photo objects using LINQ. Second, we modify the ListBox and make it show the photos:

1. **In the Silverlight project, open the `MainPage.xaml` file by double-clicking it if it's not already open.**

   This shows you the XAML for the file.

2. **Add a new ListBox control to the XAML between the `Grid` tags by adding the following code:**

   ```
   <ListBox x:Name="PhotoList"
            DisplayMemberPath="title"/>
   ```

3. **Add a new reference to `System.Xml.Linq` by right-clicking References in the Solution Explorer and selecting Add New Reference.**

   `System.Xml.Linq` is at the bottom of the list.

4. **Add a new class called Photo by right-clicking the Silverlight project name, choosing Add⇨Class, and typing the name Photo into the Name field of the dialog box.**

5. **Add the following properties to the `Photo` class by adding the following code to the class:**

   ```
   public string Id { get; set; }
   public string Secret { get; set; }
   public string Server { get; set; }
   public string Farm { get; set; }
   public string Title { get; set; }
   ```

6. **Add the `ImageUrl` property (which concatenates the other properties you added in Step 5 to properly format the URL to show the photo) by adding the following code:**

   ```
   public string ImageUrl
   {
   get
   {
           return  string.Format("http://farm{0}.static.
           flickr.com/{1}/{2}_{3}.jpg", Farm, Server, Id,
           Secret);
   }
   }
   ```

7. **To use LINQ, you need a new `XDocument` object that you create from the result of the Web service call. Replace the `MessageBox` code in the event handler with the following code:**

```
XDocument xmlPhotos = XDocument.Parse(e.Result);
```

8. **Write a LINQ statement against the new XDocument to turn the XML into a list of** `Photo` **objects by using the following code:**

   ```
   var photos = from photo in xmlPhotos.Element("rsp").
           Element("photos").Descendants().ToList()
   select new Photo{
   Id = (string)photo.Attribute("id"),
   Secret = (string)photo.Attribute("secret"),
   Server = (string)photo.Attribute("server"),
   Farm = (string)photo.Attribute("farm"),
   Title = (string)photo.Attribute("title")
   };
   ```

   This code examines the XML you downloaded, finds the different elements in it, and creates a new `Photo` object for each one it finds.

9. **Assign the newly created list of** `Photo` **objects to the** `ItemsSource` **property of the** `PhotoList` **ListBox with the following code:**

   ```
   PhotoList.ItemsSource = photos;
   ```

10. **Press F5 or click the green Play button to see a list of the first 100 photo titles in the ListBox.**

If you've followed along throughout all the step lists in this chapter, you have called the Flickr Web service, processed the XML result, and set the list of items in the ListBox control. By setting the `ItemsSource` property of the ListBox, you have Silverlight create a new ListBoxItem for each `Photo` object and add it to the ListBox. The ListBox is able to show the title of each photo because we set the `DisplayMemberPath` to `Title`. However, the ListBox has no idea how to actually show the photograph of the `Photo` object; at this point it can only show Title because the only property we have set is the `DisplayMemberPath` to show the Title of the photo.

The really cool thing about this is that each `ListBoxItem` in the ListBox knows which `Photo` object it has. This means that you can add other controls to the ListBox and show different parts of the Photo object. So the next task is to define what each item in the ListBox should look like by telling the ListBox what its ItemTemplate is.

For this task, you use a cool feature of Silverlight called binding. You can think of *binding* as a way to tell the Silverlight XAML what to put in controls. In this example, you want to show the photograph associated with each item you get back from the Flickr Web service. To do this, you add an Image control to the ListBox control's `ItemTemplate` and then bind the source of the Image control to the `ImageUrl` property of the `Photo` object associated with that item. (See Chapter 9 for more information on binding.)

Follow these steps to show the photos from the Web service:

1. **Open the** `MainPage.xaml` **file by double-clicking it.**
2. **Remove the** `DisplayMemberPath` **property from the PhotoList ListBox control.**
3. **Create a data template for the ListBox control that shows the photo in an ImageControl by adding the following code to the ListBox:**

   ```
   <ListBox x:Name="PhotoList">
   <ListBox.ItemTemplate>
   <DataTemplate>
   <Image Source="{Binding ImageUrl}"/>
   </DataTemplate>
   </ListBox.ItemTemplate>
   </ListBox>
   ```

4. **Run the application by pressing F5 or clicking the green Play button.**

   You should now see a list of photos.

REST-based Web services such as the Flickr service are becoming more and more popular, especially for public-facing services. However, other types of protocols for accessing Web services are available, and we discuss those in the following sections.

Programming against a Web service that has a WSDL

What's a WSDL? This acronym — pronounced *wiz-del* — stands for Web Service Description Language and is an XML file that describes everything about a Web service, such as the methods it contains and the types of objects it can interact with. The Flickr REST service discussed in the previous section did not have a WSDL, so you have to rely on written documentation to discover how to construct your calls to the Web service. If the Web service has a WSDL, however, you can use a tool such as Visual Studio to help you out when programming against it.

The beautiful thing about programming against a Web service with a tool like Visual Studio is that you simply add a reference to the Web service as you would add a reference to a local assembly. Visual Studio then adds all of the "plumbing" code that is needed to write code against the Web service. Part of this "plumbing" code is called a *proxy class,* which includes all of the methods that the Web service exposes. A proxy class means that the class is a local

Chapter 10: Accessing Data in Silverlight 233

representation of the class and not the real class, hence the term *proxy*. The proxy class generation by Visual Studio is what makes programming against a Web service so easy.

The proxy class generation means that you get full IntelliSense when programming against the Web service. (IntelliSense makes programming much easier and means you have less chance to create bugs.)

The best way to see all this in action is with a demonstration that shows you how to add a Service Reference and then demonstrates IntelliSense for a Web service. Follow these steps to use a WSDL to create the proxy class and show IntelliSense with Visual Studio:

1. **Open Visual Studio.**

2. **Create a new Silverlight Application by choosing File**⇨**New Project, selecting Silverlight Project from the dialog box that appears, and calling the new application** SilverlightForDummiesWSDL.

3. **In the Solution Explorer, right-click the Silverlight application's References node.**

4. **Select Add Service Reference from the menu that appears.**

5. **In the dialog box, enter the following:**

    ```
    http://api.search.live.net/search.wsdl
    ```

6. **Press Go to see the service show up in the window just below the address, as shown in Figure 10-2.**

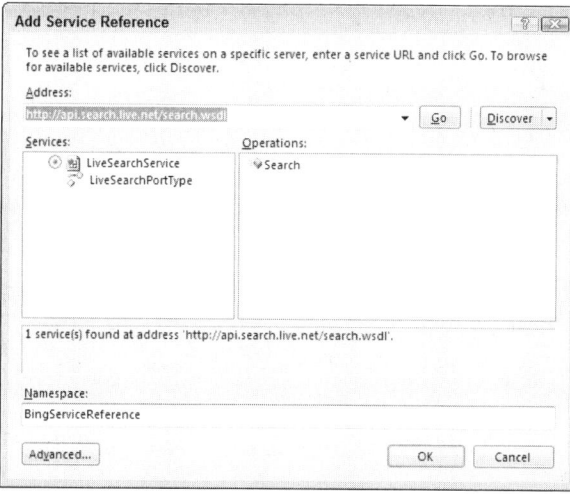

Figure 10-2:
The Add Service Reference dialog box.

7. **In the Name Space field, type** BingServiceReference **and click OK.**

   This causes Visual Studio to generate all the required files so that you can easily program against this service as if it were a local assembly.

8. **Open the** `MainPage.xaml.cs` **file.**

9. **In the Constructor, where it says** `public MainPage()`**, add the following code:**

   ```
   var service = new BingServiceReference();
   ```

10. **On the next line, type** service **and then a period, like so:**

    ```
    service.
    ```

11. **Select any of the available methods from the IntelliSense listing that appears.**

Having a WSDL for a Web service makes programming against it much easier. This is because you don't need to use classes such as `WebClient` or `HttpWebRequest` to call the methods on the Web service. You use the `ServiceReference` object that you created; then, IntelliSense lists all the available methods, which you then program against as if it were a local assembly. We discuss how to call these methods on the `ServiceReference` object in the next section.

Creating your own WSDL Web service

In this chapter thus far, we've looked at a few different ways in which Web services manifest themselves on the Internet. But what about when you want to create your own? Visual Studio makes it very easy to create your own Web services. In this section, we look at creating your own ASP.NET Web service and using it in a Silverlight application.

When you create a Web service with Visual Studio, Visual Studio automatically creates the WSDL file for you, which makes the service much easier to program against. When you create a Web service with Visual Studio, the template also creates a `HelloWorld` method for you, so you get a fully functioning Web service without writing any code at all!

In this example, you see how to create an ASP.NET Web service and then call the `HelloWorld` method to display the results of the method in your Silverlight application. You do it in two parts: first by creating the Web service, and then by showing the results of the `HelloWorld` method in your Silverlight application.

Follow these steps to create the Web service:

1. **Open Visual Studio.**
2. **Create a new project by choosing File⇨New Project and selecting Silverlight Application from the dialog box.**
3. **Call the new Application** SilverlightForDummiesWebService.
4. **In the Solution Explorer, right-click the SilverlightForDummiesWebService.Web project and select Add New Item from the menu that appears.**

   The Add New Item dialog box appears.
5. **Select Web Service and call it** HelloWorldWebService.
6. **Press Ctrl+Shift+B to build your solution, or press F6.**
7. **Add a new Service Reference to the Silverlight Application by right-clicking References in the Solution Explorer inside the SilverlightForDummiesWebService project.**

   The Add Service Reference dialog box appears.
8. **Click the Discover button in the Add Service Reference dialog box.**

   This locates the newly created HelloWorldWebService.
9. **Name the service reference** HelloWorldServiceReference.
10. **If the** MainPage.xaml **file is not already open, double-click it in the Solution Explorer to open it.**
11. **Add a StackPanel control between the** Grid **tags by adding the following XAML:**

    ```
    <StackPanel>
    </StackPanel>
    ```
12. **Add a button with a** Click **event inside the StackPanel with the following code:**

    ```
    <Button Click="Button_Click" Content="Submit"/>
    ```
13. **Add a TextBlock to show the formatted string you get back from the** HelloWorld **Web service:**

    ```
    <TextBlock x:Name="ContentText" />
    ```
14. **In the Button tag, right-click the words** Button_Click **and select Navigate to Event Handler from the menu that appears.**

    This adds the event handler code to the MainPage.xaml.cs file and takes you directly to the event handler.

15. **Create a new service object with the following code inside the** `Button_Click` **event handler:**

    ```
    var service = new HelloWorldServiceReference.
            HelloWorldWebServiceSoapClient();
    ```

16. **Create a new event handler for the completed event of the service object by typing the following code:**

    ```
    service.HelloWorldCompleted
    ```

17. **Use the Visual Studio shortcut to automatically generate the event handler code by typing a plus sign and an equal sign and then pressing the Tab button twice immediately after entering the code in Step 16.**

18. **Inside the new event handler, replace the exception code that is automatically generated with the following code:**

    ```
    ContentText.Text = e.Result;
    ```

19. **Add the call to the Web service by adding the following line of code to the end of the** `Button_Click` **event handler:**

    ```
    service.HelloWorldAsync();
    ```

20. **Press F5 or click the green Play button to run the application.**

    A button appears.

21. **Click the button to see the words** `Hello World` **display on your screen.**

Understanding Cross-Domain Security

The Silverlight plug-in for your browser runs inside the browser and is therefore subject to the same security restrictions that a browser is. One of the restrictions that is imposed on Silverlight is that it can only retrieve resources from the same domain that the Silverlight application is running on. For example, if your Silverlight application is running on `www.mydomain.com/MySilverlightApplication.aspx`, by default, the application can only access resources that have the same domain name. If you call a Web service on `www.mydomain.com/MyWebService.asmx`, it will work perfectly, exactly as it did in the previous example. However, if you hosted that exact same Web service on a different domain, you would get a cross-domain security exception, as shown in Figure 10-3.

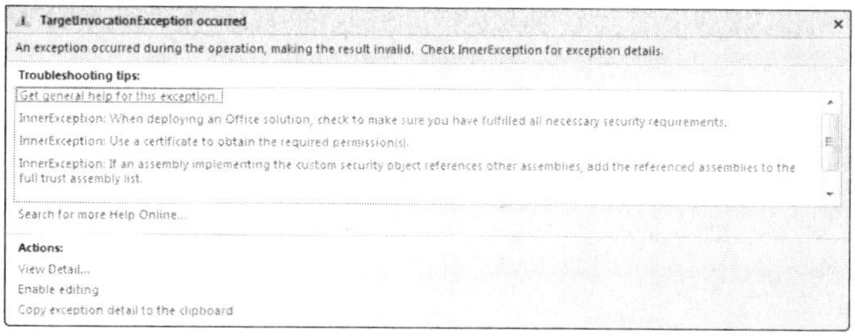

Figure 10-3: Cross-domain security.

Creating a cross-domain policy file

The Internet would be not be very useful if applications could access resources only on their own domain names. Instead, a cross-domain policy file makes it safe to use other resources. A *cross-domain policy file* is an XML file that you can add to your site to allow specific access to your resources from Silverlight applications. The following code shows a cross-domain policy file. This file must be named `crossdomainpolicy.xml`.

```
<?xml version="1.0" encoding="utf-8"?>
<access-policy>
  <cross-domain-access>
    <policy>
      <allow-from http-request-headers="*">
        <domain uri="*"/>
      </allow-from>
      <grant-to>
        <resource path="/api" include-subpaths="true"/>
      </grant-to>
    </policy>
  </cross-domain-access>
</access-policy>
```

Accessing a Web service without a cross-domain policy file

As mentioned earlier in this chapter, you don't have to simply give up on using services that Silverlight thinks you shouldn't use (in other words, services that don't have a cross-domain policy). You can use a workaround to get that important data into your application. All it takes is a little ingenuity and some knowledge of how the Silverlight .NET Framework is slightly different than its bigger brother the .NET Framework. The Silverlight .NET Framework has some built-in security restrictions that make it secure for running on your user's machine without having to worry about viruses. This means that Silverlight allows you to call only a Web service that is running on the same domain as your Silverlight application. Using this workaround does not compromise the security of your Silverlight application because the Silverlight application is still following the rules of accessing only a service that's on its own domain.

The full version of the .NET framework does not have this restriction, so you can use this fact to build a workaround for Web services with no cross-domain policy.

All you need to do to implement the workaround is to create your own Web service that runs on the same domain as your Silverlight application. You then use this Web service to call the Web service you are interested in and implement the methods you need to call from your Silverlight application. Your Silverlight application calls your new Web service, which then calls the external Web service. When your new Web service has the results, it returns the data to your Silverlight application. Voilà! You have that elusive data in your application.

Using the workaround: An example

In the following example, we take you through accessing the weather service from The Weather Channel Web site (`www.weather.com`) and downloading the weather forecast for the next four days. The Weather Channel site does not have a cross-domain policy set up, so you cannot access the service directly. To access the weather data, we show you how to build your own weather Web service that you know you can access from your Silverlight application because it runs on the same domain. This new Web service will then access The Weather Channel weather service and get the data you require for your Silverlight application. Remember that the full .NET runtime does not have the cross-domain restrictions that Silverlight has, so it can access the weather data even though there is no cross-domain policy in place.

After you have built your own weather service, you then access that service from our Silverlight application and display the weather forecast.

Before you can get started with this example, you first need to register and get an access key from `https://registration.weather.com/ursa/xmloap/step1`. It's a simple registration form that asks you for information such as your e-mail address, ZIP Code, Web site name, and so on.

After you have an access account, you're ready to get started. You do this in three steps. First, you create the new Web service and get the data from `www.weather.com`. Second, you write the XAML required to show the weather forecast data. Third, you get the data from your new service and show it in the Silverlight application.

Build the new Web service by following these steps:

1. **Open Visual Studio.**
2. **Create a new project by choosing File**➪**New Project and selecting Silverlight Application from the dialog box.**
3. **Call the new Application** SilverlightForDummiesWeatherForecast.
4. **In the Solution Explorer, right-click the SilverlightForDummiesWeatherForecast.Web project and select Add New Item from the menu that appears.**
5. **Select Web Service from the dialog box from Step 4 and call it WeatherWebService.**
6. **Delete the HelloWorld Web method.**

   This is added by default when you create a new Web service, and you don't need it here.

7. **Add a new Web method called** GetWeatherForecastXml **by adding the following code:**

   ```
   [WebMethod]
   public string GetWeatherForecastXml()
   {
   }
   ```

8. **Open a Web browser, go to** www.weather.com, **type your location into the Search box at the top of the page, and click Search.**

   In the address bar of the Web browser, you see a new address that contains the word local followed by a forward slash and then a code. This is your locality key. The locality key should look similar to this one, which is for Melbourne, Australia: ASXX0075.

9. **Declare the address of the** www.weather.com **Web service you want to access by adding the following code to the new method:**

   You need to use your own PAR, KEY, and locality for this that you were sent in the e-mail you received when you signed up for the service.

   ```
   var sUrl ="http://xoap.weather.com/weather/local/
       YOURLOCAL?=*&dayf=5&link=xoap&par=YOURPAR&key=YOURKEY&
           unit=m";
   ```

10. **Create a new** XmlDocument **object to store the result of the call to The Weather Channel Web service with the following code:**

    ```
    var xmlDoc = new XmlDocument();
    ```

11. **Load the XML from the address and return it to the method with the following code:**

    ```
    xmlDoc.Load(sUrl);
    return xmlDoc.OuterXml;
    ```

12. **Press Ctrl+Shift+B to build your solution, or press F6.**

Your new Web service is ready to go. You can try it using the following steps:

1. **Right-click the `WeatherService.asmx` file in the Solution Explorer.**
2. **Select View in Browser from the menu that appears.**

    You should see a Web page with the XML returned from the `www.weather.com` Web service.

After you've got the new Web service working, you need to write the XAML required to show the results of your Web service in your Silverlight application.

Follow these steps to create the user interface for the weather forecast:

1. **In the SilverlightForDummiesWeatherForecast project, open the `MainPage.xaml` file by double-clicking it.**
2. **Add an ItemsControl to the XAML and call it WeatherForecastList by adding the following code:**

    ```
    <ItemsControl x:Name="WeatherForecastList" >
    </ItemsControl>
    ```

3. **Add an ItemTemplate to the ItemsControl by adding the following code between the ItemsControl tags:**

    ```
    <ItemsControl.ItemTemplate>
    <DataTemplate>
    </DataTemplate>
    </ItemsControl.ItemTemplate>
    ```

4. **Add a StackPanel control inside the DataTemplate tags with the following code:**

    ```
    <StackPanel></StackPanel>
    ```

5. **Inside the StackPanel, add a TextBox control for the Day, Low Temperature, High Temperature, and Description with the following code:**

    ```
    <TextBlock Text="{Binding Day}"/>
    <StackPanel Orientation="Horizontal">
    <TextBlock Text="Low: "/>
    <TextBlock Text="{Binding TemperatureLow}"/>
    <TextBlock Text=" High: "/>
    <TextBlock Text="{Binding TemperatureHigh}"/>
    </StackPanel>
    <TextBlock Text="{Binding Description}"/>
    ```

    Notice that you are using binding again; refer to Chapter 9 for more information on binding.

6. **Add an ImageControl immediately after the last TextBlock to show the icon for the weather with the following code:**

    ```
    <Image Source="{Binding Icon}" />
    ```

 7. **Press F6 to build the solution.**

You have now built a new Web service that will access the weather forecast data from The Weather Channel Web site and have built the XAML to display the weather forecast. When you signed up to The Weather Channel Web site, you were sent an e-mail with some instructions and a .zip file that contains all of the icons used in the weather forecast. Before you write any code in the Silverlight application, you need to get those icons into the application. Follow these steps to do this:

 1. **Unzip the file you were sent.**

    You now have access to a folder called Weather Icons.

 2. **Copy the Weather Icons folder by right-clicking it and selecting Copy from the menu that appears.**

 3. **Open the SilverlightForDummiesWeatherForecast project; right-click it and select Paste from the menu that appears.**

    You now see the Weather Icons folder in your project.

You are now ready to tackle the last phase of the workaround for accessing a Web service that does not have a cross-domain policy in place. In this last phase, you create a service reference to your new Web service exactly as you did in the section on creating your own WSDL Web service. This generates the proxy classes you need to access the Web service. After you add the service reference, we show you how to write some code to call the Web service and process the returned XML data exactly as you did with the Flickr example earlier in this chapter. Then you set the ItemsSource property of the ItemsControl to the list of WeatherForecast objects we created. When this is done, you will be able to see the weather forecast in your Silverlight application.

To access your new Web service and display the results, follow these steps:

 1. **Add a new service reference to the Silverlight application by right-clicking References in the Solution Explorer inside the SilverlightForDummiesWeatherForecast project.**

    The Add Service Reference dialog box appears.

 2. **Click the Discover button.**

    This finds the WeatherWebService.

 3. **Name the service reference** WeatherServiceReference.

4. **Open the** `MainPage.xaml.cs` **file.**

5. **Find the constructor of the page that says**

   ```
   public MainPage()
   ```

6. **In the constructor, create a new WeatherServiceSoapClient by adding the following code:**

   ```
   var proxy = new WeatherServiceReference.
           WeatherServiceSoapClient();
   ```

7. **Create a new event handler for the** `GetWeatherForecastXmlCompleted` **event by typing**

   ```
   proxy.GetWeatherForecastXmlCompleted
   ```

   followed by a plus sign and an equal sign and then pressing the Tab button twice.

8. **Add a new class called** `WeatherForecast` **to the project by right-clicking the SilverlightForDummiesWeatherForecast project and choosing Add**⇨**Class.**

9. **Add the properties to the class by adding the following code inside the class:**

   ```
   public string Day { get; set; }
   public string TemperatureHigh { get; set; }
   public string TemperatureLow { get; set; }
   public string Icon { get; set; }
   public string Description { get; set; }
   ```

10. **Add a reference to** `System.Xml.Linq.dll` **by right-clicking the References node in Solution Explorer and selecting Add Reference.**

11. **Click the Browse tab and select the assembly in the folder C:\Program Files\Microsoft SDKs\Silverlight\v4.0\Libraries\Client; then click OK.**

12. **Inside the newly generated** `GetWeatherForecastXmlCompleted` **event handler, write the following LINQ statement:**

    ```
    var weatherXml = XDocument.Parse(e.Result);
    var forecast = (from f in weatherXml.
            Descendants("day")
    select new WeatherForecast{Day = f.Attribute("t").
            Value,Description = f.Element("part").
            Element("t").Value, Icon = string.Format("/
            SilverlightData;Component/Assets/WeatherIcons/
            {0}.png", f.Element("part").Element("icon").
            Value),TemperatureHigh = f.Element("hi").
            Value,TemperatureLow = f.Element("low").
            Value}).ToList();
    ```

    This code creates a list of WeatherForecast objects from the XML you got back from the Web service.

Chapter 10: Accessing Data in Silverlight

13. **Set the** `ItemsSource` **property of the WeatherForecastList control to** `forecast` **by adding the following code immediately after the code from Step 12.**

    ```
    WeatherForecastList.ItemsSource = forecast;
    ```

14. **Call the Web service by adding the following code to the end of the constructor:**

    ```
    proxy.GetWeatherForecastXmlAsync();
    ```

15. **Run the application by pressing F5 or by clicking the green Play button.**

    You should see a screen similar to the one in Figure 10-4.

You probably noticed that it takes a few seconds for the weather forecast to display. That's because it takes time to get the data from The Weather Channel Web site's service. This is a great feature of asynchronous programming: The users see your application before the data is ready, so they perceive a greater speed and thus a better user experience.

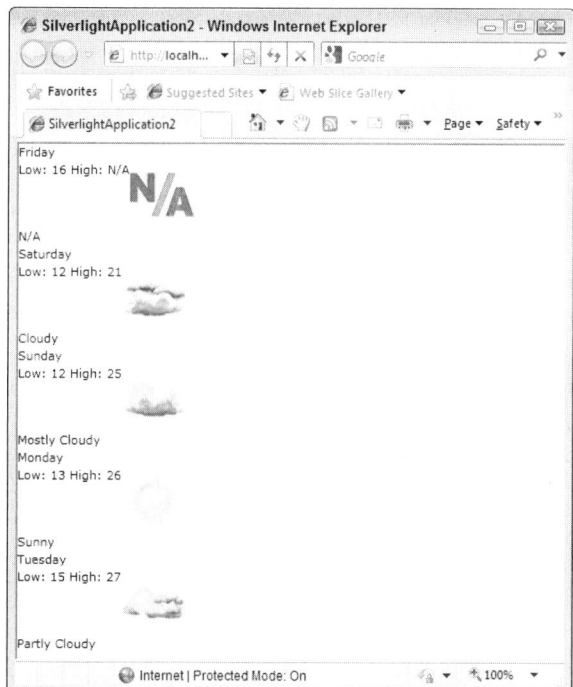

Figure 10-4: The weather forecast Web service.

Authenticating Users

When you build a Web service, you generally need some sort of method to identify the person calling the Web service. Unless your service is a free-for-all and you don't care who uses it, you should put logic in place to require your user to log in to your service. When users log in to your service, they are authenticated because you now know who they are.

ASP.NET has a built-in authentication system, which means you don't need to write your own. This makes it relatively simple to add authentication to your Web service with only a small amount of code. To use the ASP.NET authentication system, you need to add an attribute to your WeatherService class from the previous section's example to tell .NET that your class is ASP.NET-compatible. You also need to write a new method, which we call Login here, to use the ASP.NET authentication system to log in and authenticate the user.

Follow these steps to implement authentication on your WCF service:

1. **Open the SilverlightForDummiesWeatherForecast solution from the previous section.**

2. **In the Web site part of the SilverlightForDummiesWeatherForecast. Web solution, find your Web Service called WeatherService and double-click it to open it.**

3. **Near the top of the file where it says** `public class WeatherService`**, add the ASP.NET Compatibility attribute by using the following code:**

    ```
    [AspNetCompatibilityRequirements(RequirementsMode =
            AspNetCompatibilityRequirementsMode.Allowed)]
    public class WeatherService : : System.Web.Services.
            WebService
    ```

    A Web service by default does not maintain its state between requests. This means that if you set a variable in one call, it will not be set the next time you want to use it. To overcome this problem, set `AspNetCompatibilityRequirements` to `Allowed`, which then maintains the state for you by allowing the use of cookies and session states. The code in bold in the code block for this step does this for you.

4. **Open the** `WeatherService.asmx.cs` **file and implement the new** `Login` **method by adding the following code:**

    ```
    public void Login(string userName, string password)
    {if(userName=="Dummies" && password=="Dummies")
       {
       FormsAuthentication.SetAuthCookie(userName,true);
    }
    }
    ```

5. **Find the** `GetWeatherForecastXML` **method and add some logic to check whether the user is logged in. Do this by adding the code in bold to the method:**

```
public string GetWeatherForecastXml()
{      if(HttpContext.Current.User.Identity.
       IsAuthenticated)
{          const string sUrl = "http://xoap.weather.com/
           weather/local/ASXX0075?cc=*&dayf=5&link=xoap∏=
           xoap&par=your par&key=your key&unit=m";
var xmlDoc = new XmlDocument();
xmlDoc.Load(sUrl);
return xmlDoc.OuterXml;
}
else
{
       return "";
}
}
```

 6. **Build your solution by pressing Ctrl+Shift+B.**

Your weather service now implements some authentication. Now, anyone who logs in to your Web service with the username and password of `Dummies` is granted access to the service. All you need to do is modify your Silverlight application to require login. It's simple: You just need to call the `Login` method from your Silverlight application and pass it the username and password combination. The service runs the `Login` method and sets the Authentication cookie so that you can then access the service.

Follow these steps to implement the login procedure:

 1. **Open the SilverlightData project in Visual Studio.**

 2. **Update the Service Reference by right-clicking the WeatherServiceReference under the ServiceReferences folder and selecting Update Service Reference from the menu that appears.**

 3. **Find the** `Weather.xaml.cs` **file and open it by double-clicking the file.**

 4. **Declare a new variable to hold the instance of your WeatherServiceClient by adding the following code just above the** `OnNavigatedTo` **event:**

```
private WeatherServiceReference.WeatherServiceClient
        proxy;
```

 5. **Remove the** `var` **keyword from the line of code that says**

```
var proxy = new WeatherServiceReference.
        WeatherServiceClient();
```

6. **Start creating a new event handler for the new login method immediately after the line you changed in Step 5 by typing proxy followed by a period (.), and then selecting LoginCompleted from the list of options shown to you in Visual Studio, like this:**

   ```
   proxy.LoginCompleted
   ```

7. **Type a plus and then an equal sign and then press Tab twice.**

   This automatically generates the rest of the code you need for the LoginCompleted event handler. Two pieces of code are generated. One looks like this:

   ```
   proxy.LoginCompleted += new EventHandler<System.
           ComponentModel.AsyncCompletedEventArgs>(proxy_
           LoginCompleted);
   ```

   The other part looks like this:

   ```
   void proxy_LoginCompleted(object sender, System.
           ComponentModel.AsyncCompletedEventArgs e)
   {
   throw new NotImplementedException();
   }
   ```

8. **Move the line that says**

   ```
   proxy.GetWeatherForecastXmlAsync();
   ```

   from the `OnNavigatedTo` **event code to the new method** `proxy_LoginCompleted` **event.**

9. **Delete the line that says**

   ```
   throw new NotImplementedException();
   ```

10. **Call the** `Login` **method on your service by adding the following code to the** `OnNavigatedTo` **event immediately after you create the** `LoginCompleted` **event by adding the following code:**

    ```
    proxy.LoginAsync("Dummies", "Dummies");
    ```

Your final code should look like the following:

```
private WeatherWCFServiceReference.
        WeatherWCFServiceClient proxy;
protected override void OnNavigatedTo(NavigationEvent
        Args e)

{

  proxy = new WeatherServiceReference.
        WeatherServiceClient();
```

```
        proxy.GetWeatherForecastXmlCompleted += proxy_
            GetWeatherForecastXmlCompleted;

        proxy.LoginCompleted += new EventHandler<System.
            ComponentModel.AsyncCompletedEventArgs>(proxy_
            LoginCompleted);

        proxy.LoginAsync("Dummies", "Dummies");
}

void proxy_LoginCompleted(object sender, System.
        ComponentModel.AsyncCompletedEventArgs e)

{

    proxy.GetWeatherForecastXmlAsync();

}
```

You may have noticed that you moved the call to the `GetWeatherForecast` method in the completed event for the `Login`. You do this to allow the service time to actually log in before you try to call the service. If you don't do this, the asynchronous nature of Silverlight may let the GetWeatherForecast service be called before the login service. If that happens, you receive no weather forecast information.

Chapter 11

Using WCF Data Services to Store and Manage Data

In This Chapter

▶ Getting started with WCF Data Services
▶ Using WCF Data Services in a Silverlight application
▶ Tracking and saving changes
▶ Handling data concurrency
▶ How to use query and change interceptors
▶ Controlling access to entity sets

*T*his part of the book is, of course, all about connecting your Web site with the data you need to access for it, and this chapter shows you how to access data over the Internet from your Silverlight application using one of two types of Web services discussed in this part. In this chapter, that service uses The Software Formerly Known as Astoria — which now goes by the name of WCF Data Services — for data access. (The next two chapters delve into using WCF RIA Services, thereby introducing you to the next generation of data access from a Rich Internet Application [RIA]). You can use both services together, too, so you'll find it helpful to get comfortable with this chapter's material before you go on to the rest of this part.

WCF Data Services and WCF RIA Services are both free downloads from Microsoft that you need to install on the machine you use for application development. The version of WCF Data Services that this chapter is based on is the 1.5 Community Technical Preview (CTP). Microsoft releases tools such as this into the community before final release so that the company can gather community feedback from early adopters before the final product is released. The main reason for using the 1.5 CTP release is that it introduces a vital feature missing in the 1.0 release, two-way data binding. (Chapter 9 tells you about data binding.)

In this chapter, we demonstrate the use of WCF Data Services by developing a very simple blogging engine. (We use the same example in the WCF RIA Services chapters as well to highlight the differences between the two technologies.) In this chapter, you find out how to create an Entity Framework model of your data, add a WCF Data Service to your solution to access the data through the Entity Framework, and manage the data in your Silverlight application.

Getting Started with WCF Data Services

Obviously, you can't get much service out of data access technology without having a data source from which to access the data. Data sources come in various programs, such as SQL Server, SQL Server Express, Access, Oracle, MySQL, and a variety of lesser-known databases. In this chapter, the source we use for examples is Microsoft SQL Server Express (SQL Express), which you can download for free and easily install using the Web Platform Installer (WPI). The WPI is a common installation tool for a lot of great platforms, tools, and applications. It makes installing these applications, including SQL Express, very simple.

After you've established a place to store your data, you need to design the database tables for your blogging engine. Two tables in the blogging engine are created for the example in this chapter, as follows:

- Post: For storing blog posts
- Comment: For storing comment posts

Note that the table names are singular, not plural, even though it might seem more logical to make them plural. We make them singular for two reasons. One is that it is a best practice in database design to use singular names for database tables. Also, to access your data from a Silverlight application using WCF Data Services, you need one more piece of the puzzle: the ADO.NET Entity Framework.

The ADO.NET Entity Framework allows you to develop your application against a representation of a data source rather than the actual data source. This means that you end up writing less code because the Entity Framework classes that are generated for you by Visual Studio do a lot of the heavy lifting for you, leaving you to concentrate on the interesting parts of your application.

When you use WCF Data Services with ADO.NET Entity Framework in Visual Studio, the tools automatically generate a set of proxy classes based on the design of the database. So, for example, the Post and Comment tables

Chapter 11: Using WCF Data Services to Store and Manage Data

will generate code that has `Posts` and `Comments` collections of `Post` and `Comment` objects. The letter *s* appended to the name of the table in the database is part of the process of generating the Entity Framework class code. Therefore, if you had called a table `Posts`, as is a common way to name a table, the code generator would create a collection of `Posts` objects. Plus it would name the collection of these `Posts` objects `Postss` because it adds an *s* to the name of the `Posts` table to generate the collection name. This is the second reason for naming your database tables correctly when using ADO. NET Entity Framework.

A *proxy class* is a class that is generated on the client side of the application but that represents a server-side class.

To recap, SQL Server Express contains a database. You then create a set of classes with Visual Studio that represents those database tables by adding an Entity Framework to the project. After you have created those classes, you use WCF Data Services to generate the client-side proxy classes that you use in your application to access the data.

What, Exactly, Is WCF Data Services?

When you build a Silverlight application, 99.9 percent of the time you will be interacting with a database to store and update data. Even simple applications such as a blogging engine require numerous operations to be useful. At a minimum, the blogging engine needs the ability to create a new `Post` entry, update a `Post` entry, read a `Post`, and delete a `Post`. These operations — CREATE, READ, UPDATE, and DELETE — are commonly referred to as CRUD operations and are generally needed for every table in your database no matter what the application is for. So you can see that the number of operations can get quite large very quickly.

After you have your database established, you have to give it a way to interact with your database from your Silverlight application. It's nowhere near the database; instead, it sits on a user's machine, running in the browser. Therefore, you need some sort of Web service to connect your data with your application across the Internet. Several technologies are available that are designed to help you do this, as follows:

- **Simple Web services:** In Microsoft land, these are called ASMX Web services, and files used with these services have an `.asmx` extension. We talk about these extensively in Chapter 10.

- **Windows Communication Foundation (WCF) Services:** This is a more advanced set of Web services that allows you to provide security and reliability more easily than you can using ASMX Web services.

- **Java Script Object Notation (JSON):** This provides serialization services. JSON is a text-based way to describe an object and its property values so that the object can be sent over a Web service and translated at the other end.

Each of these types of technology allows you to make a call to the backend server to perform the CRUD operations. The downside to each of these services, however, is that for every single different operation, such as `CreatePost`, `UpdatePost`, `ReadPost`, and `DeletePost`, you need to create a method in your service and then call it explicitly from your application. You also have to write a separate method to return a list of `Posts` ordered by date and a separate method to return the `Posts` ordered by title. So you can imagine that for an application of any complexity, the number of methods you need to write and maintain gets to be quite a heavy workload.

Of course, we wouldn't be telling you all of this unless we had a way to make your life easier. Enter WCF Data Services, which makes handling CRUD operations — and others that we get into later — much easier and simpler to maintain than do the services described previously. WCF Data Services uses what's called a RESTful interface. REST, which stands for Representational State Transfer, works by defining an address for your service and passing that service a query. This way, the service itself can figure out what you want returned. The great advantage of this method is that you don't need to write all those CRUD operations on the server side anymore; you can simply pass a query to the service and be returned a result.

For example, the URL `http://host/service.svc/Posts?$orderby=Date` would return all the `Posts` ordered by the `Date` property. But you don't have to write a special method on the service to make this happen; instead, the service itself creates the method and interrogates the data source itself. You can also use a URL such as `http://host/service.svc/Posts(5)`, which would return the `Post` with a unique identifier of 5. When you design a database table, there will be a primary key that uniquely identifies the row in the database; this is the key that is being referred to here.

Don't worry too much about these URLs, because you won't see them unless you are accessing the service directly through a browser. Silverlight hides this complexity and makes it very easy to use WCF Data Services.

Both of these URLs will return an XML document with all the data you need, as shown in Figure 11-1. Again, don't worry too much about the complexity of this document; Silverlight uses this data to make it very easy for you to program against the WCF Data Service.

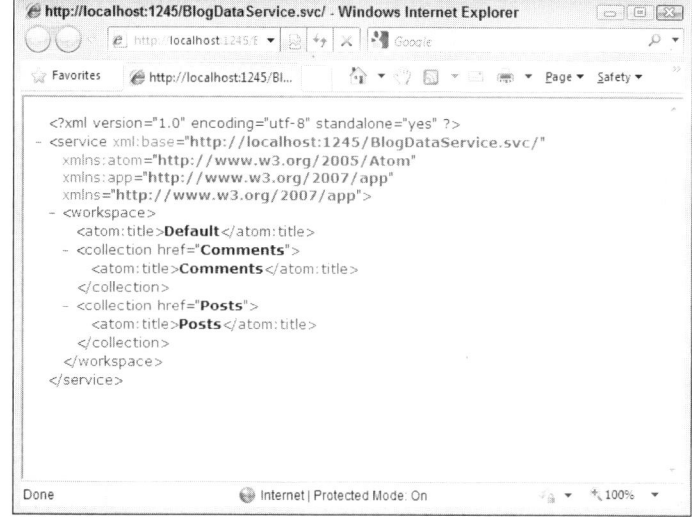

Figure 11-1: WCF Data Service in a Web browser.

The example we take you through in this chapter shows you how to query your data source using WCF Data Services, which is the equivalent of the READ operation we discussed previously. But what about the others? Well, another really elegant part of the story is that the four operations for CRUD just happen to correspond beautifully with the well-known verbs of standard HTTP. These are GET, PUT, POST, and DELETE, and the following table shows how the CRUD operations of CREATE, READ, UPDATE, and DELETE correspond to the HTTP verbs of PUT, GET, POST, and DELETE.

Database Operation	HTTP Verb
CREATE	PUT
READ	GET
UPDATE	POST
DELETE	DELETE

And the story just gets better. Because you use HTTP for all your request operations, you can employ all the standard HTTP header tags in the response message from the server to do things such as return error messages from your database. You can also manage data concurrency issues (which we look at in detail a little later in this chapter).

Creating a WCF Data Service

The preceding sections of this chapter briefly discuss the different parts of the application's structure and how they work. Now you can start building a sample application.

In this section, we show you how to do the following:

1. Create a database to store the data.
2. Add the ADO.NET Entity Framework and WCF Data Service to the Web application part of the Silverlight application. (Remember that Visual Studio automatically adds a Web application when you create a new Silverlight Application.)
3. Create the proxy classes for a Silverlight application.

    After you have those proxy classes in place, you can then start to write some code to manipulate the data in the database.

Creating the database

In this part, we show you how to create a new database, add two tables to it, and add a set of columns to each table. After you have the tables in place, you see how to tell SQL Server how the tables relate to each other to form a relational database.

Creating the database

To create the database, follow these steps:

1. **Open SQL Server Express Management Studio.**
2. **In the left pane, called the Object Explorer, right-click Databases and choose New Database.**
3. **Set the name to Silverlight For Dummies.**
4. **Click OK.**

Adding the tables

You add tables as follows:

1. **Click the plus sign next to the newly created database.**
2. **Right-click Tables and select New Table.**
3. **In the Column Name field, type Id.**

4. In the Data Type column, select `int`.
5. Deselect the check box for the Allow Nulls column.
6. To the left of where you added Id, right-click and choose Set Primary Key from the menu that appears.
7. In the Column Properties pane at the bottom of the screen, click the plus sign next to Identity Specification.
8. Change the `Is Identity` property to Yes.
9. Add another column to the table by clicking in the next row down, underneath where you added Id, and call this column Title.
10. Set the Title column's Data Type to `nvarchar(50)`.
11. Set the Allow Nulls property to Off.
12. Add another column, call it Content, set its Data Type to `ntext`, and set Allow Nulls to Off.
13. Add a column called Date, set its Data Type to `datetime`, and set Allow Nulls to Off.
14. Click the Save button and name the table `Post`.
15. Create another table by right-clicking Tables and selecting New Table.
16. Follow Steps 7 to 12 to add an Id column to the new table.
17. Add another column, call it Comment, set its Data Type to `ntext`, and set Allow Nulls to Off.
18. Add a column called Date, set its Data Type to `datetime`, and set Allow Nulls to Off.
19. Add a final column, call it PostId, set its Data Type to `int`, and set Allow Nulls to Off.
20. Click the Save button and call the table Comment.

Create the relationship between the tables

Follow these steps to create table relationships:

1. In the Object Explorer, right-click Database Diagrams and select New Database Diagram to create the relationship.

   The Add Table dialog box appears, with an option to create support objects.

2. Click Yes to create support objects.
3. In the Add Table dialog box, double-click the Post and Comment tables.

   These tables are added to the design surface behind the dialog box.

4. Click OK.

5. **Click your mouse and hold it down on top of the PostId column in the Comment table; then drag it on top of the Id column on the Post table and release.**

    The relationship is created for you.

 6. **Click the Save button and leave the default name as is for the diagram.**

 7. **Click OK.**

 8. **Press F6 to build your solution.**

    You now have the two tables related to each other by the `PostId` in the Comment table and the `Id` field in the Post table (see Figure 11-2).

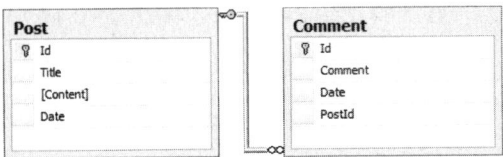

Figure 11-2: SQL Server Express database diagram for the Post and Comment tables.

Adding the ADO.NET Entity Framework

To perform this part of the process, you need a new Silverlight application that you build with Visual Studio 2010. We are using Visual Studio because it's the tool of choice for building Web services and other code-related tasks. Expression Blend is more suitable for design- and interaction-oriented tasks.

 1. **Open Visual Studio.**

 2. **Choose File➪New Project➪Silverlight Application.**

 3. **Name the project SilverlightForDummiesWCFDataServices.**

 4. **In the next dialog box, leave the default values as they are and click OK.**

Now that you have a standard Silverlight application started, it's a good time to add the ADO.NET Entity Framework classes to the application. To do so, follow these steps:

 1. **Locate the Web Application part of the Visual Studio solution in the Solution Explorer window.**

    If you left the defaults in the previous task, the Web Application part of the solution will be at the bottom of the window.

2. **Right-click the project called** `SilverlightForDummiesWCFData Services.Web` **and select Add New Item.**

 3. **Select ADO.NET Entity Data Model.**

 4. **In the Name text box at the bottom of the dialog box, enter** BlogModel. edmx, **as shown in Figure 11-3, and click the Add button.**

    Clicking the Add button starts the Entity Data Model Wizard.

Figure 11-3: The dialog box for adding new entity framework classes.

 5. **In the Entity Data Model Wizard, select Generate from Database.**

 6. **Click the Next button.**

    The Data Connection screen appears, showing your database selected by default.

 7. **In the data connection drop-down list, select Silverlight For Dummies.**

    This should be selected by default.

 8. **At the bottom of the dialog box, enter** `BlogEntities` **as the name of the Entity Data Model, as shown in Figure 11-4.**

 9. **Click the plus sign next to the word Tables.**

    This expands the list of tables in your database, allowing you to select the tables for which you want to generate an Entity Framework.

10. **Select the Post and Comment tables.**

11. **Click Finish.**

    Visual Studio generates a model from the tables you selected.

12. **Locate the file** `BlogModel.edmx` **and double-click it to see the model of the database tables.**

    You see the Entity Data Model design surface in Visual Studio, which looks like Figure 11-5.

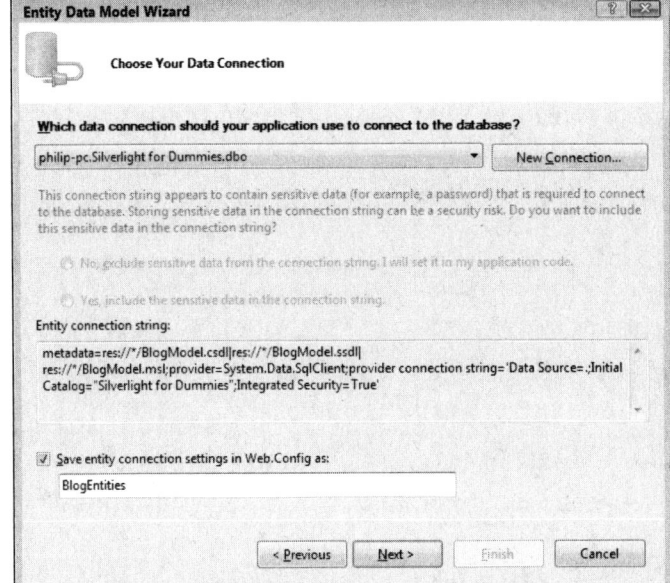

Figure 11-4: Entity Data Model Wizard showing the Entity Name step of the wizard.

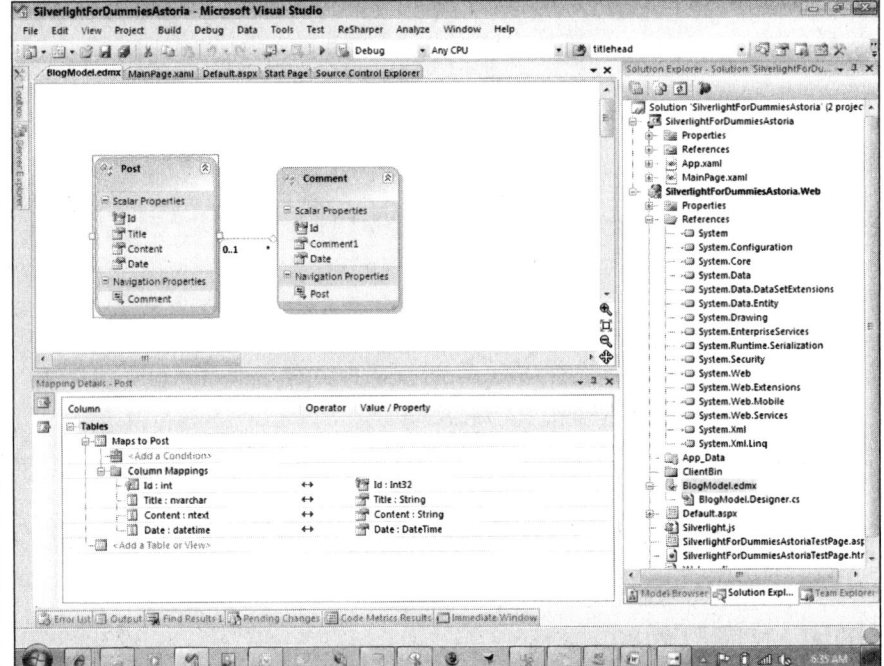

Figure 11-5: Entity Data Model design surface.

Looking at the figure, you're probably thinking that it looks just like the tables in the database. Well, it does — except for a couple of things. Have a close look at the bottom of the Post object and you'll see the word Comment; also, at the bottom of the Comment object is the word Post. These are the navigation properties that tell the entity model what the relationship is between the two objects.

Just below the two objects is the Mapping Details section. In this section, you can modify the default settings of the wizard. You can change which field maps to which other field; also, you can edit the names of the fields. Click the button in the red circle (see Figure 11-6, although you can't see the red here, of course) to set up the model to use stored procedures in the database, thereby taking care of all the data access. But hang on a minute: Where's the function to just read the data? To set that up, you need to import your stored procedure and associate it to a function. We don't go into that here, however, because we use the Entity Model to generate any database access code we need (and because using stored procedures is outside the scope of this book).

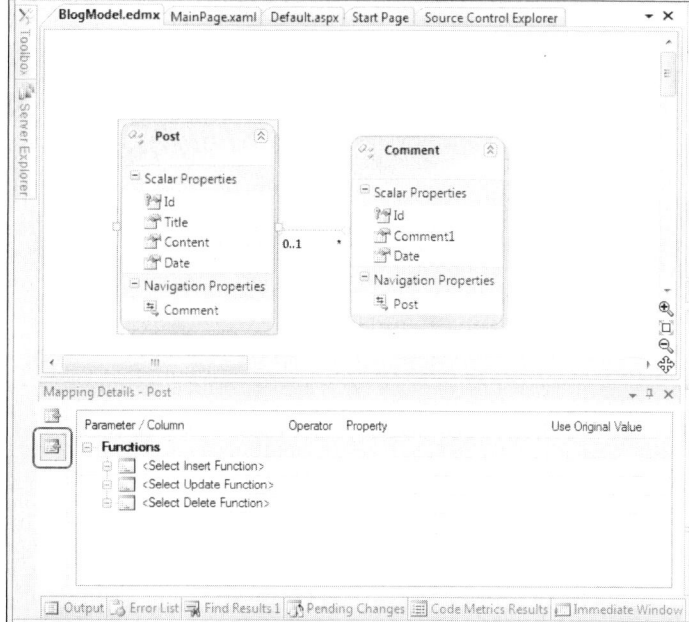

Figure 11-6: Entity Data Model mapping details.

Adding the WCF Data Service

At the beginning of the chapter, we discuss using services to interact with the database and how this ability to interact is necessary because the Silverlight application runs inside the browser, not on the server as a typical Web page

Part III: Connecting with Data

does. The Silverlight application has to be able to "talk" to the server, which means that it needs to communicate across the Internet from the user's computer to the backend server. This is where the WCF Data Service comes in. Adding that service is easy; just follow these steps:

1. **Right-click the Web project and select Add New Item.**

   The Add New Item dialog box appears.

2. **Select WCF Data Service and name it BlogService.svc, as shown in Figure 11-7.**

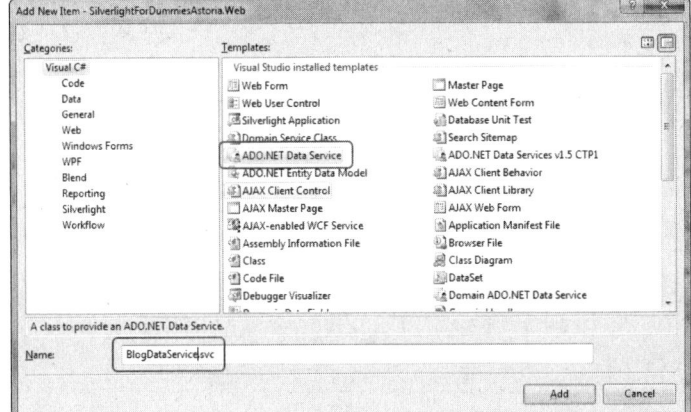

Figure 11-7: Adding the WCF Data Service.

As you've probably noticed, the service name that you're adding here has an .svc extension. This is because WCF Data Services are actually a type of WCF Service. That's a good thing, too, because they have the good security, reliability, and configurability of WCF Services.

3. **Open the `BlogService.svc.cs` file by double-clicking it in the Solution Explorer.**

4. **Locate the following line of code in that file:**

   ```
   /* TODO: put your data source class name here */
   ```

5. **You use the preceding line to define the entities that the service will interact with, so to fill out this line, open the `BlogModel.designer.cs` file and look at the line containing the class definition:**

   ```
   public partial class BlogEntities : global::System.Data.Objects.
           ObjectContext
   ```

Chapter 11: Using WCF Data Services to Store and Manage Data

6. **All the entities you need to interact with are contained in this class, so go back to the** `BlogService.svc.cs` **file and type** BlogEntities **in place of the** `TODO` **section.**

   If you remove the `/* TODO: put your data source class name here */` text and start typing **Blog**, Visual Studio IntelliSense will show you a list of options for completing the class name `BlogEntities`. You can then select BlogEntities from the list and press Tab.

7. **In the** `BlogService.svc.cs` **file, you can see that there are two commented-out lines below the word Examples. Uncomment them by removing the // from the beginning of each line.**

   You can do this easily by selecting both lines and pressing Ctrl+K+U.

8. **At this point, you are not going to restrict the use of the Entity Sets or Service Operations, so change** `MyEntitySet` **to an asterisk (*) and change** `EntitySetRights` **to All. Then change** `MyServiceOperation` **to an asterisk (*).**

   We return to this topic a bit later, in "Controlling Access to Entity Sets," to refine your application access strategy.

Using the WCF Data Service in a Silverlight Application

The previous section shows you how to set up everything needed to access the database via WCF Data Services on the server. In this section, we show you how to interact with the database from your Silverlight application.

Generating the proxy classes in the Silverlight application

In this section, you find out how to create the proxy classes inside the Silverlight application. Creating proxy classes makes it very easy for you to program against the functionality of the WCF Data Service described in the previous section. Even though the WCF Data Service is on the server, the generated proxy classes are part of the Silverlight application. Visual Studio generates the proxy classes for you when you add a Service Reference to the Silverlight application. A *Service Reference* is similar to a normal reference except that instead of referencing a local assembly such as System.Net, you add a reference, such as `http://localhost:80/ BlogService.svc`, to a service.

To add a Service Reference, follow these steps:

1. **With your `SilverlightForDummiesWCFDataServices` Silverlight project open, locate the node in the Visual Studio Solution Explorer called References.**

    You find that node just under the project name `SilverlightForDummies WCFDataServices`.

2. **Right-click that node and select Add Service Reference.**

3. **Click Discover.**

    The services in your solution appear in a drop-down list. If all goes well and you created the `BlogService.svc` we describe in the previous section, that file appears in the Address drop-down list. (It's in the Services section. If you don't see this file, Visual Studio can't find it. Try again by pressing Ctrl+Shift+B or choosing Build➪Rebuild Solution.)

4. **Click the + (plus sign) next to `BlogService.svc` to expand it (see Figure 11-8).**

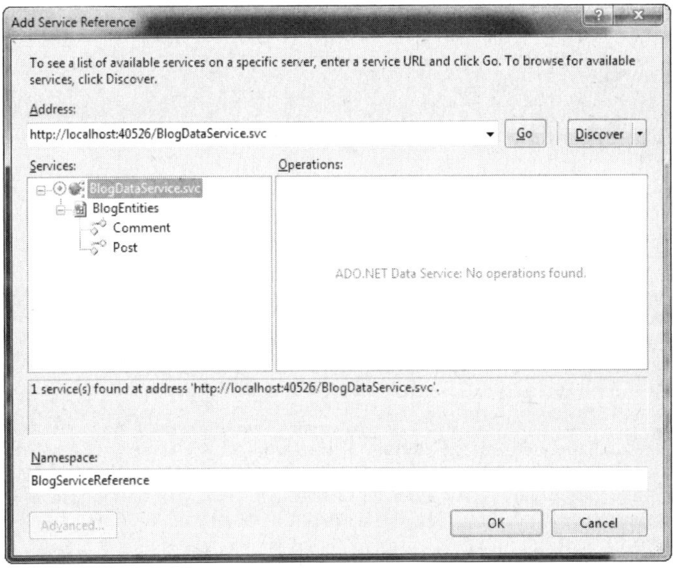

Figure 11-8: Adding the Service Reference.

Here's what just happened when you created the Service Reference. Several times, we have referred to proxy classes, and those are what we want you to look at now. To do so, click the Silverlight Application project and then select the Show All Files option so that you can see the hidden files. Now expand the Service References folder and then the BlogServiceReference; under that, you see more files. Open all the folders so that you see what's shown in Figure 11-9. If you don't see all the files shown, choose Project➪Show All Files.

The `Reference.datasvcmap` file contains information about where the service is located. It also has some meta data about the Entity Framework model.

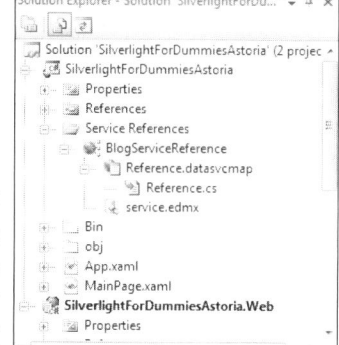

Figure 11-9: Investigating the proxy classes.

The `Reference.cs` file defines three classes:

- `BlogEntities`
- `Post`
- `Comment`

`Post` and `Comment` represent the objects you will be working with, and `BlogEntities` is the parent class that allows you to work with these objects. Note that one of the properties of the `Post` class is a collection of `Comment` objects. This makes sense because there is a one-to-many relationship between Post and Comment. A one-to-many relationship means that for any one `Post` record in the database, there can be many `Comment` records. As you would expect, the `Comment` class has a `Post` property, as well.

Reading data from the database

To read data from your database, you need to have at least a few records to read! So if you have a database already established, you can use that, or manually add a few records to both the Post and Comment tables from the blog example in this chapter.

You use the `BlogEntities` class to query the service for the data you need for your application. To use this class, you first have to create a new instance of it, which is called the *context*. Then you tell Silverlight both what to do when it has finished reading the data and to actually read the data. (If this sounds confusing, remember that all actions on services from Silverlight are asynchronous, so you have to tell it what to do when finished before you tell it to start; otherwise, your application won't know what to do when it has the data.)

The next steps will seem familiar to you if you have read Chapter 10. To read some data from the database with WCF Data Services, follow these steps:

1. **In the `SilverlightForDummiesWCFDataServices` project, open the `MainPage.xaml.cs` file by double-clicking it in the Solution Explorer.**

2. **Find the following piece of code:**

   ```
   public partial class MainPage : UserControl
   {
   ```

   This is the class declaration.

3. **Immediately after the beginning brace ({), create a new Context object by adding the following code:**

   ```
   private BlogEntities _ctx = new BlogEntities(new
           Uri("BlogDataService.svc", UriKind.Relative));
   ```

4. **Open the `MainPage.xaml` file by double-clicking it in the Solution Explorer.**

5. **At the top of the file is the `UserControl` header. Immediately after `<UserControl`, type a space and then start typing the word *Loaded*.**

   A feature of Visual Studio called IntelliSense springs into action when you begin typing. IntelliSense is a tool to help you write better code faster by giving you the options available at that point in the code. Use this feature often to be more productive in Visual Studio.

6. **Select the word Loaded from the IntelliSense list.**

7. **Type an equal sign.**

8. **Select <Add New Event Handler> from the IntelliSense list that appears.**

9. **Right-click `UserControl_Loaded` and select Navigate to Event Handler from the IntelliSense options that appear.**

   The `MainPage.xaml.cs` opens and goes to the newly created event handler for `UserControl_Loaded` (see Figure 11-10).

10. **Inside the `UserControl_Loaded` event handler, create a LINQ query by adding the following code to the event handler:**

    ```
    private void UserControl_Loaded(object sender,
            RoutedEventArgs e)
    {
        var query = (from p in _ctx.Post select p);
        var dq = (query) as DataServiceQuery<Post>;
        dq.BeginExecute(PostsLoaded, dq);
    }
    ```

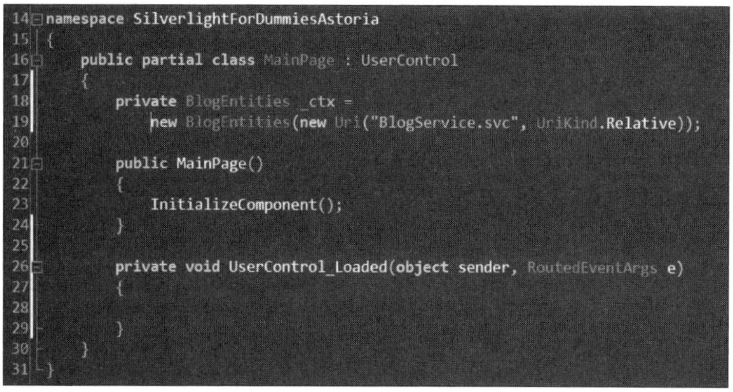

Figure 11-10:
The `Loaded` event and context declaration.

```
namespace SilverlightForDummiesAstoria
{
    public partial class MainPage : UserControl
    {
        private BlogEntities _ctx =
            new BlogEntities(new Uri("BlogService.svc", UriKind.Relative));

        public MainPage()
        {
            InitializeComponent();
        }

        private void UserControl_Loaded(object sender, RoutedEventArgs e)
        {

        }
    }
}
```

The first line creates a query that asks for all the `Post` objects in the database. The second line creates a `DataServiceQuery` object that will return a list of `Post` objects. The third line indicates that all the `Post` objects in the database should be returned to the `PostsLoaded` method when the query is finished.

11. **Create a new method called** `PostsLoaded` **by adding the following code directly after the** `UserControl_Loaded` **event handler:**

    ```
    private void PostsLoaded(IAsyncResult ar)
    {
    }
    ```

    The `IAsynchResult` is the parameter passed back from the WCF Data Service when you call the following code in the `UserControl_Loaded` event:

    ```
    dq.BeginExecute(PostsLoaded, dq);
    ```

12. **Retrieve the query from the** `IAsynchResult` **returned to the** `PostsLoaded` **method** WCF Data Service **by adding the following code:**

    ```
    private void PostsLoaded(IAsyncResult ar)
    {
        var query = (DataServiceQuery<Post>)ar.AsyncState;
    }
    ```

13. **Extract the list of** `Post` **objects from the** `IAsynchResult` **object by adding the following code:**

    ```
    private void PostsLoaded(IAsyncResult ar)
    {
        var query = (DataServiceQuery<Post>)ar.AsyncState;
        var entities = query.EndExecute(ar).ToList();
    }
    ```

Part III: Connecting with Data

14. **Open the `MainPage.xaml` file by double-clicking it in the Solution Explorer.**

15. **Add a DataGrid control to the XAML between the Grid tags by adding the following code:**

    ```
    <Grid x:Name="LayoutRoot" Background="White">
        <data:DataGrid x:Name="PostsDataGrid">
            </data:DataGrid>
    </Grid>
    ```

16. **Set the `ItemsSource` property of the DataGrid control to the entities you retrieved from the database in Step 13 by adding the following code to the end of the `PostsLoaded` event (added in Step 11):**

    ```
    private void PostsLoaded(IAsyncResult ar)
    {
        var query = (DataServiceQuery<Post>)ar.AsyncState;
        var entities = query.EndExecute(ar).ToList();
        PostsDataGrid.ItemsSource = entities;
    }
    ```

17. **Run the application by pressing F5 or clicking the green Play button.**

    There you have it; your Silverlight application should now retrieve the `Posts` and show them in the DataGrid control. You should get a result similar to the one shown in Figure 11-11.

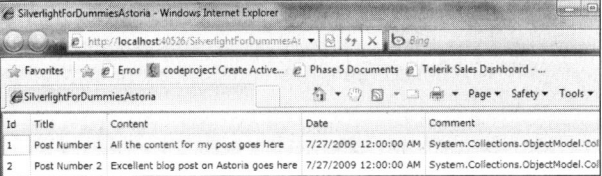

Figure 11-11: Posts showing in the DataGrid.

In a nutshell, here's what you accomplish with the preceding steps: In the `UserControl_Loaded` event, you create a query object that is cast into a `DataServiceQuery` of type `Post`. This step turns a normal LINQ query into a `DataServiceQuery`, which is the type of object you need to be able to call the WCF Data Service. If you put a break point on the next line and check the value of `dq`, you see that it is the URL {`http://localhost:40526/BlogDataService.svc/Post()`}.Entering that URL into a browser would display the resulting list of Posts from the database.

After the `DataServiceQuery` is set up, you start the execution by calling `BeginExecute` and passing it the Data Service Query and the method to call when it has finished querying the database The last line of code in Step 10 calls the `BeginExecute` method on the `DataServiceQuery` object.

The `PostsLoaded` method fires when the query has finished and the data service is ready to show you the results. In the preceding steps, `DataServiceQuery` of type `Post` comes from the Asynchronous result and runs `EndExecute` on it.

To get the LINQ query to execute and return a result, you call the `ToList()` method (see Step 13). You then set the `PostsDataGrid ItemsSource` property to the entities list that appears as a result Step 13.

Excellent — you can now query your Post table via WCF Data Services! But we can hear you saying, "How do I get the comments to show?" You can load all the comments for each post in one query and then use another DataGrid control to show those comments. To do so, you use the `Expand` command. Follow these steps to load the comments for each post in the database:

1. **Open the `MainPage.xaml.cs` file by double-clicking it in the Solution Explorer.**
2. **Find the `UserControl_Loaded` event.**
3. **Locate the following line of code:**

    ```
    var query = (from p in _ctx.Post select p);
    ```

4. **Change that line of code to the following:**

    ```
    var query = (from p in _ctx.Post.Expand("Comments")
            select p);
    ```

5. **Open the `MainPage.xaml` file by double-clicking it in the Solution Explorer.**
6. **Add a StackPanel control inside the `Grid` tags by adding the following bolded code:**

    ```
    <Grid x:Name="LayoutRoot" Background="White">
        <StackPanel></StackPanel>
    </Grid>
    ```

7. **Highlight the XAML for the existing PostsDataGrid control and drag it inside the StackPanel control tags.**

    ```
    <Grid x:Name="LayoutRoot" Background="White">
        <StackPanel>
            <my:DataGrid x:Name="PostsDataGrid" >
            </my:DataGrid>
        </StackPanel>
    </Grid>
    ```

You need to use a StackPanel control when you add more than one control to the page so that the controls do not draw over the top of each other.

8. **Add a new DataGrid control directly below the PostsDataGrid control by adding the following bolded code:**

```
<Grid x:Name="LayoutRoot" Background="White">
    <StackPanel>
        <my:DataGrid x:Name="PostsDataGrid" >
        </my:DataGrid>
        <my:DataGrid x:Name="CommentsDataGrid">
        </my:DataGrid>
    </StackPanel>
</Grid>
```

9. **Add a** `SelectionChanged` **event to the PostsDataGrid control by adding the code in bold to it:**

```
<data:DataGrid x:Name="PostsDataGrid"
        SelectionChanged="PostsDataGrid_
        SelectionChanged"></data:DataGrid>
```

10. **Right-click the words** PostsDataGrid_SelectionChanged **and select Navigate to Event Handler in the IntelliSense context menu that shows up.**

    The `MainPage.xaml.cs` file opens, showing the code that Visual Studio automatically added for the new event handler. The code looks like this:

```
private void PostsDataGrid_SelectionChanged(object
        sender, SelectionChangedEventArgs e)
{
}
```

11. **Add the following code to set the** `ItemsSource` **property of the new CommentsDataGrid control to the** `Comment` **property of the selected** `Post` **item in the PostsDataGrid control when a user clicks the grid:**

```
private void PostsDataGrid_SelectionChanged(object
        sender, SelectionChangedEventArgs e)
{
    CommentsDataGrid.ItemsSource = ((Post)
        PostsDataGrid.SelectedItem).Comments;
}
```

12. **Run the application by pressing F5 or clicking the green Play button.**

13. **Click a** `Post` **item in the PostsDataGrid control and watch how the CommentsDataGrid changes to the list of comments associated to that post in the database.**

Updating data in the database

After the data grids for the posts and comments show the information in the database, you need to be able to keep any changes a user makes to this data in your application. The data grids make it very easy for a user to make changes. If a user types something into one of the grids, the data is changed in your Silverlight application but is not saved to the database. If the user navigates away from your Silverlight application, the changes he or she made are not stored.

To make sure that the application saves any changes a user makes to the data in the PostsDataGrid, add a Button control to the StackPanel. Then add a `Click` event to the Button, use the `BeginSaveChanges` method on the data context, and provide a callback method for when the `SaveChanges` method has finished. Follow these steps to implement data saving:

1. **Open the Visual Studio solution called** `SilverlightForDummies WCFDataServices`.

2. **Open the** `MainPage.xaml` **file by double-clicking it in the Solution Explorer.**

3. **Inside the bottom of the StackPanel control, add a new Button control by adding the following code that appears in bold:**

   ```
   <StackPanel>
       <data:DataGrid x:Name="PostsDataGrid"
           SelectionChanged="PostsDataGrid_
           SelectionChanged"></data:DataGrid>
       <data:DataGrid x:Name="CommentsDataGrid"></
           data:DataGrid>
       <Button Click="Button_Click" Content="Save"/>
   </StackPanel>
   ```

4. **Right-click** `Button_Click` **and select Navigate to Event Handler in the drop-down list that appears.**

   The automatically added code looks like this:

   ```
   private void Button_Click(object sender,
           RoutedEventArgs e)
   {
   }
   ```

5. **Inside the event handler, call the** `BeginSaveChanges` **method of the data context you created previously (Step 4) with the following code:**

   ```
   private void Button_Click(object sender,
           RoutedEventArgs e)
   {
       _ctx.BeginSaveChanges(SaveChangesOptions.Batch,
           Save_Complete, null);
   }
   ```

6. **Create a new method called** `Save_Complete` **as the callback method for the** `BeginSaveChanges` **method by adding the following code:**

   ```
   private void Save_Complete(IAsyncResult result)
   {
   }
   ```

7. **Add a Boolean variable called** `succeeded` **and set it to true inside the** `Save_Complete` **method by adding the following code:**

   ```
   private void Save_Complete(IAsyncResult result)
   {
       var succeeded = true;
   }
   ```

   The succeeded variable is going to be used to test whether the Save operation was successful and used to display the appropriate message to the user.

8. **Add the following code to add a try-catch block that sets the success Boolean variable to false if an error occurs when you try to save:**

   ```
   private void Save_Complete(IAsyncResult result)
   {
       var succeeded = true;
       try
       {
       }
       catch (Exception ex)
       {
           Debug.WriteLine(string.Concat("Save
           Operation Threw an Exception: ", ex));
           succeeded = false;
       }
   }
   ```

   This code also writes the exception to the Output window. You can see the Output window in Visual Studio by choosing View➪Output.

9. **Add the following code that appears in bold to extract the response from the** `IAsynchResult` **parameter that is passed back to the** `Save_Complete` **method inside the** `try` **part of the try-catch block by the** `BeginSaveChanges` **method:**

   ```
   try
   {
       var response = _ctx.EndSaveChanges(result);
   }
   catch (Exception ex)
   {
       succeeded = false;
   }
   ```

Chapter 11: Using WCF Data Services to Store and Manage Data

10. **Process the response and check it for errors by adding the following code to the `try` section of the try-catch block directly under the line you added in Step 9:**

    ```
    foreach (var opResponse in response)
    {
        if (opResponse.Error != null)
        {
            Debug.WriteLine(string.Concat("Failed to save: ", opResponse.StatusCode));
            succeeded = false;
        }
    }
    ```

11. **Check the `succeeded` Boolean variable and display a MessageBox dialog box showing the success or failure of the Save operation by adding the following code after the try-catch block.**

    ```
    if (succeeded)
        MessageBox.Show("Saved!");
    else
        MessageBox.Show("Failed to save!");
    ```

12. **Build the solution by pressing F6.**

13. **Run the application by pressing F5 or clicking the green Play button.**

14. **Click in the PostsDataGrid control and change the title of a post.**

15. **Click the Save button.**

16. **Click the refresh button for your browser (or press F5, which works as a refresh command for most browsers).**

    A message box pops up with `Saved!` in it.

When you run the application with this function included, after you edit the content of a post in the data grid and click the Save button, you should see a message box appear. However, when you check the database or refresh the page to see whether the change was saved, you find that it's not there. That's because the `Context` object that you're using to read and save changes does not know that you edited the data in the data grid. By default, the `Context` object does not track its own changes. To remedy this problem, you need to make sure that the `Context` object knows that a change has been made each time you edit a property of one of the `Post` objects.

The `Post` class generated by Visual Studio when you add the Service Reference is called a partial class. With a partial class, you can create another partial class called `Post` and add extra functionality to the `Post` class without touching the generated class. You need to do it this way because if you update the Service Reference without creating a partial class, the `Post` class will be generated again and any changes you made to it will be lost.

Follow these steps to make sure that the Context object knows that changes have been made to it and that it should track those changes for saving to the database:

1. **In Visual Studio, show all the files in the solution by choosing Project⇨Show All Files.**
2. **Right-click the** SilverlightForDummiesWCFDataServices **project and select Add Class from the context menu that appears.**
3. **Name the class** Post **and click OK.**
4. **Wrap the new** Post **class in a namespace by adding the following code:**

    ```
    namespace SilverlightForDummiesWCFDataServices.
            BlogServiceReference
    {
        public partial class Post
        {

        }
    }
    ```

    This namespace has to be the same as the one in the generated code so that the extra functionality you add here is available to the application.

5. **Add the following code to inherit the new** Post **class from** INotify PropertyChanged **so that any time a change is made to the class by the user, the class is notified:**

    ```
    public partial class Post : INotifyPropertyChanged
    {
    }
    ```

6. **Click** INotifyPropertyChanged **and then press Ctrl+. (period).**

    The context menu for implementing the interface appears.

7. **Select Implement Interface INotifyPropertyChanged from the context menu.**

    The code you need to implement the INotifyPropertyChanged interface is automatically added. This interface has one public event called PropertyChanged that must be implemented, which is how you notify the Context object that one of the Post objects has been changed by the user.

8. **Add the following code to add a method that will handle the notification of the change made to the** Post **object:**

    ```
    private void FirePropertyChanged(string propertyName)
    {
        var handler = PropertyChanged;
        if (handler != null)
            handler(this, new PropertyChangedEventArgs
                (propertyName));
    }
    ```

Chapter 11: Using WCF Data Services to Store and Manage Data

A Public event is added to the `Post` class that you can access in your Silverlight application to tell the `Context` object whenever a change happens to the `Post` object.

9. **Track whenever a change is made to the title of a post by adding the following code:**

    ```
    partial void OnTitleChanged()
    {
      FirePropertyChanged("Title");
    }
    ```

    The method `OnTitleChanged` is one of the methods generated by Visual Studio when the Service Reference is added. It has no code, so it does nothing in the generated `Post` class. You can add some logic to tell the `Context` that the `Title` has been changed and it should keep track of that change. This method fires the `PropertyChanged` event on the `Post` object whenever the title of a post is changed.

10. **Open the `MainPage.xaml.cs` file by double-clicking it in the Solution Explorer.**

11. **Tell the `Context` object to keep track of changes whenever the `PropertyChanged` event is fired by adding the following code that appears in bold to the `PostsLoaded` method:**

    ```
    private void PostsLoaded(IAsyncResult ar)
    {
        var query = (DataServiceQuery<Post>)ar.AsyncState;
        var entities = query.EndExecute(ar).ToList();
        foreach (var post in entities)
        {
            post.PropertyChanged += ((sender, e) =>
            {
                var entity = (Post)sender;
                _ctx.UpdateObject(entity);
            });
        }
        PostsDataGrid.ItemsSource = entities;
    }
    ```

12. **Run the application again by pressing F5 or clicking the green Play button.**

13. **Make a change to a title of a Post object and click the Save button.**

When you check the database or refresh the page, you see that the change has been saved to the database. This is because the `Context` object was informed that a change had been made to a `Post` object and it tracked that change and saved it.

Adding new items to the database

So far, we have shown you how to Read and Update data with WCF Data Services so far — the *R* and the *U* in CRUD. Next in the list in our CRUD adventure is the *C*, which stands for Creating (a new entity). To enable your Silverlight application to create a new post, follow these steps:

1. **Open the** `MainPage.xaml` **file by double-clicking it in the Solution Explorer.**

2. **Add a new Button control immediately after the Save button by adding the following code that appears in bold:**

    ```
    <StackPanel>
        <data:DataGrid x:Name="PostsDataGrid"
            SelectionChanged="PostsDataGrid_
            SelectionChanged"></data:DataGrid>
        <data:DataGrid x:Name="CommentsDataGrid">
            </data:DataGrid>
        <Button Click="Button_Click" Content="Save"/>
        <Button Click="Button_Click_1" Content="Add"/>
    </StackPanel>
    ```

3. **Right-click** `Button_Click_1` **and select Navigate to Event Handler from the IntelliSense list that appears.**

4. **Create a new** `Post` **object and set the properties on it by adding the following code:**

    ```
    var post = new Post { Title = "Just added", Content =
          "New content", Date = DateTime.Now };
    ```

5. **Tell the** `Context` **object to add that new** `Post` **object to itself with the following code:**

    ```
    _ctx.AddToPost(post);
    ```

6. **Run the application by pressing F5 or clicking the green Play button.**

7. **Press the Add Button.**

8. **Press the Save Button.**

    A new Post record appears in the database. You can check this by refreshing the page (press F5 while in your browser).

Now you're probably wondering how you add a comment to your new post as well. The process is the same for the `Comment` object that you just implemented for the Post object: You create a new `Comment` object and then add it to the context. However, you need to take an extra step to associate the `Comment` object with the correct `Post` object. That step involves the `SetLink` method, which sets the link between the `Comment` and `Post` objects in the `Context` object. The relationship between the `Post` and `Comment` objects is then translated into the database for you.

Follow these steps to add a `Comment` and `Post` object and link them together:

1. **Open `MainPage.xaml.cs` by double-clicking it in the Solution Explorer.**
2. **Find the `Button_Click_1` event handler.**
3. **Create a new `Comment` object by adding the following code that appears in bold:**

   ```
   private void Button_Click_1(object sender,
           RoutedEventArgs e)
   {
       var post = new Post { Title = "Just added",
           Content = "New content", Date = DateTime.Now
           };
       var comment = new Comment { Comment1 = "New
           comment for the new post", Date = DateTime.Now
           };
       _ctx.AddToPost(post);
   }
   ```

4. **Add the new `Comment` to the `Context` object by adding the following code directly after the line of code that adds the new `Post` object to the `Context`:**

   ```
   _ctx.AddToComment(comment);
   ```

5. **Set the link between the new `Comment` object and the new `Post` object by adding the following code directly after the line of code that adds the new `Comment` object to the `Context`:**

   ```
   _ctx.SetLink(comment, "Post", post);
   ```

6. **Run the application by pressing F5 or clicking the green Play button.**
7. **Click the Add button.**
8. **Click the Save Button.**
9. **Refresh the page by pressing F5 while in the browser.**
10. **Click the new `Post` record in the PostsDataGrid.**

    The new comment appears in the CommentsDataGrid.

Deleting entities from the database

The final CRUD operation to cover is the *D*, for deleting an item. To delete an item, you call `DeleteObject` on the `Context`. One caveat, though: You cannot delete a post that has comments without first deleting the comments. To delete a post, follow these steps:

1. **Open** `MainPage.xaml.cs` **by double-clicking it in the Solution Explorer.**
2. **Add a Button control called Delete directly after the Add Button by adding the following code that appears in bold:**

   ```
   <StackPanel>
       <data:DataGrid x:Name="PostsDataGrid"
           SelectionChanged="PostsDataGrid_
           SelectionChanged"></data:DataGrid>
       <data:DataGrid x:Name="CommentsDataGrid">
           </data:DataGrid>
       <Button Click="Button_Click" Content="Save"/>
       <Button Click="Button_Click_1" Content="Add"/>
       <Button Click="Button_Click_2" Content="Delete"/>
   </StackPanel>
   ```

3. **Right-click** `Button_Click_2` **and select Navigate to Event Handler from the IntelliSense list that appears.**
4. **Delete the** `Post` **item that is selected in the PostsDataGrid by adding the following code to the** `Button_Click_2` **event handler:**

   ```
   _ctx.DeleteObject(PostsDataGrid.SelectedItem);
   ```

5. **Run the application by pressing F5 or clicking the green Play button.**
6. **Click in the PostsDataGrid on a post that has no comments.**
7. **Click the Delete button.**
8. **Click the Save button.**

   The Saved! message box appears, showing that the post was successfully deleted.

9. **Refresh the page by pressing F5 while in the browser.**
10. **In the PostsDataGrid, click a post that you know has at least one comment.**
11. **Click the Delete button.**
12. **Click the Save button.**

    The Failed to Save! message box appears, showing that the post was not deleted.

You can't delete a post with associated comments because when you created the database tables, you created a link between the Post and Comment tables, and the Comment records must have a `Post` object associated to them. If you deleted a post without deleting the comments first, the database would have to leave some orphaned Comment records, which is not allowed.

Handling Data Concurrency

In the example Silverlight application in this chapter, you perform a simple retrieve to show the blog posts in the data grid. The simple retrieve lets you edit a post and save it to the database. However, in its current form, the save action writes into the database no matter what has happened to the data in the meantime, even if someone has edited the post. You shouldn't just write straight over the top of some else's hard work if you can help it. Instead, you need to establish a way to deal with concurrent use of data. You need a way to determine whether the data you are about to update has been changed. If it has, you need to handle it elegantly. To do so, you need to see exactly what requests and data your application is sending over the Internet. One of the best ways to find out exactly what is happening is to use a very cool and necessary tool called Fiddler. You use Fiddler to trace http requests from your machine and easily see the results of the trace.

To investigate what is happening on your development machine with Fiddler, follow these steps:

1. **Start Fiddler from the Windows Start menu.**

    If you don't already have Fiddler installed, go to http://www.fiddler2.com/Fiddler2/ to download it and install it. (It's a free download.)

2. **Open the** SilverlightForDummiesWCFDataServices **project in Visual Studio.**

3. **Right-click the** BlogDataService.svc **file and select View in Browser.**

    The XML that is returned by the WCF Data Service appears in the browser window.

4. **Switch to Fiddler and look at the Web Sessions window on the left.**

    Fiddler shows you every http request that is happening in real time. You may even see some that you didn't realize were happening, such as for your e-mail programs and chat windows.

Nothing happens in Fiddler because you haven't sent your localhost http requests through Fiddler yet. To do so, change the address to http://localhost.:40526/BlogDataService.svc/Post(2). (Don't overlook the extra period after localhost and before the colon.) Fiddler can now trace your http requests, as shown in Figure 11-12, which reveals the request and response headers.

Take some time to have a look around Fiddler; it's a great tool for really getting to know how the Internet works.

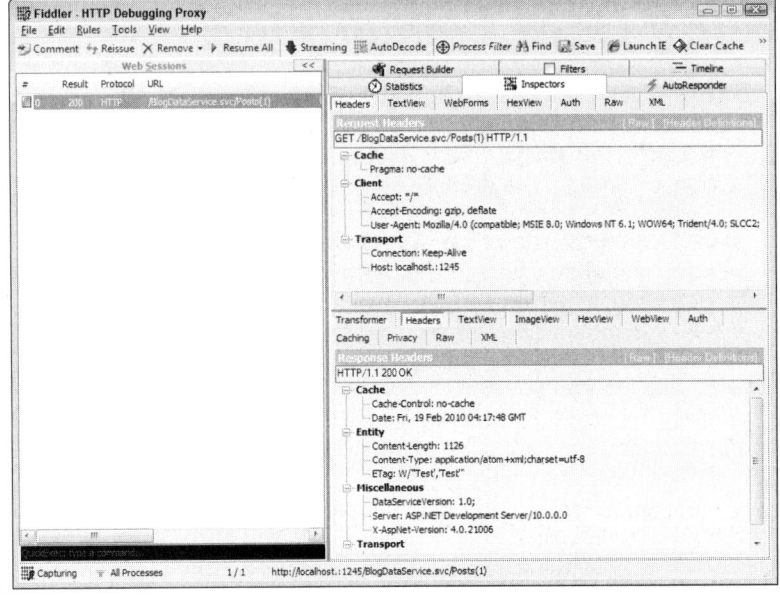

Figure 11-12: Fiddler showing the `http` trace for `BlogDataService.svc`.

Now that you have seen a little of how Fiddler works, you can use this new knowledge to investigate the requests from your Silverlight application and see how to use the built-in `http` standard tags to manage data concurrency. Follow these steps:

1. **Open Visual Studio 2010.**

2. **Open the `SilverlightForDummiesWCFDataServices` solution.**

3. **In the `SilverlightForDummiesWCFDataServices.Web` project, double-click the `BlogModel.edmx` file.**

4. **Click the `Title` field in the `Post` object on the design surface for the `BlogModel.edmx` file.**

5. **In the Concurrency Mode field of the Properties window, change the Concurrency Mode property to Fixed.**

   The Properties window is at the bottom right of the Visual Studio window.

6. **Click the Save button in Visual Studio to save the solution.**

7. **Right-click the `BlogDataService.svc` file and select View in Browser.**

8. **Insert the period after `localhost` in the Web browser's address bar.**

   The URL in the address bar of your browser should look like this:

   ```
   http://localhost.:1245/BlogDataService.svc/
   ```

   Fiddler requires that you insert the period each time you start the browser.

Chapter 11: Using WCF Data Services to Store and Manage Data

 9. **Open Fiddler.**
 10. **Refresh the Web page that shows the** `BlogDataService.svc` **so that the session data is captured by Fiddler.**
 11. **Click the session in Fiddler that shows the URL for the** `BlogData Service.svc` **service.**
 12. **Click the Inspectors tab on the right side of the screen in Fiddler.**
 13. **Click the Headers tab in the window that appears at the bottom of Fiddler.**

    In the response headers under `Entity`, a new line for ETag appears, as shown in Figure 11-13. ETag stands for *entity tag* and is part of the `http` protocol standard. The value is the value of the title for that post in the database. Now, if you save this post to the database and someone else has changed that value, you get an error.

Figure 11-13: Fiddler showing the ETag (entity tag).

```
--batchresponse_343cfe4d-47c2-4a62-81e7-b25d2e64b4e1
Content-Type: multipart/mixed; boundary=changesetresponse_92bc8df5-be45-47be-980b-635cec1f1ec4

--changesetresponse_92bc8df5-be45-47be-980b-635cec1f1ec4
Content-Type: application/http
Content-Transfer-Encoding: binary

HTTP/1.1 412 Precondition Failed
Content-ID: 11
Content-Type: application/xml
DataServiceVersion: 1.0;

<?xml version="1.0" encoding="utf-8" standalone="yes"?>
<error xmlns="http://schemas.microsoft.com/ado/2007/08/dataservices/metadata">
  <code></code>
  <message xml:lang="en-AU">The etag value in the request header does not match with the current etag value of the object.</message>
</error>
--changesetresponse_92bc8df5-be45-47be-980b-635cec1f1ec4--
--batchresponse_343cfe4d-47c2-4a62-81e7-b25d2e64b4e1--
```

You use ETags to maintain data concurrency. When your application requests some data from the database, each entity will have an ETag with it for fields that you want to maintain data integrity on. If some other process updates the field and you try to save your data, an error occurs because the ETag no longer matches the data in the database. This is a beautifully simple way to manage concurrency.

Follow these steps to see how to use ETags to maintain data concurrency:

 1. **With the** `SilverlightForDummiesWCFDataServices` **solution open in Visual Studio, press F5 or the green play button.**
 2. **Edit the title of the first post in the PostsDataGrid.**

    Do not press Save yet.
 3. **Open the database by clicking the Server Explorer tab in Visual Studio.**
 4. **Click the small triangle next to** `SilverlightForDummies.mdf`**.**

    Visual Studio connects to your database so that you can manipulate the data in it.

5. **Click the small triangle next to Tables.**

   The list of tables in the database expands.

6. **Right-click the Post table and select Show Table Data from the context menu that appears.**

7. **Find the Post record you edited in your Silverlight application and change the title to "Edited Title" by typing** Edited Title **into the Title field.**

8. **Use the Windows taskbar to switch back to the Silverlight application and click the Save button.**

   The Failed To Save! message box appears.

Changing the Concurrency mode to Fixed for the `Title` property in the `BlogModel.edmx` file instantly gives you data concurrency checking. Also, you can see the error reported back to the Silverlight application in Fiddler. A message appears stating that the ETag value in the request header does not match with the current ETag value of the object. You can now use this information to manage how you will handle data concurrency issues.

Using Query and Change Interceptors to Control Data Querying and Updates

Many applications need to be able to control which users can access data and other functionality that you cannot build into the client application because anyone using Fiddler can get detailed information about the requests and responses your application uses. This makes it a great tool for hackers to figure out how to attack your application. One of the ways to control data access is to intercept the queries as they come through and apply additional processing to them.

Controlling server-side queries with query interceptor

A query interceptor allows you to change the way a query works on the server side. For example, earlier in the chapter, you wrote the following query that retrieved all the posts in the database:

```
var query = from p in _ctx.Post select p;
```

Chapter 11: Using WCF Data Services to Store and Manage Data

In another scenario, you might want to have the application return only posts that have comments related to them. To perform this task on the server side, you create a query interceptor for the `Posts` entity collection by adding the code in the following steps to the `BlogDataService.svc.cs` file. To create the query interceptor, follow these steps:

1. **In the** `SilverlightForDummiesWCFDataServices.Web` **project, double-click the** `BlogDataService.svc.cs` **file.**

2. **Create the** `QueryInterceptor` **method by adding the following code immediately after the** `InitializeService` **method:**

    ```
    public class BlogDataService :
            DataService<BlogEntities>
    {
        // This method is called only once to initialize
            service-wide policies.
        public static void InitializeService(DataService
            Configuration config)
        {
            // TODO: set rules to indicate which entity
            sets and service operations are visible,
            updatable, etc.
            // Examples:
            config.SetEntitySetAccessRule("*",
            EntitySetRights.All);
            config.SetServiceOperationAccessRule("*",
            ServiceOperationRights.All);
            config.DataServiceBehavior.MaxProtocolVersion
            = DataServiceProtocolVersion.V2;
        }

        [QueryInterceptor("Posts")]
        public Expression<Func<Post, bool>> QueryPosts()
        {
            return p => p.Comment.Count > 0;
        }
    }
    ```

    This code tells any query that has `Post` objects in the return data to return a Post object only if it has at least one comment attached to it.

3. **Run the application by pressing F5 or clicking the green Play button in Visual Studio.**

    Only Posts with related comments are returned now. The great advantage to this approach is that any query you write on the client side will have this extra restriction added to it each time it's executed. As you can imagine, this is an excellent way to restrict data access based on who is logged in. It's also a way to remove unwanted data from the client application without changing the client application.

Enforcing rules using change interceptors

You use change interceptors to intercept any query that will change an entity in the database. This type of interceptor is excellent for ensuring that changes to the database follow the business rules for the application. For example, the business rule may be that a post can't be saved if it has no title. Adding a change interceptor on the server side ensures that any changes to the database are checked before being saved to the database. You can also add some auditing features to log which user made the changes or the time the data was changed.

The following steps show you how to ensure that no posts that have no title are saved. (By the way, this approach is also a very good way to ensure that any client-side validation you add is not bypassed on the way to the server.)

Follow these steps to add the change interceptor to the blog example used in this chapter:

1. **In the** `SilverlightForDummiesWCFDataServices.Web` **project, double-click the** `BlogDataService.svc.cs` **file.**

2. **Create the** `ChangeInterceptor` **method by adding the following code immediately after the** `QueryPosts` **method added in Step 2 in the previous section about change interceptors.**

   ```
   [ChangeInterceptor("Posts")]
   public void PostInterceptor(Post post,
           UpdateOperations ops)
   {
       if (ops == UpdateOperations.Change || ops ==
       UpdateOperations.Add)
       {
           if(post.Title==string.Empty)
           {
               throw new ArgumentNullException("The title
                   must be filled out");
           }
       }
   }
   ```

   This code checks what type of operation is occurring to the `Post` object. If a change to a post or a new post is being added, the code checks to see whether the `Title` property of the `Post` object has at least one character in it. If it has an empty value, an exception is created, which gets transferred back to the Silverlight Application and results in the `Save Failed!` message box being displayed.

3. **Run the application by pressing F5 or clicking the green Play button in Visual Studio.**

4. **In the Silverlight application, click in the PostsDataGrid and delete the title of the first post.**

5. **Click the Save button.**

   The `Save Failed!` message box appears, indicating that your change interceptor is enforcing the rule concerning saving posts without titles.

Controlling Access to Entity Sets

Early in this chapter, in the "Adding the WCF Data Service" section, we have you set `EntitySetRights` to `All`, which allows you to do whatever you want to any entity in your data model. The primary reason for the example application used throughout this chapter is to be able to manipulate the `Post` and `Comment` entities. In many cases, though, you need to be able to control the changes made to an entity.

For example, you might have a system that uses a Country entity, and countries are used as reference data in an application that millions of people use worldwide. You don't want your users to be able to change the spelling of a country; instead, that ability should be a back-office function that's kept under strict control. You want your users only to be able to read a list of countries. In that case, you need to set `EntitySetRights` to something other than `All`, and you do so by setting the rules when the WCF Data Service is first initialized in the `InitializeService` method. To see the `InitializeService` method, follow these steps:

1. **In the** `SilverlightForDummiesWCFDataServices.Web` **project, double-click the** `BlogDataService.svc.cs` **file to open it.**

2. **Press Ctrl+F to open the Find dialog box.**

3. **Enter** InitializeService **into the Find What field of the Find dialog box and click Find.**

   Inside the `InitializeService` method, the Entity Access rules are set to `All` for all Entity sets. You can add as many different rule sets as required in this section of code; the options for doing so are listed in Table 11-1.

Table 11-1	Rules for Accessing an Entity Set
EntitySetRights Setting	*What It Authorizes*
None	Denies all rights to access data.
ReadSingle	Read single data items.
ReadMultiple	Read sets of data.
WriteAppend	Create new data items in data sets.
WriteReplace	Replace data.
WriteDelete	Delete data items from data sets.
WriteMerge	Merge data.
AllRead	Read data.
AllWrite	Write data.
All	Create, read, update, and delete data.

Chapter 12
Using WCF RIA Services in Silverlight

In This Chapter
- Getting Started with WCF RIA Services
- Authenticating your users
- Creating a custom authentication system

*W*CF RIA Services is a new framework from Microsoft that you can use to easily build Silverlight applications that require users to log in to access data. In fact, although we cover WCF Data Services in Chapter 11, WCF RIA Services makes the same tasks much easier to accomplish.

RIA stands for Rich Internet Application, which, of course, is what a Silverlight application is. WCF RIA Services uses some "magic" in Visual Studio to generate files in both the server side of your application and the client side. This bit of magic makes it much faster to build your application and perform validation because you need to implement validation only once to have it executed on both the client and the server. WCF RIA Services uses the ideas of context and entities similarly to how WCF Data Services uses them.

In this chapter, we show you how to use WCF RIA Services to authenticate your users easily, and you create a custom authentication system as an example of how you might implement some custom logic when a user logs in to your site.

Getting Started with WCF RIA Services

Microsoft WCF RIA Services is installed as part of the Silverlight 4 Tools for Visual Studio 2010. When you create a new Silverlight application with these tools installed, some new templates show up, including the Silverlight Business Application template and the WCF RIA Services Class Library (see Figure 12-1).

Part III: Connecting with Data

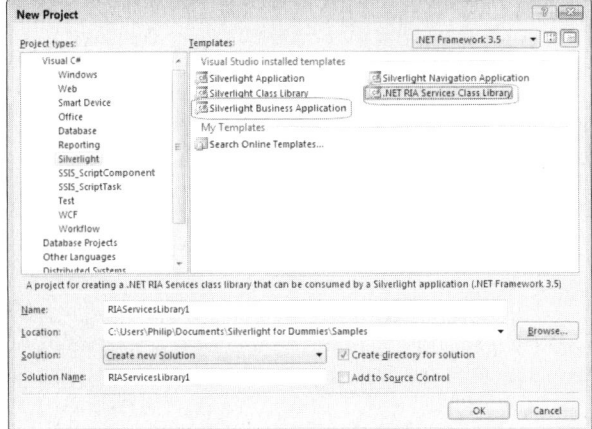

Figure 12-1: New WCF RIA Services templates for Silverlight in Visual Studio 2010.

Also, whenever you create a new Silverlight application with WCF RIA Services installed, the Enable WCF RIA Services check box appears in the Add New ASP.NET Web Application dialog box. Selecting this check box tells Visual Studio to perform its code generation magic for you. (If you use the new Business Application template, you don't see this check box because the template takes care of this setting for you.)

In this section, we show you how to build an application using the Business Application template. You work with the tools that you get "out of the box," and in the final section of this chapter, you customize the application to suit your specific needs.

Authenticating Your Users

We discuss the reasons for authenticating users in Chapter 10.

This example starts with one of the more difficult tasks involved with building online applications: authentication. In years gone by, to complete this task you would have to build a database, write a bunch of stored procedures, and then build a login control and a way for your users to register themselves and be provided with feedback. ASP.NET introduced the membership system with some login controls, which made life easier. (See Chapter 10 for details about the ASP.NET membership system.)

Now, WCF RIA Services makes the situation even better. WCF RIA Services has a built-in authentication system that takes advantage of the existing ASP.NET authentication system and adds to it. You can build a login system more easily now, but even better, your users can log in to your Web site using the ASP.NET system, and your RIA application can detect that login and use it. This means that your users need to log in to your Web site only once; if they then navigate to a page that contains your Silverlight RIA application, they don't need to log in again!

Authenticating users with the Business Application template

In this section, we show you how to use an application template in Silverlight to authenticate your users. This template, called the Business Application template, contains all the required parts of a Silverlight application that use WCF RIA Services to authenticate a user, so you don't have to write any code for that purpose at all. To create an application using the Business Application template, follow these steps:

1. **Open Visual Studio 2010 and choose File**➪**New Project.**

    The New Project dialog box opens.

2. **Select the Business Application template under the Silverlight group in the dialog box.**

3. **Name the project SilverlightForDummiesRIA.**

    This will add two projects to the solution, one called SilverlightForDummiesRIA and another called SilverlightForDummiesRIA.Web.

4. **Click OK.**

As mentioned previously, WCF RIA Services uses the same authentication system as ASP.NET, so you can use the ASP.NET Configuration tool built in to Visual Studio to manage the users. Using the ASP.NET Configuration tool, you add a user to the ASP.NET membership database that you later use to log in with. So make sure you remember the username and password that you enter in the following steps. To add a new user to the ASP.NET membership system with the built-in Visual Studio tools, follow these steps:

1. **Right-click the `SilverlightForDummiesRIA.Web` project in the Solution Explorer and select Add New Item from the dialog box that appears.**

2. **Select Data from the installed templates.**

3. **Select SQL Server database from the options in the dialog box.**

4. **Name the new database** SilverlightForDummies.

5. **Click Yes in the dialog box when it asks whether you want to place the database in the `App_Data` folder.**

6. **Choose Project**⇨**ASP.NET Configuration.**

   The ASP.NET Web Site Administration tool opens.

7. **In the ASP.NET Web Site Administration tool, click** `Select Authentication Type` **link.**

   If this link is not showing by default, click the Security tab on the Web site.

8. **Select the From the Internet option and click Done.**

9. **Click the** `Create User` **link.**

10. **Fill out the new user form and click Create User.**

    You should see a form like the one shown in Figure 12-2.

    You will need to enter a password that has at least seven characters, with at least one character that is not a number or a letter.

11. **Run the application by pressing F5 or clicking the green Play button.**

12. **Click the Login button on the right side of the application.**

13. **Log in with the credentials you created in Step 10.**

    The application should log in and your name should appear on the application next to the Logout button.

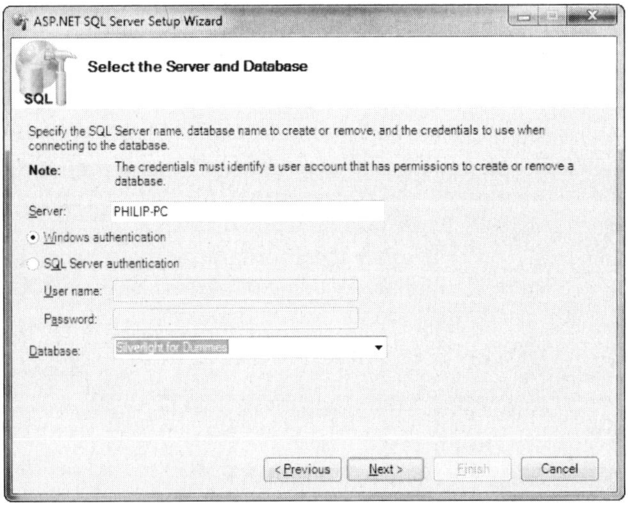

Figure 12-2: ASP.NET Web Site Administration tool — Create User.

When you create the Business Application from the template, the Business Application adds a complete application to Visual Studio. That application has two pages: One provides the ability to log in and the other lets you create new users from the Silverlight application. The ability to log in and manage users is provided by an object called the `WebContext`. This is a similar concept to the Data Context object that we describe in Chapter 11 for WCF Data Services. The Context object keeps track of what's going on with the data; it also uses a set of methods it executes to log in and create users. `WebContext` also contains the currently logged-in user so that you can easily access the user, as we explain next.

Understanding the client side of the Business Application template

The Business Application template adds files to both the Silverlight application and the Web application when you create a new solution, which means that it adds files to both parts of the solution: client and server.

When you create a new Silverlight application from the Business Application template, you get a set of files added to the solution. Open the XAML file for the `MainPage.xaml` and you see that it is a Navigation application with two pages, Home and About. Next, open the Views folder and you see the Home and About pages and three files that look as though they may have something to do with logging in! The Password control is just a password box that gets used twice on the registration form. The LoginControl is located on the `MainPage.xaml` and shows the logged-in user's name or the word *Login* with a link to the LoginWindow. The LoginWindow pops up when the user clicks the LoginControl.

Open the XAML file for `LoginControl.xaml` and you see the data context of the user control set to `RiaContext`. The `WebContext` is the object that allows you to log in to the system; it is declared in the `app.xaml` file. Open `app.xaml` and you see a section called ApplicationLifetimeObjects, which is where the `WebContext` object is instantiated for the lifetime of the application.

Investigating the server side of the Business Application template

The Business Application template adds files that manage the login of your users and creation of new users. These files also provide places for you to extend the standard login and creation of users. To investigate the files added, follow these steps:

1. **In the `SilverlightForDummiesRIA.Web` project, locate the Services folder.**

    This folder has two files. The first one, `AuthenticationService.cs`, contains the `AuthenticationService` class, which inherits from `AuthenticationBase`. You use the `AuthenticationService` class to write your own authentication logic (which we cover later in this chapter).

    The second file, `UserRegistrationServices.cs`, contains a class and methods for managing the user list for your Web site.

2. **Open the Models folder.**

    This folder also contains two files. The `User.cs` file contains the `User` class, which inherits from `UserBase`. The `UserBase` class allows you to create your own `User` object to pass back to the client when you write your own authentication methods. (We show you how to write authentication methods in "Creating a Custom Authentication System," later in this chapter.)

    The other file in the Models folder, `RegistrationData.cs`, contains the class definition for the object that gets passed to the `UserRegistration Service` when a user is created.

This completes your tour of the Business Application template files on both the client and server sides of the application. The next section delves into how they all work together to create a complete application.

Understanding how the template files work together

The `WebContext` object, which we discuss earlier, is used to perform the user's login. You simply call the `Login` method and tell it what to do when it's finished. Follow these steps to look closely at what the code is doing:

1. **Open the `LoginForm.xaml.cs` file by double-clicking it in the `SilverlightForDummiesRIA` project in the Solution Explorer.**

2. **Locate the `LoginButton_Click` event handler in the code.**

    The code looks like this:

    ```
    private void LoginButton_Click(object sender,
            EventArgs e)
    {
        // If there was a validation error in a previous
            login attempt, clear it
    this.loginForm.ValidationSummary.Errors.Clear();
    ```

```
if (this.loginForm.ValidateItem())
    {
LoginOperationloginOperation = WebContext.Current.
        Authentication.Login(this.loginInfo.
        ToLoginParameters(), this.LoginOperation_
        Completed, null);

this.BindUIToOperation(loginOperation);
this.parentWindow.AddPendingOperation(loginOperation);
this.lastLoginOperation = loginOperation;
    }
}
```

When the application is running and you click the Login button, the Login method is called on the WebContext object, in this case with the username and password. Remember that all calls to the server are asynchronous in Silverlight, so you need to provide a callback for when the operation is finished. You provide this callback by specifying a completed event on the Login Operation called LoginOperation_Completed. As the preceding code shows, when the Login method is called, the LoginOperation_Completed event is passed in as one of the parameters. The code for the LoginOperation_Completed event looks like this:

```
private void LoginOperation_Completed(LoginOperation
        loginOperation)
{
if (loginOperation.LoginSuccess)
    {
this.parentWindow.Close();
    }
else
    {
if (loginOperation.HasError)
    {
ErrorWindow.CreateNew(loginOperation.Error);
loginOperation.MarkErrorAsHandled();
    }
else if (!loginOperation.IsCanceled)
    {
this.loginForm.ValidationSummary.Errors.Add(new
        ValidationSummaryItem(ErrorResources.
        ErrorBadUserNameOrPassword));
    }

this.loginForm.BeginEdit();
    }
}
```

In this code, if the login is successful, the login window is closed. If an error occurred, the error is reported to the ErrorWindow, and if the user entered details that did not validate correctly, a message appears saying that either the username or the password was not valid.

When you call `Login`, a call is made back to the server to the `Authentication Service` object, and the default implementation of logging in to a standard ASP.NET Membership system is done for you. When the call to the server is finished, the `WebContext.Current.User` object is populated with the identity of the user you logged in as. You can then use this identity in your application anywhere you like.

To see the results of using the Business Application template for authenticating users, run the application by pressing F5 or clicking the green Play button. Then click the `Login` link on the right side of the Web page. After you have logged in, you should see your name in the top right (see Figure 12-3).

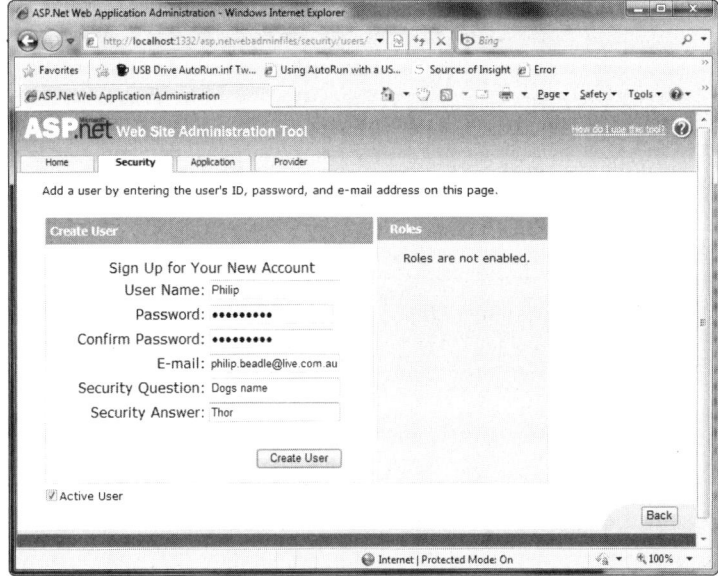

Figure 12-3: Logging in to the application.

The next section tells you how to modify the login process to use your own business logic and return a custom `User` object.

Creating a Custom Authentication System

In many scenarios, the standard ASP.NET Membership system is not used because other systems and legacy authentication systems are already in place. Therefore, it's a good idea to know how to implement authentication for one of these systems. The process is actually very simple because all the WCF RIA Services server-side classes are designed to be easily extended.

Implementing custom user validation logic

Essentially, a custom authentication system needs to validate the user and then return the custom `User` object to the client application based on some custom logic. In the following example, you see how to override the standard logic with your own very simple logic. To implement your own login logic, follow these steps:

1. **Open the** `AuthenticationService.cs` **file in the** `SilverlightFor DummiesRIA.Web` **project by double-clicking it in Solution Explorer.**

    The C# code for this file is displayed.

2. **Override the** `ValidateUser` **method by typing** override **immediately inside the** `AuthenticationService` **class.**

3. **Press the spacebar and select ValidateUser from the IntelliSense list that appears.**

    The following code is added:

    ```
    protected override boolValidateUser(string userName,
            string password)
    {
    returnbase.ValidateUser(userName, password);
    }
    ```

    As you can see, Visual Studio automatically calls the `base. ValidateUser` method, which is what happens anyway if you don't override the method. This method is declared in the base class `AuthenticationBase<User>`. Because you are overriding the method, you need to implement your own logic, which may or may not include a call to the base class method. For this example, you simply return true so that anyone who logs in will be validated.

4. **Implement your custom logic by changing the line that returns** `base. ValidateUser` **to return true.**

    Your `ValidateUser` method should look like the following code now:

    ```
    protected override boolValidateUser(string userName,
            string password)
    {
    return true;
    }
    ```

    At this point, you call whatever authentication system you are using and actually validate the user.

Returning a custom user object to the Silverlight application

After you validate the user on the server side, you need to return the authenticated user to the client (the Silverlight application, in this case). The standard `User` object is very basic, containing only a few properties, so in this example, we show you how to extend it by adding some of your own properties, as follows:

1. **Locate the Models folder in the** `SilverlightForDummiesRIA.Web` **project.**

2. **Open the** `User.cs` **file by double-clicking it in Solution Explorer.**

    The User class code looks like this:

    ```
    public partial class User : UserBase
    {
        //// NOTE: Profile properties can be added for use
        ////    in Silverlight application.
        //// To enable profiles, edit the appropriate
        ////    section of web.config file.
        ////
        //// [DataMember]
        //// public string MyProfileProperty{ get; set; }

        [DataMember]
        public string FriendlyName { get; set; }
    }
    ```

3. **Add a property called** `Email` **of type** `string` **by adding the following code inside the** `User` **class immediately after the** `FriendlyName` **property, as shown:**

    ```
    public partial class User : UserBase
    {
        //// NOTE: Profile properties can be added for use
        ////    in Silverlight application.
        //// To enable profiles, edit the appropriate
        ////    section of web.config file.
        ////
        //// [DataMember]
        //// public string MyProfileProperty{ get; set; }

        [DataMember]
        public string FriendlyName { get; set; }

        [DataMember]
        public string Email { get; set; }
    }
    ```

4. **Add a property called** `FirstName` **of type** `string` **by adding the following code inside the** `User` **class:**

   ```
   public string FirstName { get; set; }
   ```

5. **Add the following code to override the** `GetAuthenticatedUser` **method in the** `AuthenticationService` **class by typing the word** override **immediately after the** `ValidateUser` **method that you override in Step 2 of the "Implementing custom user validation logic" section.**

   ```
   protected override User GetAuthenticatedUser(System.
           Security.Principal.IPrincipal principal)
   {
   returnbase.GetAuthenticatedUser(principal);
   }
   ```

6. **Return a new instance of your custom** `User` **object by deleting the following line of code:**

   ```
   returnbase.GetAuthenticatedUser(principal);
   ```

   and changing it to

   ```
   var user = new User
       {
   DisplayName = "My Custom Display Name",
           Email = "philip.beadle@live.com.au",
   FirstName = "Philip",
           Name = "Philip",
           Roles = new List<string>{ "Administrator",
           "Registered User" }
       };
   return user;
   ```

   This code creates a new `User` object, populates its properties, and returns it whenever a user logs in. At this point in the code for a genuine user, you would interrogate a database or some other data store, such as Active Directory or a Web service, for real user data and return the correct details for the logged-in user.

7. **Run the application by pressing F5 or clicking the green Play button.**

8. **Log in to the application with any old nonsense.**

   For this example, it doesn't matter what credentials you enter because the code always returns the same result.

   The application logs in fine and returns the values you set in the `GetAuthenticatedUser` method (see Figure 12-4).

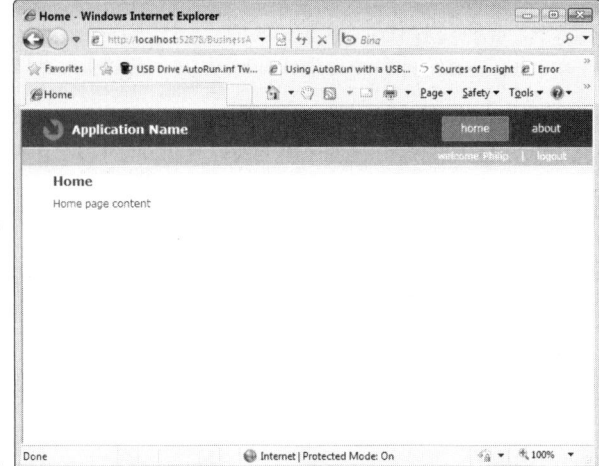

Figure 12-4:
Logging in to the application with a custom authentication.

Chapter 13

Accessing Data with WCF RIA Services

In This Chapter

▶ Creating the domain data service
▶ Writing your own Service Methods using LINQ to Entity Framework
▶ Writing your own Service Methods using LINQ to SQL
▶ Using WCF RIA Services with WCF Data Services
▶ Securing your service
▶ Validating data on the client and server sides

*E*ven though WCF RIA Services is a Community Technical Preview (CTP), it is very well developed and makes building applications that require authentication and database storage much simpler. WCF RIA Services has some excellent support for authenticating users and intercepting processing on the server side as well as for making client-side development easier.

WCF RIA Services is an excellent way to handle all your CRUD operations on a database. WCF RIA Services is more complete than WCF Data Services for use in Silverlight and requires much less work to get working. You no longer have to write code to track the data context, as we cover in Chapter 11; also, authentication is handled very nicely for you, as described in Chapter 12. You can use WCF RIA Services with both LINQ to Entity Framework and LINQ to SQL, in contrast to WCF Data Services, which works only with Entity Framework. You can even use WCF RIA Services against WCF Data Services, which is fantastic if you have to keep your database in a secure network area that's not accessible by the public Internet and you have only Port 80 open.

WCF RIA Services connects Silverlight applications to server-side data stores very effectively. Most business applications have a database, some Web services that manage the data in the database, and a user interface. The same is true for a Silverlight application that uses WCF RIA Services.

In this chapter, we use the blogging application that we discuss in Chapter 11 again to demonstrate the enhanced abilities of WCF RIA Services. The solution is essentially the same as in Chapter 11. Here, you find out how to access the database in SQL Express, use a data model created with the ADO.NET Entity Framework, employ a set of services called Domain Data Service, and connect all these to the Silverlight user interface.

Creating the Domain Data Service

You use a domain data service to access server-side functionality through the HyperText Transfer Protocol (HTTP). In the case of the blogging example, the domain data service is used to access the data stored in the database and to provide some server-side validation of any data entered by the user.

The domain data service you create in this section functions the same as the one we describe in Chapter 11 — this time using WCF RIA Services rather than WCF Data Services. The one difference is that here you use LINQ to Entity Framework, not LINQ to SQL classes. You employ the same database structure as well.

First, create a new Silverlight Application by following these steps:

1. **Open Visual Studio.**
2. **Choose File**⇨**New Project.**

    The New Project dialog box appears.

3. **Select Silverlight Business Application and name it** `SilverlightForDummiesBusinessApplication`.
4. **Click OK.**

Now, to set up the database for this example application, see Chapter 11 and follow the steps in the section about creating a database. Then follow the steps in the section that describes how to add the ADO.NET Entity Framework.

As a shortcut, follow these steps if you have previously created the database and want to reuse it for this chapter:

1. **Locate the** `SilverlightForDummies.mdf` **file from Chapter 11.**

    You can find this file in the `App_Data` folder from the Chapter 11 example.

2. **Copy the** `SilverlightForDummies.mdf` **file.**
3. **In the new** `SilverlightForDummiesBusinessApplication.Web` **project, right-click the** `App_Data` **folder and select Paste.**
4. **Press Ctrl+Shift+B to build the project.**

Following the steps from Chapter 11 provides you with a database and an ADO.NET Entity Framework data model created from that database. Up to this point, the solution is exactly the same as for the WCF Data Services example from Chapter 11. Using this database and a data model, you can create the Domain Data Service. To do so, follow these steps:

1. **In the Solution Explorer, right-click the Services folder in the** `SilverlightForDummiesBusinessApplication.Web` **project and select Add New Item from the menu that appears.**

   The Add New Item dialog box appears.

2. **Select Domain Service Class, which is located in the Web category in the installed templates.**

3. **Enter** BlogDomainService.cs **in the Name field.**

4. **Select all the check boxes on the form so that it looks like Figure 13-1.**

5. **Click OK.**

   Your Web application should now have two new files: `BlogDomainService.cs`, which has all the methods you can call to perform your CRUD operations; and `BlogDomainService.metadata.cs`, in which you can specify elements such as validation and navigation properties. (See Chapter 11 for more information about CRUD operations.)

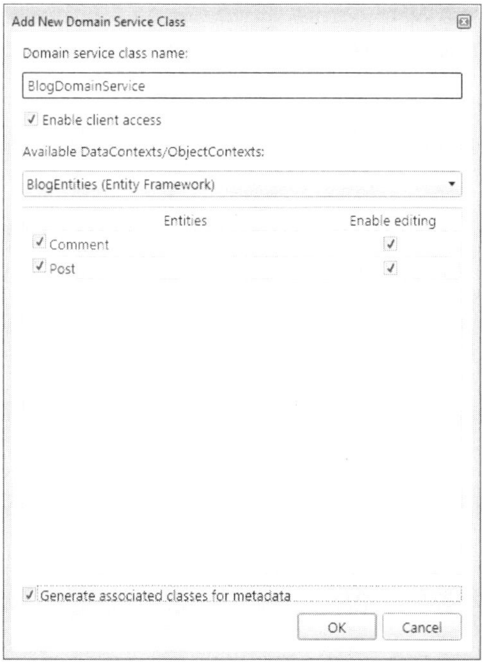

Figure 13-1: Adding a new domain service class.

 If you didn't see the list of the tables that should have been added in the Entity Framework step from Chapter 11 (which shows you how to add the Entity Framework), you haven't rebuilt your project. Cancel this form, rebuild your project, and have another go.

Understanding the generated files

The `BlogDomainService.cs` file contains the CRUD operation methods for the `Post` and `Comment` entities. The `BlogDomainService.metadata.cs` file contains the corresponding classes, which are called `PostMetaData` and `CommentMetaData`. (Meta data is simply additional information; in this case, it's a description of how you want the class to function.)

The `PostMetaData` and `CommentMetaData` class names have `MetaData` as a suffix so that WCF RIA Services knows that any meta data you want to include is contained here. For example, to specify a description in the user interface (UI) for the `Post` entity, you specify the `Display` attribute on the `Title` property by adding the following code to the `PostMetaData` class immediately on top of the `Title` property, as follows:

```
[Display(Description = "The title of the blog post.")]
public string Title;
```

You can also specify validation rules in the `MetaData` class, which we cover in the "Validating Data on the Client and Server Sides" section, later in this chapter.

Creating the user interface

In this section, you use the Business Application template and add blog functions to the home page. The Business Application template is added to the list of installed templates for new projects when you install the Silverlight Tools for Visual Studio. The template gives you a complete application, including the user interface, screens to log in and create users, and the domain data services required to handle authentication and adding new users. You can then customize the files for your purposes, which is what you do in the following example.

To create the user interface, follow these steps:

1. **Open the Views folder in the** `SilverlightForDummiesBusiness Application` **project by clicking the triangle next to the Views node in the Solution Explorer.**

2. **Open the** `Home.xaml` **file in the** `SilverlightForDummiesBusiness Application` **project by double-clicking it in the Solution Explorer.**

3. **Delete the two TextBox controls called HeaderText and ContentText.**

    You don't need these controls for this particular application.

 4. **From the Toolbox in Visual Studio 2010, select the DataGrid control and drag it onto the Stack Panel control.**

    The DataGrid control is chosen because it automatically shows data that is added to it. This makes showing data on the screen easy without having to format the control.

 5. **Enter** PostsDataGrid **in the Name field of the Properties window to change the name of the DataGrid control to PostsDataGrid.**

    You need to name your controls so that it is easier to reference them in the code later. Leaving the default name of DataGrid1 won't make much sense to you later, especially if you have lots of DataGrid controls in your application.

Retrieving the data

Retrieving the data from the database is a very similar process to that of WCF Data Services, covered in Chapter 11. To retrieve the data, you create a new `DomainContext` object.

You then create a callback method that accepts the list of `Posts` returned and updates the `PostsDataGrid ItemsSource` property to show the data. The final task is to write a piece of code that runs when the page is shown to the user, with that code using the Domain Context to actually retrieve the data. This last piece of code uses the callback method you will create as one of the parameters it has to pass to the `DomainContext` when calling the `Load` method.

If you have a database from having followed the example in Chapter 11, you already have some data available that you can use now. If you created a new database in the section "Creating the Domain Data Service" and didn't copy an existing database, you need to add some data to it by following these steps:

 1. **Hover your mouse on the tab called Server Explorer on the left side of the screen in Visual Studio.**

    The Server Explorer tool opens.

 2. **Click the triangle next to** SilverlightForDummies.mdf**, which appears directly under Data Connections.**

    This step connects Visual Studio to SQL Server Express so that you can add data directly to the database.

 3. **Click the triangle next to Tables.**

    You see the list of tables in the database, which should include the Post and Comment tables.

Part III: Connecting with Data

4. **Right-click the Post table.**

   The context menu appears.

5. **In the context menu, select Show Table Data.**

6. **In the table that appears, fill in the Title, Content, and Date fields for as many records as you want to add.**

To retrieve data using WCF RIA Services, follow these steps:

1. **In Visual Studio, open the** `Home.xaml.cs` **file by double-clicking it in the Solution Explorer.**

2. **Create a new `DomainContext` object by adding the following code immediately after the class declaration:**

   ```
   public partial class Home : Page
   {
   private BlogDomainContext _context = new
           BlogDomainContext();
   ```

   Your code-behind file doesn't know where the `BlogDomainContext` class is, so click the word BlogDomainContext to make a small blue square appear at the end of the word. Click that blue square and then select the top option from the list that appears to add a `using` statement to your class. Alternatively, press Ctrl+. (period). A `using` statement imports the namespace of a referenced assembly so that you can use shorter and more concise notation in your code.

3. **Create a new callback method to be used when the data is returned by adding the following code immediately after the** `OnNavigatedTo` **event handler:**

   ```
   private void LoadPostsDataGrid(IEnumerable<Post>
           posts)
   {
       PostsDataGrid.ItemsSource = posts;
   }
   ```

   The `IEnumerable<Post>` argument gets passed back from the `LoadOperation`'s `Entities` property.

   To import the correct `using` statement for the Post object, press Ctrl+. (period) and select the `using SilverlightForDummiesBusiness Application.Web` option from the list that appears. Do the same for the `IEnumerable` namespace to import its `using` statement, selecting the `using System.Collections.Generic` option after you press Ctrl+. (period).

4. **Call the** `Load` **method on the Domain Context by adding the following code that appears in bold to the** `OnNaviagetedTo` **event handler:**

   ```
   var query = _context.GetPostsQuery();
   _context.Load(query, op => LoadPostsDataGrid (op.
           Entities), null);
   ```

Chapter 13: Accessing Data with WCF RIA Services

This code creates a new `EntityQuery` object from the Domain Service classes that are added when you build the solution. The code then calls the `Load` method, which requires an `EntityQuery` object and a callback method to execute when the data is returned.

5. **Run the application by pressing F5 or clicking the green Play button.**

   You should see a result similar to Figure 13-2 with your sample data.

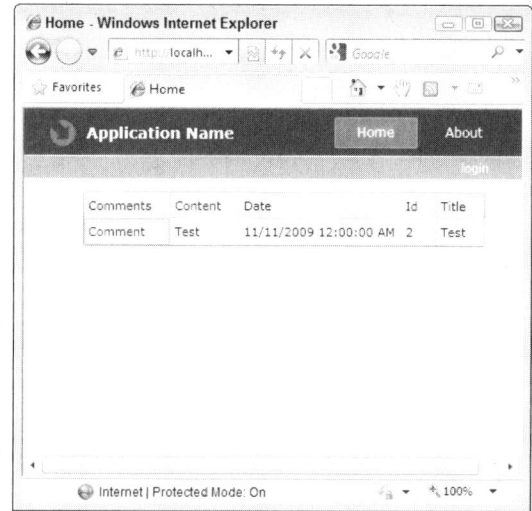

Figure 13-2: Blog Grid with Data from RIA Service call.

Updating your data

To update the database when data is changed, follow these steps:

1. **Open the `Home.xaml` file by double-clicking it in the Solution Explorer.**

2. **Drag a new Button control onto the design surface just below the Data Grid control.**

3. **In the `Text` property of the new Button control, enter Save.**

   The word *Save* will now appear on the button when the application is running.

4. **Double-click the Button control.**

   Visual Studio automatically creates the Button control's `Click` event handler in the code-behind file.

5. **Tell the Domain Context to update by adding the following code to the Button control's `Click` event handler:**

   ```
   _context.SubmitChanges();
   ```

6. **Run the application by pressing F5 or clicking the green Play button.**
7. **Click the title of one of your records.**
8. **Change the title to a meaningful name that identifies the record.**
9. **Click the new Save button.**
10. **Open the database table with the Server Explorer.**

    The change you made should be saved in the database.

The change was saved for you; in contrast to doing this same task through WCF Data Services, you did no work at all. WCF RIA Services tracks all the changes for you; all you have to do is tell it when to submit those changes.

Writing Your Own Service Methods — LINQ to Entity Framework

When you create a new Domain Service and associate it with a table in the database, Visual Studio generates a series of methods that can be used for CRUD operations. If the database has related tables such as Post and Comment, the CRUD operations do not cover the operations required to manage the related tables but instead generate only the CRUD operations for each table, independently. This means that to show related entities in the data returned by WCF RIA Services, you need to write a custom method called a service method. A *service method* is simply a public method that is exposed over the network or the Internet as part of a service. In this case, the service method is added to the automatically generated service methods created when you added the domain data service.

Writing a service method involves writing a method that returns an IQueryable list of the objects you are interested in. The query is written in LINQ and uses the Include operator to include the related entities. The object must also have the [Include] attribute on the related property.

In the database for this application, the Comment table is related to the Post table so that you can add comments to the posts. To return the associated comments with the post, you need to use the [Include] attribute on the Comment property of the Post object in the meta data file. You also need to write a new service method that uses the Include operator on the Posts property of the Context.

In this section, you associate a DataGrid of the comments with the selected post in the PostsDataGrid. First, the following steps show you how people make a very common mistake by expecting the associated Comment records to be returned by default. The second part of this section shows you how to avoid this and make sure your associated records are returned.

A common mistake (Psst — This won't work!)

To see how comments associated with a post are not retrieved by default, follow these steps:

1. **Open the** `Home.xaml` **file by double-clicking it in the Solution Explorer.**

2. **Add a new DataGrid directly below the PostsDataGrid by adding the following code:**

   ```
   <data:DataGrid x:Name="CommentsDataGrid"></
         data:DataGrid>
   ```

3. **Add a** `SelectionChanged` **event to the PostsDataGrid by adding the code that appears in bold to it:**

   ```
   <data:DataGrid x:Name="PostsDataGrid"
         SelectionChanged="PostsDataGrid_
         SelectionChanged"></data:DataGrid>
   ```

4. **Right-click** `PostsDataGrid_SelectionChanged` **and select Navigate to Event Handler.**

   This takes you to the `MainPage.xaml.cs` file at the automatically added code for the event handler.

5. **Add the following code to set the** `ItemsSource` **property of the new CommentsDataGrid control to the** `Comment` **property of the selected** `Post` **item in the PostsDataGrid when a user clicks the grid:**

   ```
   CommentsDataGrid.ItemsSource = ((Post)PostsDataGrid.
         SelectedItem).Comment;
   ```

6. **Run the application by pressing F5 or clicking the green Play button.**

7. **Click a** `Post` **item in the PostsDataGrid.**

   Note how the CommentsDataGrid gets no records.

This, on the other hand, DOES work

To associate the `Comments` to a `Post` and really, truly retrieve them from the database, follow these steps:

1. **Open the** `BlogDomainService.metadata.cs` **file by double-clicking it in the Solution Explorer.**

   This file is in the `SilverlightForDummiesBusinessApplication.Web` project.

2. **Locate the** `Post` **class by selecting it from the Class Browser drop-down list at the top left of the Code Editing window.**

3. **Add the** `[Include]` **attribute to the** `Comments` **property by adding the following code that appears in bold immediately on top of the Comments property:**

   ```
   [Include]
   public EntityCollection<Comment> Comment;
   ```

4. **Open the** `BlogDomainService.cs` **file by double-clicking it in the Solution Explorer.**

5. **Add a new service method to retrieve the comments associated with a post by adding the following code:**

   ```
   public IQueryable<Post> GetPostWithComments()
   {
       var a = this.Context.Post.Include("Comment");
       return a;
   }
   ```

6. **Open the** `Blog.xaml.cs` **file by double-clicking it in the Solution Explorer.**

7. **Change the** `OnNavigatedTo` **event to use the new service method by changing the following code that appears in bold:**

   ```
   private void LoadPosts(Action<IEnumerable<Post>>
           action)
   {
       var query = _context.GetPostWithCommentsQuery();
       _context.Load(query, op => action(op.Entities),
           null);
   }
   ```

8. **Run the application by pressing F5 or clicking the green Play button.**

9. **Click a post in the PostsDataGrid to see how the associated comments appear in the CommentsDataGrid.**

Writing Your Own Service Methods — LINQ to SQL

LINQ to SQL is very similar to LINQ to Entity Framework. To use it, you build a data model using LINQ to SQL Data Classes and then a Domain Service based on the new LINQ to SQL Data Classes. The Domain Service contains the same methods as the LINQ to Entity Framework, but the implementation is different and uses LINQ to SQL code. In this section, you change the solution to use LINQ to SQL from its current use of LINQ to Entity Framework. To change the solution to use LINQ to SQL, follow these steps:

1. **Open the** `SilverlightForDummiesBusinessApplication` **solution in Visual Studio.**

2. **Right-click the** `BlogModel.edmx` **file and select Exclude from Project. Do the same for the** `BlogDomainService.cs` **and** `BlogDomain.metadata.cs` **files.**

3. **Right-click the Web Application project file and select Add New Item.**

   The Add New Item dialog box appears.

4. **Select LINQ to SQL Data Classes and call the new LINQ to SQL Data Class** `BlogDataClasses.dbml`**.**

5. **Open the Server Explorer.**

6. **Click the Post table and drag it onto the LINQ to SQL design surface.**

7. **Click the Comment table and drag it onto the LINQ to SQL design surface.**

8. **Right-click the** `SilverlightForDummiesBusinessApplication.Web` **project and select Build.**

   Don't build the whole solution by pressing Ctrl+Shift+B or right-clicking the solution and selecting Build; you need to make a few more changes first.

9. **Right-click the Web Application project file and select Add New Item.**

   The Add New Item dialog box appears.

10. **Select Domain Service Class and call the new Domain Service Class** `BlogL2SDomainService.cs`**.**

    Figure 13-3 shows the Add New Item dialog box with the Domain Service Class selected.

11. **Select all the check boxes on the form, refer to Figure 13-1.**

12. **Right-click the** `SilverlightForDummiesBusinessApplication.Web` **project and select Build.**

13. **Open the** `Blog.xaml.cs` **file by double-clicking it in the Solution Explorer.**

14. **Change the code** `BlogDomainContext` **to** `BlogL2SDomainContext`**.**

15. **Change the** `OnNavigatedTo` **event handler to make it use the** `GetPostsQuery` **method by changing the following code that appears in bold:**

    ```
    protected override void OnNavigatedTo(NavigationEventA
          rgs e)
    {
        var query = _context.GetPostsQuery();
        _context.Load(query, op => LoadPostsDataGrid(op.
           Entities), null);
    }
    ```

16. **Rebuild the whole solution by right-clicking the solution name in the Solution Explorer, selecting Build from the menu, and running it.**

    You should now see exactly what Figure 13-2 shows: A list of the Post records in the database.

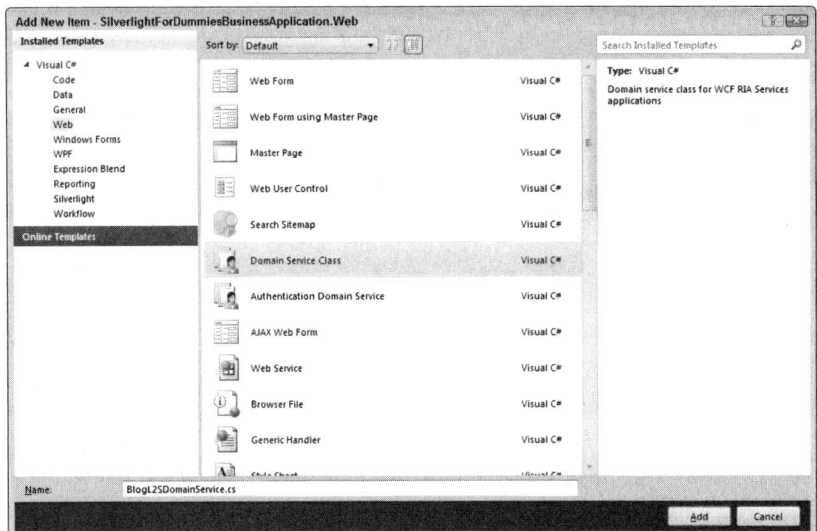

Figure 13-3: Adding LINQ to SQL Data Classes.

The application uses LINQ to SQL rather than Entity Framework as a result of the preceding steps. Next, you need to retrieve comments associated with each post. Do so by following these steps:

 1. **Open** the `BlogL2SDomainService.metadata.cs` **file by double-clicking it in the Solution Explorer.**

 2. **Add the** `[Include]` **attribute to the** `Comment` **property of the** `Post` **class in the** `BlogL2SDomainService.metadata.cs` **file by adding the following code immediately above the** `Comments` **property:**

    ```
    [Include]
    public EntitySet<Comment> Comments;
    ```

 3. **Create a new service method by adding the following code to the** `BlogL2SDomainService.cs` **file immediately after the** `GetPosts` **method:**

    ```
    public IQueryable<Post> GetPostsWithComments()
    {
        var loadOptions = new DataLoadOptions();
        loadOptions.LoadWith<Post>(p => p.Comments);
        Context.LoadOptions = loadOptions;
        return Context.Posts;
    }
    ```

This code tells WCF RIA Services to load the associated comments when it loads each post entity.

4. **Run the application by pressing F5 or clicking the green Play button.**

5. **Click a post in the PostsDataGrid to see how the associated comments are shown in the CommentsDataGrid.**

You can edit a post in the data grid and then click Save to save it.

Validating Data on the Client and Server Sides

The *R* in WCF RIA Services stands for *rich,* so you'd expect some richness out of the box without too much work to do. That's exactly what you get.

With regular Web programming, validation of user input is quite a complicated task that takes a lot of time to implement. You usually have to use some JavaScript on the client side to ensure that the text box you want to validate has the correct value in it; as a result, you have to make sure that your JavaScript works in all browsers because they all work slightly differently. The client-side validation code needs to provide some feedback to the user as well, so you have to not only validate the input but also design a way to tell users when they get it wrong.

You also have to write validation code on the server side because you can never rely entirely on client-side validation; intercepting messages from the client with a tool such as Fiddler is just far too easy. Therefore, you have to write code in two different languages, which means you can't share the code. Consequently, you have to write the same logic twice — and test it all.

Using WCF RIA Services, however, implementing validation is very simple. You just apply the correct attribute to the field in the meta data class that's associated with your domain service and you're done!

When you build your solution, WCF RIA Services does a bit of magic in Visual Studio and creates a copy of the server-side classes in your Silverlight application. Follow these steps to open the solution and see what it contains:

1. **Click the Silverlight application and then click the Show All Files button (shown in Figure 13-4) to show all the files in the Silverlight application folder.**

2. **Open the Generated Code folder and double-click the** `Silverlight ForDummiesBusinessApplication.Web.g.cs` **file.**

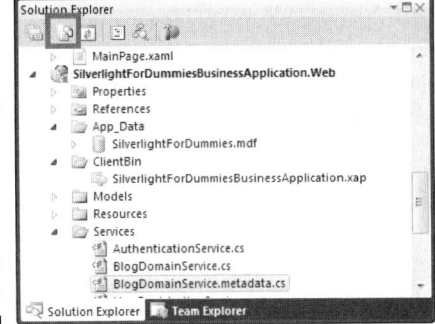

Figure 13-4: The code generated for the business application.

3. Use the drop-down list at the top left of the Code Editing window, as shown in Figure 13-5, to find the `Post` class.

4. Inside the `Post` class, find the `Content` property and look at the code in the `Set` method.

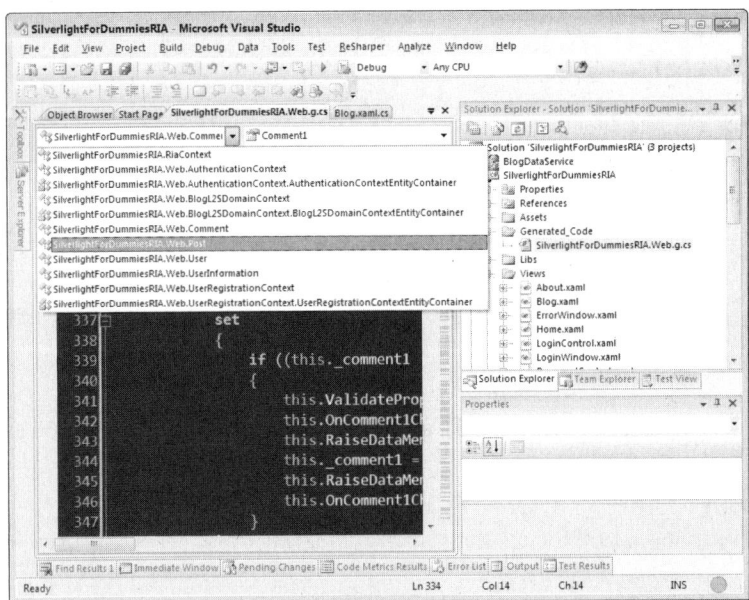

Figure 13-5: Navigating to the `Post` class.

The first line, `ValidateProperty`, is the method that evaluates all the `System.ComponentModel.DataAnnotations.Validation Attributes` on any property that has validation attributes marked against it. If any of the attributes don't validate correctly, a `Validation Exception` is thrown.

Adding validation attributes

You can specify validation rules on any property using validation attributes. A very common validation rule is that the property must be filled out. If the property is empty, a Validation Exception is thrown and you receive an error message similar to that shown in Figure 13-6.

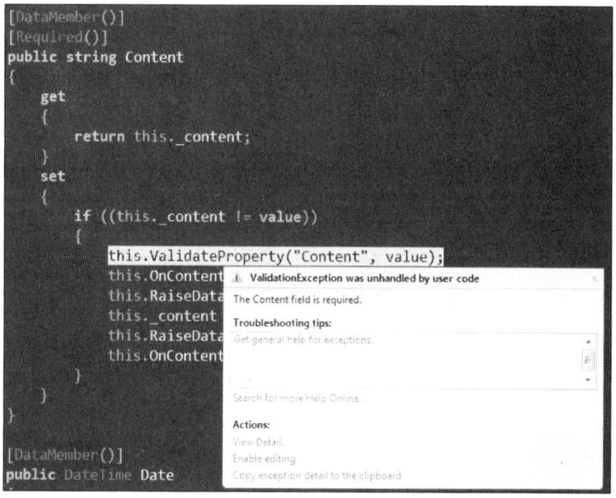

Figure 13-6: Validation error in Visual Studio.

You can try this by adding a validation attribute to the `Content` property and then making the validation fail, as follows:

1. **Open the `BlogL2SDomainService.metadata.cs` file by double-clicking it in the Solution Explorer.**

2. **Find the `PostMetaData` class.**

3. **Add the `[Required]` attribute to the `Content` property like so:**

   ```
   [Required]
   public string Content;
   ```

4. **Now run the application by pressing F5 or clicking the green Play button.**

5. **Delete the value in the `Content` field and press Tab to move your cursor out of the field.**

   Doing so causes a validation error; Visual Studio should show an error message similar to that shown in Figure 13-6. The error drops you into Visual Studio from your application.

 Being interrupted by validation errors all the time gets annoying during development. To suppress this particular error in Visual Studio, choose Debug⇨Exceptions and select Add. Select Common Language Runtime and enter **System.ComponentModel.DataAnnotations.ValidationException**. Then deselect the box next to that item.

Using a DataForm for great validation

It's good practice to provide users with a helpful way to correct data they enter incorrectly, and the easiest way to provide that is through a DataForm control. This control is part of the Silverlight Toolkit. The DataForm control provides a great data entry form, with all the fields you need to enter data (which in this example is a blog post), and validation feedback. You can get the latest copy of this control from `http://silverlight.codeplex.com/`. (Be sure to check for additions to this toolkit from time to time; you can find lots of useful items there.)

To add the DataForm control to the application and use its built-in feature that will automatically show the data entry fields, follow these steps:

1. **Add a reference to the Silverlight Toolkit by right-clicking the** `SilverlightForDummiesBusinessApplication` **project References node.**

   Adding the reference to the Silverlight Toolkit allows you to use it in your application. Without the reference, your solution won't work.

   The Add Reference menu appears.

2. **Select Add Reference.**

3. **Click the Browse tab and use the File Explorer to locate the** `System.Windows.Controls.Data.Toolkit.dll` **and** `System.Windows.Controls.Data.DataForm.Toolkit.dll` **files.**

   These files are in the C:\Program Files\Microsoft SDKs\Silverlight\v4.0\Toolkit\Nov09\Bin folder of your computer, as shown in Figure 13-7.

   The two references are added to your application. You should be able to see these two references underneath the project's References node now.

4. **Open the** `Blog.xaml` **file by double-clicking it in the Solution Explorer.**

5. **Add a new DataForm control immediately after the Comments Grid by dragging it onto the design surface from the toolbox.**

6. **Name the control PostsDataForm.**

7. **Set the** `CommandButtonsVisibility` **property to All.**

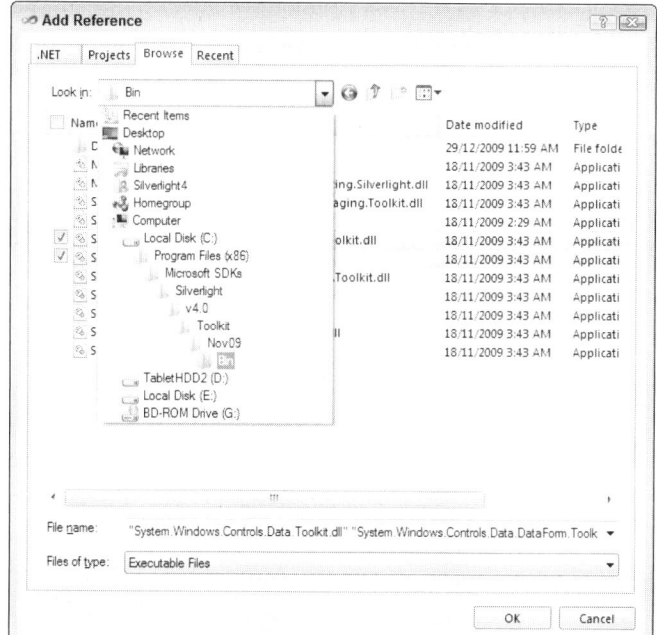

Figure 13-7: Adding the Silverlight Toolkit References.

 8. **Open the `Blog.xaml.cs` file and set the Items Source of the PostsData Form to `posts` by adding the bold code to the `LoadPostsDataGrid` method.**

    ```
    private void LoadPostsDataGrid(IEnumerable<Post>
         posts)
    {
       PostsDataGrid.ItemsSource = posts;
       PostsDataForm.ItemsSource = posts;
    }
    ```

 9. **Run the application and delete the content from the `Content` field.**

    Note that when you run the application, the Content field is bold in the data form, which indicates that it's a required field.

    Add some meta data such as a `Display` attribute. (See "Creating the Domain Data Service," earlier in this chapter, for more information about meta data.)

10. **Press Tab to leave the content field.**

    When you delete the text from the `Content` field and leave the data entry box, the validation is executed and the validation feedback appears as a red box for the data entry field. The field name is also red and the error is shown at the bottom of the form, as shown in Figure 13-8.

Building a solid validation experience is very simple using WCF RIA Services. Of course, if you don't like the standard look of the validation in the DataForm control, you can easily modify the template using Expression Blend (see Figure 13-9).

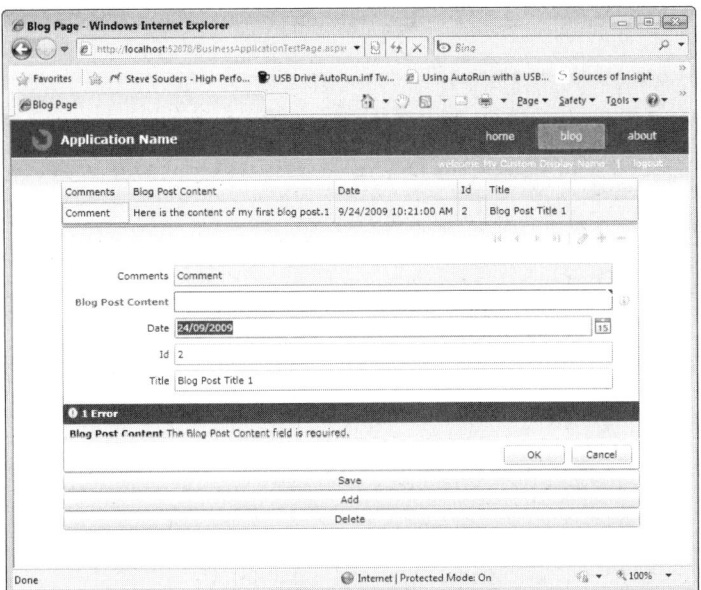

Figure 13-8: Dataform validation.

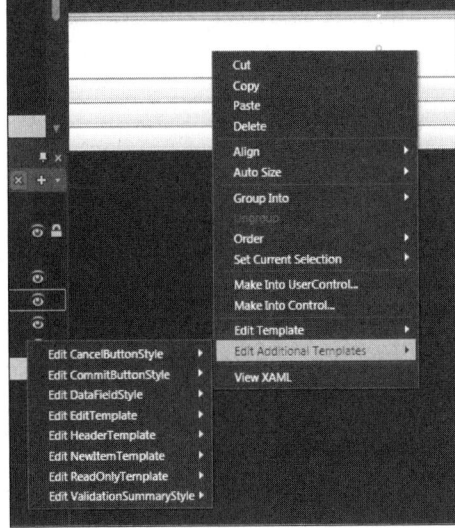

Figure 13-9: Modifying the DataForm using Expression Blend.

Securing Your WCF RIA Service

When you build an application such as a blog engine, you need to make sure that only users who are logged in to the system can make changes and read sensitive data. WCF RIA Services handles this requirement for you when you include the [RequiresAuthentication] attribute in the Service Method you use. (See the "Writing Your Own Service Methods — LINQ to Entity Framework" section, earlier in this chapter, for an explanation of a service method.) With a blog application, for example, you use this attribute with the GetPostsWithComments service method to ensure that only logged-in, authenticated users have access to the data in the database. For this example, all data access will be locked down and available only to the logged-in user.

To secure the GetPostsWithComments method on the WCF RIA Service, follow these steps:

1. **Open the** BlogDomainService.cs **file by double-clicking it in the Solution Explorer.**

2. **Locate the** GetPostsWithComments **method.**

3. **Add the [RequiresAuthentication] attribute immediately above the** GetPostsWithComments **method.**

   Your code should look like this now, with the added attribute in bold.

   ```
   [RequiresAuthentication]
   public IQueryable<Post> GetPostsWithComments()
   {
       var loadOptions = new DataLoadOptions();
       loadOptions.LoadWith<Post>(p => p.Comments);
       DataContext.LoadOptions = loadOptions;
       return DataContext.Posts;
   }
   ```

4. **Run the application by pressing F5 or clicking the green Play button.**

   No results appear in the PostsDataGrid at this point because you are not logged in.

5. **Close the browser.**

6. **Choose Project**➪**ASP.NET Configuration.**

   The ASP.NET Web Site Administration tool appears so that you can configure some users for the site. (You can use the database from the application example in Chapter 12, if you've already created it; if you have, ignore Steps 6–10.)

7. **In the ASP.NET Web Site Administration tool, click the** `Select Authentication Type` **link.**

    If you don't see this link by default, click the Security tab on the Web site to make the link appear.

8. **Select the From the Internet option and click Done.**

9. **Click the Create User link.**

    The Create User Webform appears.

10. **Fill out the new user form and click Create User.**

11. **Close the browser.**

12. **Run the application again by pressing F5 or clicking the green Play button.**

13. **Click the login link and enter the details of the user you created in Step 10.**

    You can now see the posts in the data grid.

Many applications use the idea of user roles to manage the tasks each user can perform when he or she accesses the application. You are probably familiar with the idea of a computer administrator who has complete access to a computer, allowing that person to do tasks that require some extra skills. Everyday users may not have the skills required to be an administrator, so they do not get access to those features, which stops them from accidentally breaking the computer. Therefore, user roles are assigned to users so that when they log in, the tasks they are allowed to perform are managed by their assigned role.

In the following example, you want only people who are readers of your blog to be able to access the contents of the database because you want to keep the contents private. First, you need to establish the user role, which is entered into the database via the ASP.NET Configuration Manager. You can use the built-in standard ASP.NET membership system and tools in Visual Studio to establish user roles on an application such as a blog, and use the [RequiredRole] security attribute to enforce those roles. To add this attribute to your application, follow these steps (using the blog application as an example):

1. **Open the** `web.config` **file in the** `SilverlightForDummiesBusiness Application.Web` **project by double-clicking it in the Solution Explorer.**

2. **Enable the ASP.NET Role Manager feature by adding the following code immediately after the** `<authentication>` **node in the** `web.config` **file: You can see where it goes by looking at the whole code snippet below and adding the code that is in bold.**

```
<system.web>
  <httpModules>
    <add name="DomainServiceModule" type="System.Web.
        Ria.Services.DomainServiceHttpModule, System.
        Web.Ria, Version=4.0.0.0, Culture=neutral, Pub
        licKeyToken=31BF3856AD364E35" />
  </httpModules>
  <compilation debug="true" targetFramework="4.0">
    <assemblies>
      <add assembly="System.Data.Entity,
          Version=4.0.0.0, Culture=neutral, PublicKeyTok
          en=b77a5c561934e089" />
    </assemblies>
  </compilation>
  <roleManager enabled="true" />
  <authentication mode="Forms">
```

3. **Open the Site Administration tool in Visual Studio by choosing Project➪ ASP.NET Configuration.**

   The Web page shown in Figure 13-10 appears.

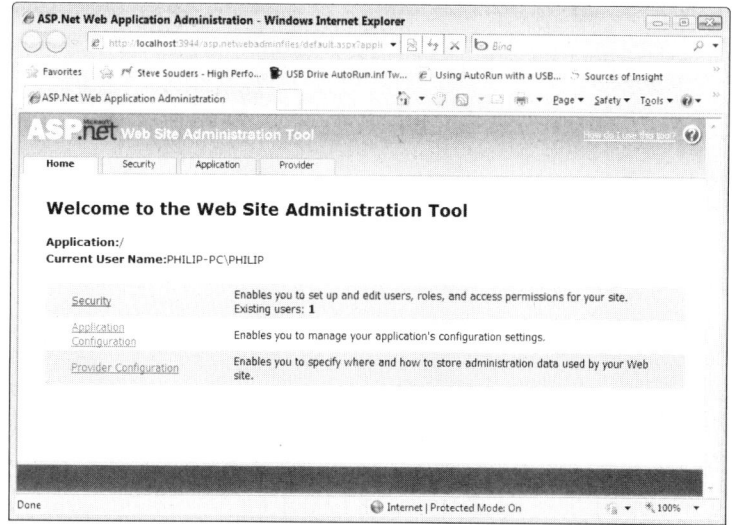

Figure 13-10: ASP.NET Configuration tool.

4. **Click the Security tab.**
5. **Click the Create or Manage Roles link in the Roles box.**

6. **Enter** Blog Reader **in the New Role Name text box and click the Add Role button.**

   A new role is added to the database and appears in a list under the New Role Name text box.

7. **Under Add/Remove Users, click the Manage link next to the new role you created.**

8. **Click the All link at the far right of the Search for Users box.**

9. **Select the User Is In Role check box to add your user to the new role.**

10. **Open the** `BlogDomainService.cs` **file.**

11. **Add the** `[RequiresRole("Blog Reader")]` **attribute to the** `GetPostsWithComments` **method.**

    Your code should now look like this, with the new attribute in bold:

    ```
    [RequiresAuthentication]
    [RequiresRole("Blog Reader")]
    public IQueryable<Post> GetPostsWithComments()
    {
        var loadOptions = new DataLoadOptions();
        loadOptions.LoadWith<Post>(p => p.Comments);
        DataContext.LoadOptions = loadOptions;
        return DataContext.Posts;
    }
    ```

12. **Run the application and log in.**

    You should see your posts.

Now you need to test the whether the code for assigning roles is working. You do so by removing the user from the Blog Reader role and trying to access the data. Follow these steps:

1. **Open the Site Administration tool in Visual Studio by choosing Project➪ASP.NET Configuration.**

2. **Click the Security tab.**

3. **Click the Manage Users link.**

   The Search for Users box appears.

4. **Next to the username, click the Manage Roles link.**

   A new column called Roles appears in the list of users.

5. **Deselect the check box next to the Blog Reader role.**

6. **Run the application again and log in.**

   You should be denied access to the data because you are not in the correct role. This is a very powerful way to restrict access to your important domain services.

Part IV
The Part of Tens

In this part . . .

The Part of Tens offers you a look at some of the things that aren't covered in the other parts of this book, in the form of lists that contain ten items each.

Chapter 14 gives you a taste of ten cool controls that you will use often in your Silverlight applications. In Chapter 15, we tell you how to get more out of Silverlight; check this chapter out for lots of tools, techniques, and tips.

Chapter 16 provides even more tips, including keyboard shortcuts, how to find additional Silverlight resources, and much more.

Chapter 14

Ten Cool Controls for Collecting and Displaying Data

In This Chapter

▶ Displaying multiple controls within a ListBox
▶ Managing tabular data in a DataGrid
▶ Editing data in a DataForm
▶ Expanding a view with the Expander
▶ Showing graphs and charts with the Chart control
▶ Picking dates with the DatePicker
▶ Showing progress using a ProgressBar
▶ Displaying hierarchical data using a TreeView
▶ Managing ratings with the Rating control
▶ Auto-completing a TextBox using AutoCompleteBox

Silverlight and the Silverlight Toolkit come with a bunch of controls out of the box, many of which are described elsewhere in this book. This chapter highlights some additional controls that you will find really useful for not only displaying data but also collecting them from the user.

ListBox

The ListBox is underrated as a control, mainly because of how it is traditionally used: to display a list of string values and have the user select one of them. Chapter 4 shows you how to use the ListBox, as well as the ComboBox, which is nothing more than a drop-down ListBox.

A single ListBox item in Silverlight can actually take a complex form and contain multiple controls that are nicely formatted, as opposed to containing just one line of string in traditional list boxes. As an example, if you had an object that contained the name, address, and e-mail of a person, you could display all those items in a single ListBox item, with name, address, and e-mail nicely formatted, as shown in Figure 14-1. The markup to represent this in a single item would look something like this:

```
<ListBox ItemsSource="{Binding Collection}" >
    <ListBox.ItemTemplate>
        <DataTemplate>
            <StackPanel>
                <TextBlock Text="{Binding Name}" FontSize="16"/>
                <TextBlock Text="{Binding Address}"/>
                <TextBlock Text="{Binding Email}" FontSize="9" FontStyle="Italic"
                />
            </StackPanel>
        </DataTemplate>
    </ListBox.ItemTemplate>
</ListBox>
```

You use the `ItemTemplate` element of the ListBox to specify how the ListBox actually looks. In spite of the way it looks, it still acts and works like a standard ListBox.

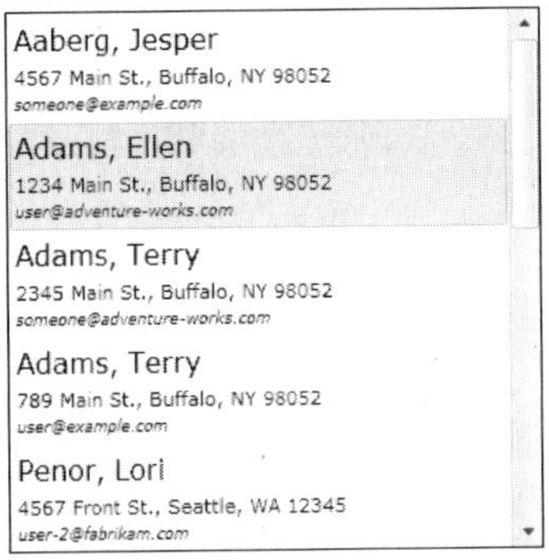

Figure 14-1: ListBox with items nicely formatted.

DataGrid

You can use the DataGrid control to display data in a nice spreadsheet-like Grid and support tasks such as editing the data inline, resizing and moving columns, sorting, and more. The markup for a simple grid that supports all these features looks something like this:

```
<data:DataGrid AutoGenerateColumns="True" ItemsSource="{Binding Collection}">
</data:DataGrid>
```

When you specify the `AutoGenerateColumns` property as true, Silverlight will automatically pick up the column names from the data specified in the `ItemsSource` property and, depending on the type of data, display the columns appropriately. You can edit the data by double-clicking a cell. You can also sort by clicking the column headings, and you can even reorder the columns by dragging the column headers around. All this functionality is available without writing a single line of code or adding markup. A data grid sorted by the name column is shown in Figure 14-2.

Name ▲	Address	Email
Aaberg, Jesper	4567 Main St., Buffalo, NY 98052	someone@example.com
Aaberg, Jesper	4567 Main St., Buffalo, NY 98052	someone@example.com
Aaberg, Jesper	4567 Main St., Buffalo, NY 98052	user@adventure-works.com
Adams, Ellen	1234 Main St., Buffalo, NY 98052	user@adventure-works.com
Adams, Ellen	1234 Main St., Buffalo, NY 98052	someone@adventure-works.com
Adams, Terry	2345 Main St., Buffalo, NY 98052	someone@adventure-works.com
Adams, Terry	789 Main St., Buffalo, NY 98052	user@example.com
Adams, Terry	2345 Main St., Buffalo, NY 98052	user@example.com
Adams, Terry	789 Main St., Buffalo, NY 98052	user-2@fabrikam.com
Argentiero, Luca	1234 1st Ave, San Francisco, CA 99999	user-7@fabrikam.com

Figure 14-2: DataGrid showing name column sorted and a column selected.

The DataGrid control is also discussed in Chapter 9.

DataForm

As the name suggests, you can use the DataForm when you want to edit data in a form. As is the DataGrid control, which is described in the previous section, this control is extremely simple to use. All you need to do is bind it to the data and let the control do all the work. In its simplest form, the markup for the DataForm looks something like this:

```
<dataFormToolkit:DataForm ItemsSource="{Binding Collection}"/>
```

This brings up a DataForm that contains buttons enabling the user to navigate the list of records in the collection. It also contains buttons to add and remove items. The labels for the data will automatically be displayed, as shown in Figure 14-3.

WCF RIA Services, which we describe in Chapters 12 and 13, use DataForms to edit data.

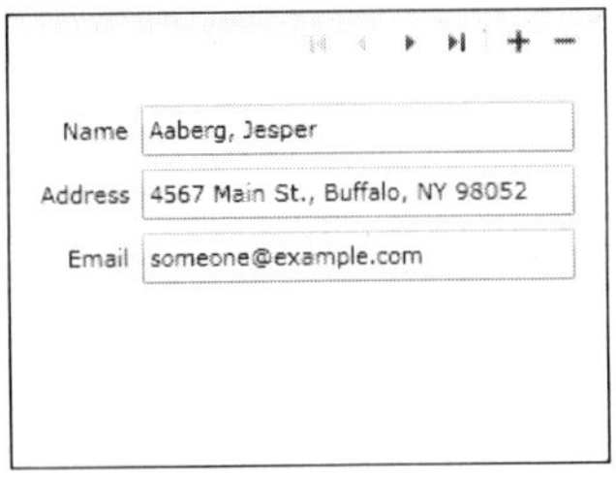

Figure 14-3: A DataForm in which you can edit the data in a collection.

Expander

You use the Expander control to collapse and expand the contents in a page. Strictly speaking, the Expander isn't used for displaying or collecting data. But it can be very useful when you do not want to show all the data on the screen all the time. With the Expander control, you can hide the content and make it appear when you click a button. This removes screen clutter and makes the page look cleaner. The markup for displaying a DataGrid in an Expander will look something like this:

```xml
<controlsToolkit:Expander HorizontalAlignment="Left" VerticalAlignment="Top" >
    <controlsToolkit:HeaderedContentControl.Header>
        <TextBlock Text="Expander that hides/displays the DataGrid" FontSize="18"
            TextDecorations="Underline" />
    </controlsToolkit:HeaderedContentControl.Header>
    <controlsToolkit:HeaderedContentControl.Content>
        <data:DataGrid AutoGenerateColumns="True" Height="300"
            ItemsSource="{Binding Collection}" />
    </controlsToolkit:HeaderedContentControl.Content>
</controlsToolkit:Expander>
```

When the application is run and the Expander is collapsed, it resembles Figure 14-4.

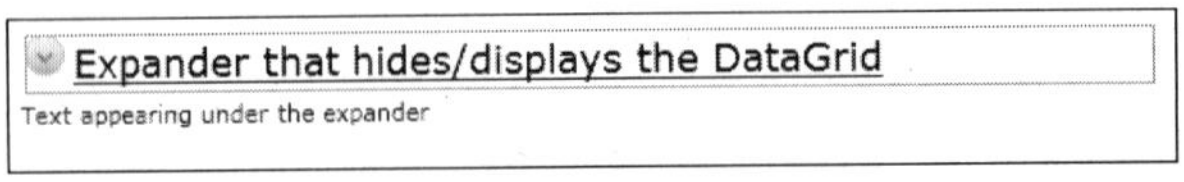

Figure 14-4: Expander with collapsed content.

When the user clicks the down arrow, the content is displayed as shown in Figure 14-5.

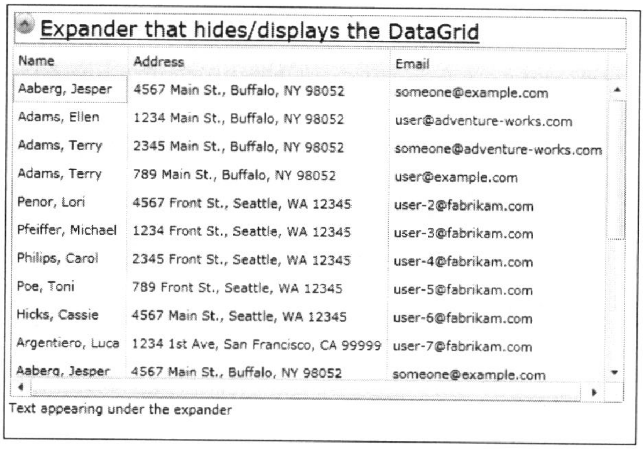

Figure 14-5: Expander with expanded content.

Chart

You can use the Chart control to display various kinds of charts in Silverlight. Following is an example of markup that creates a simple bar chart using this control:

```
<StackPanel x:Name="LayoutRoot" Background="White" Margin="10" >
    <chartingToolkit:Chart
            Title="Population(Top 5 countries)"
            Height="440"
            DataContext="{Binding Collection, Source={StaticResource
                SampleDataSource1}}">
        <chartingToolkit:ColumnSeries
            Title="Population in Millions"
            AnimationSequence="FirstToLast"
            DependentValuePath="Population"
            IndependentValuePath="Country"
            ItemsSource="{Binding}"/>
    </chartingToolkit:Chart>
</StackPanel>
```

This displays a bar chart that looks like Figure 14-6.

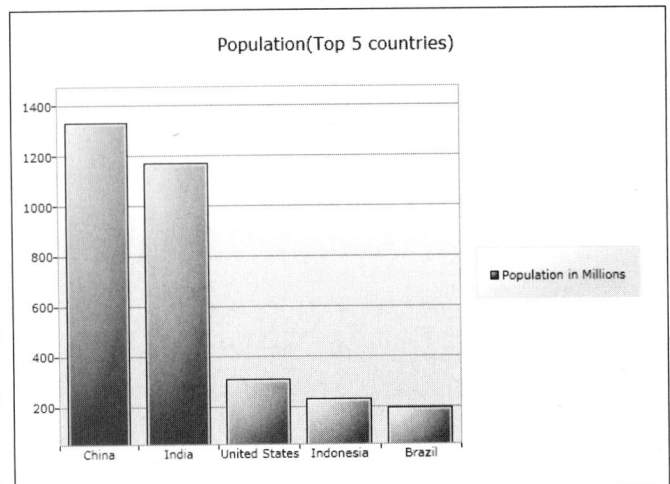

Figure 14-6:
Bar chart showing population.

DatePicker

The DatePicker control provides a simple user interface for selecting dates from a calendar. It shows a TextBox followed by a small calendar icon. The user can either type the date directly in the TextBox or click the calendar icon, as shown in Figure 14-7. Clicking the icon makes a calendar drop down, from which the user can pick a date.

Figure 14-7:
DatePicker control.

ProgressBar

You can use the ProgressBar control to display the progress of long-running activities in Silverlight. The ProgressBar is typically used to display the percentage of work that has been completed, such as download percentage. You can use data binding, explained in Chapter 9, to show the progress automatically, when the `Value` property is updated. The ProgressBar is shown in Figure 14-8.

Figure 14-8:
A Progress Bar in action.

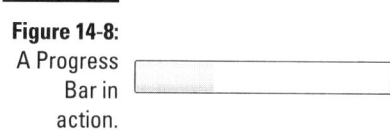

TreeView

You use the TreeView control to display hierarchical data such as an Organization chart or a directory structure that contains other directories and files. The tree is displayed in the form of nodes. The user can click a node either to select it or expand it to reveal other child nodes.

A TreeView created using sample data in Expression Blend is shown in Figure 14-9.

Figure 14-9: TreeView created from sample data.

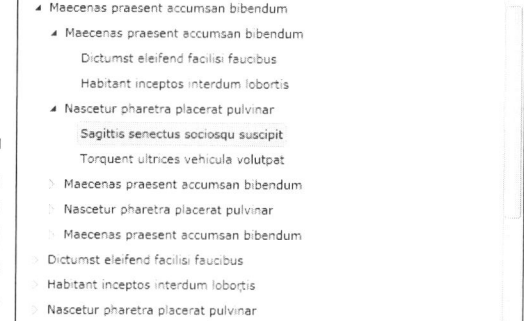

Rating

As its name suggests, you use the Rating control to select a rating for any type of field. For example, you can use it to rate a movie, vote for something, or even grade a student's assignment. The default view displays the ratings as stars, as shown in Figure 14-10.

You can pick a rating by clicking the star. The Value property of the control contains the value that you've picked.

Figure 14-10: Rating control.

AutoCompleteBox

The AutoCompleteBox is a TextBox that provides the user with a drop-down list of values based on the text that is being typed into the TextBox.

Figure 14-11 shows an AutoCompleteBox in which the values Australia and Austria show up when the user types **Au** in the TextBox. The values that need to be shown in the drop-down list are databound to the ItemsSource property of the AutoCompleteBox control, as shown in the XAML snippet below:

```
<input:AutoCompleteBox ItemsSource="{Binding Countries}" />
```

Figure 14-11: AutoCompleteBox for a Country field.

Chapter 15

Ten Ways to Get More Out of Silverlight

In This Chapter

- Using SketchFlow to prototype your application
- Using Deep Zoom Composer
- Creating designs using Expression Design
- Importing designs into Expression Blend
- Creating your own behaviors
- Printing in Silverlight
- Calling Silverlight code via JavaScript
- Accessing HTML from Silverlight
- Storing data locally in the client
- Running Silverlight out of the browser

In this chapter, you will look at a bunch of different ways to get more out of Silverlight. The chapter includes a wide range of topics, including using SketchFlow to create a prototype that you can showcase to a business client before you create the actual application; using tools such as Deep Zoom Composer and Expression Design; interacting between the browser and the Silverlight SketchFlow application; and much more.

Using SketchFlow to Prototype Your Application

SketchFlow is an application that comes with Expression Blend and helps you to quickly prototype applications. To use it, you choose File⇨New Project and select Silverlight SketchFlow Application to create a prototyping project.

You can add new pages in SketchFlow Map and specify the flow among the various pages visually, as shown in Figure 15-1.

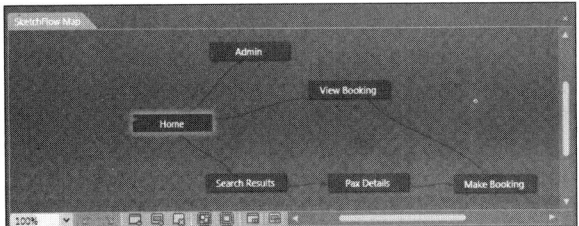

Figure 15-1: Adding new pages in SketchFlow Map.

You can then add controls to each page from the Tools panel, and a wireframe of the user interface gets created, as shown in Figure 15-2.

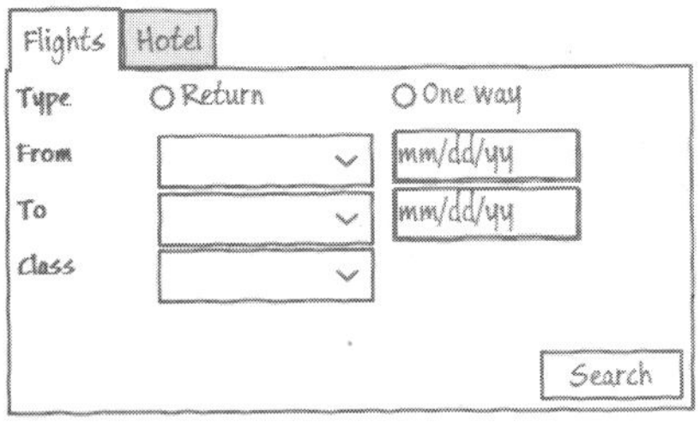

Figure 15-2: A Prototyped screen.

If you are working in a corporate environment or need to get approval of your design from others, you can get the project owners and business analysts to look at the prototype you've created using the SketchFlow Player and provide feedback. The SketchFlow Player is shown in Figure 15-3. You can also export the prototypes you create in SketchFlow into a Word document to share it with others.

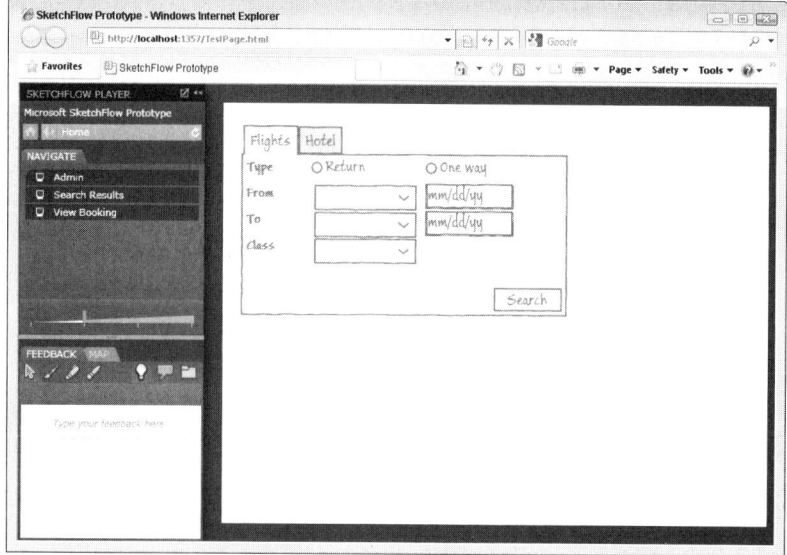

Figure 15-3: Use SketchFlow Player to let clients review the prototype.

Using Deep Zoom Composer

Using Deep Zoom composer (downloadable free from Microsoft), you can create a composition of high-resolution images to use in your Silverlight application. These images can be individual images from a collection (such as works of art or photographs) or high-resolution pictures of a single image that are stitched together to form a large, high-resolution canvas.

When the user views these images in a Silverlight application, they are downloaded progressively, initially displaying a blurry image that gets crisper as the complete image is loaded. This provides the user with a much better experience than waiting through a blank screen until the images are downloaded completely.

The Deep Zoom Composer application is extremely simple to use. You can create a Deep Zoom application with a three-step process: Import, Compose, and Export.

For the Import step, you choose the images you want to use. For the Compose step, you put the images together. Finally, for the Export step, you specify the type of output you want to create. Deep Zoom Composer allows you to create outputs in more than one form — the one that you need to choose is Silverlight Deep Zoom. Deep Zoom Composer is shown in Figure 15-4.

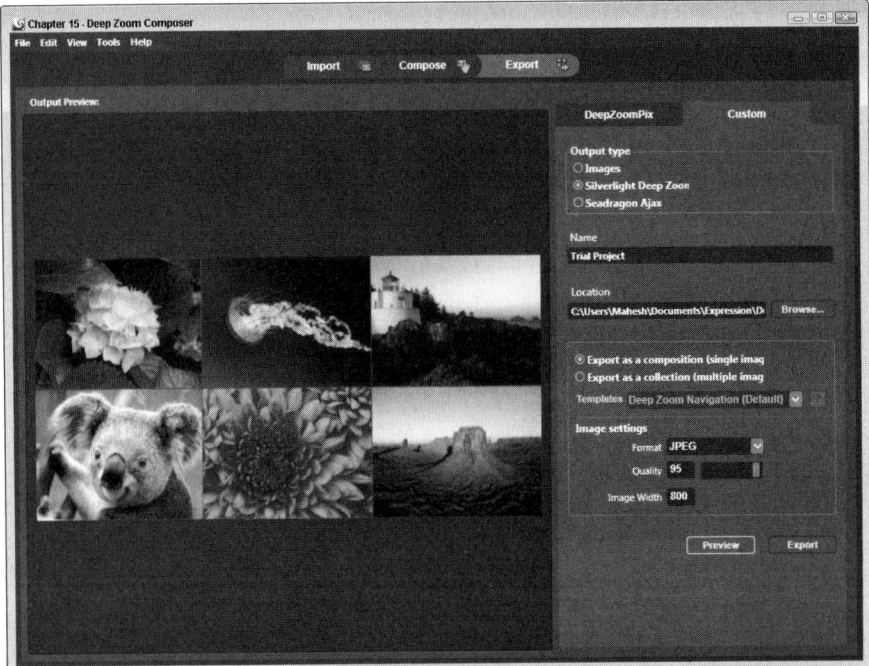

Figure 15-4: Deep Zoom Composer.

Creating Designs Using Expression Design

User interface design forms an important component of any Silverlight application. You can use Expression Blend to create your screen designs visually, but designers need something a lot more sophisticated, which is where Expression Design comes in.

Expression Design helps you create complex graphics using vector paths and bitmap graphics. Vector paths make use of points and lines to draw your image, whereas bitmap images use an array of pixels to represent it. Raster paths scale well when resized, whereas bitmaps don't.

Chapter 15: Ten Ways to Get More Out of Silverlight

In Expression Design, you can compose designs in a layered fashion, separating each part of the overall image into layers that overlap one another. You can then choose to hide or show individual layers, thereby affecting how the image looks.

You can also use the application to convert bitmap images into vector paths. For example, you might start with a bitmapped image, as shown in Figure 15-5, and choose Object⇨Image⇨Auto Trace Image.

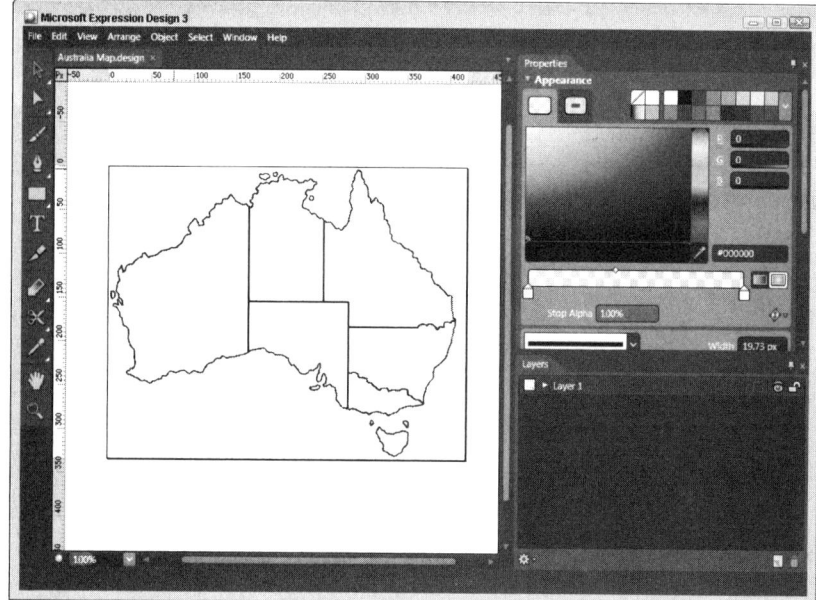

Figure 15-5: A bitmapped image of a map in Expression Design.

This action automatically traces the image using vector paths, as shown in Figure 15-6. In Chapter 3, you find out how to use the Pencil and Pen tools in Expression Blend to draw freehand sketches. Auto-tracing an image will automatically create a freehand sketch for you without the need to use these tools; it does this by copying the XAML equivalent when you choose Edit⇨Copy XAML and pasting that equivalent into markup in your XAML file.

This is just a sampling of what you can do using Expression Design. It is a very sophisticated tool and needs a separate book to do it any justice.

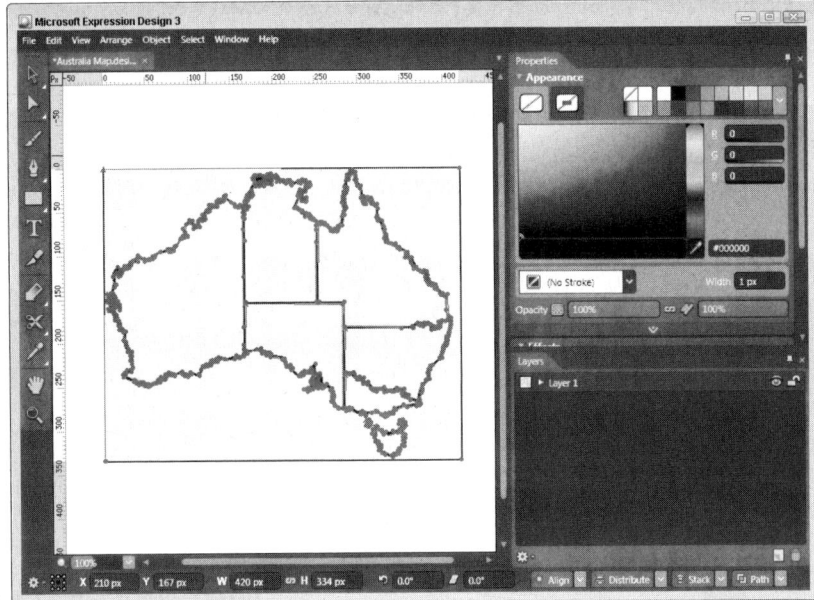

Figure 15-6:
Auto-traced path of the bitmap image.

Importing Designs from Other Applications

Expression Design and Expression Blend are slowly growing in popularity, but a lot of designers are still creating Web page designs using Adobe Photoshop and Illustrator.

You can import from these two formats in both Expression Design and Blend. In Expression Blend, you can import from these two formats by choosing File➪Import Adobe Photoshop File and File➪Import Adobe Illustrator File.

After you select the file that you want to import, Expression Blend opens the Import tool, as shown in Figure 15-7, which allows you to pick the design layers you want and bring them into the application as XAML.

Figure 15-7: Import Adobe Photoshop file.

Creating Your Own Behaviors

Behaviors let you add a certain functionality or behavior to your control without the need to write code. These behaviors are available in the Assets panel and can be added to a control from within Expression Blend. Chapter 7 tells you how to apply Silverlight's built-in behaviors to your controls.

You're not limited to those built-in behaviors, however; you can add your own to the mix. To create a behavior from Expression Blend, click the name of the project in the Projects panel to select it. Then right-click and choose New Item. When the New Item dialog box opens, select Behavior from the list and click OK.

You can then override the methods `OnAttached` and `OnDetaching` to attach to events and manipulate the way the controls behave.

Here's an example of creating a simple behavior to set the opacity of any control to 25 percent when a mouse moves on top of a control, and to set it to 100 percent when the mouse moves out of it:

```csharp
public class TransparentBehavior : Behavior<UIElement>
{
    protected override void OnAttached()
    {
        base.OnAttached();

        this.AssociatedObject.MouseEnter +=
            new MouseEventHandler(AssociatedObject_
        MouseEnter);
        this.AssociatedObject.MouseLeave +=
            new MouseEventHandler(AssociatedObject_
        MouseLeave);
    }

    void AssociatedObject_MouseLeave(object sender,
        MouseEventArgs e)
    {
        this.AssociatedObject.Opacity = 1;
    }

    void AssociatedObject_MouseEnter(object sender,
        MouseEventArgs e)
    {
        this.AssociatedObject.Opacity = 0.25;
    }

    protected override void OnDetaching()
    {
        base.OnDetaching();

        this.AssociatedObject.MouseEnter
            -= new MouseEventHandler(AssociatedObject_
        MouseEnter);
        this.AssociatedObject.MouseLeave
            -= new MouseEventHandler(AssociatedObject_
        MouseLeave);
    }
}
```

Running Silverlight Out of the Browser

With Silverlight 4, you can run your Silverlight application out of the browser, which means that you can run it from your desktop without having to start your Internet browser application. To enable this option from Expression Blend, choose Project⇨Silverlight Project Options⇨Enable Application Outside Browser. Doing so automatically adds the necessary settings to your project.

When this feature is enabled, you can install the application you've created onto your machine by right-clicking the application on the browser and choosing the "Install *Application Name* onto this Computer" option from the menu, as shown in Figure 15-8.

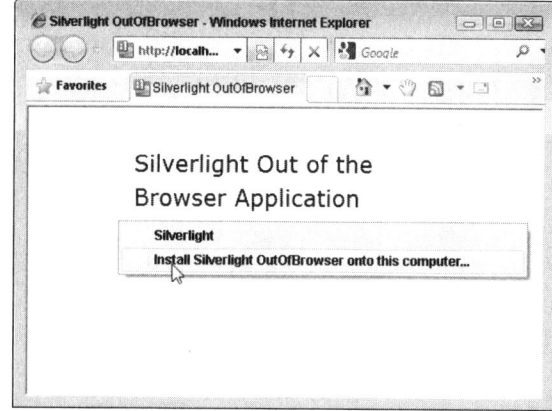

Figure 15-8: Installing a Silverlight application to run from the browser.

To enable this option in Visual Studio, you right-click the project name in the Solution Explorer and choose Properties. In the Silverlight tab, select the Enable Running Application Out of the Browser option and then click the Out-of-Browser Settings button. This brings up the Out-of-Browser Settings dialog box, shown in Figure 15-9, which you can use to set more properties for this setting.

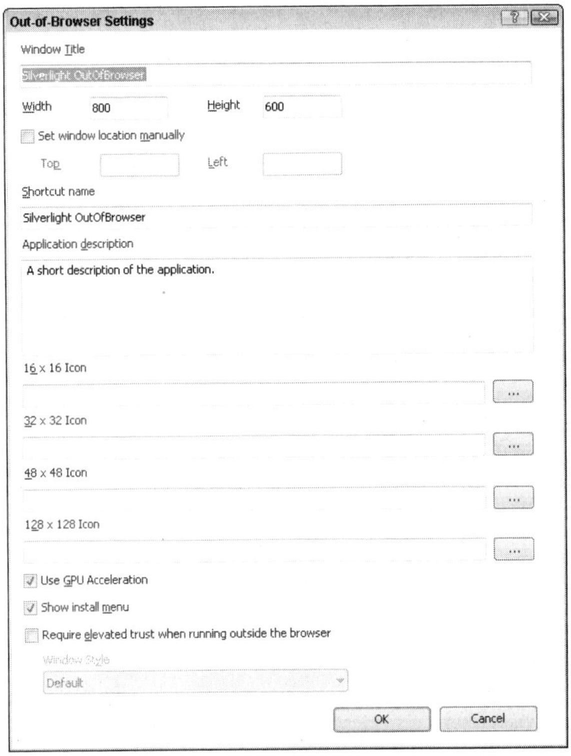

Figure 15-9: Out-of-Browser settings in Visual Studio.

Calling Silverlight code via JavaScript

You can call Silverlight code written in C# or VB.NET directly from your HTML page using JavaScript and a feature called the HTML Bridge. This allows for a better integration between a Silverlight application and the page in which the application is hosted. Using the HTML Bridge, here's an overview of the steps to call Silverlight code:

1. Create methods in Silverlight that can be called using JavaScript.
2. Register the object so that it can be called from the HTML page.
3. Call it from JavaScript.

Read on for an example.

Create a scriptable method

To create a simple method that returns a simple "Hello World" string, create a new class called `SilverlightHelper` and add the method `GetHelloMessage`, as follows:

```
public class SilverlightHelper
{
    [ScriptableMember]
    public string GetHelloMessage()
    {
        return "Hello World";
    }
}
```

The `ScriptableMember` attribute in front of the function makes it callable from JavaScript. This attribute is present in the `System.Windows.Browser` namespace.

Create and register the object

Open the `App.xaml.cs` file, and in the `Application_Startup` method, add the following two lines shown in bold:

```
private void Application_Startup(object sender,
        StartupEventArgs e)
{
    this.RootVisual = new MainPage();

    SilverlightHelper helper = new SilverlightHelper();
    HtmlPage.RegisterScriptableObject("SilverlightHelper",
        helper);
}
```

These two lines create an instance of the `SilverlightHelper` class and register them in the HTML page so that they can be accessed via JavaScript. Remember to add the following line at the top of the file:

```
using System.Windows.Browser;
```

Call the ScriptableMember function

In the HTML page that contains the Silverlight application, you need to make two changes. First, you need to add a parameter to the object that holds the Silverlight plug-in so that it calls a function as soon as the plug-in `object` element is loaded, as shown in the following line in bold:

```
    <object data="data:application/x-silverlight,"
        type="application/x-silverlight-2" width="100%"
        height="100%">
    <param name="source" value="ClientBin/Chapter 15
        Import.xap"/>
    <param name="onLoad" value="onPluginLoaded" />
    <param name="onerror" value="onSilverlightError" />
    <param name="background" value="white" />
    <param name="minRuntimeVersion" value="3.0.40624.0" />
    <param name="autoUpgrade" value="true" />
    <a href="http://go.microsoft.com/fwlink/?LinkID=14
        9156&v=3.0.40624.0" style="text-decoration:
        none;">
        <img src="http://go.microsoft.com/
            fwlink/?LinkId=108181" alt="Get Microsoft
            Silverlight" style="border-style: none"/>
    </a>
</object>
...
```

Next, you need to add the `onPluginLoaded` function in the HTML page so that it executes the scriptable method, as follows:

```
<script type="text/javascript">
    function onPluginLoaded(sender, args) {
        var silverLightControl = sender.getHost();
        alert(silverLightControl.Content.
            SilverlightHelper.GetHelloMessage());
    }
...
```

This displays a JavaScript alert message with the text that is generated by the `GetHelloMessage` in Silverlight.

Accessing HTML from Silverlight

The previous section shows an example of how to access Silverlight from HTML. What if you want to do it the other way around — that is access HTML from Silverlight? Silverlight supports that, too. Silverlight 4 provides two ways to access HTML:

- Using the WebBrowser control
- Via the Document Object Model (DOM) that holds the elements of the HTML hosting the Silverlight application

Using the WebBrowser control

Silverlight 4 introduces a new WebBrowser control for displaying Web pages within a Silverlight application. To use it within an application, follow these steps:

1. **In Expression Blend, open the Silverlight project and the XAML file to which you want to add a Web page.**

2. **Open the Assets panel and type** WebBrowser **in the Search field. When the control appears in the list, double-click the item to add it to the XAML page.**

   The WebBrowser control gets added to the XAML page with the default width and height and is displayed on the Artboard. Adjust the height and width of the control to the desired dimensions by dragging the resizing handles of the control.

3. **In the Properties panel, change the Source property, which you find under the Miscellaneous group, to the Web page address (such as** http://dummies.com**) you want displayed.**

   This sets the Web page that should be displayed in the Silverlight application. But it's important to note that the WebBrowser control will display pages only when run in Out-of-Browser mode; also, it needs to run in an elevated trust mode. An elevated trust mode allows Silverlight to directly access things such as the Clipboard, the user's folder in the computer, and much, much more. When you try to install an application that requires elevated permissions, Silverlight prompts you with a Security Warning dialog box mentioning that the application can access your personal data.

4. **Choose Project➪Silverlight Project Options➪Enable Application Outside Browser.**

   This lets you run your application outside the browser.

5. **Choose Project➪Silverlight Project Options➪Application Requires Elevated Permission.**

   This makes the application run under elevated permissions.

6. **Press F5 to run the application.**

   The application runs in a browser and the Web page that was specified in the Source property is displayed in the Silverlight application.

Apart from using the Source property, you can set the HTML displayed in the WebBrowser control in the following ways:

- Use the Navigate method of the WebBrowser control to navigate to another URL.
- Use the NavigateToString method to display HTML that you pass to it.

Using the DOM to access HTML

You can obtain the HTML DOM using the `HtmlPage.Document` object using C# or VB.NET within Silverlight. When you have the object, you can manipulate individual HTML elements in C# as shown in the following example:

```
HtmlDocument document = HtmlPage.Document;
HtmlElement element = document.
        GetElementById("elementID");
element.SetStyleAttribute("color", "Red");
```

You are not restricted to calling just the HTML elements in the page, you also have access to things like cookies. You can access the cookies in the page by calling `HtmlPage.Document.Cookies`.

"How can I call a JavaScript function from Silverlight?" you ask. Easy: Instead of using the `HtmlPage.Document` object, you use `HtmlPage.Window`. For example, to call a function called `javaScriptFunction` that takes two parameters, `parameter1` and `parameter2`, your call from C# code will look something like following:

```
HtmlPage.Window.Invoke("javaScriptFunction", new object[]
        { parameter1, parameter2 });
```

Storing Data Locally in the Client

Silverlight allows you to use the local storage on the client machine to store application-specific data or even to cache some data from the server. The sample markup that follows shows how you can access the local storage:

```
using (IsolatedStorageFile storage = IsolatedStorageFile.
        GetUserStoreForApplication())
{
    using (IsolatedStorageFileStream fileStream = new Isol
            atedStorageFileStream(LogFileName,
        FileMode.OpenOrCreate, storage))
    {
        //Do stuff with the fileStream object
        ...
    }
}
```

Each user of the application gets his or her own isolated storage in the client machine, which is initially set to 1MB capacity. When the application needs additional storage, the user receives a prompt asking whether he or she wants to grant the application additional storage. When you run the application out of the browser, this starting storage limit is set to 25MB.

Chapter 16
Ten Handy Tips for Writing Silverlight Applications

In This Chapter
- Finding resources and utilities to increase your productivity
- Writing applications with accessibility and worldwide users in mind
- Putting handy shortcuts to good use
- Debugging Silverlight applications
- Designing large Silverlight applications

Resources about Silverlight Beyond This Book

You can find out a lot more about Silverlight than we have space to cover in this book — and it's free on the Internet. The best place to start is at `www.silverlight.net`. This site contains blogs, video tutorials, community samples, forums, and much, much more.

The site also contains links to download all the software you need to get started with Silverlight. Other sites worth investigating are `www.silverlightshow.net` and `www.silverlightcream.com`.

Ten Handy Expression Blend Shortcuts

In addition to using a series of mouse clicks to perform an action in Expression Blend, you can also use keyboard shortcuts to speed up your work. Table 16-1 shows the top ten keyboard shortcuts that you will find useful.

Table 16-1	Expression Blend Keyboard Shortcuts
Shortcut	**Purpose**
F4	Hide all other panels and show only the Artboard
F5	Run the application
F6	Switch from one workspace to another
F11	Toggle the Artboard between Design, XAML, and Split views
Alt+Drag	Create a copy of the selected object
Ctrl++, Ctrl+-	Zoom the Artboard in and out
Space+Drag	Pan the Artboard
Ctrl+0	Fit the Artboard onto the screen
Ctrl+1	Zoom to actual size (100%)
Ctrl+.	Open asset library

Ten Handy Visual Studio Shortcuts

As does Expression Blend, Visual Studio provides keyboard shortcuts to speed up your work. Table 16-2 lists ten keyboard shortcuts that you will find useful when you are working in Visual Studio.

Table 16-2	Visual Studio Keyboard Shortcuts
Shortcut	**Purpose**
Ctrl+Shift+B	Build your application
F5	Debug the application
Ctrl+.	Display the Smart tag menu, from which you can add references, implement interfaces, and so on
Ctrl+Shift+F	Find files
Ctrl+I	Interactive search; allows you to start typing the search text interactively after you press Ctrl+I
Ctrl+Spacebar	Activate IntelliSense
F10/F11	Step over and into code while debugging
F7/Shift+F7	Switch between XAML and code-behind file
Ctrl+Tab	Switch among open documents
Ctrl+K+C and Ctrl+K+U; Ctrl+E+C and Ctrl+E+U	Comment and uncomment code

Debugging Silverlight Applications

If you would like to debug your application from Visual Studio, make sure that the Silverlight check box under Debuggers on the Web tab of Project properties for the Web application is selected. You may need to deselect this check box when you want to debug JavaScript in Visual Studio.

To get to this option, select the Silverlight project from the Solution Explorer and then right-click to bring up the menu. Choose Properties from the menu and click the Debug tab, which is shown in Figure 16-1.

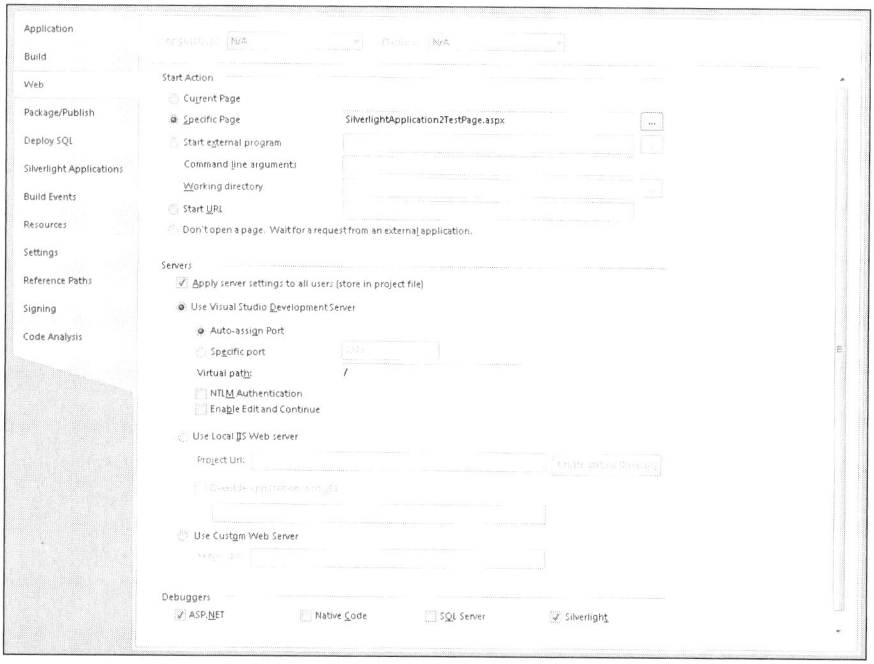

Figure 16-1: Enabling the Debugger for Silverlight in Visual Studio.

Looking Out for Performance Pitfalls

One of the good things about Silverlight is that it can use the processing power and memory of the machine on which it is running quite well. However, you still have to be careful not to write code that takes up too much valuable CPU cycles and other resources. While writing applications in Silverlight, always keep in mind that operations such as animations, Pixel Shader effects, transparencies, and other high-performance features can hog the CPU.

You can fix some graphic issues by turning Graphics Processing Unit (GPU) acceleration on, but this does not always improve performance — in fact, if not used properly, it will have the exact opposite effect.

You can also try setting the `EnableRedrawRegions` property of the Silverlight plug-in control to `true` during development to see which regions are being repainted on your screen often. Silverlight shows the repainted regions in a different color to give the developer a visual cue.

Another issue is that your application could be chewing up bandwidth by having large XAP files, which contain the complete Silverlight application and thereby require downloading large volumes of data from the Internet. It is better to load the data you need on demand, and to perform optimizations such as using binary XML with WCF or encoding media elements such as streaming video at a lower resolution.

Microsoft provides abundant advice on how to avoid performance pitfalls for Silverlight in the MSDN article "Performance Tips," which, at the time of writing, is found at `msdn.microsoft.com/en-us/library/cc189071(VS.95).aspx`.

Building for Accessibility

The goal of accessibility is to make an application available for use by as many people as possible, including people with a disability that has an impact on how they can use some or all of the application's features. For instance, a visually impaired person may use a screen reader to use the application, so you need to design your application to accomodate that possibility.

Silverlight 4 by itself provides accessibility support out of the box, but it's still up to you to ensure that your application is highly accessible. Here are a few handy tips for doing so:

- Use colors that have high contrast settings. In fact, don't use colors alone to differentiate between object states; use additional visual indicators as well, such as a different font attribute, so that people who can't distinguish colors can still see the difference.
- Provide keyboard shortcuts or alternative ways of doing things rather than relying solely on mouse movements.
- To help screen readers interpret elements such as Image controls and Buttons that do not have text, add the attached properties `AutomationProperties.Name` and `AutomationProperties.HelpText` to the control, as shown in the following XAML:

Chapter 16: Ten Handy Tips for Writing Silverlight Applications

```
<Image Source="Logo.png" AutomationProperties.
    Name="Company Logo"/>
<Button Content="<"
    Width="20"
    AutomationProperties.Name="Previous"
    AutomationProperties.HelpText="Move to
    Previous Record"
    x:Name="prevButton" />
```

✔ Use the attached property `AutomationProperties.LabeledBy` with an input field such as a TextBox to link it to the TextBlock it is associated with, as shown in the following code snippet:

```
<TextBlock x:Name="lblLastName" Text="Last Name" />
<TextBox AutomationProperties.LabeledBy="{Binding
    ElementName=lblLastName, Mode=OneWay}" />
```

For more about attached properties, see Chapter 2.

Internationalization and Localization

Internationalization and Localization are means by which you can adapt your software for a different language or local culture. The way it works is that you put all the text or string you use in your application into a specific resource file, which then gets compiled into a DLL. You can modify the resource file for each country or region, thereby providing support for other languages and cultures.

There is more to localization than just translating strings into another language. You need to take into consideration aspects of a culture such as currencies, date formats, number formats, calendars, and so on.

You can find out more about Internationalization and Localization from the MSDN reference `msdn.microsoft.com/en-us/library/cc838238(VS.95).aspx`.

Build Composite Applications Using Prism

Consider the scenario in which you are building a very large Silverlight application for your company, and the application has many pages. Some of these pages can be combined to form some kind of module — for example, an Administrator or a Financial module. These modules can be built independently of the each other and are even being built at different periods in time.

Although they are independent, you would still like to bring them together to work like one single application.

This is not an uncommon scenario. Many people have a very similar requirement and end up building all the necessary classes and libraries to make this happen. This is a lot of work and people end up putting extensive effort into building the framework — effort that could be better spent on developing business functionality.

Rather than build your own solution to this problem, you can use Prism, which is a framework released by the Microsoft patterns and practices group that specifically targets this scenario. Prism helps you to create what it calls Composite Applications, which are loosely coupled applications that don't know much about other applications or modules but can be brought together to work as a single application.

Prism is free, and you can find more details about this library at www.codeplex.com/CompositeWPF.

Use the Model-View-ViewModel (MVVM) Pattern to Manage Large Applications

When the size of your application gets bigger and bigger, spilling over with screens and features, it may become increasingly complex. Over time, the complexity may become unmanageable unless you have a good architecture in place.

Sometimes, good architecture is all about reusing concepts and ideas from previously successful implementations of your current project. These are known as patterns, and among the several good patterns that you can use is the Model-View-ViewModel (MVVM).

The MVVM pattern helps in separating the various components of your user interface. It's a variation of other patterns such as Model View Controller (MVC) and Model View Presenter (MVP), but it is particularly well suited for data binding, which Silverlight supports.

The MVVM separates a user interface into three parts:

- **Model:** This part represents the data Model and holds the data used in the application, such as Customer, Product, and Address.

- **View:** This part refers to the visual representation of the data. This component is expressed declaratively in Silverlight using XAML and can be created by a designer using Expression Blend. The Model can consist of data bound directly to the View, but in many cases, the Model may contain elements that are not directly bindable. For example, in the Model, you may store a person's Date of Birth, but on the View, you may only want to display Age.

- **ViewModel:** The ViewModel is a specialization of the Model whose specific purpose is to make all elements of the Model bindable. In the example previously provided, the ViewModel will have a field for Age that is calculated based on the Date of Birth and can be directly databound to a field on the view. In addition, this component may contain code to load the data Model from a service, as well as event handlers to handle events.

You can create MVVM applications from Expression Blend by selecting the Silverlight Data-driven Application (MVVM) option in the New Project dialog box.

Handy Tools

There are quite a few applications that you can use to make your Silverlight development more productive while trying to see how something has been implemented or just trying to fix problems while developing the application. Here are several of those tools that you will be glad to know about:

- **Red Gate's Reflector:** Whether you want to look at how Microsoft has implemented Silverlight code or see the code from XAP files, you can use Red Gate's Reflector tool. It is a free download and can be obtained from www.red-gate.com/products/reflector/index.htm. Figure 16-2 shows the source code for the Slider, one of Silverlight's controls.

- **Windows Performance Analysis Tools:** These tools include XPerf.exe and XPerfView.exe, which you can use to analyze performance bottlenecks in your Silverlight application, You can download them from msdn.microsoft.com/en-us/performance/cc825801.aspx.

- **Fiddler:** If you want to monitor your HTTP requests and responses, Fiddler is what you need. You can download Fiddler from www.fiddler2.com/fiddler2/.

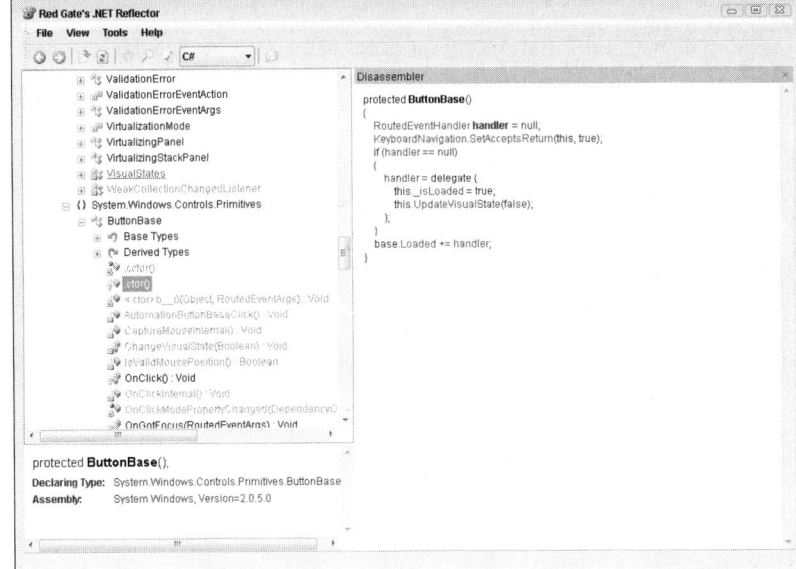

Figure 16-2: Using Reflector to look up the source for the `OnApplyTemplate` function for Slider.

Index

Special Characters and Numerics

... (ellipsis), 4
{} (curly brackets)
　`Style` property, 130
　`Value` property, 194
< > (angle brackets)
　XAML, 37
　XML, 34
3-D perspective transformations, 60, 63–64

• A •

A (Alpha) property, Expression Blend, 66–67
absolute positioning
　Canvas control, 121–122
　defined, 107
accessibility, 21, 346–347
accessing data
　authenticating users, 244–247
　cross-domain security, 236–243
　downloading files, 214–226
　overview, 213–214
　WCF RIA Services, 297–318
　Web services, 226–236
Add New Project dialog box, Visual Studio, 162–163
Add Service Reference dialog box, Visual Studio, 233, 235, 262
Add Sample Data Source button, Expression Blend, 205
Add Simple Property button, Expression Blend, 206
Add State button, Expression Blend, 159
Add States Group button, Expression Blend, 159
`Address` class
　creating, 198
　data binding, 198–199
　`StreetName` property, changing value of, 199–201
　`UseAsMailingAddress` property, adding, 201–204
Address fields, binding TextBox control to, 195–198
AddressUserControl
　creating, 195–196
　data binding, 196–197
　overview, 150–153
　properties for, 154–156
　reusing, 153–154
Adobe Illustrator, importing designs from, 334
Adobe Photoshop, importing designs from, 334–335
ADO.NET Entity Framework, 250–251, 256–259
Advanced Property options, Properties panel, Expression Blend, 51–52, 133
aligning controls, 110–111
`All` setting, `EntitySetRights`, 284
`AllRead` setting, `EntitySetRights`, 284
`AllWrite` setting, `EntitySetRights`, 284
Alpha (A) property, Expression Blend, 66–67
angle brackets (< >)
　XAML, 37
　XML, 34
animation
　bouncing ball, 171–185, 187
　running, 180–185
　of states of controls, 188–189
Animation workspace, Expression Blend, 174
Appearance properties group, Properties panel, Expression Blend, 52
application tier, purpose of, 19
`App.xaml` file, 46
`App.xaml.cs` file, 46–47
Artboard, Expression Blend
　adding controls to, 35
　clearing margins from, 112
　columns, changing width of, 117
　overview, 28
　purpose of, 26–27
　rows, changing height of, 117
　shapes, drawing, 53–56
Artboard controls, Expression Blend, 28–29
Artboard element picker, Expression Blend, 169
ASMX (simple) Web services, 251
ASP.NET Configuration tool, Visual Studio, 287
ASP.NET Web Site Administration tool, Visual Studio, 288, 315–316

`AspNetCompatibilityRequirements`, 244
assemblies, defined, 47
Asset Library window, Expression Blend, 93
Assets panel, Expression Blend
　behaviors, 169
　controls, 153–154, 166–167
　images, adding to Button controls, 93–94
　purpose of, 30–31
　SketchFlow, 330
Assets panel tool, Expression Blend, 30
attached properties
　accessibility, 346–347
　defined, 40
attributes (properties)
　defined, 34, 38
　setting, 38, 50
　that control layout, 109–110
　XAML, 37–41
audio
　microphones, 78–79
　playing, 74–75
　Silverlight support for, 20
authenticating users
　blogging engine, 315–318
　custom authentication system, 292–296
　overview, 244–247
　WCF RIA Services, 286–292
　Weather Channel Web service, 244
`AuthenticationService` class, 290, 293, 295
auto sizes, 116–117
AutoCompleteBox control, 327–328
`AutoGenerateColumns` property, DataGrid control, 323
`AutomationProperties.HelpText` property, 346–347
`AutomationProperties.LabeledBy` property, 346–347
`AutomationProperties.Name` property, 346–347
`AutoPlay` property, MediaElement control, 75
`AutoReverse` property, 181
auto-tracing feature, Expression Design, 333–334
axis of rotation, Expression Blend, 61

• B •

B (Blue) property, Expression Blend, 66–67
Back easing function, 185
`Background` attribute, `Grid` element, 36
bar charts, 325–326
Barber, Corrina, 144
`Begin` method, 180
`BeginExecute` method, 266
`BeginInvoke` method, TextBlock control, 226
`BeginSaveChanges` method, 269–270
`Behavior<T>` class, 335
behaviors
　controlling, 168–170
　creating, 335–336
　defined, 168
Bezier curves, defined, 186
binding
　controls to each other, 192–195
　to data objects, 195–205
　defined, 13
　Flickr Web service photos, displaying, 231
　overview, 191–192
　to sample data, 205–210
　values in templates, 143
bitmap graphics
　Expression Design, 332–334
　vector graphics versus, 53
`BlogEntities` class, 263
blogging engine
　authentication, 315–318
　change interceptors, 282–283
　concurrency, 277–280
　databases, 254–256, 263–276
　Domain Data Service, 298–304
　Entity Framework, 255–259
　entity sets, 283–284
　LINQ to Entity Framework, 304–306
　LINQ to SQL, 306–309
　query interceptors, 280–281
　validating data, 309–314
　WCF Data Service, 259–263
Blue (B) property, Expression Blend, 66–67
BlurEffect, 71, 73, 336–337
`Bold` element, RichTextArea control, 102
Border container, 108
Border tool, Expression Blend, 30
`BorderBrush` property, 143
Bounce easing function, 185

Index

bouncing ball animation
  ball, 172–173
  easing, 182–185
  KeySplines, 187
  looping, 182
  overview, 171–172
  reversing, 181
  running, 180
  switching to Animation workspace, 174
  timeline, 172–174
  XAML for, 177–180
bounding box, Expression Blend, 57
Brush Resources tab, Expression Blend
  function of, 66
  video brushes, 76
Brush Transform tool, Expression Blend
  displaying, 30, 70
  gradients, 70–71
Brushes properties group, Properties panel, Expression Blend
  filling objects with color, 65–66
  overview, 52
Bubble Creme theme, Silverlight Toolkit, 144–145
Business Application template
  applications, creating, 287
  client side of, 289
  overview, 287–289
  server side of, 289–290
  user interfaces, creating, 300
Button control
  adding, 91
  animating captions in, 188–189
  event handler, writing, 91–92
  images, adding to, 93–95
  overview, 90–92
  setting content of, 92–93
  skinning, 138–139
Button tool, Expression Blend, 30
`Button_Click` event
  adding, 140
  automatic creation of, 303
  event handlers, generating, 91, 104–105
  SmileyUserControl, 162
`BytesReceived` value, 221

• C •

C#, 1
calendars, 326
`cameraSource` data member, 77–78
Canvas control
  absolute positioning, 121–122
  purpose of, 108

Canvas tool, Expression Blend
  displaying, 30
  figure of, 121
`CaptureSource` class, 77
change interceptors, 280, 282–283
`ChangeInterceptor` method, 282
Chart control, 325–326
CheckBox control, 97
CheckBox tool, Expression Blend, 30
child controls, 107
child elements
  defined, 34
  setting properties with, 38
Circle easing function, 185
`ClickFace` event, 167
client-side validation, 309
Close Storyboard button, Expression Blend, 177
code-behind files, 44
CodePlex, 337
color
  Eyedropper tool, 66
  filling objects with, 65–66
  gradients, 67–71, 138, 141
  high contrast, 346
  mixing, 66–67
  overview, 64
  special effects, 71–72
  text, changing, 73
Color Eyedropper button, Expression Blend, 66
`Color` properties
  function of, 40
  simple animation, 178
`ColorAnimation` class, 178
`ColorAnimationUsing KeyFrames` class, 179
`Column` property, Grid control, 116
`ColumnDefinition` element, 116
columns
  adding controls to, 114–115
  overview, 112–113
  setting up, 113–114
  width of, 116–117
  XAML for, 115–116
ComboBox control
  creating, 100–101
  overview, 98
ComboBox tool, Expression Blend
  displaying, 30
  figure of, 100
`Comment` table, blogging engine, 250
`CommentMetaData` class, 300
common controls, 39

Common properties group, Properties panel, Expression Blend, 52
CommonStates group, 136–137
Community Technical Preview (CTP) releases, 249
Completed event
 controlling animation, 181–182
 LoginOperation, 291
Composite Applications, 348
concurrency, 277–280
consistency, defined, 127
containers, defined, 107. *See also names of specific containers*
Content property
 Button control, setting, 91–92
 HyperlinkButton control, setting, 96
 ListBox control, setting, 99
 UserControl element, function of, 109
ContentControl control, 92–93
contentPresenter, animating, 189
context, defined, 263
controls. *See also* data binding; *names of specific controls*
 adding themes to, 146–147
 behavior of, controlling, 168–170
 defined, 21
 grouping to create UserControl, 149–156
 layout, 107–126
 skinning, 134–144
 Smiley UserControl, 156–168
 styles, 127–134
 themes, 144–147
conventions used in book, 4
copying objects, 73
corner radius handles, Expression Blend, 59
Crawford, David, 144
CREATE, READ, UPDATE, DELETE (CRUD operations)
 creating data, 274–275
 deleting data, 275–276
 LINQ to Entity Framework, 304
 overview, 251–253
 reading data, 263–268, 301–303
 updating data, 269–273, 303–304
Create Data Binding dialog box, Expression Blend, 192–193, 204
Create Style Resource dialog box, Expression Blend, 128–129
cross-domain exchanges, 227–232
cross-domain policy file
 accessing Web services without, 237–238
 creating, 237
 defined, 227

cross-domain security
 cross-domain policy file, 237–238
 overview, 236–237
 workaround, 238–243
CRUD operations (CREATE, READ, UPDATE, DELETE)
 creating data, 274–275
 deleting data, 275–276
 LINQ to Entity Framework, 304
 overview, 251–253
 reading data, 263–268, 301–303
 updating data, 269–273, 303–304
CTP (Community Technical Preview) releases, 249
Cubic easing function, 185
curly brackets ({})
 Style property, 130
 Value property, 194
cursors, Expression Blend, 50, 57–59, 61
custom controls (templatable controls; templated controls)
 defined, 149, 156
 Smiley UserControl, 162–168

data binding
 controls to each other, 192–195
 to data objects, 195–205
 defined, 13
 Flickr Web service photos, displaying, 231
 overview, 191–192
 to sample data, 205–210
 values in templates, 143
data objects, binding to
 automatically updating changes to data, 199–201
 binding data object to control, 198–199
 binding to property name, 196–198
 converting data while binding, 201–205
 creating data class, 198
 creating UserControl for, 195–196
Data panel, Expression Blend, 32–33
Data parameter, 56
data tier, purpose of, 19
databases
 creating, 254
 creating data, 274–275
 deleting data, 275–276
 reading data, 263–268, 301–303
 tables, 254–256
 updating data, 269–273
DataContext property, Slider control, 194

Index

DataForm control
  overview, 323–324
  validating data, 312–314
DataGrid control
  binding to sample data, 207–208
  displaying in Expander control, 324–325
  `ItemsSource` property, 266
  LINQ to Entity Framework, 304–306
  overview, 322–323
  user interfaces, creating, 301–302
`DataServiceQuery` object, 265–266
DatePicker control, 326
debugging applications, 345
Deep Zoom Composer, 19–20
Deep Zoom Composer, 331–332
`DeleteObject` method, 275–276
Design view, Expression Blend, 28–29
design-time resizing handles, 112
Details mode button, Expression Blend, 209
Direct Selection tool, Expression Blend, 30
`Disabled` button state, 137
discrete interpolation, 179
`DisplayMemberPath` property, 231–232
.dll (libraries), 47
docking controls, 124–126
DockPanel control
  overview, 124–126
  purpose of, 108
Documents tab, Expression Blend, 28–29
DOM (Document Object Model)
  accessing HTML, 342
  Silverlight support for, 21
domain data service
  generated files, 300
  overview, 298–300
  retrieving data, 301–303
  updating data, 303–304
  user interface, 300–301
`DomainContext` object, 301–302
`Double` properties, 177
`DoubleAnimation` class, 178
`DoubleAnimationUsingKeyFrames` class, 179–180
double-headed arrow cursor, Expression Blend, 57
downloading files
  `HTTPWebRequest` class, 222–226
  overview, 214–215
  `WebClient` class, 216–221
`DownloadProgressChanged` event, 219–221
`DownloadStringCompleted` event, 229
DropShadowEffect, 71–72, 336–337
`Duration` attribute, `DoubleAnimation` element, 178

• E •

easing animation
  Easing functions, 185–186
  KeySplines, 186–187
  overview, 182–185
Easing functions, Expression Blend
  kinds of, 185–186
  list of, 185
  overview, 183–185
Edit menu, Expression Blend, 27
Edit Sample Values button, Expression Blend, 209
Edit Sample Values dialog box, Expression Blend, 209–210
Editor panel, Visual Studio, 42–43
`Effect` property, 71
effects (.fx extension), 337
Elastic easing function, 185
`ElementName` property, Slider control, 194
elements
  defined, 34
  XAML, 37–41
Ellipse tool, Expression Blend
  creating SmileyUserControl, 157–158
  displaying, 30, 53–54
ellipsis (. . .), 4
ellipses button, Expression Blend, 94
Enable Sample Data When Application Is Running check box, Expression Blend, 205, 208
Enable WCF RIA Services check box, Visual Studio, 286
`EnableRedrawRegions` property, 346
Entity Data Model design surface, Visual Studio, 257–258
Entity Data Model Wizard, Visual Studio, 257–258
entity sets, 283–284
entity tags (ETags), 279–280
`EntityQuery` object, 303
`EntitySetRights`, 283–284
ETags (entity tags), 279–280
event handlers, defined, 45, 199
events. *See names of specific events*
Events button, Properties panel, Expression Blend, 51–52
Expander control, 324–325
Exponential easing function, 186
Expression Blend
  importing designs from Adobe applications, 334–335
  keyboard shortcuts, 343–344
  overview, 16–18, 23–26

Expression Blend *(continued)*
  running Silverlight out of Web browser, 337
  SketchFlow, 329–331
  user interface, 26–34
  using in tandem with Visual Studio, 48
Expression Dark theme, Silverlight Toolkit, 144–147
Expression Design, 17–18, 332–334
Expression Encoder, 17–18
Expression Studio, 16–17
Expression Web, 16–17
Extensible Application Markup Language (XAML)
  AddressUserControl, 151–153
  appearance of code in book, 4
  blank Silverlight page, 108
  bouncing ball animation, 173, 177–180
  Button control content, 92, 95
  columns, 115–116
  data binding, 194, 196–197
  defined, 1
  DockPanel control, 126
  elements and attributes, 37–41
  Expression Dark theme, 146
  ListBox control, 100
  overview, 35–41
  POST requests, 222–223
  RichTextArea control, 102–103
  rows, 115–116
  SmileyCustomControl, 164–166
  SmileyUserControl, 158
  StackPanel container, 120
  Style property, 131
  styles, 128, 130–131
  templates, 136–137
  TextBlock control, 84, 87–90, 131
  UI framework, 12
Extensible Markup Language (XML)
  defined, 34
  Flickr Web service, 228
Eyedropper tool, Expression Blend
  color, 66
  figure of, 30
  gradients, 69

• F •

Fiddler tool, 277–280, 349
File menu, Expression Blend, 27
Flickr Web service
  accessing, 229
  developer account, 228
  displaying photos, 232
  modifying ListBox control, 230–231
  overview, 227
  XML data, 228
Flip tab, Properties panel, Expression Blend, 160
Flip Y axis button, Expression Blend, 160
Focused button state, 137
font
  changing using Properties panel, 85
  increasing size of, 72
FontSize attribute, TextBlock tags, 37–38
Foreground attribute, TextBlock tags, 37–38
four-sided arrow cursor, Expression Blend, 50
From attribute, DoubleAnimation element, 178
.fx extension (effects), 337

• G •

G (Green) property, Expression Blend, 66–67
GET request, 215
GetAuthenticatedUser method, 295
GetDefaultAudioCaptureDevice( ) method, 78
GetDefaultVideoCaptureDevice( ) method, 77
GetPostsWithComments method, 315
GetRequestStream method, 225–226
GetResponseResult method, 225
GetWeatherForecastXml method, 239, 245
GoToStateAction behavior, 168–169
GPU (Graphics Processing Unit) acceleration, 346
Gradient brush tab, Expression Blend
  function of, 66
  setting, 67
gradient brushes, Expression Blend, 67
Gradient eyedropper, Expression Blend, 68–69
Gradient slider, Expression Blend, 67–68
gradient stops, Expression Blend, 68
Gradient tool, Expression Blend
  displaying Brush Transform tool, 70
  figure of, 30
  overview, 69–70
gradients
  Brush Transform tool, 70–71
  Button controls, 138, 141
  Gradient tool, 69–70
  Properties panel, 67–69

graphics, Silverlight support for, 20
Graphics Processing Unit (GPU)
    acceleration, 346
Green (G) property, Expression Blend,
    66–67
Grid control
    converting to StackPanel, 118–119
    laying out controls in tabular fashion,
        112–116
    purpose of, 108
grid divider, Expression Blend, 113
Grid element
    eliminating, 37
    function of, 36
    using TextBlock element within, 40
Grid tool, Expression Blend, 30
grouping controls
    to create UserControl, 149–156
    into tabbed pages, 122–124
GroupName property, RadioButton
    control, 97

• H •

Hard Rock Café Memorabilia site, 10–11
Height property
    function of, 56, 109–110
    UserControl, setting at design time, 111–112
"Hello, World" application, 34
    attached properties, 40
    creating, 24–25, 44
    eliminating Grid element, 37
    XAML for, 35–36
HelloWorld method, 234–236
Help menu, Expression Blend, 27
Help tab, Expression Blend, 24
High Level Shader Language (HLSL), 337
HorizontalAlignment property
    function of, 110
    setting, 122
hosting applications
    with Visual Studio, 47–48
    in Web pages, 14–15
HTML (HyperText Markup Language)
    accessing, 341–342
    hosting Silverlight applications in, 14–15
    overview, 340
HTML Bridge, 338–340
HtmlPage.Document object, 342
HTTP (HyperText Transfer Protocol)
    verbs, 253
HttpWebRequest class
    downloading files, 222–226
    overview, 215

Hungarian notation, 87
Hyperlink element, RichTextArea
    control, 103
HyperlinkButton control, 95–96
HyperText Markup Language (HTML)
    accessing, 341–342
    hosting Silverlight applications in, 14–15
    overview, 340
HyperText Transfer Protocol (HTTP)
    verbs, 253

• I •

IAsynchResult parameter, 265, 270
icons used in book, 4–5
IDE (Integrated Development
    Environment), 16, 42–43
IEnumerable namespace, 302
Illustrator, importing designs from, 334
image brushes, 76
Image control, 215
images, as content for Button control,
    93–95
ImageUrl property, 230
importing designs, 334–335
Include operator, 304
[Include] attribute, 304, 306, 308
InitializeComponent method, 45
InitializeService method, 283
InlineUIContainer element,
    RichTextArea control, 103
INotifyPropertyChanged interface,
    200, 272
Integrated Development Environment
    (IDE), 16, 42–43
IntelliSense feature
    defined, 87, 264
    proxy classes, 233–234
internationalization
    overview, 347
    Silverlight support for, 21
interpolation, defined, 178–179
IQueryable list, 304
IsChecked property
    CheckBox control, 202, 204–205
    RadioButton control, 97
IsMuted property, MediaElement
    control, 75
IsSelected property, ListBox
    control, 100
Italic element, RichTextArea
    control, 102

`ItemsSource` property, DataGrid
    control, 266–268, 323
`ItemTemplate` element, ListBox
    control, 322

• J •

Java Script Object Notation (JSON), 252
JavaScript
    creating and registering objects, 339
    overview, 338–340
    scriptable method, creating, 339
    `ScriptableMember` function, 339–340
    Silverlight support for, 21
JSON (Java Script Object Notation), 252

• K •

keyboard shortcuts
    accessibility, 346
    Expression Blend, 343–344
    Visual Studio, 344
`KeyDown` event, 88
keyframe animation, XAML for, 178–180
keyframes, defined, 175
KeySpline editor, Expression Blend,
    186–187
KeySplines, 186–187
Kothari, Nikhil, 349

• L •

Language Integrated Query (LINQ)
    Flickr Web service, 228, 230–231
    LINQ to Entity Framework, 304–306
    LINQ to SQL, 306–309
layers (tiers), defined, 19
layout
    absolute positioning, 121–122
    docking controls, 124–126
    grouping controls into tabbed pages,
        122–124
    layout containers, 107–112
    rows and columns, 112–117
    stacking controls, 117–120
    wrapping controls, 120–121
layout containers
    aligning controls, 110–111
    clearing margins from Artboard, 112
    function of, 39
    `Height` and `Width` properties, setting at
        design time, 111–112
    overview, 107–108
    properties that control layout, 109–110
    root container, 108–109
    selecting incorrect, 126
Layout group, Properties panel, Expression
    Blend, 58
layout management, defined, 13
layout properties, 40
Layout properties group, Properties panel,
    Expression Blend, 52
`LeftButtonUp` function, 168
libraries (.dll), 47
Line tool, Expression Blend, 30, 53–54
Linear Gradient button, Expression Blend,
    67–68
linear interpolation, defined, 179
`LinExpression` element, RichTextBox
    control, 103
LINQ (Language Integrated Query)
    Flickr Web service, 228, 230–231
    LINQ to Entity Framework, 304–306
    LINQ to SQL, 306–309
LINQ to Entity Framework, 304–306
LINQ to SQL, 306–309
ListBox control
    creating, 98–100
    displaying photos in, 230–232
    overview, 321–322
ListBox tool, Expression Blend
    displaying, 30
    figure of, 98
`ListBoxItem` property, ListBox control,
    100
ListMode button, Expression Blend, 209
`Load` method, 302
`Loaded` event, 264–266
Local Resource menu item, Expression
    Blend, 133
localization
    overview, 347
    Silverlight support for, 21
`Login` method, 245–247, 290–292
looping animation, 182

• M •

`MainPage.xaml` file, 44
`MainPage.xaml.cs` file, 44
Make Into UserControl dialog box,
    Expression Blend, 152
Mapping Details section, Visual Studio,
    258–259
margin adorners, Expression Blend, 112
`Margin` property, 56, 109

Index

margins
  clearing from Artboard, 112
  values, 110–111
Master-Detail view, Expression Blend, 209
MaxHeight property, 108, 109
MaxWidth property, 108, 110
media elements, function of, 39
MediaElement control
  adding, 75
  source files, 215
Menu bar, Expression Blend
  overview, 27
  purpose of, 26–27
microphones
  connecting to applications, 78
  selecting default, 79
Microsoft Expression Blend
  importing designs from Adobe applications, 334–335
  keyboard shortcuts, 343–344
  overview, 16–18, 23–26
  running Silverlight out of Web browser, 337
  SketchFlow, 329–331
  user interface, 26–34
  using in tandem with Visual Studio, 48
Microsoft Expression Design, 17–18, 332–334
Microsoft Expression Encoder, 17–18
Microsoft Expression Studio, 16–17
Microsoft Expression Web, 16–17
Microsoft Silverlight. *See* Silverlight
Microsoft Silverlight Configuration dialog box, 25
Microsoft SQL Server Express (SQL Express)
  database diagram, 256
  overview, 250–251
Microsoft Visual Studio
  creating applications, 44
  debugging applications, 345
  files, 46–47
  hosting applications, 47–48
  keyboard shortcuts, 344
  overview, 16
  running Silverlight out of Web browser, 338
  Solution Explorer, 44–45
  starting, 41–48
  user interface, 42–43
  using in tandem with Expression Blend, 48
MinHeight property, 108, 109
MinWidth property, 108, 109
mirror effect, 73

Miscellaneous properties group, Properties panel, Expression Blend, 52
mixing colors, 66–67
Mode parameter, Slider control, 194–195
Model-View-ViewModel (MVVM) pattern, 348–349
mouse, shaping objects using, 57–58
MouseEnter event, 88
MouseLeftButtonUp event, 167
MouseOver button state
  defined, 137
  setting, 140–141
moving gradients, 71
multi-touch, defined, 13
MVVM (Model-View-ViewModel) pattern, 348–349

Name property, Button control, 103–104
naming
  database tables, 250–251
  styles, 130
Navigate method, WebBrowser control, 341
NavigateToString method, WebBrowser control, 341
NavigateUri property, HyperlinkButton control, 96
nested containers, 109, 118–119
.NET Framework
  Silverlight .NET Framework versus, 237–238
  using to write applications, 12
New Project dialog box
  Expression Blend, 24
  Visual Studio, 41
New Resources Dictionary button, Expression Blend, 132
New Silverlight Application dialog box, Visual Studio, 41–42
No brush tab, Expression Blend, 65
None setting, EntitySetRights, 284
Normal button state, 137
NumericUpDown control, 192–194

Object Collection Editor: Items dialog box, Expression Blend, 99
Object menu, Expression Blend, 27
object tags, 15
ObjectAnimationUsingKeyFrames class, 179

Objects and Timeline panel, Expression Blend
  bouncing ball animation, 175–176
  displaying, 174
  purpose of, 30–31
  selecting controls, 111
obtaining Silverlight, 9–10
OnAttached method, 335
OnDetaching method, 335
OneTime value, Slider control, 194–195
one-to-many relationship, defined, 263
OneWay value, Slider control, 194–195
onPluginLoaded function, 340
OnTitleChanged method, 273
opacity of controls, setting, 335–336
OpenReadAsync method
  downloading files using WebClient class, 216, 218
  progress bars, 220
OpenReadCompleted method, 216–218
operating systems, 10
Orientation property, StackPanel control, 118–120
Oscillations property, Elastic easing function, 185
Out-of-Browser Settings dialog box, Visual Studio, 338

• P •

padlock icon, Expression Blend, 117
Paint Bucket, Expression Blend, 30
Palette icon, 138
panning. See Deep Zoom Composer
Panning tool, Expression Blend, 30
Paragraph element, RichTextArea control, 102–103
param name "source" tag, 15
parent controls, defined, 107
partial classes, 271
Password property, PasswordBox control, 87–88
PasswordBox control
  function of, 84
  overview, 83–90
  user input, 86–87
PasswordBox tool, Expression Blend, 30
PasswordChanged event handler, 90
Path object
  function of, 20
  XAML for, 56
Pause method, 181

Pen tool, Expression Blend
  drawing shapes, 53–55
  figure of, 30
Pencil tool, Expression Blend
  creating SmileyUserControl, 157–158
  displaying, 30
  drawing shapes, 53–55
  performance issues, 345–346
Photoshop, importing designs from, 334–335
pin button, Expression Blend, 29
Pixel Shader (.ps) files, 337
pixel sizes, 116–117
playing
  audio, 74–75
  video, 74–75
plug-ins, defined, 9
plus sign cursor, Expression Blend, 59
Point properties, 178
PointAnimation class, 178
PointAnimationUsingKeyFrames class, 179
Position property, MediaElement control, 75
POST method, 215
POST request
  HttpWebRequest class, 222–226
  overview, 215
Post table, blogging engine, 250
PostMetaData class, 300
PostsDataGrid ItemsSource property, 301
PostsLoaded method, 265, 267, 273
Power easing function, 186
Power property, easing functions, 186
presentation tier, purpose of, 19
Pressed button state, 141–142
Prism, 347–348
.prj (project files), 25, 44
progress bars, 219–221
ProgressBar control, 220–221, 326–327
project files (.prj), 25, 44
Project menu, Expression Blend, 27
projection
  3-D perspective transformations, 63–64
  defined, 60
Projection ball, Expression Blend, 63–64
Projects panel, Expression Blend, 30–31
Projects tab, Expression Blend, 24
properties (attributes)
  defined, 34, 38
  setting, 38, 50
  that control layout, 109–110
  XAML, 37–41

Properties button, Properties panel, Expression Blend, 51–52
Properties folder, Visual Studio, 47
Properties panel, Expression Blend
  color, 64–72
  GoToStateAction behavior, 169
  gradients, 67–69
  overview, 49–52
  purpose of, 31–32
  setting properties, 50
  shaping objects, 58–59
  sizing objects, 58–59
  styles, applying to existing elements, 133
Properties window, Visual Studio, 43
Property groups, Properties panel, Expression Blend, 51–52
`PropertyChanged` event, 200–201, 273
protocols, defined, 227
proxy classes
  defined, 232–233, 251
  displaying, 262–263
  overview, 261–263
`.ps` (Pixel Shader) files, 337

• Q •

Quadratic easing function, 186
Quartic easing function, 186
query interceptors, 280–281
`QueryInterceptor` method, 281
Quintic easing function, 186

• R •

R (Red) property, Expression Blend, 66–67
Radial Gradient button, Expression Blend, 67–68, 70
RadioButton control, 96–97
RadioButton tool, Expression Blend
  displaying, 30
  figure of, 96
RadiusX property, Properties panel, Expression Blend, 60
RadiusY property, Properties panel, Expression Blend, 60
raster paths, 332
Rating control, 327–328
`rctWebcam_MouseLeftButtonDown` method, 77–78
reading data
  WCF Data Services, 263–268
  WCF RIA Services, 301–303

`ReadMultiple` setting, `EntitySetRights`, 284
`ReadSingle` setting, `EntitySetRights`, 284
Record Keyframe button, Expression Blend, 175, 183
Rectangle control, Expression Blend, 55–56
Rectangle object, rounding corners of, 59–60
Rectangle tool, Expression Blend
  displaying Ellipse and Line tools, 53–54
  figure of, 30
Red (R) property, Expression Blend, 66–67
Red Gate Reflector tool, 349, 350
References folder, Visual Studio, 47
Reflector tool, 349–350
`RegistrationData` class, 290
`RepeatBehavior` property, 182
Representational State Transfer (REST)
  accessing Web services, 228–232
  defined, 227
  overview, 22
  RESTful interfaces, 252
`[RequiredRole]` attribute, 316
`[RequiresAuthentication]` attribute, 315
resizing
  gradients, 70
  scaling versus, 60
  using Properties panel, 58–59
Resource brushes, Expression Blend
  images, 76
  video, 76
resource dictionaries, 132
resource elements, 39
Resources panel, Expression Blend
  purpose of, 31–32
  styles, 132–133
REST (Representational State Transfer)
  accessing Web services, 228–232
  defined, 227
  overview, 22
RESTful interfaces, 252
RESTful services, 22
Results panel, Expression Blend, 33
`Resume` method, 181
reusing UserControls, 153–154
Reverse Gradient Stops button, Expression Blend, 68
reversing animation, 181
Rich Internet Applications (RIA), 9, 285. *See also* WCF RIA Services

RichTextArea control
  formatting text at runtime, 103–105
  function of, 84
  overview, 83–90, 101–102
  XAML for, 102–103
root container, 108–109
rotating
  gradients, 70
  objects, 60–61
round selection handle, Expression Blend, 55
rounding corners, 59–60
RoutedEventHandler, 167
Row property, Grid control, 116
RowDefinition element, 116
rows
  adding controls to, 114–115
  height of, 116–117
  overview, 112–113
  setting up, 113–114
  XAML for, 115–116
rulers, Expression Blend, 113
Run element, RichTextArea control, 103
running Silverlight
  out of Web browser, 337–338
  overview, 9–10

• S •

sample data
  binding to, 205–210
  TreeView control using, 327
SampleDataSource item, 205–206
Samples tab, Expression Blend, 24
sandboxed environment, 13
scaling objects
  defined, 60
  resizing versus, 60
screen readers, 346
ScriptableMember function, 339–340
ScrollBar tool, Expression Blend, 30
ScrollViewer tool, Expression Blend, 30
Search field, Properties panel, Expression Blend
  overview, 51
  setting properties, 50–51
security
  cross-domain, 236–243
  WCF RIA Services, 315–318
SelectedIndex property, ListBox control, 100
selection handles, Expression Blend, 57

Selection tool, Expression Blend
  figure of, 30
  setting properties, 50
SelectionChanged event, 268
server-side validation, 309
service methods
  LINQ to Entity Framework, 304–306
  LINQ to SQL, 306–309
Service References
  adding, 233, 235, 262
  defined, 261
  updating, 245
Services API page, Flickr, 227
Set to Auto button, Expression Blend, 111
SetLink method, 274–275
Setter child elements, 131
shadow effect, 73–74
shape elements, 39
shapes
  drawing, 53–55
  XAML for, 55–56
shaping objects
  overview, 56
  rounding corners of Rectangle object, 59–60
  using mouse, 57–58
  using Properties panel, 58–59
Show Advanced Properties button, Expression Blend, 204
Show Annotations control, Expression Blend, 29
Show Grid control, Expression Blend, 29
Silverlight
  browser support for, 10
  compatibility with other technologies, 21
  examples of sites enhanced with, 10–12
  Expression Blend, 16–18, 23–34, 48
  features of, 12–14, 21–22
  help resources, 343
  hosting applications in Web pages, 14–15
  name of, 14
  obtaining, 9–10
  operating system support for, 10
  running, 9–10, 337–338
  tools needed to create applications, 15–20
  user experience, 20–21
  versions of, 14
  Visual Studio, 16, 41–48
  Web sites, 343, 346–347
  XAML, 35–41
Silverlight 4 Application + Website option, Expression Blend, 24
Silverlight Configuration dialog box, 79

Index

Silverlight Toolkit
  adding references to, 312–313
  overview, 19
  themes, 144
Silverlight Tools for Visual Studio, 16
`SilverlightApplication1` project, 44
`SilverlightApplication1.Web` project, 47–48
simple (ASMX) Web services, 251
simple animation, 177–178
Sine easing function, 186
sizing. *See* resizing
SketchFlow, 329–331
SketchFlow Map, 330
SketchFlow Player, 330–331
skewing
  gradients, 71
  objects, 60–63
  text, 73–74
skinning (templating)
  controls, 134–144
  defined, 3, 135
  styles versus, 135
Slider control, 192–194
Slider tool, Expression Blend, 30
.sln (solution files), 25, 44
SmileyCustomControl
  adding, 166–167
  behaviors, 168–170
  creating in Visual Studio, 162–166
  events, 167
SmileyUserControl
  creating, 157–159
  overview, 156–157
  states, 159–162
  testing, 161–162
Snap to Grid control, Expression Blend, 29
Snap to Snaplines control, 29
Solid Color brush tab, Expression Blend
  function of, 65
  setting text color, 73
Solution Explorer, Visual Studio, 43–45
solution files (.sln), 25, 44
Source property
  MediaElement control, 75
  WebBrowser control, 341
`Span` element, RichTextArea control, 103
special effects
  color, 71–72
  overview, 72–74
splined interpolation, defined, 179
Split view button, Expression Blend
  function of, 35
  location of, 29
Split view, Expression Blend
  function of, 28–29
  skinning Button controls, 139
`Springiness` property, Elastic easing function, 185
SQL Express (Microsoft SQL Server Express)
  database diagram, 256
  overview, 250–251
stacking controls
  adding controls to StackPanel, 117–118
  converting Grid to StackPanel, 118–119
  XAML for StackPanel, 120
StackPanel control
  adding controls to, 117–118
  converting Grid to, 118–119
  creating AddressUserControl, 150
  purpose of, 108
  XAML for, 120
StackPanel tool, Expression Blend
  adding controls to StackPanel, 117–118
  displaying, 30
star sizes, 116–117
starting Visual Studio, 41–48
`Startup` event, 47
startup file, specifying, 46–47
Startup screen, Expression Blend, 23–24
states
  animation of, 188–189
  Smiley UserControl, 159–162
  specifying, 140–142
States panel, Expression Blend
  purpose of, 30, 32
  specifying state, 140–141
static resource, defined, 130
`Stop` method, 181
storing data locally, 342
`StoryBoard` class
  `AutoReverse` property, 181
  `Completed` event, 181–182
  controlling animations, 180
  `RepeatBehavior` property, 182
Storyboard element, 177
`Storyboard.TargetName` attribute, `DoubleAnimation` element, 178
`Storyboard.TargetProperty` attribute, `DoubleAnimation` element, 178
`Stretch` property, MediaElement control, 75
`StringToBooleanConverter` class, 202–204
`Stroke` property
  binding to `BorderBrush` property, 143
  function of, 56

Style menu item, Expression Blend, 133
`Style` property
  overview, 130
  XAML for, 131
styles
  applying to existing elements, 132–133
  creating, 128–130, 134
  defined, 128
  editing existing, 134
  overview, 127–128
  Resources panel, 132
  skinning versus, 135
  `Style` property, 130–131
styling, defined, 3
`succeeded` variable, 270–271
Super Preview feature, Expression Web, 16

• T •

tabbed pages, grouping controls into, 122–124
TabControl control, 122–123
TabItem control, 122–124
`TargetType` attribute, 131
templatable controls (templated controls; custom controls)
  defined, 149, 156
  Smiley UserControl, 162–168
templates. *See also* templating (skinning)
  Business Application, 287–290
  defined, 135
  editing visually, 138–140
  how work together, 290–292
  WCF RIA Services, 285–286
templating (skinning)
  controls, 134–143
  defined, 3, 135
  styles versus, 135
text
  color, changing, 73
  displaying, 84–85
  font, 72, 85
  formatting at runtime, 103–105
  skewing, 73–74
Text group, Properties panel, Expression Blend, 72
text properties, 40
Text properties group, Properties panel, Expression Blend, 52
`Text` property, TextBox control, 87–88
TextBlock control
  adding to rows and columns, 114–115
  creating AddressUserControl, 151
  displaying text, 84–85

downloading files using `WebClient` class, 217–218
function of, 84
overview, 83–90
special effects, 72–73
styles, 128–129
`TextBlock` element
  drop-shadow effect, 38
  function of, 36
  using within `Grid` element, 40
`TextBlock` tags, 37–38
TextBlock tool, Expression Blend
  figure of, 30
  function of, 33–34
TextBox control
  accessing values in XAML markup, 87–90
  binding to Address fields, 195–198
  creating AddressUserControl, 151–152
  function of, 84
  user input, 86–87
TextBox tool, Expression Blend, 30
`TextChanged` event handler, 88–89
themes
  adding controls to, 146–147
  overview, 144–147
3-D perspective transformations, 60, 63–64
tiers (layers), defined, 19
Tile Brush tab, Expression Blend
  function of, 66
  image brushes, 76
timeline, animation, 172–174
Timeline Recording mode, Expression Blend
  starting, 173
  stopping, 177
`TimeSpan` parameter, `RepeatBehavior` property, 182
`To` attribute, `DoubleAnimation` element, 178
`ToList( )` method, 267
Toolbox panel, Visual Studio, 42–43
Tools menu, Expression Blend, 27
Tools panel, Expression Blend
  drawing shapes, 53–54
  overview, 28
  purpose of, 26–27
`TotalBytesToReceive` value, 221
Transform group, Properties panel, Expression Blend, 62–63
Transform properties group, Properties panel, Expression Blend, 52
transformation properties, 40
transformations, defined, 60

Translate transforms, Expression Blend, 62–63
transparency, 67
TreeView control, 327
Turn on Effects control, Expression Blend, 29
two-sided arrow at angle cursor, Expression Blend, 61
TwoWay value, Slider control, 194–195

• U •

UI (user interface)
  audio, 74–75, 79
  Button control, 90–95
  colors, 64–72
  ComboBox control, 98, 100–101
  domain data service, 300–301
  Expression Blend, 26–34, 49–52
  features of, 12–13
  HyperlinkButton control, 95–96
  ListBox control, 98–100
  PasswordBox control, 83–84, 86–90
  properties, setting, 50
  RadioButton control, 96–97
  RichTextArea control, 83–90, 101–105
  rotating objects, 60–61
  shapes, drawing, 53–56
  shaping objects, 56–60
  sizing objects, 58–59
  skewing objects, 60–63
  special effects, 72–74
  TextBlock control, 83–90
  TextBox control, 86–90
  3-D perspective transformations, 60, 63–64
  video, 74–79
  Visual Studio, 42–43
Underline element, RichTextArea control, 103
Unfocused button state, 137
Universal Resource Indicators (URIs), 22
updating data. *See also* data binding
  WCF Data Services, 269–273
  WCF RIA Services, 303–304
URIs (Universal Resource Indicators), 22
UseAsMailingAddress property, Address class, 201–204
User class, 293–295
user interface (UI)
  audio, 74–75, 79
  Button control, 90–95
  colors, 64–72
  ComboBox control, 98, 100–101
  domain data service, 300–301
  Expression Blend, 26–34, 49–52
  features of, 12–13
  HyperlinkButton control, 95–96
  ListBox control, 98–100
  PasswordBox control, 83–90
  properties, setting, 50
  RadioButton control, 96–97
  RichTextArea control, 83–90, 101–105
  rotating objects, 60–61
  shapes, drawing, 53–56
  shaping objects, 56–60
  sizing objects, 58–59
  skewing objects, 60–63
  special effects, 72–74
  TextBlock control, 83–90
  TextBox control, 86–90
  3-D perspective transformations, 60, 63–64
  video, 74–79
  Visual Studio, 42–43
UserBase class, 290
UserControl element, 36
UserControls
  data binding, 195–198
  defined, 149
  grouping controls to create, 149–156
UserRegistrationServices class, 290

• V •

ValidateEntry( ) method, 89
ValidateProperty method, 310
ValidateUser method, 293, 295
validating data
  DataForm control, 312–314
  overview, 309–310
  validation attributes, 311
Validation Exception, 310–311
Value property
  NumericUpDown control, 192
  Rating control, 327
  Slider control, 192, 194
VB.NET, 1
vector graphics
  bitmapped graphics versus, 53
  defined, 53
vector paths, 332–333
VerticalAlignment property
  function of, 110
  setting, 122
video
  playing, 74–75
  Silverlight support for, 20

video *(continued)*
  video brush, creating, 76
  webcams, 77–79
View buttons, Expression Blend, 28–29
View menu, Expression Blend, 27
Visual Studio
  creating applications, 44
  debugging applications, 345
  files, 46–47
  hosting applications, 47–48
  keyboard shortcuts, 344
  overview, 16
  running Silverlight out of Web browser, 338
  Solution Explorer, 44–45
  starting, 41–48
  user interface, 42–43
  using in tandem with Expression Blend, 48
VisualState group, 136–137
VisualStateManager class, 161
Volume property, MediaElement control, 75

• W •

WCF (Windows Communication Foundation) Data Services
  change interceptors, 280, 282–283
  concurrency, 277–280
  creating, 254–261
  database operations, 22
  defined, 251–253
  entity sets, 283–284
  overview, 249–251
  query interceptors, 280–281
  using in Silverlight applications, 261–276
WCF RIA (Windows Communication Foundation Rich Internet Application) Services
  accessing data with, 297–318
  authenticating users, 286–292
  custom authentication system, 292–296
  overview, 19, 285–286
Weather Channel Web service
  accessing, 241–243
  authentication, 244
  building, 239–240
  displaying results of, 240–241
  installing icons, 241
  login procedure, 244–247
  overview, 238
  using, 240

Web browsers
  running Silverlight out of, 337–338
  support for Silverlight, 10
Web pages
  adding UI elements to, 33–34
  hosting Silverlight applications in, 14–15
Web Platform Installer (WPI), 250
Web Service Description Language (WSDL) Web service
  creating, 234–236
  programming against, 232–234
Web services
  creating WSDL Web service, 234–236
  defined, 22
  overview, 226–227
  programming against WSDL Web service, 232–234
  that allow cross-domain exchanges, accessing, 227–232
  without cross-domain policy file, accessing, 237–238
Web sites
  Barber, Corrina, 144
  CodePlex, 337
  Crawford, David, 144
  DataGrid control, 312
  examples of Silverlight-enhanced, 10–12
  Fiddler tool, 277, 349
  Flickr, 227–228
  free application development tools, 15
  Hard Rock Café Memorabilia, 10–11
  MVVM pattern, 349
  Prism, 348
  Red Gate Reflector tool, 349
  Silverlight, 343, 346–347
  Weather Channel, 238
  Windows Performance Analysis Tools, 349
  Woodgrove Financials sample application, 11–12
  Yahoo!, 228
  YouTube, 213
WebBrowser control, 341
Webcam / Mic dialog box, 79
webcams
  displaying video from, 77–78
  selecting default, 79
WebClient class
  downloading files, 216–221
  overview, 215
WebContext object, 289–291
Width property
  function of, 56, 109–110
  UserControl, setting at design time, 111–112
Window menu, Expression Blend, 27

Windows Communication Foundation Rich Internet Application (WCF RIA) Services
  accessing data with, 297–318
  authenticating users, 286–292
  custom authentication system, 292–296
  overview, 19, 285–286
Windows Communication Foundation (WCF) Data Services
  change interceptors, 280, 282–283
  concurrency, 277–280
  creating, 254–261
  database operations, 22
  defined, 251–253
  entity sets, 283–284
  overview, 249–251
  query interceptors, 280–281
  using in Silverlight applications, 261–276
Windows Performance Analysis Tools, 349
Windows Presentation Foundation (WPF), 12
Woodgrove Financials sample application, 11–12
workspace panels, Expression Blend
  moving, 29
  overview, 26–27, 28–33
  purpose of, 26–27
  resetting to default position, 30
  saving, 29
  toggling between, 29
WPF (Windows Presentation Foundation), 12
WPF/e (WPF everywhere), 14
WPI (Web Platform Installer), 250
WrapPanel control
  overview, 120–121
  purpose of, 108
WrapPanel tool, Expression Blend, 120
wrapping controls, 120–121
WriteAppend setting, EntitySetRights, 284
WriteDelete setting, EntitySetRights, 284
WriteMerge setting, EntitySetRights, 284
WriteReplace setting, EntitySetRights, 284
WSDL (Web Service Description Language) Web service
  creating, 234–236
  programming against, 232–234

XAML (Extensible Application Markup Language)
  AddressUserControl, 151–153
  appearance of code in book, 4
  blank Silverlight page, 108
  bouncing ball animation, 173, 177–180
  Button control content, 92, 95
  columns, 115–116
  data binding, 194, 196–197
  defined, 1
  DockPanel control, 126
  elements and attributes, 37–41
  Expression Dark theme, 146
  ListBox control, 100
  overview, 35–41
  POST requests, 222–223
  RichTextArea control, 102–103
  rows, 115–116
  SmileyCustomControl, 164–166
  SmileyUserControl, 158
  StackPanel container, 120
  Style property, 131
  styles, 128, 130–131
  templates, 136–137
  TextBlock control, 84, 87–90, 131
  UI framework, 12
XAML view, Expression Blend, 28–29
XAML view button, Expression Blend
  function of, 35
  location of, 29
  overview, 55
XAP files, 14, 346
x:Class attribute, UserControl element, 36
x:Key attribute, 131
XML (Extensible Markup Language)
  defined, 34
  Flickr Web service, 228
XmlDocument object, 239
x:Name property
  Grid element, 36
  ProgressBar control, 220
XPerf.exe tool, 349
XPerfView.exe tool, 349

Yahoo!, 228
YouTube, 213

Z-Index property, 110
.zip extension, 14
zooming. See also Deep Zoom Composer
Zooming tool, Expression Blend, 29, 30